The Road to Delhi

*On the road to Delhi I met a hundred men,
and they were all my brothers.*
                                    Indian Proverb

Who was a neighbor to this man?
                                    Jesus

The Road to Delhi

J. Waskom Pickett Remembered

Arthur G. McPhee

SAIACS PRESS
BANGALORE, INDIA

Arthur G. McPhee teaches Intercultural Studies at Associated Mennonite Biblical Seminary, Elkhart, Indiana, USA.

SAIACS Press
P.O. Box 7747
Kothanur Post
Bangalore-560 077

ISBN 81-87712-11-2

Comments and Questions

www.roadtodelhi.info

For Douglas, Margaret, Miriam, and Elizabeth

the children of J. Waskom Pickett

and Ruth Robinson Pickett

Contents

Introduction 9

The Early Years (1890-1909) 11
  1 The Picketts of Hallelujah Hill 15
  2 The Application 20
  3 Dreaming of India 32
  4 American Methodists in India 38

The Settling Down Years (1910-1915) 43
  5 Passage to India 47
  6 Lal Bagh, Lucknow 54
  7 The Long Journey Home 70

The Arrah Years (1916-1924) 91
  8 Arrah, Bihar 95
  9 War and Other Challenges 105
  10 Working with a Mass Movement 117
  11 Meeting Gandhi 135
  12 In Famine and Flood 144

The Lucknow Years (1925-1935) 153
  13 *The Indian Witness* 158
  14 Mott's Proposal 177
  15 The Mass Movement Study 188
  16 The Survey Underway 198
  17 Applause and Dissent 210
  18 Lessons from the Survey 218
  19 Sudra Movements 226

20 Ambedkar 237
21 The Mid-India Survey 248

The Bombay Years (1936-1944) 253
22 Politics and Conversion 258
23 The McGavran Controversy 267
24 From Tambaram 279
25 Jones' Dissent 286

The Delhi Years (1945-1956) 293
26 Finally, Delhi 299
27 Independence! 310
28 Orphans of the Storm 317
29 The Last Days of Gandhi 331
30 The I-3s 337
31 Birth of the Republic 345
32 Ambassador-at-Large 356
33 Mission to Nepal 363
34 "Leaving Home, Going to America" 369

Abbreviations 377
Glossary 378
Sources and Acknowledgments 384
Index 388

Maps:

"Pickett's India," page 8

"Christ Church and the Butler Road Area," page 294

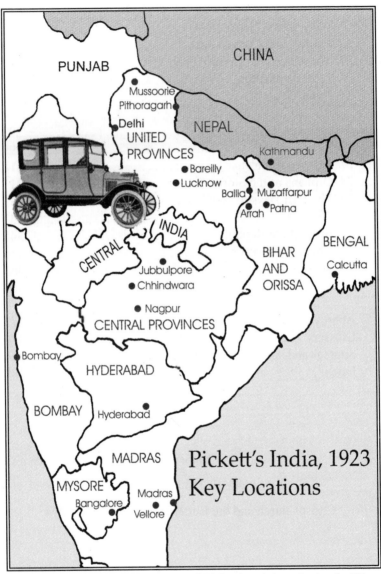

This map of India in the last year of Pickett's ministry in Arrah, Bihar, shows the places that appear most commonly in his life story overall.

Introduction

J awaharlal Nehru, the first Prime Minister, told him, "If I ever do something counter to Christian ethics, I want you to tell me." M.K. Gandhi, "Father of the Nation," criticized him in print and "accidentally" read his mail, yet commended his candor. B.R. Ambedkar, chief drafter of the constitution and first law minister of independent India, permanently borrowed dozens of his books and twice asked him for baptism. And H.C. Mookerjee, vice president of the Constituent Assembly, consulted him on language for the new constitution's statement on religious freedom. Unofficially, but with Nehru's implicit consent, he met with two American presidents, as well as U.S. senators, secretaries of state, and ambassadors on behalf of India. Yet he was not a politician. He was not even an Indian. He was a missionary.

It was in that capacity that Bishop J. Waskom Pickett, an American Methodist, made his mark on his adopted country. He came to India in 1910. By the end of the decade he had made a name for himself as a leader in the national temperance movement. Later, he would become known for his editorials in the influential *Indian Witness*, his leadership in health care, and a massive study of untouchable Christians—until then the largest social survey ever done outside America and Great Britain. During the 1947 communal riots that followed partition, Pickett did more to organize relief efforts than any nongovernmental person. Through his efforts and those of the Christian volunteers he recruited, tens of thousands of lives were saved. In the late 1940s, Pickett served as president of India's National Christian Council. At mid-century, he organized and became the first president of the remarkable United Mission to Nepal. However, most mission historians remember him not for those contributions but for his influence on Donald A. McGavran, missionary theorist and father of the late 20th century Church Growth Movement.

When Indian Methodists elected Pickett to the episcopacy, author and missionary E. Stanley Jones wrote: "It would have been very difficult to have made a better choice." Bishop James K. Mathews, who served as a missionary under Pickett in the 1940s, remembered:

> He lent an unusual degree of stability to the church and nation as Indian independence emerged. His friendship with Mahatma Gandhi (with whom he did not always agree and with whom he frequently took issue), with Ambedkar, . . . especially with Jawaharlal Nehru and then his daughter, Indira, and other Indian leaders was of crucial importance and incalculable value to the Christian community.

Another colleague, Bishop B.T. Badley, saw in him all the qualities one would wish for in a bishop: "a strong preacher, an able administrator, an untiring pastor, an effective writer, an inspired leader, a skilled presiding officer, and a Christian statesman."

In what follows you will accompany the man they described. Along the way, you will get to know him yourself. However, in theses pages you will meet more than a son of Kentucky, whose extraordinary life-journey paralleled the blossoming and fruition of India's independence movement and the end of empire, for this is not just about him. Featured, also, are the times and forces that shaped him along the road to Delhi—movements, institutions, events, places, and people. I hope this portrayal capably reflects all of these—not just J. Waskom Pickett's extraordinary life but, also, the Indian milieu he encountered, the movements and events he knew, and the missionary enterprise as it functioned in his time.

The Early Years (1890-1909)

The Pickett Brothers. Back: James
Lowry and Elbert Deets; front: Ludo
Carradine and Jarrell Waskom

Leander Lycurgus (L.L.) Pickett   Ludie Day Pickett

The new Pickett house in Wilmore, Kentucky. Built after the first house burned in 1907, L.L. Pickett had even the interior walls constructed of concrete.

Asbury College original Administration Building

Asbury College senior class, 1907. J. Waskom Pickett is second from left, top row. E. Stanley Jones is on the right, bottom row.

Main Street in Wilmore, Kentucky (1911), looking toward the depot

The opposite side of Main Street, looking in the same direction

1 The Picketts of Hallelujah Hill

W hen, in 1909, Professor J. Waskom Pickett and his brother, Willard Lee, arrived home for Christmas, the professor was only 19. Waskom had just completed his first semester of teaching at Taylor University in Indiana. Willard, who was five years younger, was a student at a related school and roomed with Waskom. As they walked from the Wilmore, Kentucky train station up Main Street, they passed the Wilmore Deposit Bank, J.R. Prather's Livery Stable, and an eating establishment with a sign that said, "LUNCH ROOM." A smaller sign, attached to the bottom read, "DINNER 30¢." Main Street was the only "real" street in Wilmore. Lower Main Street, near the depot, had not changed much since the Pickett family came to the town 15 years earlier. Without sidewalks, pedestrians still had to dodge horses, carriages, and wagons. Even so, because the village was the main stock shipping point in that part of the state, folks liked to call it "the biggest town of its size in central Kentucky."

A little farther up the street, on the right, the boys passed Asbury College, a Christian college of the Methodist stream of the American Holiness Movement. Although its roots went back to the 1830s, the Holiness Movement came into full bloom after the American Civil War. The movement taught that salvation involves two crisis experiences. In the first experience (conversion), God forgives your sins. In the second one (variously called "entire sanctification," "Christian perfection," "the second blessing," "the second work of grace," "the higher Christian life," "the rest of faith," and "full salvation"), God gives you power not to sin and to live a pure and holy life. John Wesley's *Plain Account of Christian Perfection* (1794), the Bible commentaries of Adam Clark, and John Fletcher's *Last Check to Antinomianism* (1907) were instrumental in launching the movement. Early leaders of the movement had included Charles G. Finney and Phoebe Palmer, but a new generation of leaders was in place now, including the Pickett boys' father, L.L. Pickett.

The emergence of camp meetings, holiness organizations, annual conventions, prayer bands, holiness publishers and publications, a growing holiness hymnody, and itinerating holiness preachers all contributed to the spread of the movement. Methodist denominational leaders tolerated, then trivialized, and finally opposed it. From the 1880s on, clashes between supporters of the movement and church hierarchies led to the starting of many independent holiness churches and denominations.

Asbury College, which had briefly been called Kentucky Holiness College, was Waskom's alma mater. Nine months earlier, fire had leveled the largest two buildings. For Waskom, passing by the blackened remains of the former Administration Building and Music Hall must have evoked a litany of memories: classes taken and taught; missionary conversations about Africa, India, and Japan; literary society debates with his roommate, E. Stanley Jones, now a pastor in India; campus revivals, especially the one in 1905; his 1907 graduating class of 16 (four women, 12 men), or possibly another fire—one that had destroyed his family home two years earlier.

Or was there, at that moment, something else on his mind? Perhaps he was thinking of a two-year-old decision he made while a student at the college, which he was just now ready to act on. That was what the large envelope tucked away in his luggage was about.

At the top of the street, the young men turned left. From there, it was a five-minute walk to the new Pickett house on four acres of hillside land purchased when the family arrived in town in 1894. L.L. Pickett had dubbed it, "Hallelujah Hill." The Greek Revival style residence built to replace their fire-wasted, original house was constructed of concrete. To fend off another disaster, L.L. had ordered that even the inside partition walls be concrete.

CHRISTMAS ON "HALLELUJAH HILL," (later, "Pickett Hill") was never dull—not with eight boys under one roof, although by now Waskom's two older stepbrothers were, like himself, on their own. If all the Picketts had been at home that Christmas—though they weren't—Waskom and Willard Lee would have been welcomed by their father and mother (Leander Lycurgus and Ludie Day Pickett), their eldest stepbrother (the Reverend James Lowry Pickett) and his family, another stepbrother (Elbert Deets) and wife, Annie, and younger brothers Ludo Carradine, Wilbur Crafts, Eulice, and Leroy Woodson.

Waskom, five foot nine, with black hair, gray eyes, and ruddy complexion, looked at least as youthful as his 19 years—no asset to a professor younger than most of his students. But this was nothing new. Before signing on at Taylor, Waskom had already taught at two other colleges, and from his first day in school he had always been the youngest in his grade.

FOLKS KNEW WASKOM'S FATHER, fifty-year-old Leander Lycurgus Pickett, as L.L. He was an evangelist, hymn writer, composer, editor, publisher, author, public debater, and sometime political candidate. He was also an astute businessman and expert fundraiser. L.L. was handsome and fit looking, though, in fact, he was habitually exhausted from overwork. Always impeccably groomed when he was itinerating—and he usually was—his usual uniform was a dark suit, starched shirt, and necktie, which had succeeded the Western style bow tie he once favored. L.L.'s strong, yet warm eyes were rivaled only by a conspicuous mustache, which had grayed long before his ebony hair. From these, other facial features stood back, even his prominent nose and eyebrows. More striking than L.L.'s physical appearance, though, was his intensity. To be with him was to be left in no doubt about his decided standards. Perhaps this is what Waskom had in mind when he admitted, "I was always a bit afraid of him."

Although L.L. spent most of his adult life in Kentucky, he established his reputation in Texas. That is where he put out his first collection of hymns and set up his publishing company. In the years after that, he edited and published the weekly King's Herald, produced dozens of booklets on religious themes, wrote 49 books, and composed the words and usually the music for more than 440 hymns. One of his best-known compositions, "Where the Healing Waters Flow" was the theme song in Oral Robert's early ministry. From it came the title of Robert's magazine, Healing Waters. Through his publishing, L.L. Pickett rose to prominence in the holiness revival of his era.

In the late 1870s L.L. married Mellie Dorough. They had two sons, James Lowry, born in 1880, and Elbert Deets, born August 29, 1885. Like Waskom, both would go by their middle names. Soon after Deets' birth, Mellie died. L.L.'s mother, Melissa, a widow for two years, came to help with the children. She lived with L.L.'s family the whole time Waskom was growing up. She died in her mid-seventies, only a month after the Pickett house fire. L.L. had little formal education—five months to be exact—but he had acquired a self-taught mastery of several fields of study. Most remarkable was his knowledge of the Bible, including the ability to read the Greek New Testament. In his public debates, he astonished opponents by not only stating the reference for whatever biblical text they cited, but by repeating its context word for word. As E. Stanley Jones, who boarded with the Picketts during college, remembered, [L.L.] "had the most amazing knowledge of the scriptures of any man I have ever known." Though such knowledge brought L.L. Pickett much respect, the lack of a college degree kept L.L. from his fulfilling his great dream of becoming a missionary to Asia. But his enthusiasm for missions never waned, as this excerpt from his writings shows:

> Some people . . . take no interest in the great work of filling the dark corners of earth's habitations of cruelty with "the knowledge of the glory of the Lord." But it is a spurious holiness that can say daily "Thy kingdom come," and yet tighten the purse strings or give stingy pittances when money is being raised to send the representatives of Jesus into the "regions beyond."

IN THE LATE 1880S, L.L. PICKETT preached often across the state line in Louisiana. During the 1887-1888 school year, he preached a series of sermons at Mansfield Female College. There he met the woman who would become his second wife—and Waskom's mother. Her name was Ludie Carrington Day. Born March 31, 1867 in Bayou Tunica, Louisiana, her parents were Lemuel P. and Emily (Alexander) Day.

Ludie, who had earned Bachelor of Arts and Master of English Literature degrees at Mansfield, had stayed on to teach English grammar and literature. She also served as organist in the college church, which is where she and L.L. met. Just two weeks after the close of the revival services, Pickett wrote to her and invited her to become his wife. She accepted, even though she had often declared that she would never marry a preacher, a widower, or a Texan. The 30-year-old evangelist and the 21-year-old teacher married on the fifth of December, or thereabout, in 1888.

Like her husband, Ludie had applied to the Board of Foreign Missions. Unlike him, she was accepted. But she needed to pass a medical exam in Nashville. Though she felt fine when she got to Nashville, her temperature was one degree above normal. They sent her home with instructions to record her temperature for a month and come back. Because her temperature remained slightly above the normal mark, the secretary reported to the Board that Miss Ludie Day was prone to developing tuberculosis. He added that she probably would not last a year in Asia.

Ludie gave birth to seven sons, one of whom—Vernon Day—died in infancy. When Leroy Woodson was born and the Picketts learned they would have no more children, L.L., who had hoped for at least one daughter, wept. As a kind of assuagement, a succession of temporary daughters (Asbury College students) stayed with the Picketts. They sought to adopt one of them. Three of them became missionaries.

Ludie Day Pickett was slight in build. Her demeanor was serene. Stanley Jones could not recall ever seeing her ruffled. When the first Pickett house caught fire, he was riveted by a plaque on a hallway wall. It was still readable through the flames. Later, he told "Sister Pickett" that the "Trust in the Lord" motto was the last thing he saw of home's interior. Ludie replied, "Stanley, that is exactly what I am doing." Confidence in Christ was her constant refrain, as expressed her hymn, "Never Alone."

Though all around me is darkness, earthly joys all flown;
My Savior whispers His promise, never to leave me alone!

This was the family from which Waskom Pickett came, to which he went home in 1909 for his 19th Christmas: passionate in convictions, literate and informed on the news and issues of the day, keenly interested in international missions, and deeply involved in the American holiness and temperance movements. But this Christmas Waskom had more on his mind than gathering around the piano for carols, catching up on family news, and seasonal services at the Methodist church. It had to do with that two-year-old decision. It had to do with the contents of that envelope in his luggage. It had to do with an unfulfilled dream inherited from both his parents. It had to do with a cablegram he had recently received from his friend and former roommate, Stanley Jones. Sometime on Christmas Day, perhaps with Papa and Mama Pickett close by, Waskom removed from the envelope in his luggage, a four-page form. In the form's upper left corner was a return address, typeset in small caps. It read: BOARD OF FOREIGN MISSIONS OF THE METHODIST EPISCOPAL CHURCH, 150 FIFTH AVENUE, NEW YORK. Just below, horizontally centered, in Courier typeface, the form's title announced: "APPLICATION OF THE CANDIDATE."

2 The Application

Waskom smoothed the application and dipped his pen into a jar of black ink. Under PERSONAL HISTORY—*Full name*, he wrote: "Jarrell Waskom Pickett." Under *Residence*, he answered: "Wilmore, Kentucky." Under *When and where born*, he added: "February 21, 1890, near Marshall, Texas."

Waskom Pickett never got to know the town of his birth. When he was three weeks old, the Pickett family rode a train to Columbia, South Carolina where L.L. took on the pastorate of the Gospel Mission Tabernacle and the editorship of a weekly paper called *The Way of Faith*. Besides those duties, L.L. was also heavily involved in itinerant preaching. A letter dated February 7, 1891, to "Masters Lowry and Deets Pickett," gives a glimpse of his multifarious lifestyle.

> My Dear Little Boys,
>   I must take time in the rush and strain of much hard work to write to you. I do not write to you as often as I might if I was not so hard pressed with work. I write from 5 or 6 to 12 or 15 letters a day these times, besides preaching twice a day & trying to study a little in a general way & particularly for my book on the Sabbath.
>   I want you boys to be studious, work hard and try to make noble, earnest men that Grandma, Mama & I may never be ashamed of. I see some young men who drink whiskey, lounge around the saloons, and waste their lives in idleness and sin . . .
>   I want my boys to keep entirely clear of such things as these. I count on you shunning sin in all its forms, so that you may love God and everybody, live to a noble purpose, a life of genuine usefulness and consequent happiness.

This life of loving God and working for Him will be a life of sweet memory to all who love you, leave many friends to miss you and weep over you when you are gone, and will bring you a crown of life and great glory when in the last great Day of Judgement, you stand before God.

God bless & save you both. Love to Grandma, Mama, Little brother [Waskom] & you both.

From y'r Papa

The Picketts stayed in South Carolina until Waskom was four. Then they moved to Wilmore, Kentucky.

THE NEXT QUESTION asked, *In what institution or institutions were you educated?* Waskom wrote: "Asbury College."

John Wesley Hughes, founder of Wilmore's Asbury College, wanted to birth "a real salvation school," one "where unsaved and unsanctified students could not only be encouraged but urged to get saved and sanctified and prepared educationally for their life's work." Hughes chose Wilmore because it was centrally located in the state and because of its accessability by rail. The chief commercial centers in Kentucky were Louisville, Lexington and Frankfort. Wilmore enjoyed regional rail service from these centers, as well as long-distance connections. In fact, for a time, Wilmore was the Q & C (Queen & Crescent) Railroad's greatest stock shipping point between Cincinnati and Chattanooga. At the same time, Wilmore preserved the reputation of a laid-back, clean-living community with no saloons, no crime, and a population who intended to keep it that way. In fact, the *Jessamine Journal* had recently suggested that, if Wilmore had a police court it would "die of rot." (Ironically, less than a month later, there were two bold attempts to rob the Wilmore Deposit Bank.)

A few days after Waskom entered Asbury College in 1903, two students wanting to escape the overcrowded boys' dormitories inquired about boarding at the Pickett house. One of them, a new student, was Stanley Jones from Baltimore. Ludie reported she had agreed to take them both. For 10 dollars a month, they would receive board and have the room that contained L.L.'s library. In subsequent years, Stanley and Waskom would share Waskom's room.

By the time he was 18, Waskom had earned his masters degree. From the beginning, he had shown unusual aptitude and intelligence. His mother's philosophy of educating children served to strengthen those qualities. Ludie Day Pickett believed that children should be reading fluently by four. So, by age two, she had taught Waskom the lower and uppercase alphabets. By four, when they came to Wilmore, he was reading the morning paper and, at breakfast, reporting on the noteworthy events of the day. And, by six, he had read all the New Testament and portions of the Old. Since Waskom's birthday came in February, he could not enroll in kindergarten until he was six and a half. But he soon made up for his "late" start. He entered kindergarten at nine o'clock, advanced to first grade an hour later, and to second grade after lunch. The next day they promoted him to grade three and the next month, to grade four. He finished high school one May and entered college in September of his 13th year.

TWO OF THE NEXT QUESTIONS had to do with languages. The first asked, *What languages other than English have you studied?* Waskom wrote: "Latin 6 years, Greek 4, German 1, Spanish ½ year." The second asked, *Do you acquire languages readily?* Without hesitation, he answered, "Yes."

Waskom had already taught several languages courses. In the 1908-1909 school year at Arkansas Holiness College he taught Latin. And the year before, while completing his Master of Arts degree at Asbury, he had lectured in Greek and Latin. New Testament Greek was his specialty. When he was just seven years old, his father began to teach him. By eight, he had become reasonably proficient, so L.L. bought two copies of Westcott & Hort's Greek New Testament. Each evening, the father chose a passage and read and translated the first verse. Then he called on the son to take the next verse. The two continued to take turns reading and translating until they finished the passage. Because of his language skills, classmates often called on Waskom for tutoring. One beneficiary of his competence with Greek was Stanley Jones who, because of a conflict with another class, was not able to take Asbury's introductory Greek course in his first semester.

WASKOM MUST HAVE SMILED as he penned his answer to a question about the applicant's ability to play the piano or organ, or lead in singing. While he shared his parents' appreciation for music, the closest he came to musical accomplishment himself was selling his father's hymnbooks at camp meetings. In that way, though, he earned enough to cover half of his college tuition.

THE PROFESSOR SKIMMED over the second section of the application, which asked about the applicant's physical condition. Waskom, who would live to be 91, signaled in his answers that his health was good.

As well as certifying the status of the applicant's health, the medical report also described his appearance. Waskom, it revealed, weighed 146 pounds, had a 33-inch waist and a 34-inch chest. For a little while, this would be all the description the mission board had of Pickett. As requested, he had a photo made, which he mailed separately. But since he forgot to include his name, the board's correspondence secretary could not know whose photo he had received.

The final question under "physical condition" asked: *Are you a total abstainer from the use of tobacco, from all forms of alcoholic beverages, and from opium, cocaine, and other narcotic drugs?* Firmly, Waskom wrote, "Yes." Just two years earlier, Waskom's father, L.L. Pickett had accepted the nomination of the Prohibition Party and had run for governor of Kentucky. Some were concerned that he had "quit preaching and gone into politics." Pickett responded to his critics, explaining, "I had my orders from the skies." He added: "God's people ought to yoke up with Him in their business, their political, their marital, home and social life, as well as in other church matters."

At first, Ludie opposed L.L.'s running for governor. But, after much prayer, husband and wife came to a consensus: L.L. would run but would campaign as a preacher, not a politician. L.L. Pickett lost the race for governor. However, he never lost his passion for preaching against alcohol and tobacco. Ludie Day took up the fight too—in fact, had already done so. Waskom could not recall a time when his mother was not active in the Women's Christian Temperance Union. And as he penned his answer on the application, he would, no doubt, have been reminded the Kentucky WCTU had just elected her as its new recording secretary, a post she would continue in for the next 15 years. She would accept other roles too: corresponding secretary; editor of the *Kentucky White Ribbon* (the

WCTU's paper); and, for 23 years, president of the Kentucky chapter of the WCTU.

ANOTHER SECTION FOCUSED ON the applicant's religious life. For example: *Give the date of your conversion.* Waskom wrote, "February, 1907."

That was Waskom's last year as a student as Asbury, but he had been counted a member of the church since he was a boy. When he was six, the Pickett family's pastor had preached on church membership. At the close he encouraged all who wished to join the church to come to the front and be welcomed as members. When he was almost 90, J. Waskom Pickett still recalled the moment: "I was sitting in the first pew in the 'Amen corner.' His invitation impressed me so much that I walked over and stood with the adults and was received into full membership." L.L. and Ludie Day Pickett knelt by him at the altar, then stood with him as he was received.

When Stanley Jones went to the altar at 15, he wanted reconciliation but later said he had settled for church membership. Waskom could have echoed Jones, for in the months and years that followed his reception into the church, he remained on the same trajectory as before. He was agreeable, respectful, and studious. He liked baseball, the daily newspaper, playing chess, and church—in that order. But he gave no real evidence of a spiritual quickening. As Stanley Jones put it, "He studied the newspaper more than he studied his books. As a young man he was distinctly a man of world affairs."

While Waskom and Stanley were students at Asbury, revival broke out almost yearly. One such visit of God happened in February 1904. "Like a thunderbolt it broke on us," said one who was there, "and for about two weeks the College was the theater of indescribable scenes in which students were saved or sanctified or called to the foreign mission fields." A year later, on February 18, 1905, revival came again. Like those that would occur in 1907 and 1908, it was unexpected. As E. Stanley Jones remembered it:

> Four or five of us students were . . . having a prayer meeting about ten o'clock at night. I remember I was almost asleep with my head against the bedclothes where I was kneeling, when suddenly we were all swept off our feet by a visitation of the Holy Spirit. We were all filled, flooded by the Spirit. Everything

that happened to the disciples on the original Pentecost happened to us. That night, Stanley paced the floor, praising God—"loudly and continuously," according to Waskom. At about two in the morning, L.L. Pickett came upstairs and said: "Stanley, the Word of God says, "The Lord giveth his beloved sleep." But the suggestion did no good; for Stanley, sleep was out of the question.

The revival of 1905 left few undisturbed. As it rippled through the school, its power intensified. Hundreds from Wilmore and beyond joined those in the Asbury community at the altar. Affected perhaps, but missing from the stream of seekers, was young Waskom. As he later recollected, "I was below the average age in my class, and I think, perhaps, I responded to that revival less than did many." The following year (1906) featured a series of smaller revivals, one of them led by Stanley Jones. But not until the year after that, during Waskom's final term as an undergraduate, did he finally turn with deep conviction to God.

The first gray days of February that year were surely among the most difficult of young Waskom's life. A month earlier, on the second of January, he had lost home and belongings by fire. Charred timber and ashes were all that remained of the house on Hallelujah Hill. Two weeks later Waskom's ill and aged step-grandmother, Melissa Pickett, who had barely gotten out of the burning house alive, passed away. Waskom had other things on his mind as well. With commencement just three months away, Stanley was preparing to leave—not just for another Baltimore summer but, perhaps, for good.

Those days must have been hard for a 16-year-old, uncertain of his future, not fully settled in his faith, about to say good-bye to his good friend. However, late in the month, another revival occurred. Though not as celebrated as some of the others, Asbury's president, B.F. Haynes, had never seen anything like it. He wrote,

It . . . has no leader and needs none, and possesses every feature of a most genuine, phenomenal and divine work of the Spirit. It just came from the Father, breaking out in the Boys' Conference and the first thing we knew there was a mighty, unprecedented, indescribable, phenomenal, spiritual conflagration among us. I haven't told half the story. It cannot be told in human words.

However, it was not the ferment of that revival that transported Waskom's life to a new level that month. His was to be a quieter, more thoughtful transformation. After Sunday morning worship at the Methodist Church, Waskom went for a long walk.

> Everywhere I went it seemed that God was speaking to me. And I came back late in the afternoon and then went to the evening service in the Methodist Church. And the pastor, who preached a very ordinary sort of sermon, closed by saying, "It seems to me that God has been speaking to someone here during the service—and maybe before the service—and that I ought to ask anyone who knows that this is true of him, or her, to come forward and kneel. And some of us can join that one in prayer."

Waskom immediately felt the invitation was for him and went forward and knelt at the altar. A minute or two later, Ludie knelt beside him and then others, praying with him as he was praying for himself, "rather quietly in contrast to a good deal of the praying that had been going on during that year in the college," he recalled.

> But in a way that has never ceased, my mind and heart were filled with wonder and with love for God, and within a week after that experience, I knew very definitely that God wanted me to be a missionary.

The thought of being a minister in the United States never occurred to Waskom. Those who wished to find God in America would have no trouble. Many would be eager to help them. So, if he were to become a minister, it would be overseas. He soon narrowed his focus to two places: Japan and India.

ANOTHER QUESTION ASKED, *Have you had success in winning souls for Christ?* Waskom responded, "I have felt that my efforts have been successful."

For Asbury boys, success in "winning souls for Christ" was substantially through preaching. In fact, some, like Stanley Jones, chose the school specifically to learn to be evangelistic preachers. One of the best opportunities for students who wished to develop their preaching skills was the "Boys' Conference." Students hoping to become ministers ran the organization. Some of them were already serving as pastors or assistant pastors in Kentucky churches. Juniors and seniors served as coaches to the younger members. Beginning at 6:30, they met for a half hour each weekday evening. After a brief prayer, one member preached a 15 minute sermon. Then a designated critic summarized the strengths and weaknesses of the sermon. Waskom did not become a member until his senior year, but Stanley joined as soon as he arrived on campus.

The next question asked, *Do you believe that you have a special call to the foreign mission field?* The limited writing space did not encourage detail. Waskom answered, "The Word of God gives me a sufficient call. I long to meet the need of the lost." *Is it your purpose to consecrate your life to missionary work in the foreign field?* Waskom responded: "It is."

This question gave Waskom the opportunity to reaffirm a decision made two years earlier. Right after his conversion, Waskom had signed a pledge card to go to the foreign field if possible. Perhaps, even now, he had the card in front of him or in his wallet. If not, it certainly came to mind.

As he responded to the question, he must have thought of his friend, Stanley too. It had been just a year since word had come from the *RMS Teutonic* that Stanley Jones was at last on his way to the field, though it was not Africa as he had long imagined, but India. Stanley had written:

> As we are nearing old England I feel constrained to let you know how I fare so far on my eastward voyage. It is really true that God will 'bless thy going out.' As I waved goodbye to my brother and sister, standing upon the docks in New York, strange sensations of holy joy flooded my soul and I knew I was in his will. Our native land, how sweet, but to the wholly surrendered soul, God is its home and His presence is its native atmosphere.

Since then, Jones' letters had reported, among other things—his wish to see the missionaries of his Lucknow church seek "the fullness of the blessing;" his plan to distribute to native preachers "thousands of holiness books"; and his struggles with Urdu, his new language.

Waskom's longing to follow Stanley was stirred, no doubt, by his friend's letters. But now, here he was actually applying, taking the first step! As he dipped his pen into the ink for the next question, he knew that his youth was still against him. However, in just two months, he would be 20. In the eyes of those searching for maturity, there was a vast difference between 19 and 20. The hour was approaching, he could feel it, when he would be on the field himself.

What special field, if any, do you prefer? Here he wrote, "I want to be led of the Lord where he can use me to the best advantage." But, in his heart, Waskom was already pondering, perhaps even dreaming of, a particular place. So, after writing the previous sentence and taking up all the allotted room, he inserted one thing more, just above the first word of the sentence. It was "India."

ASBURY HAD BEGUN A MISSIONARY society with 50 members in only its fifth year. All students were urged to join. Three years later, in 1898, the school funded its first two missionaries, both international students who would return to preach in their homelands of Persia and Japan (although only the student from Persia did so for sure). The same year, a Student Volunteer Band began with students who committed themselves to go anywhere, anytime for Jesus Christ. Weekly study classes met to learn about the countries to which students hoped to go. The idea was to become intimately acquainted with the challenges of those lands ahead of time. The band's noonday prayer meetings were passionate affairs, described by one student as "Pentecostal." Each week, one of the student volunteer members of the band led Sunday afternoon services. In addition, the students were responsible for one evening service each month.

In those days the influence of the Student Volunteer Movement for Foreign Missions (SVM) was widespread on college campuses. But it may be stated with some justification that nowhere was its potency felt more keenly than at Asbury. The SVM had emerged from the first Young Men's Christian Association summer conference for students in 1886, held at D.L. Moody's conference ground at Mt. Hermon School in Northfield, Massachusetts. Each evening, a group of 21 young men had prayed that, from that gathering, God would raise up a host of new missionaries. As the event continued, ever more of those present signed a pledge affirming that they were "desirous and willing, God permitting, to go to the unevangelized portions of the world." They called it, "The Princeton Declaration" because it had originated with the Princeton Foreign Missionary Society.

One of the "Mt. Hermon 100" was 21-year-old John R. Mott, a Cornell student from Iowa with exceptional organizational skills. In 1888, nervous leaders of the loosely structured SVM urged Mott (then Intercollegiate YMCA secretary) to bring order to the movement. Under his direction, a formal structure was adopted to unify and preserve SVM efforts. The declared purpose was: (1) to lead students to consider the call of foreign missions; (2) to guide volunteers in their preparation for the mission field; (3) to unite volunteers in an "organized aggressive movement"; (4) to secure enough volunteers to meet the needs of the various mission boards; and (5) to foster the interest and support of students who remain at home. Until the early 1920s, the SVM consistently met those goals. For all that time, half to three-fourths of all American missionaries going overseas were student volunteers who had signed a revised pledge card that stated: "It is my purpose, if God permit, to become a foreign missionary."

Although he came to Asbury with no idea of going to the mission field, Stanley Jones, by his junior year, was one of three representing Asbury at the Student Volunteer Convention in Nashville. So impressed were they by John R. Mott, they couldn't stop quoting him when they returned. That was Waskom's first introduction to Mott. He said, "Dr. Mott . . . became one of my heroes." Soon, Waskom, like so many other students of his generation, had put his signature to the SVM pledge.

Stanley Jones' pledge to become a missionary had SVM roots too. For one of their campus meetings, Volunteer Movement people asked him to give a speech on Africa. On his way to the speech, he prayed, "Lord . . . I want a missionary to go from this meeting, and I am not going in there until you give me one." According to Jones, God's replied, "According to your faith, so be it unto you." So, he went into the meeting and announced, "Somebody is going to the mission field from this meeting." He never guessed he was the one, but he said later, "From that moment, I was gripped."

After signing the pledge, it took Waskom Pickett two full days to get up the nerve to tell his mother. Showing her the card, he apologized, "Perhaps I should not have signed this without first talking it over with you." But, instead of being distressed, Ludie was ecstatic. "Oh, no!" she said. "Neither of us, your father or I, have failed for one day to pray that you might become a missionary in some part of Asia. This is an answer to our prayers." Not wanting to pressure him, they had never revealed their secret prayer. But, of course, Waskom knew well their deep interest in missions.

WHEN HE CAME TO the section entitled, EVANGELISTIC WORK, Waskom may have been surprised that the questions were about being licensed to preach, membership in an Annual Conference, and ordination. He wrote a series of noes. Under EDUCATIONAL WORK, the seventh section, the form asked, *Are you qualified to do administrative work, such as the principalship of an institution?* Waskom, ever sensitive about his youth, wrote, "My age alone might keep me from success in this phase." The next question asked, *What special preparation have you made for educational work?* He replied, "Independent study and research on a small scale." To the final request, *What experience have you had? Give positions held and length of time in each place*, he had more to say.

Waskom and Stanley both graduated with honors in 1907, in a commencement which featured an evening devoted to missions. But, though both young men were committed to foreign missionary service, they were, by graduation time, both planning to come back, Waskom as a graduate in the masters degree program, and Jones as an assistant in teaching Latin and Greek. Since he was already well along on his Master of Arts degree, Waskom's choice was perfunctory. Stanley, however, had hoped to be elsewhere. On April 30, he had applied to the Board of Foreign Missions of the Methodist Episcopal Church, but so far nothing had materialized. He thought of full-time preaching, but when President Haynes offered him a contract to teach, he accepted.

As expected, Stanley arrived by train just before the start of the fall term. However, he had come, not to teach, but to ask to be released from his commitment. The Methodist Board of Foreign Missions had just offered him a pastoral assignment at the English language church in Lucknow, India, and, after much prayer, he was convinced God wanted him to accept it. President Haynes told Stanley that if he could persuade Waskom to teach the classes, he could be released. Because of his age, though, Waskom was ambivalent. He had difficulty visualizing teaching Latin and Greek to students all older than he. Then there was his unfinished M.A. However, Haynes assured him that he could do both, so Stanley was freed to go to India and start the work for which he became renowned.

After earning his masters, Waskom wanted to enroll in Vanderbilt University's School of Theology, but L.L. was firmly opposed. He did not approve of seminaries, in fact, he called them "cemeteries." He urged Waskom to at least wait until he had several years of ministry experience in Asia or America. Meanwhile, Waskom got a letter from C.L. Hawkins, president of Arkansas Holiness College, in Vilonia, Arkansas. Hawkins wanted him to teach there in the fall. Enclosed with the letter was a contract, which Waskom returned signed.

Arkansas Holiness College was very small and very new. September 15, 1908 would mark the start of just its third session. When Waskom got there, he found the college community in an optimistic frame of mind. Enrollment was up. The new boys' dorm was nearing completion. And, including him, 10 eager teachers were anticipating their first classes. It was just the right place to begin a teaching career—except that all the students were at least two years older than he.

WASKOM SKIPPED THE QUESTIONS in the next two sections, which had to do with medical and industrial work. For references, he listed the following: Professor and Mrs. Newton Wray, now at Taylor but formerly members of the Asbury community; the Reverend A.P. Jones of Wilmore; and the Reverend E. Stanley Jones. With that, the application was complete.

Two days later on December 27 he got out some of his old Asbury stationery and penned a letter to go with the form. He wrote:

I enclose my application for foreign service. The physical report accompanies it. My choice of work would be the educational, but when I said I was anxious to teach or preach, I meant that I wanted to reach India and would be subject to the direction of the Board—willing to serve in either capacity. It would be a great treat, personally, to enter the educational work in Lucknow, India—my old roommate and classmate of '07 is pastor of the English speaking church there. I am praying that the Lord may lead me and feel sure that He has in applying to you at this time. My permanent address is Upland, Indiana.

Yours for Christ
(Prof) J. Waskom Pickett

3 Dreaming of India

Handling Waskom's application at the Board of Foreign Missions in New York was Associate Corresponding Secretary George M. Fowles. There were, at that time, a general corresponding secretary, A.B. Leonard, and three associate secretaries. One of Fowles' duties was overseeing missionary recruitment. When he received Waskom's application, he immediately wrote to Stanley Jones and to Professor and Mrs. Newton Wray for their assessments of Waskom.

Mary Gilbert Wray's recommendation, sent two days later, echoed her husband's. She spoke of Pickett's "high ideals, magnetic personality, and courteous manner." She described his earnestness of purpose, enthusiasm, leadership, brilliant mind, quick sympathy, and conversational ability. To these qualities, she added that he was "a logical speaker," and "deservedly popular." Stanley Jones' reply, on February 2, offers perhaps the best description we have of the personality and character of the young applicant:

> His disposition is of the type called sweet and he would no doubt win his way into the hearts of the people here. He has a good deal of tact & knowledge of men. I lived in the same room with him for several years & from my experience with him, I have seen nothing that would not allow him to work harmoniously with others. He completed his college course very early proving his perseverance and determination. As to his teachability, I cannot say very much since I have not known him in that capacity. He always had, however, a faculty for imparting knowledge which would no doubt fit him for school work. His manner is especially pleasing. He is very whole souled in all that he does. He was always keen at debating.

Jones also commented on young Waskom's background, realism, and maturity. "[Waskom's] home is an excellent Christian one—a sample of real home piety. His call is not a fancied notion, as the dark side of mission was always presented at Asbury College. Moreover, he is older than his years. He always was."

The immediate impetus for Waskom's application to the mission board had been a cable from Stanley urging him to apply for the pastorate of the Lal Bagh English Church, which he was vacating in order to plunge full time into the evangelistic work he loved. Stanley was anxious to have Waskom come, both for the rekindling of their friendship and the well-being of the Lal Bagh church. During his two years in Lucknow, he had become increasingly frustrated by the administrative demands of the pastorate, what he called "desk duties." Jones' forte was people-work not paperwork, his burden the unreached masses. He complained, "There is not a man free in our mission to do evangelistic work in all Southern Asia. Everyone is tied hand and foot with work that must be done, although it is not particularly spiritual in its nature."

Jones was referring to tasks like raising the 500 or 1,000 dollars a month needed for support. He described missionaries that had licked postage stamps until they tasted glue in everything they ate. He protested that the ledger supplanted the prayer closet and that the multitudes to whom the missionary had come to preach were being left to native workers while the missionary became a mere "office drudge, with only an occasional visit to the villages." How can you be "a man on fire," he despaired, when you must be "a man of affairs?" At the heart of Jones' complaint, however, was not the buildup of paperwork but the leveling off—even abridgement— of the missionary force.

Now back in the classroom in Indiana, Waskom, unaware of the correspondence between the board and his references, was growing restless. On February 10, he wrote to Fowles, "My heart burns within me to begin work on foreign land where I believe God wants me. I would be glad to hear from you and learn of the progress made in deciding on my application." Fowles responded that the board had not forgotten him but that, currently, no openings existed. He suggested that, unlike the situation in America, they could seldom forecast "educational vacancies" overseas. Dismayed to learn the board was only thinking of him for educational work, Waskom replied on February 16 that, although his experience best suited him for a school assignment, he was anxious to "get into the fray soon." Could he be considered for other work? "I would be glad to preach the precious truths of the gospel to the perishing of North India. Could I be sent there to study the language and help as I might be able, being in preparation for the ministry or school work as the exigencies of the situation determine?"

He also reported that he needed to advise Taylor University of his plans within the month. He enclosed the cable he had received from Stanley about the opportunity in Lucknow. "I would be especially pleased to be associated with [Jones]," he wrote.

Fowles wrote back that had the board known of Waskom's openness to evangelistic work, he could have sailed that spring, but now all the vacancies were filled. They would, however, keep Waskom in mind for future openings. Fowles' response was encouraging but also puzzling, for Waskom had all along indicated his willingness to serve in areas other than educational. Was the board dragging its feet due to his youth?

Two months later, on April 17, Waskom wrote another letter. However, this time he wrote, not to Fowles, but directly to the "Corresponding Secretary of the Board of Foreign Missions." He explained that, at the urging of Bishop John E. Robinson of Bombay, he was writing to inquire about an autumn departure for India.

John E. Robinson, born in Ireland and trained in the U.S., had been in India for 36 years. He was then 61. Owing to a long stint as editor of the *Indian Witness*, he was nearly as well known in America as in South Asia. Much in demand as a speaker, his long and slender face, compassionate eyes, prominent cheek-bones, thick mustache, and neatly-trimmed beard evoked instant attention. But it was "the reality and freshness of his religious experience" and his encouraging nature that drew folks to him. How Pickett met him is not certain, but probably Robinson visited the Taylor community as part of a Laymen's Missionary Movement national campaign. When he learned of the young professor's interest in India, he urged him to ask for an invitation from the Foreign Mission Board to the closing event of the campaign, the forthcoming Men's National Missionary Congress in Chicago. Robinson followed up with his own letter to the mission board, confirming his interest in the young professor. He proposed that Pickett be examined during the Chicago event for possible service at Bombay's Bowen Church. On or about Friday, April 29, Waskom got instructions by mail to report the following Monday to the Candidate Committee at Chicago's Hotel Stratford.

The national campaign leading to the Congress was generated by the Laymen's Missionary Movement. Over seven months, 100,000 men had assembled in 100 cities. Three thousand delegates were expected at the Chicago finale, including ministers from 40 Methodist Episcopal conferences and Methodist missionaries from Latin America, Africa, the Philippines, China, Japan, and India. Among the speakers were two of Waskom's heroes: John R. Mott and the legendary James Mills Thoburn of India. Most fitting, then, was the motto on the immense banner hung as a backdrop to the distinguished speakers: "UNTO HIM SHALL THE GATHERING OF THE NATIONS BE."

As his train steamed into Chicago, his travel and five-dollar registration fee paid, Waskom must have sensed that, after months of waiting, he was finally on the move and close to his great goal. Mayor Busse's Chicago was on the move too. Dozens of pushcart vendors were moving onto Maxwell Street, the White Sox were moving to Comisky Park, and the city was going ahead with a new master plan. However, as Waskom stepped from the train to make his way to the Stratford, whatever thoughts he had of the kaleidoscoping face of the metropolis must certainly have been secondary to those of the committee that would shortly affirm or deny his candidacy.

When his examiners were done, Waskom, for the most part, felt satisfied with his answers. At the same time he thought he had detected some guardedness concerning his holiness roots and was fearful, therefore, of the committee's response to his theological views. However, his anxiety was short lived. When the committee called him back, it was to warmly endorse his candidacy. One member, Dr. Homer Stuntz, even told the young professor he was perfectly qualified for the vacant principalship of the Methodist school in Callao, Peru. Thus, Waskom was not entirely unprepared when, on May 11, Fowles wrote asking him to consider going to Peru instead of India. Waskom responded:

> Following Bro. Stuntz's remarks at the committee meeting, I considered what I ought to do should this situation present itself, and feel that the Lord would have me say that I will bury any preference of my own and accept the decision of the Board as the providential ruling in this case. I have never felt that I could say positively where the Lord wanted me. I do know that the Lord has called me to his work, and applied to you to be sent to India because I thought I saw the Lord's hand opening the way. If Bro. Stuntz feels that my work will count most in Peru, and

our divinely commissioned Board agrees, I will be glad to go
there.

Fowles' reply came on Wednesday, May 18. Waskom knew without
a doubt that he would momentarily have his answer. Unfolding the letter,
he read the following:

Dear Brother Pickett:
    Bishop Robinson . . . insists that they want you in India and
has requested that we make arrangements for your outgoing. He
advises us to have you go to our English church at Lucknow...
Bishop Robinson has taken quite a liking to you and he says if
you will only turn out to be as good a missionary as your friend
Stanley Jones he will be satisfied.
    At the Board meeting yesterday you were appointed as a
missionary of this Board. There is nothing in the way now to
your sailing as soon as you can make arrangements to go. Please
advise S.O. Benton of this office about the date you wish to sail
so that he can secure steamship tickets for you. All questions in
regard to your passage will be answered by Dr. Benton. If you
have any freight you had better send it on to us as soon as
convenient. I presume you will not have much if any to go, as
you have no household goods to take along with you . . . You are
allowed 120 cubic feet of freight for which the Board will pay.

The news could not have been more agreeable. Though resigned to
Peru, Waskom had dreamed only of India. He immediately wrote to
Benton, reporting that he wished to confer with his parents before
finalizing a date. But he did have a date in mind: "Would August the 1st
be too soon? I have heard that a missionary should not begin his work in
the hot season."
    Waskom's concern about arriving in the hot season is not surprising.
The annual pattern of missionary migration to the hill stations to escape
the heat of the plains was well known. So was danger of heatstroke in
tropical climates. Missionary handbooks cautioned against summer
arrivals. However, whatever Waskom may have read about the dangers
of heat, cholera, tuberculosis, snakebite, mad dogs, scorpion stings or any
other perils associated with service in India, he was not deterred. On the

contrary, he told Benton, "I rejoice ... that I shall soon be preaching the gospel in needy India."

Showing the same excitement, he blurted out to Fowles:

You could hardly imagine how happy I became yesterday upon receipt of your letter ... I waited two years to get old enough to be a missionary and when I applied I felt that I just could not wait longer. My heart is full now because the realization of my desire is so near.

In response to Waskom's question about an August 1 departure, Fowles, after conferring with Benton, suggested waiting another month "on account of the heat you will encounter on your journey to Lucknow."

After consulting with L.L., Waskom settled on the first of October or thereabouts. In his response to Benton, he wrote:

My mother wants to see me off and she is to be a delegate to the Nat. Conv. of the W.C.T.U., which meets in Baltimore. If I sail just before or after the Convention, she can do as she hopes. I have been at home very little in the last two (2) years and I want to please Mamma in any way I can in these last months of my stay here. I will necessarily be away from home most of the time between now and Sept. and perhaps as Papa insists, I ought to stay at home that month.

Waskom had two more questions for Benton. First, would it be possible to spend some time in England and on the Continent "for general educational purposes?" And what bed clothing would he need? The latter question was at Ludie's prompting. Ludie fretted all summer that Waskom was going off to India without a wife, with no one to care for him.

4 American Methodists in India

Meanwhile, from June 14-23 of 1910 the historic Edinburgh World Missionary Conference had convened with John R. Mott as chair. Like several others of the "Mt. Hermon 100," Mott had become a leader in the international missionary movement—but Mott led the pack. Though still in his thirties, as secretary of the Student YMCA and chairman of the SVM, he had already promoted the work of Christian missions across the globe. The reputation and trust he had gained led naturally to his selection as chair at Edinburgh. There was no disappointment. His trademark skills: the capacity to unite diverse participants, project a clear vision, manage conflict, summarize positions and reports, and maintain rigorous control served the conference admirably. To those representing India at the Edinburgh Conference, its most impressive feature was the remarkable display of unity that prevailed. To see certain leaders side by side on the platform astonished but, also, greatly encouraged them.

Among the delegates from India were Pickett's recent advocate, Bishop John E. Robinson, and Bishop James M. Thoburn, whom Waskom had met at the National Missionary Congress in Chicago. Robinson reported on the mass conversion movements to Christianity in India which, he said, offered hope that the bulk of India's 50 million "Outcastes" could be won to Christ. Thoburn spoke of the missionary's call. Indigenous Indian participants included Dr. K.C. Chatterjee, "the Grand Old Man of the Church of North India," and V.S. Azariah, the future bishop of Dornakal. Chatterjee told about his conversion through Alexander Duff in 1854. But it was young Azariah who seized everyone's attention with his unexpected and impassioned plea against racial condescension and for friendship and cooperation between missionaries and Indian Christians.

Waskom would have heard about Edinburgh at the Chicago missionary congress, where the buzz about it was considerable. Further, throughout the summer and fall, coverage of it in the *Pentecostal Herald* and other church papers, both at home and abroad, was substantial.

For example, the *Indian Witness* had reported several matters its readers in India hoped to see discussed at Edinburgh. One concern was the practice of sending missionary recruits to the field without so much as a briefing. But though J.N. Farquhar and others would touch on the issue, the scandal of inadequate training would persist for decades. As James K. Mathews, who went to India 28 years later, wrote, "I was ill prepared: no special training for India or the missionary task; no language orientation; no anthropology, no nothing! . . . I was given a passport and a ticket and was told that India was 'thataway.'" Another subject Methodists in India hoped Edinburgh delegates would consider was the "indigenous church."

Whether Waskom appreciated the depth of missiological musing that went on in Methodism's largest mission station is not known. But he was certainly aware of the high profile of learning and literacy there. For one thing, H.C. Morrison had just published an article in the *Pentecostal Herald* detailing his visit to Lucknow's Methodist churches, colleges (Isabella Thoburn College for women and Reid College for men), and publishing house, in which he pointedly underscored the urbanity and refinement of the city's Methodists. Moreover, Lucknow's informed and literate *Indian Witness* had many stateside readers and, almost certainly, Pickett would have been among them. Beyond that, Stanley Jones had described the Lal Bagh Church in some detail in his correspondence.

METHODISTS WERE LATECOMERS to India. They did not begin their work there until the mid-1850s. In response to an appeal by Scottish missionary, Alexander Duff, the Methodist Episcopal Church, in 1852, started a fund for sending missionaries to India. But it took four years to find someone willing to go. He was Irish-born William Butler, then a preacher in the New England Conference. For some time, Butler had used his pen to promote the cause of missions. He and his wife, Clementina Rowe Butler, who became arguably the best-known missionary couple of the 19th century, sailed from Boston on April 9, 1856. They got to Calcutta on September 23, where they consulted with other missions. On November 29, they reached Lucknow, Butler's choice of a home base. The Butlers could not have arrived in North India at a more infelicitous time, for the

British were about to face the most unnerving event of their long tenure of sway over the subcontinent.

Because of anti-Western feeling among the locals and the British authorities' aversion to missionaries, the Butlers could not find a place to live in Lucknow. The cool reception forced them to move on to Bareilly. They arrived in early December. One bright spot came from the Presbyterians in Allahabad. They pointed Butler to a young Indian Christian, Joel Janvier, who signed on as Butler's aide. Thus, Janvier became the first Indian Methodist preacher.

In mid-May 1857, only four months after the work in Bareilly had begun, the Anglo-Indian War erupted. Rumors had been rife for weeks that the British-paid Indian foot-soldiers (called sepoys) of the Bengal Army might rebel. Aggravating tensions, the British hatched a regulation that allowed sending troops into such places as Burma (which caused fears among the Brahmans of caste-breaking). Another regulation allowed for harsher treatment when soldiers balked at certain commands. The last straw may have been only a rumor, but it didn't matter. Word spread that the bullets for the newly-issued breech-loading Enfield rifle, which had to be bitten before loading, were greased with animal fat from pigs (unclean to Muslims) and cows (sacred to Hindus). Under the revised regulations, when resentful sepoys balked at leading their rifles, they were pummeled and paraded in irons before their peers.

On May 10, in Meerut, a hundred miles northwest of the Butler's work, while most of their British officers were in church, three regiments struck back, releasing prisoners and killing the few officers on duty. They then marched off to Delhi where there were only a handful of British troops and where Indian soldiers welcomed them with open gates. After reinstating the old emperor, whom they made the involuntary symbol of the revolt, they set out to kill all foreigners and Christians. Overnight the rebellion spread to other outposts. It took months for the British to put it down.

Four days after the Meerut mutiny, the Butlers were warned to leave Bareilly. The Presbyterians implored them to go with them to Cawnpore. Others urged them to seek safety at Naini Tal, in the foothills of the Himalayas. At first they hesitated to leave at all, but as the situation grew more ominous, they retreated to Naini Tal. A few days later, fighting erupted in Bareilly. Janvier was preaching on the text, "Fear not, little flock, for it is the Father's good pleasure to give you the kingdom" when word came of the outbreak. Janvier immediately closed the meeting. It was none too soon. In a few moments, the insurgents were at the door. The entire congregation escaped, except one. An Anglo-Indian named Maria Bolst, she became the first Methodist martyr in India. The Butlers were fortunate to have escaped. They were the only missionaries to survive. All the others, including the Presbyterians who had fled to Cawnpore, were killed in a massacre "too shocking for the polite English to mention."

On the day Bareilly came under siege, two more families, the Humphreys and the Pierces, set sail from Boston to join the Butlers. William Butler wrote to them in Calcutta and arranged to meet them in Agra. There, under the dome of the Taj Mahal, they sang the doxology. The next day, Janvier joined them and they traveled to Naini Tal, where, for the time being, the women and children were still under British orders to stay. Butler began regular worship services there. Then, when order was restored, he returned to devastated Bareilly, and from there went to Lucknow. In contrast to their arrogantly cool reception on Butler's first visit, the British officials at Lucknow, chastened by the fall of the city and the long siege of the Residency, now welcomed him and helped him purchase property. The early work in Lucknow included open-air preaching in the bazaars, worship for British soldiers in the cantonments, group-meetings in English and Hindustani, three schools, and orphan care. By September 1859, more missionary recruits had arrived, including James M. Thoburn and Edwin W. Parker. As Butler had intended from the start, Lucknow became the administrative and educational center of what emerged as Methodism's North India Conference.

FOR SOMEONE USED TO COLLEGE TOWNS, as Waskom was, Lucknow represented an ideal setting for starting a missionary career. In 1910, Lucknow contained Methodism's largest mission station and it was still growing, especially its educational institutions. Of these facts, Waskom was well aware. Still, seen firsthand for the first time, the scale of the enterprise would surprise him, as he confirmed in an article he wrote six years later:

> Along with the common idea of the missionary as a frock coated, silk-hatted brother singing psalms to naked cannibals, is the popular misconception of a mission station as a mud hut in the jungle. A mission station, on the contrary, is usually placed in

a large city, centrally located with reference to a very wide area, and comprises an assembly of buildings, organizations and people which gives it the air of a large American University.

This, then, was the ministry setting for which Jarrell Waskom Pickett was packing that summer.

The Settling Down Years (1910-1915)

Baltic II, the ship on which Pickett began his journey to India

Methodist Bishops F.W. Warne and J.E. Robinson

Top: Lal Bagh Church, Lucknow, both
   Jones' and Pickett's first assignment
Right: E. Stanley Jones
Bottom: Lucknow Central Church and its
   pastor, J.R. Chitambar

Ruth and Miriam Robinson, 1916

Ruth and Miriam at Evanston

5 Passage to India

In late September 1910, just before Waskom's departure, Lowry and Deets came home to Wilmore for a family reunion. It would be the last time L.L., Ludie Day, and all the children then living would be together at the same time.

On September 25, 1910, Waskom gave a Sunday evening farewell address to his friends at the Methodist church. The following day, at the Wilmore station, he said goodby to his mother and brothers and, with his father, boarded a train for New York. Once in New York, they checked into their hotel and made their way to the headquarters of the Board of Foreign Missions at 150 Fifth Avenue. There they met George M. Fowles, with whom Waskom had carried on most of his correspondence. Fowles led them to the office of Dr. A.B. Leonard, the General Secretary. Leonard was sitting at his table with his back to the door when they came in. He was a big man. Fowles said, "I have brought Waskom Pickett, our newest missionary, and his father to meet you. He will leave for India tomorrow." Without turning around, Leonard said, "Well, sit down. I'm busy now. I'll be able to talk to you soon." They waited for what seemed like a half-hour to Waskom but was probably 10 minutes. Finally, Leonard gave them his attention.

Addressing himself to Fowles, he said, "Is this boy going to India? He is too young to be a missionary. You should cancel his passage. Where did you think of sending him?"

Fowles replied, "Bishop Warne, in India, has accepted him as successor to Stanley Jones at Lucknow. We can't change that."

SATURDAY, OCTOBER 1, the day Waskom's ship, the British White Star steamer, *Baltic II*, was scheduled to sail, promised to be fair and warmer according to the newspapers. If Waskom purchased a *New York Times* that morning (a virtual certainty for Waskom) he would have paid a penny and learned, among other things, that Woodrow Wilson was running for governor of New Jersey and the reclusive artist, Winslow Homer, had died at his home in Maine. Of most interest to him, however, would have been the column on departing ships on page 13. The paper announced that *Baltic II* would be one of 10 transatlantic steamships departing that day, and one of two heading for Liverpool, England.

Waskom and L.L. went to the pier from which *Baltic II* would sail. The seven-year-old ship must have been an impressive sight for the two Kentuckians. It was a handsome vessel, with four masts and two funnels. The ship was 709 feet long and 75 feet wide at the beam, with a gross weight of nearly 24,000 tons—considerably larger than the *Teutonic* on which Stanley Jones had sailed. At that time, *Baltic II* could accommodate 425 passengers in first class, 450 in second class, and 2,000 in third class. The ship had been in the news the year before when it rescued more than a thousand passengers from the *Republic* and *Florida*, which had collided at sea. A couple of years later it would be one of the ships to radio the *Titanic* that there was ice in the area. After a while, the two men said their goodbyes, and the younger of the two joined the line waiting to embark. Soon J. Waskom Pickett's Indian odyssey would be underway.

BALTIC II ARRIVED AT LIVERPOOL SIX days later. From there, Waskom set out on a two-week tour of Wales and England, visiting Cardiff, Stratford-on-Avon, and London. Along the way he visited a number of Methodist clergymen. After that, he spent three weeks in Paris, Florence, Rome, and Naples. His last two days were in Naples. From there, on a ship originating in Liverpool—probably a ship of the P&O line, Waskom had booked passage to Bombay.

The voyage across the Mediterranean must have called all sorts of schoolboy images to mind—everything from the adventures of Odysseus to the shipwrecks of Paul. However, other than the blue water and the occasional glimpse of a distant shoreline, there was little to arrest one's attention. Instead, Waskom took notice of the daily chess game of two Irish girls—sisters—one in her late teens, the other in her early twenties. But although their daily competition attracted him, their cigarette smoking repelled him. He had never before seen a woman smoking a cigarette (although he had seen Kentucky mountain women with corncob pipes). After the shock subsided, Waskom's love for chess won out and he struck up a conversation with the young women. When they offered him the chance to join them, he accepted, losing his match with the older sister but defeating the younger one.

Though their smoking disturbed him, the Christian devotion of the sisters won his admiration. On boarding the ship back in Liverpool, the young women had learned there would be no chaplain aboard. After examining the passenger list and finding no clergyman mentioned, they had gotten the captain's permission to hold a public Bible study each morning and a prayer and praise service each evening. When they learned that Waskom was a missionary, they asked him to take over the services. Waskom "mildly objected" but finally gave in. From then until their arrival in Bombay, he conducted morning and evening services.

On arrival at Port Said, arrangements were made for passage through the Suez Canal, an 80-million dollar ribbon of blue that linked Britain to its eastern empire. There the passengers got their first real glimpse of the East and met the weathered faces of those whose ancestors slashed their way to Europe claiming that theirs was the one true God and that Mohammed was his prophet. They saw their first African faces there too, as well as a sprinkle of British and French faces belonging to those charged with the operation and maintenance of the shipway.

Twelve hours and 118 miles after entering the canal, the Gulf of Suez came into view and, later, the main body of the Red Sea. For a student of the Bible, like young Waskom, this was sailing into the world we all came from. It was sailing past the world of Adam and Eve, the land of the Hebrews' 40-year sojourn, and the port of Solomon's navy. Watching the ship's wake from the fantail, Waskom knew that somewhere in the receding hills was Mt. Sinai, and somewhere behind that, old Jerusalem, and Galilee, and the Dead Sea, and the site of Jesus' Great Commission to go into all the world with the gospel. But of course the real attraction was still a long way off . . . beyond Jiddah halfway down the Arabian coast, the supposed location of the tomb of Eve . . . beyond Aden at the bottom of the peninsula . . . and beyond the Gulf of Aden, the gateway to the Arabian Sea. In fact, India was a full seven days of sailing beyond that.

Meanwhile, the Bible studies and worship services grew steadily, drawing both passengers and crew. During the last week, several passengers sought spiritual counsel from the young missionary. Among them was the captain. On the final evening of the voyage, he informed Waskom that he wished to become a follower of Jesus, and would

Waskom pray for him, his wife, and his children? From the bridge, the captain made another announcement, this one for all the passengers: sometime before breakfast, he said, they would be in Bombay Harbor.

BY SIX O'CLOCK THE NEXT MORNING, Waskom was on deck. Silhouetted against a backdrop of hills and a brightening sky, Bombay was already in view. Old Bombay looked very different from today's Bombay (Mumbai). There were no skyscrapers then, and no Gateway of India arch. That would come the following year. Instead, the inner harbor—with Elephanta Island and its cave-temples starboard, and Taj Mahal Palace Hotel on the port side—served as gateway. The subcontinent's real portal, however, was the city itself. It was on stepping ashore and wandering into Bombay's beehive streets that one got the distinct feeling of crossing a threshold. It was there that one first caught sight of—both as reflection and promise—the India beyond.

Like Calcutta, the city of Bombay was the product of colonialism. Lying midway along India's western coast on the Arabian Sea, it was an obscure island village when the Portuguese took it over in 1534. It was they who christened it Bon Bahia, or "Good Bay." Nevertheless, they preferred Goa, farther to the south, and in 1661 gave Bombay to King Charles II of England as part of a royal dowry. There followed a brief custodial period under Captain James Cook. Then the East India Company leased Bombay for an annual sum of 10 pounds in gold.

Realizing the potential for a deepwater port, Gerald Aungier, an early British governor of the islands, lured thousands of Gujarati traders, Parsi shipbuilders, and Muslim and Hindu workers to Bombay by promising them religious freedom. A few decades later, a fort, which came to be known as "the Castle," was built on Girgaum, the largest of Bombay's seven islands. Beyond the fort, a walled-in European-style town developed. And beyond the walls, a ramshackle settlement known as Native Town emerged. In between was the Esplanade—an open area that served as defensive buffer, parade ground, sports field, and community common. After the rebellion of 1857, the British Crown replaced the British East India Company as the governing authority. That was when the city really began to percolate—so much so that by now, the year of Waskom's arrival, Bombay was firmly established as the dominant industrial center on the subcontinent.

The city's surge into prominence was sparked by the emergence of a few small textile mills, strengthened by the coming of the railways, and solidified by events in America and Egypt. The first of the mills was established in 1854. By 1860, six more were in place. The first railway (in 1853) connected Bombay to Thana, a distance of 22 miles. Governor-General Dalhousie had urged further development, but it was the unnerving "mutiny" that finally fueled a full head of steam. The unexpected violence and rapid escalation of the rebellion into a widespread uprising shocked both the British public and British authorities. Although the centers of the war were Delhi, Lucknow and Cawnpore, there were uprisings at dozens of other posts as well as a simultaneous series of rural rebellions. Only a tip-off prevented a similar outbreak in Bombay. When the British finally regained control of the areas taken by revolutionaries, a stunned Parliament dissolved the East India Company, asserted the sovereignty of the British Raj over all the feudal princes, and reorganized the army to prevent a repeat of the calamity. The rapid expansion of the rail system helped make possible a smaller (therefore, less costly) and more mobile army and artillery. However, the real benefit was its catalytic effect on industrial development. By 1910, more than 25,000 miles of broad and narrow gauge track crisscrossed the country, with more than 65 million tons of raw materials freighted yearly. Much of that freight went to Bombay, which by now had two major trunks joining it to commercial centers in north and central India and to all the back country villages between.

The Bombay that greeted the 20-year-old Pickett contained 979,000 people. Eighty percent were migrants from rural districts. Most of them faced grim futures. Overcrowding, famine, disease, feculent streets and deficient drainage guaranteed it. Between 1899 and 1901, almost one fourth of the city's population died (195,000 people). In the decade leading up to 1906, deaths outnumbered births by 405,000. One of the Cowley Fathers wrote, "The vocation of the Bombay Mission seems to be especially to prepare people for death ... After being with us a short time death carries them off."

In contrast to the misery of the perimeter slums, the other Bombay—British Bombay—across the Esplanade contained elegant imperial residences, a university, the best luxury hotel in India, a yacht club, and a stadium for observing military reviews and sporting events (especially Saturday afternoon horse races). Mostly Europeans attended the horse races, but in contrast to the British Yacht Club, the races were open to moneyed non-Europeans too, including many Parsis.

Although Parsis numbered only 6 percent of the Bombay population, they were an elite and influential community. Sometime after the Islamic conquest of Persia in the seventh century, a band of Parsis migrated to Gujarat, where they found freedom to practice their Zoroastrian beliefs. A thousand years later, many Gujarat Parsis moved again—this time south to Bombay where they became wealthy as entrepreneurs, selling cotton and other goods, first to the Portuguese and then to the British. Not by accident, Parsis were often among the first Indians encountered by newcomers to Bombay. When E. Stanley Jones arrived in Bombay three years earlier, it was "a stove-pipe hatted" Parsi who guided him through customs, delivered him to the railway station, and found a pillow and a blanket for him. From the ranks of the Parsi community came some of the most celebrated leaders of the early nationalist movement in India. Chief among them in 1910 was 86-year-old Dadabhai Naoroji, who had founded the first Indian-owned firm in both London and Liverpool. Naoroji was also the first Indian elected to Britain's Parliament and a three-time president of the Indian National Congress. Although a few had become Christians, most Parsis remained Zoroastrians. Among the best-known landmarks in Bombay were the Parsis' Towers of Silence on Malabar Hill, each open-topped "tower" (or *dakhma*) a cylindrical funeral building for the disposal of the bodies of the departed.

Besides Parsis, Bombay was home to every religious and ethnic group on the subcontinent: to Hindu, Muslim, Christian, Sikh, Buddhist, Jain, and Jew; to those who spoke Hindustani, Marathi, Gujarati, Hindi, English, Punjabi, Urdu, and too many more to name. For sheer diversity and variety, even New York, London and Paris—each of which Pickett had toured on his stopover in Europe—had nothing on the streets of Bombay. As the American writer, Price Collier, put it, Bombay in 1910 was "a kaleidoscope of moving color" beside which "the Strand, Broadway, and even the boulevards of Paris [were] ... tame, and brown, and dull." On the whole of the subcontinent, Pickett could not have found a better starting place for espying the diversity and complexity and wonder that was India—its past and future, its stability and volatility, its wealth and wretchedness, its cultures and cults, and its hope and despair. It was all there on the streets of Bombay, though who could take it in?

IN A FINAL CONVERSATION WITH THE IRISH SISTERS, Waskom and the young women learned to their surprise that they were all going to Lucknow. The sisters were going to be staying with their uncle and aunt for about three months. Their uncle was lieutenant governor of the United Provinces of Agra and Oudh. "Maybe we will see you there!" they told Waskom.

Once the ship was secured, the Reverend C.B. Hill, an Anglo-Indian Methodist, boarded. He came bearing letters from Waskom's family and a telegram from Stanley Jones. Waskom opened the telegram first. It said: "HEARTY WELCOME FROM INDIA AND LUCKNOW." A scripture reference, 2 Corinthians 1:8, followed, but the verse was a mistake. Jones had given the telegrapher 2 Corinthians 9:8 ("And God is able to make all grace abound toward you; that ye, always having all sufficiency in all things, may abound to every good work"). However, the received verse read: "For we would not, brethren, have you ignorant of our trouble which came to us in Asia, that we were pressed out of measure, above strength, insomuch that we despaired even of life!" Taken aback, Waskom asked if anything had happened to Stanley lately. Hill was not aware of anything—except that Stanley was getting married!

Waskom got to Bombay on November 20. How long he spent there is not known, but since Jones had already moved 50 miles north of Lucknow to Sitapur, and the Lal Bagh Church was eager for his replacement, his stay was brief. Ludie's insistence that he bring sheets and a pillow paid off, for he learned that train passengers and hotel guests were expected to provide their own linens. He bought a second class ticket on the *Bombay Mail*, which would deliver him to Delhi or Agra, where he would have to change trains for the final stretch of his journey. In those days, the mail train was the fastest and highest priority train on the route, mainly because it carried mail. Besides the *Bombay Mail*, there were the *Punjab Mail*, *Frontier Mail*, *Kalka Mail*, and *Imperial Mail*. Mail trains would pick up and drop off mail bags on the fly at small stations. They stopped only at the larger ones. They carried first-class mail only; parcels were carried by slower, local trains. With his second class ticket, Waskom got a private compartment and, perhaps, the opportunity to catch up on some sleep. (The only added benefit of first-class would have been more luggage space.) Even so, the dust was terrific. Before the 880-mile journey was over, the young missionary had brushed off his clothes at least a dozen times.

6 Lal Bagh, Lucknow

W askom reached Lucknow on a Tuesday, probably December 6. As he stepped down from his carriage, he was greeted by a welcoming party from the English church. The welcomers included missionary bishop, Frank W. Warne; the bishop's daughter and secretary, Edith; the district superintendent, John Wesley Robinson; representatives of Lucknow's two Methodist colleges; a representative of the Methodist Publishing House; several government and railway workers; and some privately employed individuals. The *Kaukab,* the official Methodist vernacular paper, announced his arrival. The following Tuesday, the announcement was repeated in the *Indian Witness*:

> On Tuesday of last week Rev. J.W. Pickett, for some years a professor in the Taylor University, in America, arrived in Lucknow, to take the work of the English speaking Methodist Episcopal Church here. As the pastorate has been vacant for some weeks and the burden of supplying the pulpit had fallen on men busy in their own departments, he was most cordially welcomed by the missionaries, and also by the congregation.

Waskom was shown to the Lal Bagh ["Red Garden"] Church and to his bungalow, which was just left of the church building in the same yard. In India, bungalows were not the small California or Cottage-Style houses Americans were getting to know at the time, but large, high-ceiling residences with a kitchen, living room, dining area, two or three bedrooms, bath, and a large veranda. The Lal-Bagh parsonage was no exception. It was a big house for a single man, and for the next several months, Waskom would be its only occupant.

In front and around the attractive parsonage were well-kept garden areas, bordered by bricks standing on end. Nevertheless, the church itself—a gothic-style, cross-shaped structure in gray plaster finish, with soaring roofline, spire-topped tower, pointed-arch windows, and buttresses—was unimpeachably the most prominent feature of the compound. Like much of its congregation, it was manifestly of Western descent—the child of sentiment, perhaps: a place like home.

On Saturday, in the hall of the Isabella Thoburn College, the congregation held an informal reception for the new pastor. Speaking for the 200 guests, Bishop Warne mistakenly welcomed Pickett as "Prichard." Waskom corrected Warne and made a joke about the blunder. Later, he apologized to him for embarrassing him.

EVEN BEFORE THE RECEPTION, WASKOM LEARNED that members of the church were grousing about the loss of Jones as their pastor. When Helen Ingram, the church's deaconess, took him on a first round of visits to the church families, the majority asked if there wasn't someway he could take the work to which the bishop had appointed Stanley, so that Stanley could stay on. He knew then and there that his job would not be easy. To make matters worse, Waskom learned that, since Jones' departure, worship attendance had declined steadily.

Waskom was aware of at least three other obstacles he would face as he began his work. First, he learned that coming into his new responsibilities with no knowledge of British-Indian conventions could easily put him up a gum tree, as the British put it. Miss Ingram had introduced him to some older men who were British, and he had called them "Sir." In Kentucky that was how you honored your seniors. But the deaconess had been shocked. She informed the young preacher that only menials addressed others as "Sir."

Second, although he was coming to an English-speaking church, he knew that he would need to spend much of his first term concentrating on a required program of study, including courses in Urdu and Hindi. The latter, especially, were regarded as imperative, for there was general agreement that if missionaries did not overcome the main difficulties of language learning within a year, they were unlikely to overcome them at all.

Third, and most prominent, Waskom had no pastoral experience, yet as he began his work, he knew his parishioners would inevitably compare him with his predecessor.

IN JANUARY, THE NORTH INDIA ANNUAL CONFERENCE met at the Lal Bagh Church. On the final day, Sunday the eighth, J.W. Pickett was "ordained"—three times! In the morning service, he was set apart as a deacon by Bishop William F. McDowell, whom Waskom described as "the most dignified clergyman I have ever known." In the evening, Bishop Frank W. Warne ordained him as an elder. And, as Warne put it, a "third ordination" took place when Mrs. Lois Lee Parker, the saintly widow of Bishop Edwin W. Parker, added her benediction.

More than 40 years earlier, Mrs. Parker, with Mrs. Clementina Butler, had inspired Methodist women to see need for missions to women and girls. Now past 90, she approached young Pickett and said, "I have seen you ordained twice today, but in neither service did the bishop say how long you should serve in India as a minister. Kneel down here and let me pray that you may serve in India for at least 50 years." Pickett wrote of that moment, "I knelt and neither ordination earlier that day meant more to me than her prayer."

WHEN J. WASKOM PICKETT CAME TO Lucknow, the old capital of the kingdom of Awadh had a population of about 270,000, making it the largest city in the United Provinces and the fourth largest in British India. From a distance, the city said to be the purest center of the Hindustani language had a stately, architecturally rich appearance. However, up close, the splendor faded into the standard trappings of a crowded Oriental town. Situated on the banks of the Gumti River, Lucknow was known for its manufacturing, educational establishments, parks (it was called "the city of parks"), and as the headquarters of Oudh's principal court. On the eastern side of the city was a section of European shops. Also prominent was the city's large military cantonment and fort. The political fortunes of Lucknow had been in decline since the Anglo-Indian War of 1857, although positive change was in the works. The old lands of Awadh (mispronounced and spelled "Oudh" by the British) had once had their own chief commissioner, but after the uniting of Awadh with the Northwest Provinces in 1877, the chief commissioner's job was merged with that of the lieutenant governor, who resided in smaller and—to the rebuffed citizens of Lucknow—*inferior* Allahabad. Some believed that, because of its size, high culture, manufacturing, grain exports, landed power and wealth (and high tax revenues), status as an important Muslim center, and celebrated history, the eventual reincarnation of Lucknow as provincial political stronghold was fated. But the real savior of Lucknow was not its karma but a man, Harcourt Butler, who as deputy commissioner of Lucknow (1906-1908) had beautified the city and improved its amenities. Butler created gardens, rehabilitated monuments, and upgraded streets and roads. He was passionate in his advocacy of Lucknow, and he spent much tax money to insure it lived up to all he said it was.

If, in 1910, Lucknow was no longer the provincial capital, it was surely the capital of Methodism in India. Of the Methodist Episcopal Church's 341 India-based missionaries, nearly one in 10 was in Lucknow. Most were absorbed in institutional work—at Reid College for men, Isabella Thoburn College for women, the Methodist Publishing House (which ran 14 presses valued at 150,000 dollars), and the Lal Bagh Church. Lucknow then contained two thriving Methodist congregations: Central Hindustani Church, a thriving congregation of 400 under the leadership of Jashwant R. Chitambar; and the smaller, though healthy, Lal Bagh Church to which Pickett had been called.

Despite his youth and inexperience, Waskom soon began to make his mark. Though he lacked Jones' eloquence, he preached compellingly. Administratively and organizationally, he excelled. His best attribute though was his determination. While well aware of his limited experience, he refused to be bridled by it. Instead, he employed it as a goad to boost his knowledge and skills.

Waskom never hesitated to ask questions or accept advice. If Stanley Jones had been closer, he probably would have leaned heavily on him for counsel, but Stanley was recently married, headquartered more than 50 miles away, and constantly itinerating. Instead, Waskom turned to others, especially John Wesley Robinson, his district superintendent—that is, if Robinson was in town. Robinson, who had come to India in 1892, was Bishop Warne's right-hand man. The superintendent was responsible for the district of Oudh, which was 250 miles long and, on average, 50 miles wide. It contained five million people, including 3,000 Christians (mostly untouchables) scattered among 50 or 60 centers in nine circuits. Robinson was gone often, but his commitments in Lucknow—chief among them, editing the *Kaukab-I-Hind* (*Star of India*)—meant that he was seldom gone for long. The work of readying the church paper was time-consuming, but, since it touched almost every Methodist worker in the Hindustani-speaking areas of the church, it was, in Robinson's reckoning, well worth the required effort. Then, again, from church development, to administrative and editorial responsibilities, to designing church buildings, he put great energy into all he did. The dignified, yet approachable Robinson, was legendary for his capacity for sustained effort.

WHEN WASKOM HAD BEEN IN LUCKNOW for about three weeks, a uniformed Englishman came to the parsonage. He arrived in an elegant brougham and presented himself in a military manner. He had come, he said, to deliver a letter and to secure a response. On opening the letter, Waskom discovered that it was from the lieutenant governor's lady. It was an invitation to dine with Their Excellencies at Lucknow's Government House.

As soon as the aide-de-camp left, Waskom rode his bicycle to District Superintendent Robinson's house to seek his counsel, for although he was excited, he was also uneasy. How was a boy preacher from Kentucky to conduct himself among British aristocrats, he wanted to know. On his Atlantic crossing, he had noticed that cultured Britishers didn't even handle their knives, forks and spoons like Americans. He confessed that on both legs of his voyage to India he had been embarrassed by his cultural ignorance, but his discomfort had been inconsequential. Now, though, by accepting this dinner invitation stemming from his shipboard friendship with the Irish sisters, his ignorance would be on conspicuous display to people for whom settled proprieties of conduct mattered a great deal! What should he do? To all this, Superintendent Robinson listened empathetically, but since in his 18 years in India he had never been invited to the home of any high official, in the end he could only offer, "Be natural."

In 1910, the imperial governance of South Asia was ultimately under Parliament in London. In India, the highest authorities were the rulers of the princely states and the viceroy. The princes, descendants of those who remained loyal to the crown during the Anglo-Indian War of 1857, were in charge of a third of the subcontinent's 1,800,000 square miles. The remainder, "British India," was under the authority of the king's representative—the viceroy—who, when Pickett came to Lucknow, was Charles Hardinge. Three branches of authority upheld order in the provinces: the judiciary; the civil administration (under a governor, lieutenant governor or chief commissioner); and the army. In 1836, when the province of Bengal became too large, the Northwest Provinces were formed, with their own lieutenant governor. In 1877, Oudh was added and the administrative authority of the lieutenant governor of the Northwest

Provinces was expanded to include the added territory. In 1902, the name was changed to United Provinces of Agra and Oudh.

The current lieutenant governor of the United Provinces was Sir Leslie Alexander Selim Porter. An Irishman in his late fifties, Sir Leslie had entered the Indian Civil Service in 1876, when he was only 22, just two years older than Pickett was now. Since then, he had served in various posts and had only recently been temporarily appointed "officiating" lieutenant governor. Since, of the 18 who were present at the dinner, Waskom was the only cleric, he was seated at the right of Lady Aletta, the lieutenant governor's wife. Her Excellency's husband sat at the other end of the table. Seating was carefully planned, as were all details of formal dinner parties, for it was by her dinner parties that a hostess was appraised in British India. And as Maud Diver, the novelist put it in *The Englishwoman in India* (1909), "India is the land of dinners, as England is the land of five o'clock teas." As hostess, Lady Aletta called on the Reverend Pickett to offer thanks for the food.

At one point during the meal, speaking loudly enough for all to hear, Sir Leslie asked if Waskom realized how fortunate he was to be appointed as a Methodist cleric to Lucknow. Waskom replied that he would regard himself fortunate to be appointed a Methodist minister anywhere. But why, he asked, should he be grateful for being appointed to Lucknow?

"Because," replied the lieutenant governor, "the Methodists are highly respected because of the great colleges they have set up here." He then lauded Isabella Thoburn, for whom one of the colleges was named, as, perhaps, the ablest educator he had ever known. The women at the table would have agreed. Arguably, Thoburn was the best-known advocate of women's education in Asia. Her constant refrain was, "No people ever rise higher as a people than the point to which they lift their women."

After dinner, Waskom undoubtedly told Sir Leslie's nieces the details of his journey to Lucknow and his experience since then. Whether he ever saw the Irish sisters again is not known, but their brief friendship had a deep impact.

> Meeting the Irish sisters . . . on the ship en route to India has exercised a strong influence across all the rest of my years. It enabled me to serve India more acceptably than I could have done without a better understanding of British rulers than I had possessed.

IN THE MONTHS THAT FOLLOWED, the advantages of acquaintance with the lieutenant governor became clear. When a severe food shortage occurred, Porter, who had been long associated with relief work in India, invited Waskom to serve on the District Famine Relief Committee. Waskom not only welcomed the opportunity but, by accepting it, expanded further his network of relationships with public officials. The committee's first meeting was over breakfast at the home of the district magistrate, who served as chair. Also present, and seated next to Waskom, was the Nawab of Jehangirabad, a wealthy Muslim landlord with limited ruling powers. Because Muslims are forbidden to eat pork, Waskom was surprised when the cook served them pork chops, confounded when without hesitation the nawab ate two, and flabbergasted when he took still another helping. Waskom's face obviously betrayed his surprise, because the nawab turned to him, smiled, and said, "Padri, are not these the best mutton chops you have ever tasted?" The committee's goals were achieved. From the big landlords and others, they were able to solicit about 800,000 rupees—roughly $275,000—which was distributed according to need.

About midyear in 1911, Waskom was asked to bury the unbaptized infant grandson of a prominent Methodist lay member. Since, at that time, the British civil chaplains superintended all cemeteries for Christian burials, he wrote a letter requesting the Lucknow chaplain to prepare a grave for the infant's burial. However, the chaplain, having learned the child was unbaptized, refused, stressing that government cemeteries are consecrated ground. Waskom replied that Methodists had no conscience against burying unbaptized children in consecrated ground and argued that, in any event, the chaplain had no authority to prevent the burial in the Methodist section. When the chaplain would not budge, Waskom went to the magistrate on whose relief committee he had served. The magistrate strongly disapproved of the chaplain's attitude but said he had no authority to give him orders. Waskom then went to the city commissioner, Arthur Saunders, who occupied the next level of authority, but the commissioner could do nothing either. So, with much apprehension, the young preacher went to Lieutenant Governor Porter. When Pickett explained the situation, Porter immediately dispatched a letter commanding the chaplain to have the plot prepared for the baby's burial by the time requested. Further, he ordered the chaplain to apologize in person to the Reverend Pickett for interfering with his clerical duties. News of Pickett's success brought congratulations and thanks from other victims of clerical hubris. Especially gratifying, though, was word of a general order to the Anglican chaplains of Agra and Oudh to stop imposing matters of Anglican conscience on non-Anglican clergy. Pickett's early dealings with British officials taught him the value of building cordial relationships with those in authority. Without his previous contacts with the lieutenant governor, his chance of getting an immediate interview would have been remote. Not surprisingly, then, after Sir Leslie's retirement from service that year, Pickett cultivated a similar friendship with his successor, James Scorgie Meston.

THE LIEUTENANT GOVERNOR'S INTERFERENCE on Pickett's behalf punctuated the fact the British were very much in charge in India in the year of his arrival. Of the subcontinent's 300 million people, 234 million of them answered directly to British rule. Nothing better symbolized this hold than the December of 1911 grand coronation *durbar* for King George V and his announcement of the transfer of the capital from Calcutta to Delhi. Since 1857, the only alarming ripple in the calm sea of British rule had been the nationwide protests and rioting of 1905, brought on by Lord Curzon's decision—"concocted in the dark," as loyalist politician Gopal Krishna Gokhale had put it—to partition Bengal. Soon, however, most of the leaders of the antipartition and Swadeshi (home rule) movements were in jail, and the Indian National Congress was back in the hands of loyalists. Now, in 1911—the year of the king's month-long visit—the political situation seemed even more settled. Public disruptions were sporadic and not worrisome. Peasant movements remained isolated, fragmented, and focused on single issues. M.K. Gandhi was not yet on the scene. And, although young Jawaharlal Nehru was home from London, his interests at the time were more personal than political, and any small celebrity he had was as the son of Motilal Nehru. Understandably, therefore, the missionaries, sensing no change afoot and being free to preach the gospel and serve the church without state interference or control, were happy to support the status quo. The prospect of Indian self-rule anytime soon seemed as remote to them as to anyone else. And with the British bestowal of a nationwide rail system, the benefits of mostly fair and effective governance, the emergence of English as a lingua franca, the recent withdrawal of restraints on the Indian press, and the freedom to assemble, what added benefits could independence offer anyway? After the First World War broke out, the British Government would grow suddenly cautious about allowing foreigners to enter their colonies. And, beginning in 1917, even missionaries (unless they were British) would have to sign a loyalty pledge or be recommended by an approved missionary society or agency. But in 1911's political climate, missionaries were free to come and go and minister with little interference.

Of course, the Government did expect missionaries to avail themselves for certain minor duties. For example, military and civilian pensioners were required to present certificates from government officials or clerics to receive their monthly pensions. The purpose was to prove they were alive. Because he had been ill, one such pensioner—an Irishman, retired from the Indian Army and married to an Indian woman—came to Pickett for certification in the middle of the month. Dutifully, Pickett attested the pensioner was alive. However, a few days later Pickett received the following letter from the head clerk of the District Magistrate's office:

> Dear Holy Sir:
> You have signed a statement the Old Soldier Johnson was alive and appeared before Your Holiness on the 15th of October. You are kind and helpful, but for our records we must know whether the pensioner was alive on the first of the month.

Waskom suppressed his amusement long enough to decorously testify that, yes, Soldier Johnson was as fully alive at the beginning of the month as at the middle.

GIVEN THE PREVAILING TRANQUILITY in pre-World War I Lucknow, public conversations and debates about social and religious issues overshadowed political ones. In fact, among missionaries and the growing subcultures of Christian-educated Indians and university-trained devotees of other faiths, discussions of religious truth and social reform were becoming more numerous and vigorous all the time. In public discourse, newspapers, tracts, and books, Christians criticized the age of consent (10 years old), *sati* (the self-immolation of widows on their husbands' funeral pyres), caste (especially untouchability), women's rights, and temperance. They also debated Hindu and Muslim apologists on the relative authority of the Bible, *Shastras*, and Qur'an. They saw periodic adjustments of the agendas of Hindu reform movements like the Arya Samaj and Brahmo Samaj as evidence of usefulness of the critiques and debates.

How involved the youthful Reverend Pickett got in such discussions is not clear, but his main focus was necessarily on pastoral and administrative issues. For example, in 1911, Pickett's first full year as pastor of the English church, a severe plague affected the area, and the death roll for the Oudh District was unusually large. As the following incident shows, Pickett's flock was not spared the trauma. Arriving at the home of one sick churchgoer who had sent for him, Waskom could not raise a response. After a few minutes, he went into the house and found the man's corpse in the bedroom. All the other family members were also dead. The servants had run away in fear. The plague not only affected church members directly but stirred up ill-will in outlying villages. Brahmin priests and other Hindu community leaders whispered around that the Christians were intentionally spreading the disease.

Among Pickett's pivotal pastoral contacts that year was a Muslim boy in his late teens whose name was Julam Qadir. He had gotten acquainted with some Methodist young men in Moradabad and was interested in knowing God as they seemed to know God. He recounted that the previous year he had heard two young men preaching Christ and selling Bibles on a street near his home. He was so annoyed he and some friends bought one of their New Testaments, ripped it in two, and spit on it. However, when the young men who sold them the New Testament did not curse them or try to hit them, Julam didn't know what to make of it. The thought came to him that maybe they knew God in ways that Muslims didn't. So he bought another New Testament and took it home. However, his father discovered him reading it and burned it. After beating Julam, he warned him that if he ever caught him reading a Bible again he would kill him. Nevertheless, within a few weeks Julam got hold of a copy of the Gospel of Mark, which he hid and read when his father was not around. Eventually he turned his life over to Jesus.

One day, Julam's father, who was leaving for Agra on business, learned at the railway station that his train had been in a wreck. Returning home, he walked in on Julam reading a New Testament. He beat Julam severely and the next day, before traveling to Agra, ordered his four wives to confine him to his room. Instead, Julam's mother gave him a few rupees and told him to take a train to Lucknow and, once there, to go to some missionary for protection. That's how he met Pickett.

Since the detached kitchen at the parsonage was not being used, Pickett decided to let Julam stay there for the time being. He and the principal of Lucknow Christian College, Jashwant Rao Chitambar, each spent several hours a week tutoring Julam. Two months later Chitambar baptized him, and immediately after that, Julam began street preaching. Before long, though, a group of Muslims assailed him and left him lying beside the road. A Christian found him and got him to a hospital. After his release, he went back to the parsonage and took up street preaching again. With the help of Pickett and Stanley Jones, Julam eventually enrolled in the Methodist seminary in Bareilly.

AS WITH JONES, PICKETT'S TOP PRIORITY was evangelism. For example, in March 1912, Pickett arranged to pitch a *shamiana* (large tent) next to the railway headquarters at nearby Char Bagh. Waskom preached the first week, and Stanley Jones came from Sitapur for the second week. When the meetings closed, 58 persons—many of them railway workers—had decided to follow Jesus. Waskom continued to hold services at Char Bagh twice a month. The ranks of new believers grew so rapidly the railway authorities promised to build a church at the site for joint use with the local Church of England congregation.

BY THE SPRING OF 1912, J. WASKOM PICKETT was in love. On just his second Sunday in Lucknow, in December of 1910, Waskom had been walking from the parsonage to the church when he saw the District Superintendent's wife, Elizabeth Fisher Robinson, and her two daughters coming into the churchyard. The young women, Miriam and Ruth, were 11 and 15. They had been attending Wellesley School in Naini Tal. The older daughter had just graduated from high school with honors. She had been born in the parsonage of the Lal Bagh Church on March 9, 1895, for, as with Jones and Pickett, John Wesley Robinson's first appointment had been to that church. When Waskom saw Ruth Robinson that December morning, he was immediately attracted to her. The thought came to him, "God has sent me my wife." By 1912, a close friendship had developed between the 22-year-old pastor and the 17-year-old daughter of the District Superintendent—Waskom's "blond angel" as he came to call her. When, on July 9, Waskom proposed to her, she responded that her heart said yes but that she would first need her parents' consent. For that Waskom would have to wait, since Ruth's father, just elected India's newest missionary bishop, was out of the country. When the news did come, it was good; however, it contained a condition: the couple should wait until Ruth had graduated from Northwestern University, which she would enter as a sophomore after a year at Isabella Thoburn College. "That meant a four-year wait," Pickett later recalled, "but she was worth waiting for!"

When Ruth entered Isabella Thoburn College, she and the president of the college shared the same name. The other Ruth Robinson was the daughter of John E. Robinson, the bishop who had persuaded the mission board to interview Pickett in Chicago. When Waskom's Ruth took up residence in the dormitory, the chance of their mail being confused became clear. Understandably, he grew a bit nervous that his letters to his fiancée might reach the wrong bishop's daughter.

PICKETT ENJOYED SPENDING TIME AT the Robinson home, which, by all accounts, was filled with much love and laughter. Though one would never guess it from his photos, in which his demeanor was invariably grim, John Wesley Robinson had a hearty sense of humor. Among his—and the family's—favorite games was Croquinole, which was played on an octagonal wooden board by two or four people. With four, you formed two teams. The object was to get as many wooden discs as you could into—or close to— a circular area at the board's center that was guarded by eight obstacle-pegs. You did this by flicking the disks with your finger from behind a line near the edge of the board. You also tried to knock opponents' disks away from the center and even off the playing area altogether—an obligation John Robinson felt duty-bound to do with vigor!

Pets were allowed in the Robinson household. Rabbits, goats and cats were all acceptable--but no dogs. The danger of rabies kept that policy firm. One of the family's great joys was singing hymns, and John Robinson offered a standard reward of two annas (one eighth of a rupee) for each hymn the young women could learn to play correctly on the piano.

John Wesley Robinson was rarely sick. One secret of his good health was his ability to let go of pressing matters long enough to enter into one of the forms of recreation he enjoyed. One of his favorite recreations was reading detective stories. His favorite outdoor activities were tennis and baseball. That summer (1912) Robinson became a local baseball legend. The Lucknow missionaries were matched against the language students. When it was the 46-year-old Robinson's turn to bat, to the amazement of all, he hit a pitch that was almost in the dirt clear out of the Lucknow College ball field into a nearby mosque. What the others didn't know though was that, besides putting all his weight and muscle into the home run, he had (he later claimed) "a secret weapon"—a specially-made bat of sisham wood.

The Robinson family's daily routine began with the gathering around the breakfast table for pea pulao (rice with peas), John Robinson's favorite dish. Afterwards, they took turns reading the verses in the Scripture lesson for the day, and they sang a hymn. Then "Father" Robinson prayed for family and friends, with Elizabeth, Ruth, and Miriam joining him at the end in the Lord's Prayer. Table conversation included mission affairs, father's latest tour, and favorite quotations. But the young women's interests always took top billing.

According to those who knew her well, Elizabeth Robinson was an exceptional helpmate, mother, and hostess. She enthusiastically backed her husband's work and program. Her love for her daughters was palpable to anyone present. She had loved an infant son too—her firstborn—but little Paul had become ill with fever and died shortly after his first birthday. Elizabeth was a lively conversationalist. Friends spoke of her compassion, noting that she was never satisfied with less than her best for others. When her daughters were old enough to begin school in the hills, Elizabeth not only accompanied them but stayed on to provide personal care for them. That was not an unusual arrangement for missionary mothers, but her sometimes frail health may also have contributed to her decision to remain. The long separations from father were hard for the women of the Robinson family, but they were most difficult, perhaps, for John himself. He had once written to a friend:

> Mrs. Robinson has had to be away to the hills seven months this year, and I batched it down here in the heat. Most of the time, West, who was also alone, came and lived with me. That is a part of life . . . [that] to my mind . . . is the hardest thing that has to be faced.

He added:

> We have reached the place in our family also where the children have to be away from home nine months in the year. Ruth is now eleven and is in Wellesley school. She is doing nicely and will go into the sixth standard soon. She just passed her Junior Trinity College music examination and is really quite a pianist for a girl

of her age. We are beginning to plan the home going on her account. If she passes the government examinations each year she has only three years after this in Wellesley and then will be ready for college. But as that would take her through college in America in her seventeenth or eighteenth year, we will probably keep her here a year after finishing school before going home.

Thus, six years later, in 1912, when John Wesley Robinson's response to Waskom and Ruth's wish to be married was both "yes" and "but wait," it was in keeping with long-settled family plans.

Besides Waskom and Ruth's engagement, 1912 brought other changes to the Robinson household. The decision of the Methodist Episcopal General Conference to add another missionary bishop in India, and the election of John Wesley Robinson to the office, altered the life John and Elizabeth Robinson had become used to in two profound ways. First, it meant a move to Bombay; second, it meant even more travel for John.

For Elizabeth, the transition would be especially difficult, for much of her life had centered on the care of her husband and children, and the absence of either had always been difficult. Now, with John's expanded responsibilities and Ruth starting college in Lucknow (with Miriam to follow), long separations would be the rule more than ever. Yet, despite the changes John Wesley Robinson's episcopal duties would bring, the family sensed this was God's will. In fact, it seemed the Lord may have spared his life for this very purpose. For the man who had made his way to Europe and across the Atlantic for General Conference that spring, the man who on May 24 received 686 out of 738 votes for the office of missionary bishop, had held a reservation for the maiden voyage of the world's largest ship—the pride of the White Star line—the "unsinkable" *Titanic*. Had not John Wesley Robinson's connecting ship, the *Marmora*, been delayed in reaching Marseilles, the next chapters of his life would almost certainly never have been written at all.

NEAR THE END OF 1912, JOHN R. MOTT visited India as part of a larger Asian tour that would end in Japan the following April. After Edinburgh 1910, the Continuation Committee had asked Mott to work at setting up national missionary councils in various countries. This grew out of the committee's recognition that "if it were to render the largest help to the work abroad, there was need of taking counsel with missionaries and leaders of the church on the mission field as to the tasks most requiring co-operative consideration and action." Mott's planned tour of India would result in seven new provincial councils, with all their work coordinated through a National Missionary Council. This he set about doing in India through sectional conferences beginning in mid-November, followed by a national conference in Calcutta from December 18-21. The sectional conferences were held in Madras, Bombay, Jubbulpore, Allahabad, Lahore, and Calcutta. Pickett, for whom Mott had been a hero since college days, heard Mott speak twice and liked what he heard. "I was even more favorably impressed than I had expected to be," he said. Afterwards, Pickett organized a group of six Lucknow College students to study Mott's *The Decisive Hour of Christian Missions*. Five of the six would later enter Christian service as ministers or teachers in Christian schools.

In 1913, the Lal Bagh Church saw fresh conversions every month, noteworthy gains in financial stability, increased benevolence giving, and renewed interest in evangelism (expressed in the support of a new district worker in Tirhoot and in the start of Sunday worship at Char Bagh). Since many of the new converts at Char Bagh had British roots and worked for the Oudh and Rohilkhand railway line, the agent agreed to provide a permanent church—and, until then, an interim chapel. In the works, too, were new facilities at the Lal Bagh Church itself. The missionaries, students, government employees, businesspeople, railway workers, and others who called the church home welcomed with enthusiasm the additions of a social hall next door and a tennis court out back.

Just as happily, Waskom welcomed as badges of trust two new jobs with the Commission on English Work—those of secretary and editor of its official organ, *The Methodist*. Still, as year three wound down, he felt as frustrated as he did fulfilled. For one thing, Ruth Robinson—India's best benefaction to him—was off to America for her last two years of college. Further, although he was deeply grateful for the headway he had made in adapting to a new culture, learning a new language, and earning the trust and affection of the Lal Bagh Church, no one recognized better than he the difference between where he was and the missionary he hoped to be. Later, in a retrospective look at the boy preacher from Kentucky, he would shake his head. How had he managed at all? Not by resiliency, intellect or personality, he concluded. Only the providence of God, the kindness of the Lucknow congregation, and the friendship of Ruth could account for it:

I have never ceased to wonder that a congregation that included most of the officers of two great colleges could accept and allow to remain as pastor the green and immature young man that I then was or that the aforesaid young woman could accept the proposal of that young man and become engaged to marry him.

7 The Long Journey Home

In 1914, most Americans could only dream of traveling to places like India. Unless they were well-to-do or were missionaries, even the most venturesome were reduced to armchair tourists, imagining the glamor of globetrotting through the writings of others. The American reading public included many such vicarious adventurers. Exotic tales depicting life in some far-off Timbuktu were in great demand. Not surprisingly, some who had lived or traveled in strange settings were only too happy to oblige with hyperbolical accounts of humorous customs, hungry cannibals, and horrific conditions. Take, for example, A.E. Rassmann's Edgar Allan Poe-like portrait of a beleaguered Lucknow bishop in *With Jesus in India's Jungles*.

> The Bishop was awfully tormented with a bad case of prickly heat. He had been bitten nearly mad by mosquitoes, fleas and bed-bugs; he had been startled by huge muskrats running across his feet as he sat at his desk, making cold chills creep up his back, thinking that a cobra was about to finish him. He had been worried in his bath by big ants; he had his tea flavored with little ants that were hidden in the sugar, and his body had been a campagna for an army of medium-size ants. He had thrust his foot into his slipper to find a cold, slippery toad, or a stinging scorpion. He had a big lizard fall across his mouth as he was taking his first morning yawn. He had found his new silk London umbrella riddled by mice, his steamer rug cut up by moths, his writing desk inhabited by grub worms that spent their lives in the wood and left the desk worthless. His Gladstone bag was ruined by rain through the ceiling, his fountain pen stolen, and his shoes covered with mildew; his clothes damp, almost wet, when he arose to put them on in the morning. He cried out: "This is a

beastly country. Let's go to America!" Snakes are never supposed
to come into a room at night if a light is kept burning. The Bishop
was living in the great city of Lucknow. First a karait [krait]
snake coiled on the wire of the lantern which was burning in the
bed-room, the next morning a cobra was in the bathroom but
wandered out while he was hunting a stick. The advantage of
being bitten by a karait [krait] instead of a cobra is slight. The
former is warranted to kill in twenty-eight minutes and the latter
in half an hour.

Overdrawn as such caricatures were, serving abroad did involve
significant health risks. In a more restrained account of the hardships of
Indian service, Robert Stewart, in his *Life and Work in India* (1899),
reported a study which found the careers of ordained missionaries to India
lasted, on average, less than 16 years. In contrast, clergy careers in North
America lasted almost 40 years—about 150 percent longer. However, the
most menacing hazards were not the snakes and scorpions sensationalist
writers described, but, as both Jones and Pickett learned early, stress and
disease. For Stanley Jones it was mostly the former. For Waskom Pickett,
it was mostly the latter. Because of breakdowns in health, both Stanley
and Waskom were ordered home after only a few years on the
field—although both also returned.

As Stanley described it, his collapse was due to a "spiritual sag"
leading to a "physical sag."

I began to feel a pressure from within and a call from without to
enter this field of the intelligentsia of India—to present Christ
there . . .

This brought on a spiritual crisis. It was aggravated by the
fact that, while I had passed my examinations in Urdu and Hindi,
my use of these languages was confined to the surface. I couldn't
feed myself spiritually by my own preaching. I preached what
I could say, not what I wanted to say. The depths and the heights
were unplumbed—I preached surface things and my spiritual life
became surface.

This spiritual sag brought on a physical sag . . . My body did
not throw off disease as before, and I began to have nervous
collapses . . .

As a consequence, at the end of eight and a half years I was ordered home to America on furlough. So at the end of my first term as a missionary I ended up with a call and a collapse.

Waskom's withdrawal to America came even more quickly when, before the completion of his first term, he was diagnosed with tuberculosis.

Even before leaving for the foreign field, most missionary recruits knew the diseases behind missionary attrition, for they were the same diseases that struck people at home. However, the risk of succumbing to them in places like India was far greater. For example, in 1880, the mortality rate of the wives and children of British soldiers on the subcontinent was triple the rate in the British Isles.

The most menacing maladies were malaria, dysentery, cholera, and tuberculosis. Of these, tuberculosis was the best understood. By the time Jones and Pickett came to India, it had been unmasked for some time. In fact, less than three months before Waskom's arrival in Lucknow in 1910, the *Indian Witness* had carried a lengthy and learned article on the progress so far in understanding and treating it. The report described Robert Koch's discovery of the *tubercle bacilli* in 1882, dispelled the myth the disease was hereditary, discussed the practical importance of understanding tuberculosis as "a germ disease," but critiqued Koch's tuberculin, which had thus far not lived up to its promise. The account also told how tuberculosis spread, ways to avoid it, and what to do if one got it.

But understanding the disease had not mitigated its menace. It showed up regularly—even in the Lal Bagh Church. One of the infected there was an old man who, each Sunday, sat behind the organ and pumped the bellows. He had grown up a nominal Irish Catholic but had made a fresh commitment to Christ under the preaching of E. Stanley Jones. The old man lived in one of the poorest, most congested parts of Lucknow. As his condition worsened, Waskom would go to his home and attend to him through the night. Before long, Waskom was echoing his patient's cough.

When the bellows tender died, Waskom consulted Alexander Corpron, a British government physician who specialized in the diagnosis and treatment of tuberculosis. An examination and x-rays confirmed Waskom's fears. Dr. Corpron began treating him immediately, but when there was no improvement, he sent the young preacher home to die.

The news of Pickett's tuberculosis stunned the congregation. When Corpron reported that Waskom might have less than a year to live, they

were even more dismayed. On May 10, 1914, Pickett's bishop, Frank
Warne, entered the following in his journal:

> A number [of] our missionaries have been ill and among others
> Rev. J.W. Pickett, pastor of the English church, has been told by
> the best specialist in India on the subject that he has tuberculosis
> and is being given tuberculin. This is such a shock to a young
> man. I was saying to Edith this morning that I had built up my
> life work with the consciousness that I had a healthy body, but
> I do not know what would have become [of] me if, when I was
> 24 years old, I had been told I had tuberculosis. It has not been
> in our family as a family so far as I know. And yet my eldest
> sister died of that disease and was one of the most terrible
> sufferers I have ever known. How she got it is a mystery to me
> and why none of the rest of us ever got it is another mystery.

Ironically, Waskom Pickett was just beginning to hit his stride. Under
his leadership the church was again thriving. Upon his arrival three and
a half years earlier, the leaderless congregation was depressed and
declining. But within months, Sunday morning attendance had doubled,
and the evening congregations filled the sanctuary just as they had under
Jones. Brenton T. Badley, then a member of the church, remembered the
young pastor's impact well:

> J.W. Pickett, young as he was, soon made it evident that a real
> pastor had come among the people. With his special gifts, his
> capacity for organization, and his financial ability, he greatly
> strengthened the Church . . . [and] built up a membership roll that
> reminded one of the "good old days." His vision and versatility,
> together with his gifts as a financier, as well as his unfailing
> emphasis on evangelism, were all in evidence before he left
> Lucknow.

The Lal Bagh congregation did not fail to show its appreciation. When
their pastor disclosed that he had been ordered back to America, more than
a dozen families and individuals presented him with a cash gift for his
passage and other expenses. As it turned out, the gift was a godsend.
Austria's bombardment of Belgrade was about to draw all of Europe into
war. The effects on Pacific shipping would be immediate and, for

Waskom, very personal, forcing holdups in port after port and both protracting his journey and inflating his costs.

Another expression of appreciation came from the Anglo-Indian members of the congregation, who offered their pastor the following tribute for his support of "the English work."

It has been given to few men to have such an illustrious career as a missionary in so short a time. Your labor in the land of your adoption has already received marked recognition by members of your Church and a wide circle of friends. The conquest of Anglo-India for Christ has been the all-absorbing aim and ambition of your life, and to this end all your splendid powers of mind and soul were consecrated. No duty has been too hard and no cost too great. By voice and pen you have strenuously and earnestly desired to uplift a submerged community to their rightful position as citizens and Christians. Your efforts in this direction have been recognized by the Anglo-Indian community who comprise a large number of church membership and other friends, who are here this evening . . . Your support in the Anglo-Indian Methodist call for a separate English conference is an unbreakable tie which has bound not only this Church, but all Anglo-Indian Methodists from Karachi to Burma and from the Himalayas to our Mission Stations in the South.

The members of your church in Lucknow are not the only ones who say with painful emotion their sad good-bye, but Anglo-Indian Methodists all over India join in the refrain. And we with them earnestly desire and pray that your sojourn and medical treatment in your native land will enable you in God's good time to come back to India and take up the work you so unwillingly lay down.

Anglo-Indians were English-speaking Methodists of mixed European and Indian extraction who, as the tribute said, could be found from the northern border country to the "mission stations in the south," and even in what is now Pakistan ("Karachi") and Burma. In the early days of the British presence in India, many Englishmen who came to India decided to make the subcontinent their home. As one writer put it, "they settled in the country, married the women of the country, and served their time and generation in the country. When they died, they left their children as a legacy to both India and England."

From the beginning of Methodist Episcopal activity in India, tension had existed between those who championed "English work" and those who belittled it. The Missionary Society of the Methodist Episcopal Church said that its "main intent" was "the conversion of the Natives of the Country, and only incidentally to [reach out to] the European population in India." Many, however, including some in the Lal Bagh Church, felt deeply that to desert spiritually needy British residents, domiciled Europeans, and Anglo-Indians for exclusive ministry to Indians of Aryan and Dravidian decent was, to say the least, inconsistent. In the words of one writer to the *Indian Witness*:

> I am unable to comprehend how it is possible ethically or logically to justify our church in carrying on mission work in countries that are nominally Christian, where everybody is a member of the church, and at the same time to regard money expended in India for the salvation of exactly the same kind of people as practically misappropriated.

The writer went on to point out that it had not always been so:

> When William (afterwards Bishop) Taylor came to this country, he found a large section of the Anglo-Indian community unevangelized though nominally Christian. Their godless lives made them a stumbling block in the way of the evangelization of the heathen. Under his ministry many of these people were converted and became towers of strength in the church . . . I do not need to enlarge upon the growth of this work, how it spread into different parts of India, &C., that is known to most of us, but . . . [the] investment of men and money our church has put into this work has paid big interest.

A handful of missionaries—Pickett among them—agreed. One of them wrote:

> It is not surprising that many Europeans and Domiciled people in India have a suspicion that the American Missionary looks down on them when they hear some American Missionaries say

that they have been sent to India to work between . . . natives and
not between Europeans and Christians.

The writer added, "These American Missionaries make the Europeans and
Domiciled Community feel that their souls and welfare are of less value
than the souls and welfare of the natives."

In 1907, Dr. Harvey Reeves Calkins had proposed in the *Indian
Witness* that the Central Conference remedy the situation with appropriate
guidelines for English work. In line with this, a proposal surfaced at the
Central Conference of 1912 that the English-speaking churches be
organized into a mission conference of their own. However, although there
was some movement on the proposal, it never materialized. Waskom's
support of the proposal was unusual among the younger missionaries.
Most could not wait to move beyond the English community to the "real"
work of mission, but Waskom seemed perfectly content with ministering
to English speakers. One may argue that, since he was assigned to
Lucknow's English church, he might as well be content. However,
Waskom surprised and delighted the Anglo-Indian community by taking
a genuine interest in their concerns and aspirations. Now, as he readied
to leave for America, they honored him with a citation to remind him that
they would not soon forget his advocacy.

Beyond the immediate church community, Pickett heard from many
other well-wishers, including his friend (now District Superintendent)
Stanley Jones. In his conference report, Jones also prayed that Waskom
might "be restored to perfect health."

The one silver lining of Waskom's illness was the chance to see his
fiancée, who was completing her college work at Northwestern University,
near Chicago. When it became apparent that he was not improving,
Waskom had offered to release her from their engagement. Ruth's reply
was his greatest encouragement. She wished to remain engaged, she wrote,
adding that she had full faith he would recover.

WASKOM LEFT LUCKNOW FOR CALCUTTA and America on or about August
2, 1914. Next to London, Calcutta was the largest city in the British
Empire and until two years before had been India's capital. The city was
situated on the east bank of the Hooghly River. The twin city of Howrah
was on the opposite bank. Howrah was where the trains from the West
came in.

Upon arriving at Howrah Station, Waskom immediately asked directions to Thomas Cook & Sons. Before leaving Lucknow, Pickett had already been in touch with the agency about the logistics and cost of his return—780 rupees (about 260 dollars) for passage from Calcutta to San Francisco via Hong Kong. However, when he arrived to collect his tickets, he learned the price was now 840 rupees. The increase, the agent told him, was unavoidable. The British Government had requisitioned the ship on which he was booked, so he could no longer sail directly to Hong Kong as planned. He would, instead, have to transship at Rangoon and, again, at Singapore.

From the ticket office, Waskom, set out to find his new ship. It was his first time in the celebrated city. Along the way were commercial buildings, open-fronted shops, tea stalls, and a labyrinth of colorful side streets lined with ethnic bazaars, places of worship, religious merchandisers, and vendors of all kinds of food. At the river, the ghats, like the streets, were replete with people, vehicles, and animals. There were beggars, buyers, traders, travelers, religious mendicants, rickshaw wallahs, bicyclists, carriages, crows, and vagabond cows. Besides bathers, the river was filled with boats and ships of every kind—from fishing craft, to tea clippers, to passenger ships. The greatest congestion was in the vicinity of the docks, where the Hooghly was a veritable forest of masts. Somewhere in that forest Pickett found his ship.

Waskom had probably never been to a place more teeming with people. He may never have been to a damper, wetter place either. He had arrived in Calcutta in the heart of the monsoon, the time when most of the city's 64 inches of annual drenching comes in on the wind. In Calcutta, everything sweats in August. The intense humidity is, as Mark Twain once remarked, "enough to make a doorknob mushy." Given the condition of his lungs, it is not hard to imagine, then, that Waskom was anxious for ocean air. It is not hard to imagine, either, what the main topic of conversation was on Waskom's first day at sea, for on that day—August 4, 1914—word came that Great Britain had declared war on Germany.

The next day, his second day at sea, Waskom had a long conversation with God about his desire to be healed. By the time he retired that night, he knew God's answer. Since being diagnosed with tuberculosis, he had been in the habit of recording his temperature three times a day. On most mornings, it was slightly below normal, and on most evenings, it was elevated. That evening, though, his temperature was normal, which Waskom took as a sign that God would heal him. On the basis of that assurance, he wrote that he fell to his knees and thanked God repeatedly. Although the next evening his temperature was elevated again, it would be the last time. For the remainder of the journey, the thermometer showed a constant 98.6 degrees. And each day he felt a little better.

Soon Waskom's vessel arrived in Rangoon, another of Britain's far-flung outposts. After some delay, he was able to catch a cargo boat for Singapore where, he was assured, a ship to Hong Kong awaited him. However, rough seas slowed the small boat's progress, and by the time it arrived at the island port of Penang, the scheduled departure time of his Singapore connection had passed. At that point, he abandoned the sea route. Crossing to the mainland, he caught the first train heading south. In later years, Pickett said the reason for the switch was a warning from the skipper of the cargo boat about a German warship—SMS *Emden*—in the area. However, according to a letter he wrote en route, making up time seems to have been the main motivation for preferring the overland route.

As Pickett's train sped south on the 370-mile journey from Penang to Singapore, he must have been struck by the exceptional mix of peoples on the Peninsula, which would not only have been apparent in the variations of skin color, facial features, dress, and languages of those milling about the stations, but would also have been telegraphed by the depot signs, many of which displayed the station names in English, Malay, Chinese, and Tamil. In particular, the number of Chinese and Indians would have impressed the 24-year-old. Because of their strategic location on the Europe-to-the-Orient steamship routes, and because of the European demand for tropical agricultural products produced in the region, all of the Peninsula settlements along the Straits of Malacca, particularly Singapore on the southern tip, were vital economic centers. Penang, the northern gateway, had a population of just more than 100,000. About 60 percent of its population was Chinese, who had come mostly from the southern provinces of China, and who were the main entrepreneurial force behind the vibrant Malaysian economy. A rung lower on the economic ladder were Tamils from South India and Ceylon, many of whom were involved in agricultural work. Farther down were the indigenous Malays.

When Waskom's train pulled into Singapore, the small size of the railway station probably surprised him. It consisted of a single platform with a simple, one-story building whose only ornamentation was a modest clock tower rising a few feet above its pitched roof. Next to the building were covered waiting and baggage areas and a couple of small storage sheds. The explanation for the diminutive station was that the real transportation hub of the 217 square mile island was the docks. From those docks, steamships carried various spices and tropical fruits—chiefly coconuts and pineapples—to destinations in the West. They also carried rubber. Once at the docks, the beehive of activity would have amazed Pickett, but probably no more than the tremendous variety of races and languages on exhibit there—many more, even, than he had witnessed on the way. In an article called "Where East Meets West," in *World Outlook*, Arthur M. Brilant, who visited Singapore around the same time, described the scene like this:

> In the city, exclusive of the rest of the island, there are spoken sixty-nine languages. Of these not more than twenty-five are spoken by more than 500 persons, and only ten by more than 5000 persons. Babel is avoided by making Malay the lingua franca. In Singapore's hotels one meets people of all nations, bound for the remotest part of the globe, on business or pleasure bent—men and women, of all degrees.
>
> In its streets and alleys the adventurous Occidental rubs democratic elbows with an endless and delightfully kaleidoscopic procession of Malays: Filipinos, Moros, Jawi Pekkans and Javanese from Java, Boyanese from Bawean, Dyaks from Borneo, Achinese from northwest Sumatra, Bugis from the Celebes—all in picturesque sarong and baju; Chinese: Cantonese, Hok-Kiens from Amoy, Teo Chews from Swatow, Kehs from the Hakka country, Hylams from the Island of Hainan, and Babas born in the Straits; black Madrassi and Tamils from India, lank Bengalis, and Chettdies with closely shaved heads and muslin swathed limbs; Cingalese, Klings from the Cordomandel coast, Armenians, Arabs, Parsees, Jews, Hindus, Japanese, Burmese, Siamese, Persians, Egyptians, Annamese, Afghans, Somalilanders, and other races.

Colorful as the street scene was, the Reverend J. Waskom Pickett's focus was on finding the departure point for his ship. When at last he located it, the slip was empty. As he had feared, the vessel for which he had purchased his ticket two weeks before had sailed on time.

Despite the letdown, he soon obtained passage to Hong Kong on a British ship that had docked there unexpectedly. On their second day at sea, a German warship appeared on the horizon (which Pickett in later years mistakenly identified as SMS *Emden*). According to Pickett, the signal to stop flew from her foremast, but Pickett's captain, knowing that a British cruiser was nearby, decided to run for it. While radioing repeatedly for help, Pickett's ship steamed full speed ahead in the cruiser's direction. The German vessel gave chase, but when the British man-of-war came into view, it turned away.

Waskom arrived safely in Hong Kong on August 28, a Friday. But, again, there was a hitch. Although his ship was in port, its voyage had been cancelled. Moreover, Waskom learned that he would have to wait until September 16 for the next ship to the U.S., and even that was uncertain. He found out, however, that a Japanese ship, *Tenjo Maru*, in Yokohama, was scheduled to sail for San Francisco on September 14. Since that seemed his best option, he purchased second-class passage on it. Still, how would he get from Hong Kong to Yokohama?

Nearly a week later, Waskom boarded a British vessel to Shanghai where he would transship to Japan. Since he would have to wait several days for passage, upon arriving in Shanghai he took a 50-mile side trip to Soochow (Suzhou) where Bertha Attaway, who as a student had lived with the Picketts in Wilmore, was teaching in a Methodist college. From Shanghai, Waskom sailed to Nagasaki where, until earlier that year, two more of his Asbury classmates had been stationed. From there he went 350 miles by rail to Kobe where a friend of his father ran a home for missionaries.

Waskom emerged from the Kobe station onto a street filled with people. He had been unable to find anyone in the station who spoke English. He climbed into a jinrikisha and signaled the driver to go. He hoped he would see a European or American who could help him. However, the man pulling the rickshaw assumed he wanted to go to a house of prostitution.

Finally, Waskom spotted someone in western clothes. He signaled the rickshaw puller to stop. Catching up with the man, he asked, "Can you help me find someone? I am a Methodist missionary from India."

The man interrupted him. "Are you Waskom Pickett?" he asked. Pickett had stopped the man for whom he was looking.

After two days, Waskom continued to Tokyo. He was met by a senior missionary who invited him to stay with his family—a stay that would drag on for 10 days. Waskom got word almost immediately that *Tenjo Maru's* departure from nearby Yokohama had been delayed. Over the next few days, two more postponements were announced, the last one indefinite. Rumor had it that *Tenjo Maru* might not sail for weeks. Two reasons were given. First, one of the engines was out of commission. Second, the ship's owners were afraid of German cruisers in the area. (Probably the fear was fueled by Japan's declaration of war on Germany on 23 August.)

Waskom sought the counsel of his hosts. Based on the indefiniteness of the delay, they advised him to transfer to the Pacific Mail's *Mongolia,* also headed for San Francisco. The change of ships would require buying a first-class ticket at an added cost of about 75 dollars, but that was preferable to chancing the alternative.

Waskom's circuitous route to finding a ship was vexing but providential. For one thing, a young woman he met on board turned out to be his second cousin and knew his parents. But, more significantly, Waskom learned that also sailing on the *Mongolia* was Mrs. B.O. Wilcox [Rita Kinzly Wilcox] and her ten-month-old child. Mrs. Wilcox's husband, Berton Oliver Wilcox, had come to Malaysia as a lay missionary in 1910. She had come two years later. Until recently, she and her husband had been involved in work in West Borneo, but her husband had died quite suddenly, and she and her child were now forced to return to her home in Ohio. Mrs. Wilcox was herself unwell, so Waskom took the responsibility of helping her—no doubt a divinely-appointed responsibility.

BECAUSE HE HAD BEEN SO BUSY COPING with cancellations and delays, Waskom was unable to focus upon his arrival in America until he was actually underway on the *Magnolia.* There, on the open ocean, he was able to relax and think extended thoughts for the first time since leaving Lucknow. The long Pacific voyage did him good. His health improved remarkably. He learned just *how* remarkably when he debarked in San Francisco and, as instructed by the Board of Foreign Missions, called on a doctor who provided free checkups for returning missionaries.
"Who told you that you have tuberculosis?" the doctor asked after he had listened to Waskom's lungs.

Waskom retrieved the envelope containing his x-rays. The doctor scrutinized the images and admitted, "Well, you certainly had an advanced case when these were taken. But something has happened since then." Even so, he cautioned Pickett to guard his health carefully in the coming months.

Waskom's extraordinary improvement and ensuing recovery would have a deep and enduring impact upon him. He developed a lifelong interest in the healing arts and a passion for bringing modern medicine to India. He was indefatigable in his efforts to find funds for clinics, hospitals, and medicines. He was relentless in recruiting the best doctors, nurses, and technicians for service in the field. And he was instrumental in establishing Indian teaching hospitals. Indeed, renowned missionary surgeon Charles Perrill, who knew Pickett well, would say in retrospect that Waskom Pickett probably did more than any other single individual of his time to advance the cause of medical missions in South Asia.

From San Francisco, Waskom made his way to Topeka, Kansas, where Deets Pickett was serving as Research Secretary for the Temperance Society of the Methodist Episcopal Church. When he got there, Deets handed him a letter from Dr. James M. Taylor of the Foreign Mission Board. Taylor wanted Waskom to participate in a fund-raising meeting in Boston. Waskom replied that he would be happy to oblige if his expenses were covered but that he felt it unwise to undertake any extensive work for a few months. All the same, he added: "I feel like a new man."

From Topeka, Waskom traveled to Evanston, Illinois, to see Ruth and her parents who were on furlough. Perhaps it was from them that Waskom learned that his friend Fred Perrill, district missionary in Arrah, Bihar had reported at the North India Annual Conference that Waskom had returned to America due to "lung and other affections."

From Evanston, Waskom headed for St. Augustine, Florida, where he planned to do his convalescing. On the way, he stopped in Wilmore. It was election time and he was surprised, though delighted, that even though he had been away for more than four years, local voting officials were willing to let him cast his ballot. His stay in Wilmore was brief, however, for the Pickett family no longer lived there. L.L. and Ludie had, during his absence, moved to St. Augustine, Waskom's destination.

When Waskom got to Florida, he was greeted by his mother and younger brothers. His father, who had been traveling since April, was due back in a few days. L.L. planned to remain at home for the full month of December. Waskom would be recuperating on nearby Anastasia Island where his father owned a large parcel of land and six small cabins. L.L. rented the cabins to people who wanted to hunt or fish on the island.

The plan was for Waskom and his brother, Willard Lee, to lodge in adjacent cabins. While Waskom read and recuperated, Willard would tend to his small garden and do most of the cooking. They would keep their dishes and utensils separate. Among Willard's specialties was turtle soup. One large turtle made an ample enough batch to feed the whole family back on the mainland. Apparently, Willard was equipped to hunt other game as well, for one night Waskom was startled from his sleep by a gunshot. He rushed next door to find Willard standing over a lifeless wild cat that had gotten into his room.

In India, Waskom had embarked upon a program of self-education to improve his pastoral skills, but he was ill at ease over his lack of formal theological training. While in America, he hoped to take some seminary courses. But though he applied to several schools, none were agreeable to his coming. Despite his improved health, they felt that his tuberculosis presented too big a risk.

On his journey from Evanston, Waskom had met briefly in Cincinnati with James M. Taylor, whose letter he had received in Topeka. Taylor had been a missionary to South America but was now assigned to the New York office of the Board of Foreign Missions. Taylor wanted to recruit Waskom for one of his fund-raising teams. Waskom was agreeable but not until summer. His plan was to spend the last two months of 1914 resting up. Then, soon after the first of the year, he would begin deputation work in the South. He would stay in the South until summer, thus avoiding the winter cold, while also taking advantage of his and his father's many contacts with Southern pastors. Then, come summer, he would join Taylor for up to a year. After that, in the summer of 1916, he hoped to return to India with Ruth.

Waskom also discussed with Taylor the possibility of visiting some of the Holiness camp meetings. He proposed to describe the exciting potential of India's so-called "mass movements," in which thousands were coming into the church. He was convinced that, once informed, holiness people would be eager to support missionary work in mass movement areas.

THE MASS MOVEMENTS WERE THE FOCUS of much discussion in India. The previous January, for instance, at North India's Annual Conference, Pickett had J.O. Denning, superintendent of the Tirhoot District, describe a new mass movement developing there. Denning had begun by clarifying a common misconception. He cautioned that it was incorrect to say that India's masses were turning to Christ, for the masses had not yet even heard the gospel. He explained: "Where the Gospel is having success along caste lines, and whole villages of the same caste are baptized at one time, and this movement spreads from village to village in that community somewhat rapidly, this we call a 'mass movement.'" In describing the movement and the work of H.J. Schutz and Fred M. Perrill in responding to it, it was apparent the phenomenon was restricted to a single group of untouchables called Chamars. Denning described how Chamars themselves were the catalytic force of the movement:

> As they meet in the bazaars and in their social gatherings they talk of their religion and of what the *Padris* [pastors] have taught them and in that way people of new villages come to learn something of Christ and are anxious to learn more. Often people from new villages where our workers have never visited, and know only what they have heard from their converted relatives and friends, come to the missionary and beg for baptisms.

The first experience of the Methodists with mass movements in India had come in their work among a small group called Mazhabi Sikhs, first contacted in 1859 right there in Moradabad where, in 1914, the North India Conference was celebrating its fiftieth anniversary. However, conversion movements, themselves, were much older than that. For example, in all likelihood, the ancient Syrian Church of South India came from a strong mass movement. Likewise, almost all the Roman Catholics in India could trace their Christian lineage to a mass movement. Early Protestant conversion movements had occurred among the Sambavars and Nadars (then known as Shanars) in Tinnevelly and South Travancore, among the Oraons and Mudas in Chota Nagpur, among the Churas in the Punjab, and among the Mala and Madigas in what is now Andhra Pradesh. All these movements happened in groups at the bottom of the Indian social ladder. In fact, they were not even on the ladder! It was exclusively groups of untouchables who were expressing the desire to become Christians.

Having served in Lucknow, and having focused on English work, Waskom had little firsthand knowledge of these conversion movements. Nevertheless, he was well acquainted with the details of the movements, for they were discussed at length in the all church papers and in lively debates at practically every missionary gathering. Moreover, Waskom had struck up friendships with several missionaries with experience in mass movement areas.

Conversion movements were not unique to the Indian context. As missiologist Alan Tippett observed, most of the Pacific Island Christians came to faith in Christ that way. Nonetheless, the remarkable rise of Protestant conversion movements in India, beginning in Tinnevelly in 1802, but especially in the late 1800s and early 1900s, was understandably championed as the subcontinent's most consequential missional development. Certainly the numbers coming into the church were unlike anything the missionaries had experienced before. In the Punjab, in the decade preceding 1914, the total number of Christians increased from 37,000 to 163,000. In 1914 alone, Methodists were aware of 15,000 who wanted baptism in the Delhi area. During the previous two years in the Tirhoot District, 1,000 Chamars had been baptized. In the south of India, there were comparable conversion movements in the Telugu, Tinnevelly, and Travancore fields. Similar interest in Christianity existed in the Vizagapatnam district of the Madras Presidency, in Hyderabad, in parts of Maratha country, in Coorg, and in the North Lushai Hills.

The term "mass movements" was not applied to group conversions until 1892. Later, probably due to the number of emerging movements, some spoke of them collectively as "the mass movement." But although new movements were appearing, there was no single or unified mass movement. Each was distinct in origin and development. Nor did the phenomenon spread in any planned, orderly, or systematic way. On the contrary, they were spontaneous local developments in which groups were persuaded—usually by one or more of their own—to embrace the Christian faith. Western missionaries and their teams of Indian preachers did evangelize. However, for the most part, they employed the same methods used in areas where results came slowly, one person at a time. The missionaries and their co-workers were ready to shift their focus and energies when new movements emerged. However, by that time, something was already underway—something generated from within the groups in a collective decision-making process. Therefore, no outsider could take credit for what was happening. Always, the opening move was from within (or above!).

BY THE TIME WASKOM PICKETT RETURNED to America in 1914, there were a million depressed-class Christians in India, and Christianity had become the third largest faith in the country. Waskom's bishop, Canadian-born Frank Warne, was foremost among the advocates of mass movement work and was specially gifted in organizing it. On average, more than 30,000 converts a year were coming into the church under his oversight. Warne was convinced there could be even more. The bottleneck was a shortage of personnel. Thousands who wished to be baptized had to be put off because there were not enough catechists to adequately ground them in the faith. To receive them without adequate means to instruct and nurture them would leave new believers in a vulnerable state if their faith was tested as, doubtless, it would be. "What would YOU do?" Warne asked.

> Would you cry for help? Would you go on and baptize unlimited numbers whom you could not train and run the risk of later having all your Christians swept off in Mohammedanism as happened in North Africa in the early Middle Ages?

This was the predicament Waskom proposed to accentuate at the camp meetings and in churches. But he would keep his presentation positive. It would include a word of encouragement (God was already visibly at work), a word of opportunity (the need for funds and workers was pressing and plain), and a word of promise (the prospects seemed bright for millions to enter the church in the next few years).

Although he had resolved to stay in the South for the winter, by mid-January Waskom felt well enough to join Dr. Taylor for a New York fund-raising campaign. For Waskom, who had already sat at the feet of one master solicitor—his father, L.L. Pickett—this was an opportunity to learn from another seasoned fund-raiser, and as the following letter shows, Taylor was more than ready to impart his expertise.

> Now Waskom I am going to speak very frank with you for I believe you will appreciate it. I have had years of experience in Missionary Meetings and the [Mission Board] Secretaries, especially the older ones, tell me their experience has been much the same as my own, namely: Missionary <u>sermons</u> is not the thing. Begging money and lambasting the people is not the thing. But short addresses filled with facts and incidents giving the audience an illuminated version of the Field and inspiration that gladdens the heart showing that results can be had when money and lives are invested.

In March, Pickett accompanied Taylor to the First State Convention of Methodist Men at Columbus, Ohio. The convention, which began on St. Patrick's Day (Wednesday) and wound up Friday, registered 3,456 paid delegates—all men. Thursday noon the delegates formed a parade and marched to the State House. A squad of Methodist police officers, two brass bands, and a drum corps joined them. When they arrived, they assembled on the State House steps where the governor addressed them. The theme of the convention was "The Challenge of To-day." Among the speakers were such well-known leaders as John R. Mott, George Sherwood Eddy, and William F. Oldham. Taylor and Pickett each gave brief "Messages from the Foreign Field," Taylor representing South America. Not surprisingly, Waskom struck the mass movement theme. He told the assembly that, initially, the Methodists had sent missionaries to scattered locations in India but had paid little attention to the masses until recent times. He then summarized the stunning results of this change of focus.

In the last quarter of a century our Methodist Church has grown from 9,000 to nearly 300,000 members. Last year more than 37,000 converts were baptized by Methodist missionaries and their Indian associates. Years ago Dr. Rockwell Clancy crossed the Ganges River and baptized our first Methodist convert in Northwestern India. Today we have in that territory the Northwest India Conference with a Christian community of 115,000 or more, although we have turned about 18,000 of our baptized converts there over to other missions.

Then, echoing a Bishop Warne refrain, he added:

We are by no means meeting our opportunity in India. It is glorious that 37,000 people were baptized by our ministers last year, but it is tragic that several times that number who wanted to become Christians were denied baptism and the ministry of the Word.

In conclusion, the young missionary contended that, with the help of the American churches, that situation could change.

ON THE FIRST OF NOVEMBER, 1915, Waskom was in Wichita, Kansas for a convention sponsored by the National Laymen's Missionary Movement. There, he received a letter from Bishop William F. Oldham at the mission board's New York office explaining that, due to a severe personnel shortage in North India Conference, they were anticipating a request for his immediate return. Waskom immediately wrote back to Oldham, professing ambivalence about the prospect.

> My friends advise me not to return until next year. My home folks will strongly oppose it. The last physician who examined me warned that I ought to be very careful with myself and that I should by no means return to India this year.
>
> However, the threat against my lungs seems to have disappeared. I have had no serious cold for months and feel better and stronger now than I have previously felt since I started for India.
>
> If I could stay here until next August I would then be perfectly well and would have a reserve of strength that would be invaluable to me, probably.
>
> But they are tragically short of men and if I should not return the work might suffer greatly.

Waskom also had reservations about making a decision without Ruth. "My fiancée expects to graduate in June and we had hoped we could be married and make the trip out together. I would prefer to see her or at least have time to learn her views before a decision is made."

As expected, before the week was out, Bishop J.E. Robinson had cabled New York, asking that Pickett be assigned to the Moradabad School, 90 miles east of Delhi. On November 8, Waskom wrote to Dr. Taylor for advice.

> Dr. Purvis, a local expert diagnostician declares that my lungs are now alright. I also feel in well-nigh perfect condition. But it is only for the last six weeks or so that I have felt so well . . . Dr. Coole strongly advises me to stay here until next August . . . The local doctors incline to that opinion too, but do not forbid me to go. My people strongly oppose it and if I insist on going I will probably have to go directly in the face of my father's opposition.

Waskom suggested that if Taylor's fund-raising warranted his further participation, perhaps Taylor could intercede for him with Bishops Warne and Oldham, to whom he would be writing that day also. Shortly thereafter, Waskom got his reprieve.

In December, Waskom took a train to see his parents—not in Florida, however, but in Wilmore. Because Ludie Day's health had been so poor in Florida, she and L.L. had moved north again, where they would remain. Waskom arrived home three days after Christmas with a bad cough. It was not, however, a recurrence of tuberculosis but "la grippe."

The following week, Waskom got a letter from James Taylor offering him an alternative to the fund-raising circuit. Taylor proposed that he come to New York for a few months as "a kind of sub-assistant deputy secretary." The proposition appealed to him, both because he was worn out from the wear and tear of travel and, also because, in his words, "it would . . . supplement my work of the past year." That Sunday, January 9, 1916, Waskom spoke to the Asbury Student Volunteer meeting. A few days later he packed his bags for New York.

BY SUMMER, WASKOM AND RUTH knew their first assignment together would be in Arrah, Bihar, where Fred and Mary Perrill had been serving. Thus, the wedding notice they sent to friends and family announced, "At Home after the first of October . . . Arrah, India."

On July 27—a Thursday on which the temperature reached a scorching 100 degrees Fahrenheit—J. Waskom Pickett and Ruth Robinson were married at Evanston, Illinois. The wedding was on Sherman Avenue in an apartment John and Elizabeth Robinson were using as headquarters while on furlough. About 15 were present, including the Robinsons, L.L. and Deets Pickett, and two of Ruth's classmates. Both fathers, along with the local Methodist minister, Dr. T.P. Frost, officiated. The wedding took place at 6:30 p.m. Around 9:00 p.m., the newlyweds left for Kentucky. Their honeymoon began with a two-day stay at Mammoth Cave, followed by two weeks in Wilmore, thus "making it possible," said Waskom, "for my home-folk and my home-maker to become acquainted with one another."

From Wilmore, Waskom and Ruth made their way to Vancouver, British Columbia. There they would rendezvous with Ruth's parents, the mother-in-law and sister-in-law of missionary Ted Badley, and Ruth Hyneman, an Asbury College graduate leaving for her first assignment in India. On August 24, they sailed for Hong Kong on the *Empress of Japan*. From there they sailed to Colombo—but not before the familiar delays: ship's engine repairs (six-days); late departure (three days); weathering a typhoon on the China Sea (one day); a holdup in Singapore (one day); and desertion of the ship's stokers, which meant navigating with something less than a full head of steam. Upon crossing the channel from Ceylon, Waskom and Ruth boarded a train for Lucknow. The trip, via Manmad, would take two days. They would then spend a week in Lucknow—long enough to see old friends and rest up before the final leg of their journey.

Waskom and Ruth had learned that their first assignment as husband and wife would be in Arrah, Bihar, where Waskom's friend, Fred Perrill had been working with a small mass movement. So, ironically, he had come full circle, for his two-year ellipse to America and back was ending on the same rails that had taken him to Calcutta when the unsought detour began.

Waskom's long journey home was nearly concluded—ironically on the miles of track on which it had begun two years earlier. One can imagine his and Ruth's excitement as their train sprinted past fields and villages toward Arrah. The view from their carriage afforded them an initial glimpse of their new province and place of service—but only a glimpse. That is all a speeding train *can* deliver—panoramas, not close-ups. The occasional station stops did offer fleeting opportunities to observe local people, hear local conversations, sip local tea, and breathe local smells—but they were abridged opportunities—mere snapshots. Nevertheless, both the wide-angle and close-up shots attested to a substantial difference between the India to which they were going and the India from which they had come. The Methodist community of Lucknow had, at many points, been familiar—even to a Kentucky boy. It had employed a familiar tongue (English), embraced familiar issues (holiness, abstention from alcohol, and the like), played familiar games (baseball and tennis), and worshiped with familiar furnishings (pulpit, lectern, pew, and organ). Bihar, on the other hand, was another world, a new and different India that would take some time to know.

The Arrah Years (1916-1924)

The Railway Station at Arrah

The Arrah Bungalow

Meeting with Shahabad villagers

Pickett bought ponies and ekkas for each of his village preachers

Clockwise from upper left: (1) John Wesley Robinson, (2) Elizabeth, six weeks old; (3) JWP (far end) with Lucknow Christian College board, ca. 1923; (4) Elizabeth Robinson

8 Arrah, Bihar

Even as they stepped from the train at Arrah Station, the Picketts knew they must shortly pack their bags again. The Tirhoot District Conference, of which the Arrah field was a part, opened in Ballia the following Tuesday, on October 24, 1916. The Picketts were expected. That meant they would have time for a briefing, a blitz of the town, and a tour of their bungalow—not much more. However, after so long a journey, and with so little time before journeying again, their primary interest was undoubtedly the bungalow.

The bungalow was just seven years old. The Reverend and Mrs. A.L. (Arthur Lee) Grey had been the first to live there. The Greys and seven co-workers—all Americans—had come to India in 1904 under the sponsorship of an independent mission organization. When financial support dwindled, they asked the Methodist Episcopal Church to assume oversight of the work. The Methodists agreed. The new arrangement took effect in October 1907. Although their co-workers took up responsibilities elsewhere, the Greys stayed on. To that point, Lee Grey had been preaching in melas (fairs) and muhallas (sections of a town) and had gotten some Sunday schools and other educational work started. He had also recruited about seven Indian preachers, the best of whom was Brother John Sampson.

With the help of District Superintendent J.O. Denning and recent converts from the Ballia District across the Ganges, the work of the Arrah Circuit had started to flourish, especially among the lowly Chamars. In one two-week period in 1909, for example, 79 Chamars were baptized.

Early on, Grey had purchased twelve acres on the outskirts of the city on which he constructed several temporary buildings. However, due to the incursion of white ants, the structures (including Grey's small house) became unsound. The need for more acceptable housing was imperative.

In 1909 the Methodists came up with the funds for a new bungalow. It cost 13,000 rupees. They also built a boy's school on the property.

Fred and Mary Perrill were the second family to occupy the bungalow. Fred, who had arrived in India in 1906, was appointed to Arrah in January 1911. Before coming to Arrah, he was principal of the Columbia Boys' School and Orphanage in Muzaffarpur, Bihar. In that capacity, he became reacquainted with Mary Voigt, whom he had known when both were students in Evanston, Illinois. Mary was his counterpart at Muzaffarpur's Indian Girls' School. The two soon fell in love, and on May 4, 1911, at 8:00 in the morning, they married in the presence of friends and the children of the two schools. They chose the early hour to avoid the heat, which in that season was often 110 degrees by midday. They left for Arrah that afternoon.

By late 1911, the third year of the Methodist superintendency, some 1,500 persons had been baptized in the Arrah area. "The field was ripe unto the harvest," wrote Fred Perrill. "We simply thrust in the sickle."

However, Perrill found the inflow of church members as unsettling as exhilarating.

To have fifteen hundred people baptized in three years, right in the midst of a community where for centuries heathen worship has gone on undisturbed, this is startling, and the people are startled. Even the devil is startled and he is trying to tighten his grip on his slaves . . . Our task is a heavy one.

Fred Perrill was the Picketts' sole host when they arrived in Arrah. Mary and three-year-old son, Charles, had returned to the States to wait out the war. As he showed the newcomers around, Perrill must have summarized something of the history of the work. However, from some source—most likely conversations with his bishop father-in-law—Waskom already knew many of the details, even of the finances. "If you find any one in your meetings who can be persuaded to give money for property in India, you might remember Arrah," he had written James M. Taylor from Vancouver in August. "We already possess the property but there is a debt of three thousand on it which must be paid."

As they drove up to the bungalow in Fred's Model T, Waskom and Ruth must have been surprised by the large size and distinctive appearance of the house. In contrast to the typical, square-shaped missionary residence, the double-decker, flat-roofed Arrah house was rectangular—five rooms long and two rooms deep on the first floor. At the roofline a decorative cornice traced the perimeter. Beneath the cornice and running the length of the front were upper and lower multi-arched verandas. From floor level the arches rose three-fourths of the way to the tops of the verandas. The balcony had nine arches, and the lower veranda had eight (the "missing" one accounted for by a double-wide entry arch). A similar single-story porch graced the back of the house.

Inside, the bungalow's upper level had four large rooms, which, added to those on the main level, made a total of 14. There were no hallways; one room led to the next. The rooms were immense, containing 300 square feet or more. The walls were plastered. They were 18 feet tall on the first floor and 15 feet on the second floor. High ceilings were thought to aid summer cooling. They also provided vertical space for the majestic swing of a 20-inch by eight or ten-foot punkah (sweep fan) that a "punkah coolie" pulled by rope from the adjacent veranda. Light entered the rooms through doors leading to the verandas and through roshan dans (literally, "light containers"), which were high glass windows on a central pivot that were opened with a long pole. Some rooms had smoky fireplaces for removing winter chill. Bathrooms had inside and outside entrances so that servants had access for cleaning. Hot water for baths was heated outside in a heating canister. Servants carried the steaming water inside one bucket at a time.

Almost immediately, Fred, Waskom and Ruth had to leave for the district conference gathering in Tirhoot. Formed in 1913, the Tirhoot ("place of the three rivers") District took in an immense area on both sides of the Ganges that included most of Bihar and the southeast corner of the United Provinces. H.J. Schutz, the new District superintendent, described it as "so vast . . . that it took more than 24 hours of continuous traveling by train to go from one end of it to the other." Situated in the heart of the world's largest alluvial plain, the district contained the most fertile land in India. With 800 to 900 people per square mile, it was also the most densely populated rural area on the subcontinent. Methodist work in the district had three main centers: Muzaffarpur, Ballia, and Arrah. Muzaffarpur and Arrah were almost identical in size, each town having a population of 46,000. They were also alike in that they were both headquarters of the civil district of which they were a part. Ballia, on the other hand, was much smaller, with only a third as many people.

Getting to Ballia required taking the mail train to Buxar, 40 miles away, and boarding a paddle-steamer riverboat for an upstream trip of 20 more miles.

On the opening day of the conference, the 50 or so workers who were present warmly welcomed Waskom and Ruth, but their farewell to Fred Perrill, who was about to go on furlough and rejoin his family, was especially moving. Following Perrill's reading of his annual report, the preachers-in-charge and a number of others stood, one after the other, to affirm him and Mary and their achievements. Pickett, who wrote up the meeting for *the Indian Witness*, observed:

> Seldom have any of our missionaries been permitted to see the Christian community in their charge grow to such proportions from a small beginning, as Mr. Perrill has witnessed here. Yet he and all his workers agree that we are merely at the beginning of the mass movement in both the Ballia and the Arrah sections of the district.

Future Methodist bishop, Clement D. Rockey, with his thoughtful messages, fluently delivered in the vernacular, made a strong impression on Pickett. But just as strong was the impression made by the Indian workers. For example, the last day had been set aside for prayer; however, when the meeting opened, some of the Indians wanted time to discuss the subject of giving. After several short speeches, John Sampson appealed to those present to commit themselves to tithing and to declare it publicly by signing their names. More than four-fifths of the congregation did so.

THE BROTHER SAMPSONS WERE THE UNSUNG heroes of the mass movements. Without these helpers, whose stories have for the most part been lost, the missionaries would have accomplished little. As Grey and Perrill had their Brother Sampson, so the LMS missionary, W.T. Ringeltaube had his Vedamanickam, and the American Baptist missionary, J.E. Clough had his Periah. One of the most famous Indian preachers was Ditt, whose evangelistic work among his fellow Chuhras in the late 1800s is legendary. Unfortunately, many more are now forgotten, but these Indian partners in the gospel were indispensably instrumental in all the mass movement areas. The missionaries inspired, trained, and encouraged them. They often accompanied them for short periods. However, it was the Indian village preachers themselves, and their accompanying family members, who occupied the trenches day in and day out.

Like Brother Sampson and his wife, they packed their tents from village to village. They routinely put up with heat, dust storms, and other obstacles. Fred Perrill's description of his sojourns to the Sampson camp offers a glimpse of how these indigenous workers functioned, as well as how they and the missionaries partnered in village evangelism.

> I have gone out to their camp staying a few days at a time . . . I always have to carry my food with me, for a European cannot find any food arrangements out away from some European home. All my work is out in the native villages five to twenty miles away from railways and European settlements. I always carry tea and sugar with me so that when I get thirsty I can have some water boiled and have a cup of tea. I never think of drinking unboiled water . . .
>
> Brother Sampson is a shepherd to his flock and is doing fine work. It is good to see how the humble village people depend upon him and listen to his instruction. And also there are two or three young preachers who are working under Sampson and he is doing a valuable work in training them.

The Chamars were, in Fred Perrill's words, "a humble farmer caste who are almost the slaves of the landowners." In the villages, to own land was to have preposterous power over the landless. Everything was under the control of the zamindars (landlords): employment, animals to work the fields, loans for weddings, wood for repairs, even wood for funeral pyres. Moreover, the landowners could be ruthless in their efforts to preserve the status quo, as missionaries William and Charlotte Wiser wrote in *Behind Mud Walls*.

> The leaders [synonymous with landowners] of our village are so sure of their power that they make no effort to display it. The casual visitor finds little to distinguish them from other farmers. They dress as simply and cheaply as their neighbors, and do no more shouting or scolding; they work as faithfully as any in their fields; the walls enclosing their family courtyard may be high but are no better kept than those adjoining them, and their entrances are often less elaborate. And yet when one of them appears

among men of serving caste, the latter express respect and fear in every guarded word and gesture. The serving ones have learned that as long as their subservience is unquestioned, the hand which directs them rests lightly. But let there be any move toward independence or even indifference among them, and the paternal touch becomes a stranglehold.

Without the John Sampsons, the task of ministering to scattered, subjugated, and often, persecuted believers would have been impossible. Although their pay was a modest 15 rupees a month (about five dollars), in the currency of God's kingdom, the contribution of the missionaries' Indian colleagues was incomputable, as Perrill confessed.

It is impossible for me to make the rounds of the forty or more villages very often. I have had to depend on my native preachers. And I have but a handful of them. I need more before I will be able to develop the work as it should be. But I must have the ones I have to hold the work where it is. If we baptize people we must care for them, and when they come to us, sick of their heathen religion and crying out for the living God, we have no authority to deny them baptism. But with every new convert the church imposes a duty upon itself . . .

Any one supporting a native pastor should not lightly esteem the good being done: I do all I can, but without the help of these native men, I could do little. I come and preach and give out what advice I can. When I am gone the native pastor stays, and by living with people is able to amplify the teaching. May God bless the native pastor of India. With him largely is the burden of India's evangelization. I have faith in him if only he will follow in the footsteps of the Master. He needs your prayers for his temptations are very great. Living alone in the midst of heathenism is not the best condition in which to grow in grace.

WASKOM AND RUTH RETURNED TO ARRAH on November 1, just over a week after they had first arrived. They immediately set to work procuring supplies, hiring servants, arranging the bungalow, assessing the situation at the boys' school, and getting to know the community.

Arrah was 40 miles west of Patna, the capital of Bihar. It was essentially a rural town, but it was strategic. For one thing, the main trunk of the EIR (East Indian Railway) ran through it. Along those rails sailed the Punjab-Howrah Mail and other important trains. Moreover, since Arrah was the headquarters of the Shahabad civil district, it was the home of district judges and other officials.

Since no river ran through Arrah (the Ganges was 10 miles north and the Sone was seven miles east), it was an unlikely candidate for a major flood. Nevertheless, because of poor drainage, during the rainy season it was not unusual for much of the country around Arrah to be covered with standing water. In other seasons water for crops came from a large navigable canal, specially built for that purpose. It flowed out of the Sone some 60 miles south and passed through the eastern part of the city.

Because of the long periods of minor flooding and standing water, which sometimes lasted two to three months beyond the rains, mosquitos flourished and so did malarial fever—especially in September and October. High rodent and flea populations and poor sanitation, including surface drains used as privies, heightened the risk of other diseases. A particular menace was bubonic plague, which had been commonplace for 15 years. According to Pickett, other common ailments included "spleen troubles . . . ophthalmia . . . and elephantitus" [elephantiasis].

However, Arrah had its assets too. For one thing, the sun shone virtually every day, even during the rainy season. For the Picketts and their colleagues, and for the students, the open location of the compound, a mile from the most populated and unhygienic part of the city, was an asset too.

Arrah was a city of some historical importance—at least to the British. In July of 1857, during the Anglo-Indian War, 50 Sikh police and 11 Europeans had, for eight days, kept 5,000 of Babu Kunwar Singh's mutineers at bay. They had made their defense from a house that still stood and was known as "the little house."

Besides the famous house, the town consisted of the railway station, a market, a few grain shops, some municipal buildings, a church, a jail, a handful of official residences, and the huddled adobe huts of its populace. The best road was just wide enough for an oxcart—or a Model T. Other so-called roads were hardly more than paths between the fields. Elephants were the best form of transportation over these, though only the well-to-do had access to the beasts. The main crops around Arrah were wheat, barley, gram, some fruits, and bajra (a species of millet). Rice was grown in the low-lying areas near the river, but rice was not a favorite of the locals. Those who subsisted on rice were thought to be "weak" people like those in South India. Some British agricultural people still grew indigo, although since the Germans had imitated it synthetically, it was no longer in as high demand. Other Britishers grew opium, although they had to be specially licensed as government suppliers of the product.

As for the Christian community in Arrah, Pickett discovered that there was only one church large enough to have a building—an Anglican church that served British officials, their families, and a few Anglo-Indians. Indian Christians were a rarity in Arrah, and Methodist Christians were even rarer. The entire Methodist community consisted of the following: an unordained local preacher, a clerk in a government office, the wife and parents of the clerk, and an old man and his wife. The old man and his wife lived in a room on the mission compound. She worked as an ayah (nursemaid).

Among Waskom's responsibilities was oversight of the district's boys' school. Fred Perrill had started the school from a little orphanage begun by the Greys. According to District Superintendent H.J. Schutz, the school was founded to reach the sons of the new Christians in the villages. The goal was to enhance the boys' chances of an improved and happier life by getting them away from their surroundings and the slavery of child labor. When Waskom and Ruth first arrived, there were 12 primary students. The school, which was behind the bungalow, consisted of one building with three rooms—two for the boys and one for the teacher. The headmaster (the above-mentioned local preacher) served as teacher, warden of the dormitory, and chaplain.

When the Picketts came to Arrah, the boys' school and 12 inadequate village schools were the only places children could learn to read and write. Of the 2,000 school-age children of Christians in the district, only 143 were enrolled. Because the teachers were barely literate themselves, the schools offered, at best, a basic primary education. None could be counted on to develop future leaders. There was a better school in Ballia, but families from Pickett's side of the district (south of the Ganges) would not let their children go there.

After just two months in Arrah, Waskom had already made a good many trips out into the district. As he toured the villages, he discovered that many more young boys wanted to attend the Arrah school. He immediately saw that expanding its capacity and improving its program must be top priorities. He envisioned a 40-bed addition and began soliciting funds for it.

The Picketts also realized the need of a school for girls. The nearest Methodist girls' boarding school was 80 miles away in a different language area. Waskom and Ruth contacted the Women's Foreign Missionary Society for funds to get a girls' school started, but they were unable to help. Undeterred, they determined to start the school on their own.

Pickett's fund-raising mentor, James M. Taylor had urged him never to be shy about asking for money. Taylor needn't have worried. Using a little Corona typewriter provided by Taylor, Waskom wrote at least 15 letters a day, most of them seeking gifts for the work. Besides enlarging the boys' school and starting a girls' school, he described a third project. Upon arriving in Arrah, he almost immediately had become aware of the limitation of developing indigenous preachers and teachers through boys' and girls' schools. That was a good long-term approach, but a more immediate prescription was needed to the chronic shortage of workers. So Pickett also sought funds to jumpstart a local training school for preachers—if possible by the end of 1917, the conclusion of his first full year in Arrah.

The paucity of Indian co-workers was a longstanding problem with which Lee Grey and Fred Perrill had also struggled. Training schools like the one Pickett was proposing existed in other areas, but their students could rarely be persuaded to relocate. Pickett proposed to bring into the training school young men who were committed to evangelizing in the villages. There they would receive at least a year's instruction in the Bible and other subjects related to their task. Because most of them would be married, Pickett envisioned their wives receiving the training with them. His appeal, therefore, included a request for gifts to construct quarters for the young men and their families. He also asked for donations to build an assembly hall. The hall would not only serve as the classroom for training the preachers and their wives but would double as the meeting place of the Methodist Church in Arrah. The church presently gathered on the Picketts' veranda. "Think of this veranda being the only place Methodism has for its members to worship in this city of 40,000 people," he wrote.

The time spent in letter writing blended well with unpacking and settling into the bungalow, not to mention settling into his role as a married man. By Christmastime, Pickett could write: "My wife and I are now fairly established in our new home and are finding it very pleasant indeed." The presence of Ruth's parents for the holidays (a tradition they would continue) enhanced the pleasantness. That first year, 1916, John Robinson was able to stay for only nine days, but Elizabeth, who came earlier, stayed nearly a month.

The Robinsons left the day after Christmas. After two days' reprieve, the Perrills came (that is, Fred and his sister, Louise) for what Fred called "a sort of 'off again, on again, gone again' visit." The next month Fred and Louise came again for a nine-day visit. They were on their way to Calcutta and America, where Fred would join his wife and son. Since Arrah was on the main rail line to the old capital, entertaining missionaries and visitors on their way to or from the U.S. became routine for the Picketts. They became known for their hospitality. After eating Ruth's famous fried chicken and homemade candy, many—even those who came for business purposes, such as auditing the books—threatened to return. Fred Perrill always did. Some of his humorous guest book alerts were: "I'll come again the first chance I get"; and "I came this time on a scheme to sell some property—will be thinking of some other excuse for next time."

9 War and Other Challenges

As new district missionary, Pickett's main job was evangelization, which connoted much time on the road—when there was a road! In a memorial address in 1981, Pickett's one-time colleague, Bishop James K. Mathews, described what that meant in Pickett's Arrah days:

> Evangelism meant moving from village to village, often on foot; being pastor to the already Christian and witness to the not-yet-Christian; it meant getting to know profoundly Hinduism and Islam and adherents of these religions. It meant acquaintance with social customs and encountering intense opposition. It involved organizing schools and securing support for them; the recruitment and training of local leadership. It involved a ministry of healing; and dealing with a wide array of social concerns about poverty, alcoholism, drugs and oppression of outcastes; it involved also response to the Gospel by groups and individuals; it meant baptism and new life in Christ; the organizing of new churches. Life becomes very full when the agenda is set by endless human need and guided by response to these needs.

Pickett seems to have been elated with the prospect of working in a mass movement area. On the train from Lucknow, he may well have read an article in the current *Indian Witness* which catalogued mass movement "facts." The article condensed a longer piece by Bishop Warne. In it, Warne highlighted India's 50 million depressed-class people, whom he called the foundation of Indian social life. "If we can win these fifty millions," he asserted, "we shall have made the winning of the remaining millions relatively easy." Warne was not alone in his optimism. The fact that Methodists were active on nearly all the current mass movement stages—Telugu territory and the region of Travancore in the South, the Punjab, the northern part of the United Provinces, and northern Bihar and Chota Nagpur, which included Arrah—inflated the expectations of many.

In January 1917, a little over two months after the Picketts' arrival, the Methodists shifted their Arrah Circuit, which had been attached to the Tirhoot District since 1907, to the new Ballia-Arrah District. H.J. Schutz was named district superintendent. Although the circuit contained three million people, the Methodists were concentrating on three untouchable castes numbering around 200,000. In this new configuration, Pickett's duties—supervising workers, baptizing (there would be 751 new believers in 1917), and looking for better ways to handle the thousands of inquirers—remained unchanged. Nevertheless, new challenges were presenting themselves. The prime example was World War I . Its impact on mission work was enormous. It affected family life, fund-raising, communications, workloads, costs, international travel, personnel replacement, and more. As isolated as the new Ballia-Arrah District was, it escaped none of these consequences.

ONE EFFECT OF THE GREAT WAR, as it was called, was an expanded pastoral load resulting from the virtual closing of the German "Gossner Mission." American Methodists and German Lutherans had long worked together in Chota Nagpur. However, the repatriation of German missionaries due to the war meant the fruit of their work was in jeopardy. Moreover, since getting financial support from Germany was no longer possible, the Gossner Mission had to dismiss its indigenous workers. The workers had ministered in scores of villages north of the Ganges, as well as in Buxar, the next main train stop west of Arrah. The abandoned Christians from these areas pled for the Methodists to come and shepherd them. Even though it put greater strain on their limited resources, Pickett and his colleagues responded. In a subsequent letter to John R. Mott, Pickett described the situation and, also, the help they got:

> When anti-German feeling was running high, and certain British Government officials were making reckless attacks against German missionaries, the Society for the Propagation of the Gospel, the Chota Nagpur Diocese of the Church of England and the Anglican clergy in India led by the Metropolitan, who had previously been the Anglican Bishop in Chota Nagpur, defended

the character and political record of the missionaries. But they did not stop with that. The P.G. [Provincial Government] in Chota Nagpur undertook to cooperate with the Indian clergy and the Church Councils in maintaining their work. The Bihar and Orissa Council and the National Christian Council offered their services. The American United Lutheran Missionary Society loaned one of their ablest missionaries and made financial grants. An Advisory Council and a Board of Trustees were appointed and eventually the Lutherans of the area organized an autonomous church.

A second difficulty of the war was inflation. A key factor was the removal of Germany from the Indian economic picture. Before the war, many of the most salable items in Indian bazaars were imported from Germany. Now they were no longer available. Moreover, before the onset of the war Germany had become India's second largest market for exports, importing from the subcontinent fully half the value of all the goods shipped to Britain. The collapse of this important export market depressed major crop prices, including those grown in Bihar. Britain compounded the problem by requiring huge amounts of wheat and other crops to feed its troops, thereby causing food shortages. Profiteering, speculating and hoarding made matters still worse. Pickett noted that certain items, such as medicines, could no longer be purchased at any price. With food prices rising more than 90 percent and imported goods more than 190 percent, with higher taxes to support the war effort added to that, and with catastrophes like the monsoon failure of 1918, many missionaries and village preachers were barely able to hold on.

A third consequence of the war was its role in drying up missionary support from the West. To a certain extent, that was expected. It was only natural that American Methodists would choose to divert some of their giving from international missions to the home front. Notwithstanding the financial constraints of the war, however, Pickett did manage in 1917 to erect the family quarters building for those to be trained as village workers. Although he was forced to use it, instead, to accommodate more boys, he regarded the arrangement as temporary, until money could be found for a larger boarding school. He could not know the money would never come.

Most disheartening of all, though, was the opening the war gave to those who opposed the work of the missionaries. It offered the perfect backdrop for spreading false information. Evoking and embroidering the rumor that fueled the 1857 revolt, some upper class Hindus whispered the British planned to melt baptized infants into lard to be used for the greasing of bullets in the war. Others warned of a plot to conscript Indian Christians for the European front. Still others spread the word that a Government order had decreed that, because of the war, all Christians should return to their former religion. Each of these had some effect. Particularly troubling to the missionaries was the fact that there were not enough Christian workers to keep up with and refute the deceptions. Also troubling was the threat of violence against Christians. The house of one of Pickett's preachers was stoned off and on for several weeks, though he refused to be intimidated.

The surge of enthusiasm for home rule also emboldened those opposed to mission work. Among educated Hindus, there was, in Superintendent Schutz's words, an emerging "spirit of unrest," One Brahmin told him, "Yes, you are now lifting the masses; but when we get the power we will put a quietus on all your work." Another said, "When we get home rule, the English power will wane, and then the Christians will be driven out. We have only one religion—Hinduism."

Distrust was sown even in the zenanas, the living quarters of Indian women who were largely isolated from outside society. These "shut-ins" told visiting ladies from the mission: "We know you have come to see our jewels, so you can report it to the Government so we will have to pay taxes on them. We like you and your teaching, but please don't come back until the war is over."

BESIDES THE SHORTAGE OF INDIAN co-workers and adverse effects of the war, Pickett faced yet another challenge to effective ministry: the logistics of getting around. He had intended to bring a Ford car to India. A friend from Brooklyn had promised to buy it but at the last minute reneged. Instead, he gave Pickett 50 dollars, less than 14 percent of the $360 a Model T would have cost him before shipping.

Waskom and Ruth were the only missionaries of any denomination in all of Shahabad, a district of two million people. His indigenous colleagues were not only few but far apart, for the small Christian communities of the district were widely scattered. Two railways ran through Shahabad but, as Pickett explained at the time, they were not much help in getting to the villages:

[They] do not reach the communities where most of the converts live and even when they do reach a community which I wish to visit, the trains are so slow that I have to waste hours of precious time on them. I now have on my desk urgent calls from the preachers in three places for me to come to them tomorrow. To reach the first of them I would have to leave Arrah at six in the morning on a combined freight and passenger train and would arrive there at eleven o'clock, having traveled just twenty-three miles. If he would wish me to go with him to see the Christians in his care I would have to hire an ekka and drive from two to twelve miles according to the . . . community. The ekka [a horse-drawn cart] is the slowest and most uncomfortable mode of travel man has yet invented, but it is the only vehicle obtainable in the smaller places and I am wasting hours every week riding on them. Sometimes I walk for miles in preference but I don't save any time that way. To reach the second place I would have to come back through Arrah and go out on the other railroad the next day on a slightly faster train and repeat the experiences of the first day while the third place would wait for the third day.

Pickett reckoned that, by car, he could cover the 23 miles to the first place in an hour, "for the road there is excellent." Further, he figured that he could reach the second and third places the same day. Taking the preacher with him in the car, they could stop anyplace on the preacher's circuit. Pickett had at first calculated that a car would abbreviate his travel time to the villages by a third. But after talking with some of the eight local British officials·who had automobiles, he revised his estimate. He became convinced his travel time would be halved. However, though he had already collected more money towards a vehicle, he knew there was no hope of getting one at a fair price until after the war. Meanwhile, he would have to settle for less satisfactory means.

ON HIS EXCURSIONS INTO THE VILLAGES, Pickett encountered the heart of India, for the villages were where nine-tenths of India's people lived. These communities between the fields—which one writer aptly described as resembling "commodious and certainly neglected barnyard[s]"—varied considerably in size. Most had a single street featuring a temple or shrine, an adjacent bazaar, and, on either side of the street, tight clusters of baked-brick houses. The surrounding fields were owned by the wealthy and farmed by the poor.

Most villages had a large reservoir, called a tank, which would fill in the rainy season and empty slowly through the winter. The tank was the villagers' chief gathering place. It was where they washed laundry and wagons, where they watered their livestock, and where, at the end of winter, they gathered mud for repairing mortar or for building. In some villages, the tank also served as the water supply for untouchables like the Chamars. Usually, though, they had their own well, or they paid for water from caste people.

The interior of a village house contained a small, high window, a wall recess for jars or idols, a few tools for food preparation, and rope cots for sleeping. Drawings of various deities adorned the walls. The entryway opened onto the street or into a courtyard. The courtyard was the family room. It contained a mud fireplace for cooking, clay jars for storing grains and spices, millstones for grinding, a manger to which the family cows were tethered, and a sleeping area. For much of the year, it was more comfortable to sleep out-of-doors.

As one might imagine, Chamar living quarters were more ramshackle. Because of their status below recognized caste lines, Chamars and other untouchables lived in separate compounds outside the main village. Because of their poverty, they built with mud instead of bricks. They worked, not for themselves, but as "so-and-so's Chamar."

What sparked the Chamars' interest in Christianity is elusive and certainly complex. Though they embraced the Christian faith in groups, individuals within the groups described a variety of motives. There was, however, an emerging readiness among the Chamars to adopt a variety of changes. For example, more and more Chamars were taking trains to the cities in search of better-paying jobs. Some of them did well enough to buy small plots of land when they returned. This new mobility tended to benefit even those who stayed, for the shrinking labor pool and the fear the urban trickle might become a flood brought improvement in local wages too. It seems that even modest gains such as these were enough to raise the hopes of many Chamars. Some of them believed that identifying with the missionaries and their religion was yet another path to social progress—that it would bring improved social standing and more police protection from tyrannical landlords. Moreover, to a people who were socially stigmatized, relegated to drudgery, and kept from participating

WAR AND OTHER CHALLENGES

in the religion of caste Hindus, the offer of freedom in Christ, however vaguely understood, could have strong appeal.

As *achut* (untouchables), Chamars were regarded as unclean and precluded from most social interaction with caste villagers—especially Brahmins. To avoid pollution, Brahmins would neither serve as their gurus nor officiate at their ceremonies. They would not even allow them to listen to their recitations of the Vedas. Thus, Chamars never acquired a knowledge of the great Hindu traditions. On occasion a Brahmin might be persuaded to interpret horoscopes for Chamars, or call out a demon, or give religious advice, but that was the extent of it. Thus, the accepting attitude of Christian preachers and missionaries contrasted vividly with the arrogance of the Brahmins. This in itself may have been instrumental to Chamar receptivity to the Christian message.

Another contributing factor to Chamar openness to the gospel was their religious beliefs and practices. Although most Chamars claimed to be Hindus, in practice their religion was animistic. Their world was replete with spirits. The many carved and vermilion-stained stones in their villages testified to the profusion of spirits. But spirits dwelt in every leaf of every tree as well, as attested by their sighs and shudders on a stormy day. As true then as now, but not as widely understood by missionaries, was the fact that animists are uncommonly quick to embrace the gospel. Nonetheless, they were learning that mass movements were most likely to emerge among tribal and untouchable populations.

PICKETT'S EXCURSIONS TO THE VILLAGES and Chamar communities afforded him most of his early lessons in evangelism. On one such visit, though, the lesson was particularly expensive. A group of Chamars had invited Pickett to tell them about Jesus. They explained that some of their caste relatives had become followers of Jesus and were urging them to do the same. When Pickett got to the village, he found about 60 Chamars waiting to hear him. Trying to target their needs, he spoke for more than an hour on unwholesome Chamar practices. He explained, alternatively, that followers of Jesus do not worship idols, drink intoxicants, gamble, or eat the flesh of animals that have died of disease or old age. When he finished, a Hindu priest, who sometimes advised the community, asked to speak.

"If this missionary has spoken correctly, the gospel is better than I thought," he said. Then, he enumerated the list of sins on which Pickett had preached:

> *Don't drink alcoholic liquors.* "I thought all Christians drank regularly. In Calcutta I have seen many Europeans who appeared to drink alcohol every day."
> *Don't gamble.* "In Calcutta the Christians have a race track and gamble on every race."
> *Don't eat the flesh of animals that have died of old age or disease.* "Which of these things did I ever tell you to do?"
> *Don't worship idols.* "I don't object to idol worship, but I don't tell you to do it."

The priest added:

> Did I ever tell you to drink alcohol or gamble or eat the flesh he forbade you to eat? No, I go further than he does. If you must eat flesh, it is better to eat without having to kill. Does he prefer that you kill God's creatures in order to get food? I tell you not to eat any flesh. I also tell you not to eat tomatoes or beets because they are red like blood. I tell you not to eat eggplants because they look like eggs.

Pickett knew immediately that he had badly mishandled his opportunity. The Chamars were looking for good news, for God's way out of the grip of karma. Instead, he had given them rules—a litany of don'ts.

Eventually, most of the group embraced the gospel, but it took two years of many visits and hard work—much of it by Pickett's Indian co-workers—to undo the damage. The incident permanently impressed upon Pickett that, when it came to offering up don'ts, Hindus and Muslims would win overwhelmingly every time. In his book, *Dynamics of Church Growth*, he disclosed that, after that embarrassment, he resolved never again to represent the gospel as a list of laws:

> It is frightfully easy to be more against a whole assortment of actions or ideas of secondary or tertiary importance than to be effectively for something of primary importance. The missionary must be for the kingdom of God, for the rule of God, the Father

of our Lord Jesus Christ, and not just against what he considers to be evil.

The Christian faith is not a set of denials but a consistent body of affirmations. No one is made a Christian by what he denies or by what he refrains from doing. One becomes a Christian by positive decisions ... We may break the tyranny of a bad habit or an untrue creed but we will remain in a lost and perilous state if we do not come under the influence of a positive faith and dedication.

The work of building up a village church was never predictable or routine. On one occasion, Pickett accompanied several Indian village pastors and three college students to one of the newest of the district's churches. One of the pastors had been invited the year before to be the spiritual advisor and instructor for about a hundred Chamars there. Since then he had visited twice a month and had recently baptized most of the adults and children. However, for some reason—perhaps the interference of some high-caste villagers—these new believers had begun to express doubts and reservations about their decision. Not sure what to do, the pastor asked Pickett to come with him to the village. The others came to testify to how God had changed their lives, and to offer encouragement to the new believers. However, even before they got started, the pastor made two critical mistakes, which precipitated a near debacle. First, because he had not been discreet, it was already widely known throughout the village of 2,500 that the group was coming. Second, the pastor did not have the foresight to enter the village on the side where the new Christians lived. When they entered the village, therefore, they were immediately surrounded by angry, shouting men, for, expecting them, all the propertied men had stayed home.

Only after one young man appeared to switch sides and rebuke the rest, did the mob's hostility seem to subside. The man then described two women who were frightened because the son of one of them, a new Christian, had destroyed their family shrines. But he added that he and his family now saw the futility of idols and, in fact, would be pleased if the visitors would destroy *their* shrines and idols too. Upon hearing this, the relieved Indian pastor and several of the college students were only too happy to oblige. They invited Pickett to help them, but he declined. He sensed no danger, he said, but as a non-Indian, his policy was never to take part in activities that might be misconstrued or cause trouble.

It was apparent that the invitation to tear down the shrines was a setup. When the pastor and the others began dismantling the first one, an old woman, whose husband was a former caste leader, threw herself in front of it and demanded that they kill her instead. Immediately her children began crying. The result was pandemonium. Hundreds rushed in from other parts of the village. The college students were ready to bolt. But Pickett "under a strong sense of compulsion" simply knelt and prayed. The pastor and several others joined him. The crowd grew quiet. Even the woman who had seemed so agitated grew calm. Six weeks later, Pickett and the pastor returned to conduct worship for the new believers. All the shrines and idols were gone—every one of them.

DESPITE THE VICISSITUDES OF THE WAR, the difficulty of getting about, and his lack of experience in village evangelism, Pickett's first full year in Arrah was both productive and promising. In July 1917, he wrote,

> This has been the best month I have ever spent in India so far as the results can be seen. We have a real live Mass Movement in this Arrah Civil District among the Chamars and embryonic Mass Movements among two other castes.

A few weeks later he wrote,

> Within the last six weeks, despite most serious floods due to the overflow of the Ganges and Sone Rivers, we have baptized more converts than were baptized all of last year and we seem to be at the beginning of a Movement unparalleled in this section of the country.

However, 1917 ended on a somber note. In November, during the Muslim Great Feast, violence broke out in the little village of Piru, 20 miles southwest of Arrah. The annual festival, celebrated by Muslims worldwide, included the sacrifice of goats and cows. Although the Hindus of Piru and neighboring villages disapproved of the cow killing, they had been content in the past to denounce it and let it go at that. However, this year, on the morning of the sacrifice, a mob of 50,000 Hindus overwhelmed the Muslim community. Under the pretense of protecting the cows, they looted and burned houses, desecrated the mosque, murdered as many men as they could, and abused the women. That was just the start. From Piru, the mob moved to other villages and repeated their mayhem. In all, 124 Muslim villages were looted by Hindus. Most of the rioting occurred in Pickett's district and an adjoining one. Thousands of government troops were required to restore order.

After the mayhem, the Provincial Government levied a special tax on the Hindus to recover their costs. Since Muslims and Christians were exempted, many Hindus tried to claim they were Christians. Most of them were relatives of Christians, and some had been thinking of becoming Christians. But the Government served notice that, unless a clergyman could vouch they had been baptized or were under instruction for baptism, they would have to pay the tax. Under the circumstances, Pickett put a moratorium on baptisms for the remainder of the church year, which was about nine months.

"OUR FIRST HOME TOGETHER LED RUTH AND me into a vast area of discovery," Pickett was later to write of those early days in Arrah. In Shahabad, Waskom and Ruth's experiences contrasted sharply with life in Lucknow. In fact, in many respects, coming to Shahabad was like coming to India for the first time.

In those days, a new emphasis on the "Indianization" of the church was emerging. What happened in Arrah was the Indianization of Pickett. Missionaries who spent their careers in the cities—especially in a missionary hub like Lucknow—could, and sometimes did, carry on much as they had back home. Methods of preaching, orders of worship, social patterns, lifestyle—none of them needed much adjustment. But those who spent substantial spells in the villages were themselves changed. Sometimes, in the process of learning village patterns, protocols, and perspectives, they abandoned preconceptions and found in themselves a willingness to experiment and embrace new ideas. Sometimes, though, as in Pickett's case, another kind of transformation occurred: a transformation of heart. Even before coming to Arrah, Pickett had favored encouraging the mass movements, but here in Bihar, he saw, for the first time, how impoverished, how exploited, how enslaved, how maltreated, the people of the mass movements were. The shameless evil of societal stratification as it existed in the villages hit Pickett hard. Here were human beings who, because of their "untouchable" birth families, were regarded as pariahs for life. They had no rights, no status, no hope. The zamindars, upon whom they depended for a living, deliberately kept them in debt. If they missed a day of work due to illness, they had to pay the zamindar a rupee for his losses. If they worked that day—which meant dawn to dusk—they got four annas, a fourth of a rupee. "Why do you treat people like this?" Pickett would ask the landowners. "Because they are stupid," would come the response—or "dirty," or "vicious." But the only difference Pickett could see was "the cruelties inflicted upon them."

Here and there, Chamars were finding ways to save a few annas; some even managed to buy a bit of land. Overall, though, such gains were rare. The subjugation and poverty persisted as before. A firsthand awareness of this changed Pickett and led him in a different direction than he might otherwise have gone. Out of that change came a lifelong conviction, which he put like this:

Early in my missionary career I became convinced that the Church should identify itself primarily with the underprivileged. So throughout my ministry I gave much more time to people at the bottom of society than to those at the top or in between.

10 Working with a Mass Movement

As Pickett's District Superintendent, H.J. Schutz, pointed out more than once, "The real leaders of the Mass Movement [were] the converts." As they interacted with family members and others in their caste, they shared their new-found faith freely—often with great enthusiasm. As a consequence, those who heard them—groups ranging from individual families to part or all of a village caste—would invite the local missionary or an Indian colleague of the missionary to give a more complete introduction to the Christian faith and to answer their questions. The decision to convene such an inquiry almost invariably depended upon the advocacy of one or more trusted and respected leaders, to whom then would fall the responsibility of extending the invitation. A decision to embrace the Christian faith might not come until after several such meetings. Or it might not come at all. But, in the Arrah field, many Chamars were deciding affirmatively, and some people, including J. Waskom Pickett, dared to believe that in the end they all would.

This phenomenon led Pickett and some others to focus not just on individuals, but on groups. Although village castes were comprised of individuals, they concluded that the operative unit was the group. In Indian villages, individuals could exist as individuals only as *sadhus*, and even that involved the renunciation of one's *jati*—the unchanging, all-embracing womb of relatives into which one was born, and in which one was destined to live and die. The unyielding reality of caste, which had survived millennia of invasions, religious reforms, and political upheavals was a web so tightly and intricately spun the so-called mass movements constituted the only pattern by which substantial numbers could move Christward. That did not mean, however, that groups made their decisions monolithically. Nor did it mean that some individuals and families did not, on their own, apart from their castes, decide to become followers of Jesus.

As Pickett wrote: "Some participated most gladly and others [more] slowly and apparently without conviction."

> [I have] known of some villages in which all the members of one caste or of two castes have been baptized in a single service, but of many more villages in which the members of a caste group have been divided, some professing Christian discipleship and others refusing to do so.

Wherever he could, Pickett cultivated the friendship of village *chaudhris* (headmen). Their goodwill was essential to a favorable outcome. Moreover, they would be the most natural leaders in an emerging church. However, even more important than the attention Pickett gave to the *chaudhris*, was the attention he gave to his village preachers. Without them there could be no adequate response or follow-up to emerging Chamar movements. Moreover, despite the group movements, traditional methods such as open-air evangelizing and personal witnessing remained important too. And one never knew when one of those drawn by traditional methods might be the catalyst for a group movement. As Pickett wrote later, "A notable feature of the great movements in India . . . has been that one man in nearly every case started the process." Indeed, across the river in Ballia, the entire Chamar movement toward Christianity could be traced back to one key leader, a man named Ilahi Baksh.

AS EVERY MISSIONARY KNEW, specially blessed was the mission that had in its stable of preachers one or two indigenous evangelists who were gifted in obtaining a hearing. Pickett was fortunate in having several such colleagues, and he showed from the start that helping them and learning from them were among his highest priorities. On coming to Arrah, one of his first expenditures was the purchase of *ekkas* and ponies for his Indian co-workers. An *ekka* was a horse-drawn vehicle with two large wheels and a raised, canopied platform (approximately three feet square). The high clearance enabled them to navigate primitive, deeply rutted roads that were impassable by car.

Because the Shahabad District did not yet have schools capable of producing local preachers and teachers, nearly all Pickett's Indian co-workers were imported from Methodist schools in distant Agra, Oudh, and Rohilkhand. Although the baronial bearing of some of them got in the way of relating to low-caste people, four proved to be wonderfully competent village workers. In fact, Pickett called them "the main strength of the church in Shahabad." They were Julam Qadir, Andrias, Emanuel Sukh, and Ishwar Dayal.

When a new pastor was needed in Arrah, Julam Qadir, the young Muslim whom Pickett took under his wing in Lucknow and who had gone on to the seminary in Bareilly, responded to Pickett's invitation. Julam was still single, but Stanley Jones wanted him to meet a young woman in a Methodist boarding school in his district. The two were married, and they immediately joined the Picketts. Pickett regarded Julam as an outstanding pastor and member of the Annual Conference, and an exceptional evangelist too.

Andrias was first employed by the Gossner (Evangelical Lutheran) Mission. When the Gossner Mission decided not to resume work in Shahabad following the war, he enlisted with the Methodists. The number of professed believers in his circuit increased by 150 percent during his 15-year tenure. Pickett wrote: "Only twice a year was a communion service held for his people, but they all seemed to grow in grace and understanding of their rights and duties as Christians."

For the last two of this quartet of colleagues, Pickett had special regard. They were Emanuel Sukh and Ishwar Dayal and their wives, Dr. Polly Sukh and Priavati Dayal.

Emanuel and Polly Sukh were from Rohilkhand in what was then the United Provinces. Both had studied in Christian schools. Emanuel had completed high school and one year at Lucknow Christian College's School of Commerce where he had learned shorthand, typing and book-keeping. For a time, he worked as an assistant in the office of a district magistrate in Agra. When Hindus working in the office learned that Emanuel's grandparents were members of the low-caste *Mazhabi Sikhs* (a caste of Sweepers who professed the Sikh religion but were not socially recognized as Sikhs), they went on strike. However, the magistrate refused to yield to their pressure.

When the call came for help to minister to new and potential converts in the Shahabad District, Emanuel and Polly responded. By the time the Picketts came to Arrah, they had been in Raghunathpur (22 miles west of Arrah) for several years. There the Reverend Emanuel had faithfully carried on a spiritual ministry, while Dr. Polly, a licensed medical practitioner, had carried on a medical ministry.

Pickett's most valued colleagues were probably Ishwar and Priavati Dayal. As a lad of 10 or 12, Ishwar began a long search for God. His parents were respectable middle-class people but were not particularly interested in religion. Neither were his friends nor close relatives. Ishwar himself, however, had a strong yearning to know God, which he believed God had placed there. At the same time, he sensed the local Brahmin priests and others who claimed to represent God did not really know God. So he asked his parents to allow him to become a *sadhu* (a Hindu religious mendicant) so that he could travel to various temples where people were supposed to have found God. His experience was depressing. Much of what he found seemed distressingly ungodly. "If this represents God," he said, "I am against him." Along the way, Ishwar met a *sadhu* who had a band of *chelas* (disciples). They all claimed to be constantly in touch with God. However, what they described as communion with God turned out to be a marijuana high! Ishwar decided that if he were to find God he would have to search elsewhere.

Because he was dressed in the saffron-colored robe of a *sadhu*, fellow Hindus treated Ishwar warmly. This included railway employees who allowed him to ride without a ticket. Thus, when he decided to give up his search and go home, he naturally made his way to the nearest railway station. When he arrived, he learned his train would depart about 10 hours later. So he laid down in the shade and went to sleep. He awoke to the voice of a well-to-do British woman who had come to India at her own expense to witness to Jesus. She handed him a tract and explained to him the gospel message. Later, on the train, Ishwar read the tract. It seemed to contain the answer for which he had been searching. Switching trains, he went back to the station to look for the woman. He looked for 10 days and finally learned that she lived in Muzaffarpur. When he finally found her house, she was not there. So, he waited until she returned seven days later. She gave him a room and began to teach him about Christ. When he decided that he must become a Christian, she took him to a German missionary in the city and, within a few days, Ishwar Dayal gave his allegiance to Christ and was baptized. The German missionary persuaded Ishwar to forsake his *sadhu* practices, accept a monthly salary, and enter formally into a Christian marriage with the girl to whom he had already been married in childhood—if she would agree to become a Christian. She did agree, and they were married. However, one day a misunderstanding occurred, and the missionary, in a rage, struck Ishwar. Ishwar immediately left Muzaffarpur and went searching for another Christian colleague with whom he might work. He found one in Fred Perrill. Before employing him, Perrill went to the German missionary, who not only commended Ishwar but expressed regret for his uncalled for outburst.

When Pickett succeeded Perrill and began working with *Shri* and *Shrimati* (Mr. and Mrs.) Dayal, he found Ishwar to be adept at presenting the gospel to all castes. In fact, throughout his time in India, Pickett regarded Ishwar as "the best all-around village evangelist I had come to know anywhere." In *My Twentieth Century Odyssey*, Pickett described Ishwar's approach:

> When he began to speak in a village, people from houses all around came close enough to hear him. He talked about favorite gods of Hinduism and always in a way that impressed his hearers and did not offend any of them, despite the fact that he always in a very friendly way introduced a strong Christian thought.

In just one year Pickett baptized 676 persons in Ishwar's circuit. They were, he wrote, "drawn to Christ by the saintly devotion of their pastor and his wife and by the beautiful Christian life of the whole family."

THE YEAR 1918 WAS ONE OF CHANGE. One change came on February 11, when Ruth delivered Elizabeth, the Pickett's first child. From grandparents and close friends came enthusiastic congratulatory notes. However, from Indian friends, came expressions of sympathy who felt that, somehow, the Picketts had displeased God. The next year, on June 8 the great event was followed with the birth of a second daughter, Miriam Lee. The third child would be a daughter too: Margaret, born October 18, 1926. Recalling their reception, Pickett wrote: "When our second and third children were also girls, our Hindu friends were clearly distressed and very frank in talking about it." Some, according to Pickett, empathized that the sins for which they were being punished had surely not *all* been committed "in this incarnation."

The last of the Pickett children, Douglas, would be born January 27, 1929. This time, there were not only congratulations from grandparents and Christian friends, but "a veritable tornado of congratulations" from Hindu friends. "Several persons told us that we should rejoice in the proof that accounts had been settled and the gods had nothing against us," remembered Pickett.

Change was also occurring in the church. Of the 648 adults who were baptized in the Ballia-Arrah District in 1918, most were on the Arrah side of the river. Ballia was languishing. The growth of the church there had been effectively arrested due to the absence of a missionary the previous year (on furlough with no replacement) plus a severe shortage of local leaders. The shortfall led to the closing of the boys' boarding school. Most of the students were sent to Arrah. Pickett figured out a way to fit 40 of them, though 20 had to be turned away.

On a brighter note, thanks to a visiting missionary woman who made a personal contribution of 500 rupees, Waskom and Ruth were able to organize the girls' school they had dreamed of. With Bishop Warne's approval, they invited Miss Edna Abbott, a Phi Beta Kappa graduate of Ohio Wesleyan, to serve as principal. Later, she would become an exceptional village evangelist. The Picketts started the school in rented property on Monday, August 12. The first year's enrollment was limited to 20. Since the Women's Foreign Missionary Society was unable to provide funds for a new girls' boarding school, support came from Pickett friends in India and America. Pickett remembered, "Never once were we unable to meet necessary expenses, and the school achieved a reputation for excellence." Waskom and Ruth hoped the boys' school and the Sawtelle School, as they called it, could merge someday to become a coeducational high school—a dream eventually realized, but not before the end of their time in Arrah.

With 80 people now living in the compound and 170 more anticipated whenever the boys' dormitory and assembly hall could be built, Pickett had in mind yet another project—a small hospital building for medical emergencies. He was hoping to fund it with money raised in America through the new Centenary Campaign, but the funds never materialized. However, although no medical facility would be built in Arrah, Pickett was able to secure a private gift of 500 dollars for improvements at Polly Sukh's dispensary at Raghunathpur, which, along with the district's other clinic, cared for 33,000 patients that year.

PICKETT AND HIS CO-WORKERS CONTINUED to give the bulk of his energy to the accelerating mass movement, which showed no signs of slowing down. On September 17, 1918, he wrote:

Last week in a section hitherto hardly touched, and where we have no resident worker, about eight hundred Chamars gathered and voted by about 790 to 10 or 12 . . . [to] turn to the religion of Jesus for salvation and social uplift. Three of our workers from various distant points, having learned of the proposed meeting, were there and preached to them.

Elsewhere, both in India and abroad, the mass movements continued to stir debate. Some heralded them as the key to winning all India; others criticized them as unmanageable and warned that huge influxes would bring vestiges of heathen ideas and practice into the church. The previous year, at the 1917 Laymen's Convention in Washington, Bishop Oldham had asserted bluntly that India would be won through the low castes. A day or two later, Sherwood Eddy stated categorically the hope of winning India lay in the educated classes. E. Stanley Jones, whose own ministry was tending to focus on educated, English-speaking Indians, said that both were right but that "the thinking classes create the ideas by which the lower classes live." He argued:

If we can become *gurus* to the higher classes and change only their attitude toward Christianity, even if we do not change them into open Christians, if we change them from hostility to friendship, we make it possible for low castes to become Christians without so much opposition. You have gained an atmosphere in which many men may more easily become Christians, even if you have not gained a soul.

For the moment, Pickett did not have the luxury of entering into the debate. It was all he could do to keep up with the Shahabad movement. One example was the villages around Piru where the riots had begun the previous November. After just three years of preaching and teaching by two of Pickett's village preachers, 800 people had responded to the gospel. Moreover, there were hundreds more inquirers. On March 15, 1918, one month after Elizabeth's birth, James M. Taylor came for a one-day stay. Pickett took his former mentor to Piru. There Taylor got a glimpse of what Pickett could not ignore. Pickett had arranged for Taylor to preach at a noon service in a mango grove. It was anyone's guess how many would show up, for it was harvest time, the busiest time of the year—when, in Pickett's words, "a day's work . . . was worth more to the poor villager than several days work in any other season." Nonetheless, people came from 20 villages. Speaking on the love of Jesus Christ and the way in which love should distinguish all disciples of Jesus, Taylor got their attention and kept it for an hour. When he asked who among them wanted the love of Christ to reign in their hearts, 50 Hindus and several Muslims responded.

But the story does not end there. As Pickett, Taylor, and the village preachers walked back to the railway station, 10 men met them and explained that they had come many miles for the service but had misunderstood where the meeting would be. One of them had come specifically to be baptized. Having failed to get into the service, he now insisted that Taylor baptize him by the roadside.

Such interest in the gospel was on the increase. But, beyond welcoming it, Pickett knew he and his Indian colleagues needed to find better ways to nurture those who were coming to Christ. When Ishwar and Priavati Dayal suggested a fresh approach to educating the children of converts, therefore, Pickett was quick to affirm and adopt it. At the time, the Dayals were living in a rented house with three rooms. It was about a quarter of a mile from a hamlet of Chamar Christians. Their idea was to bring 12 to 15 boys into their home. The boys would come each Monday morning with enough rice and lentils to last them until Friday. With a dollar a month per boy, provided through Pickett's efforts, they could enrich the boys' diet substantially. The boys would stay in the room ordinarily occupied by the Dayals' daughters, who were being schooled at Arrah. Mrs. Dayal would direct the boys' cooking and be their teacher. Ishwar would help whenever he was not ministering the gospel in one of the villages. On Fridays, the boys would return home, which could be from one to 10 miles away. Pickett observed, "This simple, inexpensive way of life was wonderfully successful in teaching boys to read and to understand and practice their obligations as Christians."

Another idea—Pickett's own—was to use some of the village boys to teach in primary schools in their own or neighboring villages. The boys would live in their own homes or with relatives and, when school was in session, have no responsibilities except teaching. Pickett's plan was to educate the boys who would do the teaching and, in time, establish a network of home schools.

Pickett was concerned about the pattern whereby village boys who went to a boarding school ended up leaving their villages. "Through them, the whole standard of life in the village must be raised," he argued. They should remain as assets to their villages by setting up Sunday schools, giving counsel to the needy, telling the Good News, and "above all living pure, clean lives, free from idolatry, drunkenness and the other sins that so beset the community ."

THE LAST QUARTER OF 1918 and the first several months of 1919 were to be remembered for a great epidemic of influenza. Among those who became infected was Pickett himself. At the time, Ruth was in Bombay visiting her parents, so Superintendent H.J. Schutz acted as Waskom's nurse. "The Sahib was down with the flu," he wrote matter-of-factly in the guest book. But that did not tell the story. Pickett was seriously stricken and was in bed for a month.

That year's strain of flu was especially virulent. It ravaged populations all over the globe, killing 675,000 in the United States alone. However, nowhere were deaths more numerous than in India. Of the 22 million who died worldwide, more than 12 million were Indians. Perhaps the death toll was so high because hunger had already weakened so many. Famine conditions prevailed in many sections of the subcontinent throughout the war years. Of the Methodist areas, the hardest hit by the epidemic was the Northwest India Conference. During the quadrennium that closed in 1919, they recorded 32,195 deaths.

Because of the high incidence of influenza (and plague), events had to be canceled and schools had to be closed. In November 1918, the *Indian Witness* reported the Bareilly Theological Seminary had lost four students to influenza and that three school girls and several others in the mission had died in the last week. That account was typical. The Arrah District was fortunate in that few of the workers became ill and none died. Nor were any of the students in Arrah or the village schools lost. Nor was there much loss of life among village Christians. However, the larger picture was less comforting. There was, wrote Pickett, "indescribable suffering throughout the district." He added that the Ganges "was in places so congested with the bodies of the victims that the Hindus who live along the banks of the river . . . were compelled to leave their homes."

Among the saddest consequences of the epidemic were the scores of children who lost both parents. Many of the orphans were brought to neighbors, Christian hospitals, and other places where they might be helped. Pickett described it in a 1929 *Indian Witness* article:

At that time to nearly every Boarding School and Orphanage in the North of India, and perhaps in every part of India, people brought newly-orphaned babies with the plea that they be saved from the death by disease or starvation that surely awaited them otherwise, and very few Principals of such institutions were able to refuse the claim of these little ones for a chance in life. But none of these institutions were equipped to care for the babies; neither the staff nor the physical equipment needed was available, as nurses frayed by a succession of sleepless nights soon convinced nearly everyone closely connected therewith.

The flood of orphans made the need of a "baby fold" apparent to all. In 1920, they pulled it off. The North India, and Northwest India, Methodist Conferences voted to raise money for a home for the babies. They chose Bareilly because it was central. Also, space was available at the Clara Swain Hospital. Pickett himself would become deeply involved in the project and would help raise the money for the fold's own building (built in 1925). When the baby fold, which later became known as "The Warne Baby Fold," opened in 1920, Pickett brought by train from Bihar the first baby to enter the home. Some of the babies brought there would grow up to hold key positions in both the church and in government.

IN JANUARY 1919, WHEN THE EPIDEMIC was still at its height, District Superintendent Schutz was transferred to Bijnor where the first Methodist mass movement had begun under Thoburn in 1868. The two-year-old Ballia-Arrah field was divided into two districts. Pickett was appointed Superintendent of the Arrah District, and, until Fred Perrill's return in March, he was given temporary responsibility for the Ballia field. The new Arrah District was 160 miles long and 100 miles wide. Its population was three million. This vast field had just three missionaries (J. Waskom Pickett, Ruth Pickett, and Edna M. Abbott) and five village preachers (Ishwar Dayal, D.P. Sahae, A. Briscoe, Hem Raj Singh, and Emanuel Sukh). About 22 other workers assisted them.

The Christian community in the Arrah District had more than doubled since the Picketts' arrival. Moreover, there was every sign the trend would continue. Pickett felt more strongly than ever, therefore, the necessity of building a larger plant for the boys' school and freeing up the present facility as a training center for preachers. In February, he penned a long letter to B.T. Badley in New York pleading for help. He reported that the previous week he had been in the Bikramganj circuit and had baptized 52 people in two villages in one day, while men from nearby locales followed him all around begging him to go to their villages. In 1916, the Methodists had just 50 members in that region. Now, said Pickett, there were 700 members in 24 villages. Available to cover that area was just one preacher (Ishwar Dayal) and his son.

The news from Pickett's preachers in the other circuits was equally impressive. In the same month, February 1919, Briscoe and Sukh each baptized at least a hundred in the Dumraon and Raghunathpur circuits and, at Buxar, Sahae had added another 40 or 50. In addition, Pickett and his colleagues had just opened two new circuits—at Dehri-on-Sone and Dildarnagar. Therefore, argued Pickett, the need for a new boarding school was acute. With new churches now emerging in three castes, more future leaders than ever had to be turned away from the schools.

The three castes he spoke of included: Chamars (numbering 128,000 in the district); Dusadhs, a caste of farm laborers and village watchmen, with a slightly higher status than the Chamars (numbering 65,000); and Doms, often thought of as vagabond entertainers, though most had taken to agriculture, trade, money lending, and making mats (numbering about 6,000). Pickett believed that, given enough personnel, it was only a matter of time until all the Chamars became Christians. "I have not talked to a Chamar for over a year who has not said that within a few years all the Chamars of the District will be Christians," he wrote. As for the Dusadhs, several hundred had already been baptized and there were, said Pickett, perhaps a thousand inquirers. And of the Doms, he wrote, "Every Dom in the District is an enquirer . . . All of their chief *chaudhris* have asked us to make the entire caste Christians."

Given the mobility of many of the Chamars, Pickett believed new groups of Chamar believers could be gathered in many districts and even in the major cities of India. He observed that thousands of Chamars from his own district worked alongside Chamars from other areas for at least part of every year in Calcutta, Bombay, Poona, Lucknow, Lahore, and Darjeeling. In fact, he had in hand the addresses of 100 Chamars who had moved from his district—half of them in Calcutta and 29 more in Bombay. "These people," he wrote, "are in better circumstances than the converts of any of our other mass movements so far as I know." He added:

As shoemakers especially in Calcutta and Bombay they earn big money. At the same time, they do well at home. Most of them have a little land—some few have considerable holdings of land . . . The Chamars are a rising caste. They refuse to remain a depressed and a despised people. We can lift them up and make them Christians now, but if we delay they will grow impatient and rise socially, educationally and economically without our help—without our Christ.

Pickett was concerned, however, about the living conditions of the Chamars who went to Calcutta. He had a list of addresses and decided to see for himself. One of the Calcutta missionaries escorted him. What they saw stunned them.

We went into one dark room which had but one door, and it was so small that we had to stoop to go through. There was one small window not larger than 1½ by 2 feet. The room was 9' by 17'. There were sixteen men and two boys working in there then . . . They worked there by day, they ate there, and they slept there by night. Their food was cooked by the two boys on the small veranda . . . Within twenty feet from the door was another similar house, in the doorway of which, several prostitutes were visible. Not more than a hundred and fifty feet away was a liquor shop.

Pickett observed that while the men were earning good wages, some of it inevitably ended up with the liquor shop owner or the prostitutes. They brought back more than they could have earned at home, but they also brought illnesses—especially venereal diseases. Scores of these Chamars had become Christians in the mass movement, but in the city, there was no one to minister to them spiritually or help them gain better living and working conditions.

Such was the state of affairs at the start of 1919 when J.W. Pickett began his duties as Superintendent and wrote his long letter to Badley asking for funds to accommodate more boys and cultivate new pastors. Ironically, though, before the letter could be mailed, it was misplaced, for almost as soon as he had finished writing it, Pickett came down with a bout of malarial fever that dragged on into the spring. By the time the important letter was recovered and sent off, it was early May.

As the year 1919 progressed, the enlargement of the District's Christian community persisted. By year's end more than a thousand new believers had been added to the church. Every aspect of the work improved. Baptisms were up (there were 1,115); Sunday school attendance was up (by 778 students); the sale of scripture portions was up (by 11,784 pieces); and enrollments in the boys' and girls' boarding schools were at capacity.

PICKETT'S LEADERSHIP AND WORK ETHIC accounted for many of the gains. Yet, he never called attention to himself or his achievements. On the contrary, he gave liberal credit to both his predecessors and his co-workers. Reflecting on the successes, he wrote:

> I have grown increasingly conscious of the greatness of the work done by my predecessors, Rev. A.L. Grey and Rev. F.M. Perrill. The former, as the founder of the work, by rare faith and diligence through much privation and sacrifice gave the work an excellent beginning. The first converts tell stories of "Grey Sahib" that make him seem like a fountain from which flowed streams of energy and kindness. To my immediate predecessor, Mr. Perrill, many tributes are due. He brought the work to a state of great efficiency and prepared the way for the large in-gathering now taking place.

Another stamp of Pickett's leadership, to be underscored again, was his appreciation for his Indian colleagues. Not for a moment did he underestimate their contribution, and he told them so. Moreover, he regularly took the time to encourage them personally and to challenge them to be their best.

Finally, Pickett's leadership was distinguished by study and reflection. He held that "the greatest missionaries are found among those who have most conscientiously loved God with their minds." That was as much a motto as an observation. "Study the people to whom we are sent as missionaries, and how the Bible and church relate themselves to those people," he urged one group of colleagues. "Study the forces that are competing for the hearts and minds of those to whom we are to minister in Christ's name."

However, despite his leadership and organizational gifts, Pickett was deeply conscious of their limits. His abilities helped him get the most out of the resources he had, but they could not overcome the handicap of a perennial shortage of personnel. If only there were four missionaries to cover the field, he thought—one each for Arrah, Buxar, Dehri-on-Sone, and Moghalsarai. If only the training school was in place to equip new lay and ministerial workers. If only he had two women who were free to itinerate and evangelize.

Only one of those particular dreams would materialize. Late in 1919, the new district appointed its first female evangelist, Ruth Hyneman. Pickett was delighted, not only for what Miss Hyneman could contribute to the district, but because he was deeply committed to utilizing women in ministerial service.

The new evangelist, who had traveled with the Picketts from America, came with a good foundation in the language. With the Pickett bungalow as home base, she shared the gospel with low-caste women through every circuit of the district over the next year. She regarded it as her best year to date in India: "more accomplished and more enjoyed." The following year, she succeeded Miss Abbott (who was going on furlough) at the girls' school.

WASKOM PICKETT DREAMED, NOT ONLY of more workers, but of the changes they could help bring. He wrote:

> The Chamars, from among whom most of our converts are coming, have a virtual monopoly of the raw material of the leather industry which is entering upon a period of remarkable development. Also most of these people are tillers of the soil and own small plots of ground. I know of no people that are so advantageously situated for rapid and complete economic and social regeneration as they are.
>
> We are convinced that our church has here a rare opportunity for securing an extensive, compact Christian community and raising it within a generation to a position of economic prosperity, social independence and spiritual power.

WITHOUT DOUBT, THE GREATEST OBSTACLE to the success Pickett envisioned was the relentlessly aggressive opposition of the Arya Samaj and its allies. From 1915-1920, the Arya Samaj in collusion with the landlords fed the Chamar Christians across the Ganges in the Ballia field a megadose of intolerance. Utilizing scare tactics, economic squeeze plays, threats, and violence, they led a campaign of intimidation against all who had turned to Christ. Two years after his Arrah term, Pickett described what was going on:

> The men are attacked and beaten, their women folks are insulted, false charges are brought against them in the courts, their crops are cut and stolen, their animals are killed, their rights in the community are claimed by others, they are compelled to work under the *begar* system without pay or for purely nominal remuneration, access to their wells is denied them, and they are subject to innumerable other persecutions both petty and major.

At the same time, the persecutors declared that it was really they, the Arya Samaj, who had the Chamars interests at heart, not the Christians! In the words of historian J. Tremayne Copplestone in *The History of Methodist Missions*:

> The lowly Chamars were treated to the extraordinary sight of high-caste leaders rising to advocate Chamar interests. They heard themselves called brothers by men who had always treated them as outcastes. They heard their social superiors flattering them and cajoling them with offers of schools and social recognition—benefits that would come to those who rejected Christianity.

Due to their numbers, this alliance of opposition to Christian expansion was, in Ballia, quite effective. Said Schutz, "Where we had one worker, the Aryas had a dozen and humanly speaking it was impossible to cope with our foes." Schutz described the opposition as, "thick as mosquitoes, educated, powerful, rich, employing bribes, threats, expulsion from the brotherhood, annulling of all marriage arrangements among the Christians (the hardest blow of all to the Indian), [and] cessation of all social privileges."

The Ballia mass movement sagged under the pressure. It never did fully recover. However, the mass movement on Pickett's side of the Ganges fared better. Probably several factors accounted for this. Not among them was any escape from the false rumors, intimidation, and economic pressures that plagued the Ballia field. The enemies of the church were active south of the river too. What, then, accounted for the Arrah District's continued expansion?

The first reason was that, unlike Ballia, Arrah never had a void in missionary leadership. This was crucial because the fuel that kept the fire burning was the ability of the missionaries to respond to emerging mass movements. Moreover, without strong leadership, beleaguered Christian villagers did not know where to turn for help.

Second, Pickett cultivated relationships across the caste and class spectrums.

> One lesson I learned . . . was the wisdom of maintaining cordial relations with all classes of people. Hearing many complaints from poor Christian groups and from groups who were asking for Christian instruction, I found it essential that I cultivate friendly relations both with the oppressed and the oppressors. Contacts with the oppressors enabled my colleagues and me to contribute significantly to improving relations between the two groups.

Third, Pickett, as always, built friendships with local authorities. Consequently, various officials sought his counsel on policies, emergencies, and even appointments. For example, through his friendship with the Arrah District Magistrate, Pickett received a luncheon invitation from Lord Sinha, the governor of Bihar and Orissa. Lord Sinha had just been elevated to the peerage, the only Asian to be so honored up to that time. After the luncheon, the governor took Pickett to his office. He said the king-emperor had authorized him to appoint two representatives of the tribal people and one of the depressed classes to membership in the provincial legislature. Could Pickett, he wanted to know, recommend someone who could fairly represent the latter? Pickett immediately suggested Emanuel Sukh. Lord Sinha asked Pickett to send Sukh to him and gave him a generous sum of money to cover their travel costs. Pickett told Sukh that he was expected at the governor's mansion, but he did not tell him why. After interviewing with the governor, Sukh showed up at Pickett's house, his face aglow. He had received the appointment.

It did not take long for Sukh to make his mark in the assembly. Just weeks after joining the body, he introduced a resolution advising the governor to close all liquor shops. The British-owned newspapers ridiculed the idea, but, to the amazement of many, the resolution passed. Sukh had received a letter from Fred Perrill that said:

> The Government officials will argue that the money [liquor revenues] is used to maintain schools and hospitals. Don't let them deceive you. Our Lord was betrayed by Judas Iscariot, who was given thirty pieces of silver for that vile deed. If he had used that money to serve the needy people would he have been less a traitor? Certainly not!

According to Pickett, the letter reached Sukh just as he was leaving for a session of the legislature. He put it in his pocket and read it on the train to Patna. As he seated himself in the assembly, he was shocked to hear the chairman say, "Because of the illness of the member who was scheduled to present the business listed for today, we have to postpone it and will take up instead the resolution offered by the Reverend Emanuel Sukh." Sukh had left his notes at home. In the panic of the moment, he could not remember what he had written down. So, instead, he took Perrill's letter from his pocket and read it. The English spokesperson for the Government protested. "I will not allow myself . . . our governor, and other officials to be likened to Judas," he shouted. The chairman agreed. However, a Muslim rose and said, "We Muslims know about Judas . . . We despise him and it hurts us to see our government betraying the poor by selling poisonous drinks to them." After that, six others spoke and all referred to Judas the betrayer of Jesus. The resolution passed by a large majority. The governor vetoed it, but, said Pickett, "Mr. Sukh's reputation was made."

Sukh, who was also to become a Methodist district superintendent, was quite successful as a legislator. A few years later, when the king granted permission for the provincial legislatures to elect their own chair, a number of maharajahs and noted lawyers were nominated for the position. After eight ballots failed to elect one of them, the representative with the most votes suggested they all withdraw and elect the Reverend Emanuel Sukh. Sukh got the job.

A fourth reason the Arrah District continued to grow despite persecution was the willingness of Pickett and his colleagues, whenever necessary, to challenge the opposition. For example, during the census year (1921), Arrah Christians faced formidable opposition to evangelistic work and to registering Christians. Pickett reported that it kept up all year long "with unabated fury."' However, Pickett and his team stood firm. In his *History of Methodist Missions* volume, Copplestone summarizes what they faced.

> Anti-Christian teams devoted their entire time for weeks to visiting the villages to try to block the final conversion of inquirers and to win Christians back to the Hindu fold. Community councils were organized to bring about reconversion of Christian converts. Christians supported by vigorous leadership by Pickett and his preachers, had to lodge hundreds of complaints with the police in order to stop the census workers from listing them falsely. In the face of the fierce social pressures of the 1921 campaign, most of the Arrah Methodist constituency held steady.

A final reason why the Christian movement was not derailed in Arrah was the gradual expansion of Pickett's stable of workers, which he managed to establish despite limited funds and no local training facility. By 1921, Pickett's district staff included 49 full-time male workers and 44 women workers (35 of whom were the spouse-partners of male workers). Moreover, they were quite effective. By his support, affirmation, and example, Pickett brought out their best. In turn, their dedication and hard work allowed him enough breathing room to take on some added tasks, among them leadership of a remarkable campaign against the sale and consumption of liquor in India.

11 Meeting Gandhi

In January 1915, while Waskom Pickett was in America recovering from tuberculosis, Mohandas K. (Karamchand) Gandhi returned to India. The previous summer, after two decades of political activism on behalf of Indians in South Africa, he sailed to England to meet with his old friend, Krishna Gokhale, whom he regarded as his "political guru." Gokhale, who was touring Europe, had been a member of the indigenous Indian National Council since its beginning and, in 1915, he was arguably the most effective Indian critic of the British Raj. Even though he was Indian-born and had briefly practiced law in Bombay, Gandhi did not know India well. And despite the fact he was famous in South Africa, he was hardly known in his homeland. Gokhale urged him, therefore, to take some time after his arrival to study the country. For the next several months, traveling by train to many parts of India, that is what Gandhi did.

In May 1915, Gandhi founded Satyagraha Ashram just outside Ahmedabad. A Sanskrit word, "ashram" is used by Hindus to denote: (1) the house of a guru; (2) a *gurukul* (kind of school) where the guru passes on his wisdom to his *shishyas* (students); (3) a place where agreed-upon spiritual disciplines are practiced; and (4) a community of self-denial in which the residents forsake worldly pleasures and possessions for a life of study and communion with God. In exchange for the knowledge they receive, the *shishyas,* who live close to or in the same house as the guru, help the guru by cooking, washing clothes, and the like.

"Satyagraha" was Gandhi's shorthand for his strategy of nonviolent resistance for getting political and social concessions from the British Raj. Still evolving in his mind, Gandhi had first introduced satyagraha in South Africa. And, in 1917, he employed it with good success in Bihar, where the oppression of the peasantry by indigo planters and local officials of the Champaran District had become insufferable.

That, in fact, was probably how Pickett first heard of M.K. Gandhi. Though his time in Bihar was brief, Gandhi's impact on the political climate was impressive. In Champaran, not far north of Pickett's Shahabad, Indigo had once brought much money to the planters. However, with the introduction of chemical dyes, the bottom had dropped out of the market. To help offset their losses, the planters—among adding other intolerable burdens—raised the rents of their tenants so high they were virtually forced into indentureship. Their poverty was such that women could not wash their clothes, because they had no clothes to change into. Representing the desperate victims of the landlords' oppression at 1916's Indian National Congress in Lucknow, Rajkumar Shukla got Congress to pass a resolution condemning the exploitation. He also talked Gandhi into coming to Bihar to see what he could do. After the gathering, he kept after Gandhi, insistently reminding him of his promise. In April of 1917 Gandhi finally came. The Mahatma's reception was anything but warm. In fact, government officials ordered him to leave at once. Defying the order, he was arrested. But his satyagraha found strong support, and Gandhi and his campaign were on everybody's lips. Without doubt, Waskom Pickett, who shared Gandhi's concern for the poor and oppressed peoples of the province took notice with everyone else.

WHEN BRITAIN DECLARED WAR ON Germany in 1914, the British were nervous about how India's national leaders and the Indian princes would react. However, they soon breathed a sigh of relief. In the beginning, most of the established Indian leaders lent their support to the crown. They were convinced that, after the war, Britain would have little choice but to reward their loyalty with *swaraj*, self rule. Their logic went like this. If Britain was fighting to protect weaker nations from imperial aggression so they could retain self-determination, and India stood at her side, after the war Britain would do the right and consistent thing and offer India that same freedom. Thus, during the war years, a staggering 800,000 Indian soldiers and 400,000 Indian noncombatants went off to war in Europe. Of them, 26,000 were killed and another 70,000 were wounded. Ironically, even Gandhi, with his emphases on nonviolence supported Britain's decision to go to war. In fact, he told a mostly Indian audience in London that their support was "a matter of sacred duty." Afterwards, he organized an Indian Field Ambulance Corps to work with the Red Cross on the European Front.

After the war, though, Indian veterans came home from the battlefields of Europe fully expecting to see dramatic changes. In his 1933 biography, *Mahatma Gandhi,* Pickett's Lucknow colleague, J.R. Chitambar spelled out the reasons.

> They had acquired a first-hand knowledge of England and of the countries in Europe, their governments, their economic and social conditions, the status of their women, and, above all, the freedom which these nations enjoy. They saw evidences of "liberty, equality, and fraternity" everywhere. This created in the hearts of the Indian people the hope of being given an equal status with the other dependencies of the British Empire. The feeling between England and India was most amicable at that time.

An announcement made by British Secretary of State for India, Edwin Montagu, to the House of Commons seemed to buttress their hopes. On August 20, 1917, he stated that the British Government was committed to a self-governing India within the British Empire and that it had "decided that substantial steps in this direction should be taken as soon as possible." The announcement was followed in 1918 by the Montagu-Chelmsford Proposals, which envisioned a series of gradual changes leading to Indian self-rule.

However, two things deflated Indian aspirations for self rule. First, a Government of India Act in 1919, which ostensibly moved in the hoped-for direction, offered, on closer scrutiny, reforms that protracted British control. Particularly galling were two Rowlatt Bills, named for Mr. Justice Rowlatt, chair of the committee of inquiry on "revolutionary conspirators." Even though the war was now over, the proposed legislation would preserve the Defense of India Act, allowing the Government to try people without juries and intern people without trials—clearly steps backwards, not forwards. Thus, instead of expanding liberties, the bills would actually curtail them. Both the timing and the spirit of the pending Rowlatt Acts were an insult. When the British Raj introduced them, all of political India protested.

What most radicalized the Independence Movement, though, was an event that shocked everyone. In the spring of 1919, Punjab, a province in northwest India, was a hub of protest and swaraj sentiment. Despite Gandhi's insistence on peaceful noncooperation, many Punjabis spoke favorably of the Russian Revolution. Fueling their frustration, the British rulers had just arrested Gandhi. When tempers flared in Amritsar on April 10, and four Europeans were killed, martial law was imposed and all public meetings banned. On April 13, at 4:30 in the afternoon, a sizeable, but peaceful, crowd of demonstrators defied the order by gathering in the Jallianwalla Bagh to listen to a succession of speeches against the Rowlatt Acts and political arrests. The Jallianwalla Bagh was large and open but surrounded by walls. The only way out was through a gated entrance. With the enclosed area full of more than 10,000 people, the army was called in. Brigadier-General Reginald Edward Harry Dyer, without giving the crowd an opportunity to disperse, commanded his troops to fire. By the time he ordered them to cease firing, 10 minutes later, 400 Indian citizens (mostly Sikhs) were dead and a thousand more were wounded. How Waskom Pickett responded to the news from Amritsar is not known, for throughout those awful days he was sick in bed with malarial fever. But many missionaries were stunned and embarrassed.

Against this postwar backdrop, as well as the death of militant Congress leader Bal Gangadhar Tilak in 1920, M.K. Gandhi, who had gained much press since coming home in 1915, became a real force in Indian politics. He actively campaigned against the proposed legislation, formed a coalition committed to satyagraha if the acts passed, and inspired a direct action day on which businesses would close and Indians would fast and pray. In 1920, he would be elected to the leadership of the Indian National Congress. His noncooperation campaign, which would go on until 1922, led to boycotts of anything British including British made garments, British universities, and British courts. Of particular interest with regard to Pickett, though, is the often overlooked but prominent emphasis in the noncooperation movement against the sale of liquor.

WHEN, IN 1915, IT SEEMED THAT PICKETT would recover from his tuberculosis, his half-brother, Deets, and General Secretary Clarence Wilson of the Methodist Board of Temperance invited him to represent the temperance board in India if he returned.

Like most of his family and, in fact, much of the Methodist Church in that era, Waskom was a passionate Prohibitionist. When pressed, he allowed that some of the best Christians indulged in a daily whiskey and soda, but for the sake of those who were susceptible to addiction, he could not fathom why they would not set the right example. To the protest of some that drinking in moderation is biblically allowed, he responded that "the drunkard is always a man or woman who tried to be a moderate drinker but failed."

After returning to India in 1916, Pickett lectured and preached regularly against the sale and purchase of intoxicants. In ecclesiastical settings, he argued that, without a clear-cut position on the issue, the church's reputation and evangelistic success were jeopardized. In "An Open Letter to Methodists," he lamented that "so many nominal Christians have indulged in drink that non-Christians in vast numbers have thought the Christian religion was not opposed to such indulgence." This, he claimed, kept many from turning to Christ and accounted for some Indian opposition to Christianity.

In 1920, Pickett launched a campaign against the local liquor shops in the Arrah District. He and his workers urged Hindus, Muslims, and Christians alike to unite in demanding that all liquor shops be closed. The effort aroused enough support to scare away customers and put some of the shops out of business.

On April 1, 1922, Pickett finally agreed to a half-time appointment as the Methodists' Temperance Secretary for India and Burma. He did so knowing that the handicap of being a part-time Superintendent would soon be ameliorated by the formation of a new Buxar District, with Emanuel Sukh in charge. Pickett's advocacy helped bring the change, which not only reduced the number of Arrah circuits from 16 to eight, but increased the potential for new circuits.

Besides preaching and lecturing against the liquor trade, Pickett's new role included the production of various booklets, charts, and other publications. The foremost of these was *The Temperance Clip Sheet*, which he began putting out in September, 1921. The *Clip Sheet* was modeled after an American version that had been edited by Deets Pickett since 1913. Pickett's mailing list came from the Government, which provided him a directory of every authorized publication in India—more than a thousand. He added to it various opinion leaders and political figures whom he wished to influence. The response to the fortnightly publication was remarkable. It received accolades from church leaders, acclaim from editors, and approval from politicians. Over 20 newspapers printed practically the whole of every issue—most of them secular papers. When requests came for an Urdu version, Pickett recruited M.A. Phillips to edit it. It, too, was well received.

Items in the clipsheet ranged from reports of liquor raids to editorials on the need to crack down on railway engineers who consumed intoxicating beverages. It targeted not just liquor though, but *charas* (hashish), cocaine, and heroin. Here are two clipsheet samples:

"DOUBLE MURDER BY CHARAS ADDICT"

Bhagwati Prasad, a young Hindu of about 24, was charged at Lucknow with the murder of two old women servants of his household. This young man was addicted to Charas and under its influence he conceived the notion that if his owls could be given human blood they would tell him how he might become the king of Ceylon. He was found guilty of murder and sentenced to transportation for life. A recommendation was made to Government that he be detained in a lunatic asylum.

"WORLD NOTES"

Several ex-brewers of America are reported as saying that they expect Asia to furnish them with facilities for reestablishing their business and with an expanding market. Are America's outlaws going to be welcomed by the countries in Asia? God forbid.

Many items in the clipsheet were substantially longer than these. Some contained statistical information. Others commended leaders of boycotts or the sponsors of new prohibition laws.

Although the clipsheet lasted only a year, until the Picketts went on furlough, Waskom felt that it had contributed substantially to the vitality and endurance of the temperance movement in India. One who was impressed with Pickett's temperance work, even before the publication of the clipsheet, was the Hindu orator and politician, Madan Mohan Malviya. He invited Pickett to join him in a speaking tour of the United Provinces, an invitation Pickett could not accept because of his other commitments. However, the two did share in a large meeting in Delhi and became good friends. Pickett's temperance work netted him other new friends as well. Among them were the editors of the *Indian Social Reformer* and the *Servant of India*.

Pickett's anti-liquor drive also caught the attention of South Indian statesman, Chandra Chakravarti Gopal Rajagopalachari, for obvious reasons called "C.R." Well-known for developing strict alcohol regulations known as "halfway to prohibition," Rajagopalachari was so impressed with Pickett's campaign that he later called him "the father of Indian prohibition." Coming, as it did, from a leading political figure, the honorific underscored the broad impact of Pickett's offensive.

Such was Pickett's reputation that, in one three-month period, he received more than a hundred speaking invitations, including one to lecture at Shantiniketan ("Abode of Peace"), an experimental university begun by the Bengali poet, Rabindranath Tagore. All this, we should note, occurred *prior* to the publication of the first issue of *The Temperance Clip Sheet*! Later, the Methodist Central Conference adopted a resolution commending Pickett for his work. It cited his campaign against liquor advertisements in the press, his successful petition for bringing an end to liquor ads in post office publications, and the new willingness of the press to cover efforts to get anti-alcohol reforms passed.

A remarkable sidelight to all this is that, because of his influence in the Indian temperance movement, Pickett inadvertently played a role in the single aspect of Gandhi's noncooperation movement that actually worked! Judith Brown amplifies it in her biography, *Gandhi: Prisoner of Hope:*

> Non-co-operation set the mold for Gandhi's life and work in India and clarified his own Indian identity. But as a campaign to bring the Raj to a grinding halt by withdrawal of Indian co-operation it did not succeed . . . Ironically, the one area of financial embarrassment to the Raj resulted from an aspect of the campaign which Gandhi and Congress had not planned—a temperance movement which hit excise revenue! Several provinces were badly hit and in late February 1922 the Governor of Madras admitted that his government's financial position was 'really desperate' largely as a result.

DURING THIS SAME PERIOD, ANOTHER MATTER came to the fore. In 1919-20, a strident Muslim protest that became known as the Khilafat Movement arose. Its purpose was to provoke public dissent against Britain's postwar policies in the Ottoman Empire, specifically, shifting the Muslim caliph's oversight of Islamic holy places to the Arabs. Spearheading the protest movement were two brothers, Mahomed and Shaukat Ali. The campaign was most active in the United Provinces,

Bihar, and Sindh, although it was certainly not confined to those areas. Gandhi allied himself with the Ali brothers and the Muslim grievances. However, he did so, not only because he felt Muslim religious sensibilities had been violated, but, also, because doing so provided him an opportunity to pursue his dream of a transformed India.

> My interest in your release is quite selfish. We have a common goal and I want to utilize your services to the uttermost, in order to reach that goal. In the proper solution of the Mahomedan question lies the realization of Swarajya [self-rule].

Gandhi's advocacy of collaboration between Hindus and Muslims and his call for a noncooperation campaign were calculated to be a nonviolent strategy for obtaining British concessions. Instead, to Gandhi's horror, his satyagraha was spoiled by riots and killing, so in 1922, he called it off.

Sometime during this period, most likely in August of 1921, Pickett learned that Gandhi and one of the Ali brothers were to stop in Arrah. After getting the approval of the District Magistrate, Pickett drove to the area outside the city where Gandhi was to speak. He placed his folding chair about 10 feet from the platform. Looking around, he could see many Indian friends. Then he turned his attention to the platform, where Gandhi was being introduced. Alternating between Hindi and English, Gandhi spoke for 20 minutes. The speech, severely critical of British officials, stirred the crowd to indignation—enough so that Pickett became frightened of what might ensue. Also, at some point, friends began gathering around him, as if to protect him. Gandhi, however, ended on a more irenic note, reminding the crowd, "I am against violence and beg you to control your tempers, but defend your country." Then he introduced Ali, whom he said would speak and give them some valuable advice. After that, he left.

At that point, Pickett left too and followed Gandhi to the house where he was staying. When he asked the host if it would be possible to speak with his visitor, Gandhi himself came to the door and invited him in.

Sitting on the floor, Pickett, Gandhi, and some local Hindu leaders conversed for about an hour. The first focus of their discussion was on the liquor trade. Soon, though, Pickett brought up a series of run-ins he and his colleagues had experienced with non-cooperators who were interfering with their attempts to distribute Scripture portions. In so doing, said Pickett, they were invoking the name of Gandhi. On hearing this,

Gandhi expressed his displeasure and even agreed to being quoted as favoring the study of Jesus' teaching in the Gospels.

The last and longest part of their exchange focused on Jesus himself. Pickett asked Gandhi if he minded some clarifying questions about his religious beliefs. The 51-year-old Gandhi responded that he liked to talk about religion. Emboldened, Pickett asked if the reports were true that, in South Africa, Gandhi had for a time considered becoming a Christian.

"What do you mean by 'becoming a Christian?' I am a Christian," said Gandhi.

"Have you ever told India that you are a Christian?" Pickett asked.

"No, because I am not only a Christian, but a Hindu, a Moslem, a Sikh, a Buddhist, and a Jew. I worship God in the light of the teaching of all these religions. But being an Indian I prefer to worship God in the Hindu way, especially as Ram or Krishna."

When Pickett then asked what he thought of worshiping Jesus, Gandhi replied, "I worship him almost every day, just as I do our Hindu gods."

When asked what he thought of Jesus' claim to be the one and only Lord and Savior, Gandhi said, "That claim I cannot accept. I am sure it was a mistake."

What about Jesus' sinlessness, the young missionary asked. "I think he sinned like all others," said Gandhi. "His greatest sin was his approval of the man who killed a calf to honor his repentant son."

Gandhi admitted that he had once entertained Christian baptism but that his interest had evaporated following the indignity of being asked, because he was "colored," to leave the worship service of a well-known South African church. Long after Gandhi's death, Pickett remembered that the rejection by that church remained a lifelong thorn for Gandhi. He recalled hearing Gandhi tell the story, not just in Arrah, but many times more over the years.

12 In Famine and Flood

To live in rural Bihar was to reside around the corner from various emissaries of suffering, among them famines and floods. During his final years in Arrah, Pickett encountered both and, each time, was caught by surprise. He literally stumbled on the famine while on a trek, but for special circumstances, he would not have set out on. As for the flood, it seemed to have come out of nowhere—as Pickett put it, "under the steady gaze of a cloudless sky."

IN 1920, THE GENERAL CONFERENCE OF the Methodist Episcopal Church gave permission to the North and Northwest India Conferences "to divide their territories and adjust their boundaries." One outcome was the formation of a new annual conference, of which Pickett was a charter member. It convened in Lucknow, Tuesday, February 1, 1921, under the presidency of Bishop Warne. However, the delegates did not immediately settle its name. The missionaries, led by J.O. Denning, wanted to call it the Ganges Conference. The Indians, however, were horrified and protested naming the conference after a Hindu goddess. Alternatively, they proposed Oudh Conference or, possibly, Bihar Conference. Even though the name Ganges won by a single vote, no one was comfortable with the slim margin. So, the next day they looked for a compromise and settled on Lucknow Conference.

Lucknow Conference began with eight districts—two coming from the Northwest India Conference and six, including the Ballia and Arrah districts, under Perrill and Pickett, coming from the North India Conference.

In the heart of Pickett's Arrah District was an area of about 20 miles by 30 miles, where the boundaries of all but four of the district's circuits met. Pickett was committed to developing this core territory intensively, for in that small rectangle were 200 villages that had hardly been touched by the church. And, even in the villages where there were worship services, thousands remained unreached. To accomplish the goal of bringing the gospel to these population groups, the mission would have to develop new circuits. Pickett estimated that 100 more preachers would be needed. If the vision sounds enormous, we must remember that in four short years Pickett had already gone from three circuits with 17 paid workers and 1,700 Christians to 13 circuits with 46 paid workers and 6,668 Christians. In 1920 alone, five new circuits had been formed, including one based at Sassaram, a historic Muslim center with a population of 20,000, and a surrounding population of more than 400,000. Another of the new circuits was at Jagdishpur, a town of 10,000, which, by road, was about 20 miles from the Pickett bungalow. The land on which the town was built, plus swaths of land stretching nine miles to the northwest and eight miles to the southeast, were owned by an Englishman. Pickett had baptized the first converts there in the fall of 1919, and at the time the circuit was formed, there were already 200 new Christians.

Pickett's focus on the heart of the district did not lessen his interest in the more remote circuits. As part of the Conference reconfiguration, the Chunar Circuit, formerly part of the Allahabad District of the Northwestern Conference, was transferred to the Arrah District. Although it was 116 miles west of Arrah, the town of Chunar (population, 10,000) was directly accessible via the East India Railway. Twelve miles southeast of Chunar, which in turn was 20 miles south of Benares, was a place called Ahraura, the site of a sizable, but largely unfruitful, work of the Church Missionary Society. As the start of the hot season approached, Pickett was getting ready to go there. His business there was to purchase, inexpensively, a small property consisting of a church, several preachers' houses and a day school. The property had been offered by the Church Missionary Society, which had decided for financial reasons to abandon its Ahraura work. Although the buildings were badly in need of repair, it was Pickett's belief that the mass movement would soon spread that way and that they should establish a presence there.

On May 7, a Saturday, Pickett boarded a westbound train for Chunar. He would have preferred to drive his new Ford car, which he had recently uncrated and assembled, and was already using. For this trip, however, the car would not be of much use, for his ultimate destination, Ahraura, was only accessible by foot or by *ekka*, and as Pickett quipped, "Primitive roads demand primitive means!"

The sun was intense, for they were more than a month into the hot season. In March, a visitor had written in the Pickett's guest book, "Today began the blowing of the loo. It forecasts the days of heat, the flight to the hills." But, of course, only a few people—including missionaries—had that option. Also, in March, Pickett had read a brief item in the paper about famine in some remote part of the state. He took note of it but did not give it much more thought. He assumed that, like the famine reported two years earlier, in 1919, it was serious but not widespread. But as the rugged road unfurled into the hills, he was confronted by a scene that made the purchase of the property suddenly insignificant. Lying all along the road were dozens of sick and starving people. "I had no idea of the situation being so bad," he wrote the mission board when he got back. "The local people are not suffering seriously as the crops have been fairly good, but in the mountains back of Ahraura there has been an almost complete failure of the crops for three successive years and hundreds . . . have come here to beg."

Pickett gave away most of the money he had brought with him—enough to feed about a hundred people. But there were hundreds more he could not feed. The 12,000 permanent residents of the town seemed unmoved by the plight of their mountain neighbors. The only beggars they helped, Pickett lamented, were the ones they bribed to go away. Nevertheless, by day's end he had managed to set up a little relief center and was thinking of how to appeal for help. Forgoing his planned "flight" to the hills with Ruth and his two little daughters, he instead decided to go to the heart of the stricken area. "I dread going further back toward the mountains," he wrote, "but will have to do it." He estimated victims of the drought would need help for at least four months, after which, with a modicum of rain, the strong ones could earn a little by putting in the next crops. "But some," he wrote, "will probably have to be cared for until the next rice harvest in December . . . [and] we will probably need to adopt a few dozen famine children."

FLOODING WAS NOT AN INFREQUENT occurrence around Arrah. But by far the worst flood came in late summer 1923. Around the first of August, Waskom Pickett went to Naini Tal to be with Ruth and the girls. He had been there two weeks and was planning to stay a third when he got a telegram from Bishop Frederick Bonn Fisher summoning him to a meeting at Ranchi, Bihar—a meeting to which Fisher had also summoned E.

Stanley Jones and J.R. Chitambar. Fisher's wire was followed by a second telegram from Chitambar, who was now president of Lucknow Christian College. He proposed that he and Pickett go together from Lucknow and lay over in Arrah. They arrived there on August 18, a Saturday. After supper at the Pickett bungalow, they met with about a dozen residents of the compound who were deeply troubled by the failure of the seasonal rains. Before retiring, the group prayed for the needed rain, Chitambar and the local pastor leading them.

Because of the heat, Pickett and Chitambar slept outside on the second floor veranda. At about 4:30 in the morning, Pickett awoke to the sound of running water. He went downstairs and discovered a river, 40 feet from the house. It was flowing eastward. Since it had not rained during the night, Pickett was mystified. Where the river had come from, he could not imagine—certainly not from the Ganges, eight miles to the east, for that was the direction in which it was flowing. And the Sone river, 10 miles to the southeast, flowed into the Ganges.

Chitambar awoke about a half hour later. By then, the nearby "Mission House" and part of the public road were under water. As they watched the flow from the balcony, Pickett told Chitambar not to worry, that he had witnessed similar flooding before—though not without rain! Though the sun was shining, the waters continued to rise—in fact, they rose by seven inches per hour—until, by midmorning, much of the compound was knee deep in the flow. At that point, Pickett waded from the back of the house to the boys' dormitory, 200 yards away. He instructed Morris Phillips, the school manager, to move the boys, their possessions, and all foodstuff to the bungalow. At about 11:00 in the morning, Pickett, Chitambar, Phillips, and four of the tallest boys waded to the girls' school to make sure all were safe. Finding a route where the water was not over their heads took some doing. When they got there, Miss Hyneman, the principal, and her assistants had already moved the girls from their quarters to the nearby, four-room bungalow of the lady missionaries. However, since it too seemed destined to flood, Pickett and the others attached ladders to the flat-roofed house and left the boys "to assist." The real reason for leaving them, though, was that the water had gotten too deep for the boys to safely return. When the house flooded, everyone climbed the ladders to the roof. Just as night fell, the women were rescued by boat. Because there was not enough room in the boat for everyone, the boys remained on the roof. They would spend three nights there.

Pickett's gravest concern was for drinking water. Flood water had filled and overflowed the compound's well, and he could think of no other accessible source of potable water. Then a thought came to him. He remembered that putting alum in a container of dirty water was supposed to make the dirt sink to the bottom. And Ruth had, in a closet drawer, a two-pound sack of alum. Pickett and Chitambar filled the bath-tub with flood water and deposited a handful of crushed alum. The water cleared. The kitchen stove was still above the water line, so they boiled water from the tub for tea and coffee.

Throughout the duration of the flood, Pickett worked tirelessly. Chitambar was in awe of his "cool courage." On Sunday and Monday, Pickett spent 15 hours in the water. Chitambar wrote, "He was tireless in his efforts to save and help the people, non-Christian and Christian."

On Monday, the second day of the flood, Pickett and a helper rescued eight 25-pound sacks of rice and wheat that were beached above the waterline in one of the two small buildings used for the boys' school. When some railway ties floated into the compound, Pickett retrieved them and tied them into a raft. With the raft, he attempted to rescue a group of village people who had climbed a tree for safety. By the time he got to them, two elderly men had already fallen and been swept away, but he managed to get the rest onto the raft and floated them to the bungalow. By now, everyone in the compound had joined Pickett and Chitambar in the bungalow. Altogether nearly a hundred people took shelter in the second story of the large house.

For most of two days, Pickett waded up to his armpits in the mystery flood. Sometimes it was so deep he had to swim from place to place. The current was overpowering, even where it was only waist deep. Standing was nearly impossible. Snakes were a problem too. Cobras and kraits, driven out of their holes by the water, sought shelter on verandas or in houses. More than a dozen swept into the downstairs rooms of the bungalow and had to be killed. Two of the rescued Hindus expressed their disapproval. In contrast, Miss Hyneman had been cheered and "nearly won the 'Kaiser-I-Hind'" medal for helping to kill a cobra that sought refuge on her veranda.

"While the flood was in progress," wrote Pickett, "it seemed that the loss of life would be terrible." And there were tragedies. A resident of the compound saw the body of an infant float by. The bridge of the Chota Ganga was washed away along with 30 people and their cattle. They had been warned not to take refuge on the bridge but had ignored the warnings.

Mercifully, though, although thousands of cattle drowned, the loss of human life was small.

The new upstairs residents in the Pickett house were stranded there for three days, for although only two feet of water covered the ground floor, everywhere else in the compound the water was six feet deep. Pickett expressed concern about the bungalow's foundations. To some extent, they had been previously undermined, and there were numerous cracks in the walls. At about 9:00 a.m. on Tuesday, one of those making rounds fell into an 18-inch hole at a corner of the kitchen, confirming Pickett's fears. They promptly filled the hole with 14 bricks. The same morning, Pickett became ill. His temperature soared to 103 degrees. He had no choice but to rest. At that point, Chitambar took charge.

Only on the fourth day did the flood begin to recede. Fortunately, the bungalow had withstood the assault. In fact, all of the buildings in the mission compound survived. The inundation caved two veranda walls—that was all.

But the same could not be said of many buildings in the region. In the countryside about 65 percent of the structures in an area of 150 square miles collapsed. In Arrah, the loss of houses was more like 40 percent. Thousands were left homeless. Pickett described the situation like this:

> Several of the most densely populated mohallas are on high ground and escaped, but practically every kachcha [mud or clay] house in the flooded area came down, as did also many kachcha-pakka [mud and brick] and a few pakka [brick] houses. In the villages, with their houses, people have lost their year's grain supply stored from the last harvest, including their seed grain, many of their cattle and practically the whole of their standing crops.

Arrah itself was flooded for nearly a week before the outside world heard the details. Both roads and rails were submerged. The only way to get from place to place was through the water. One solution that caught on was boat-riding in tin bath tubs. It became "fashionable" for men to pilot their women around in a tub. Pickett was relieved to learn that the great majority of the village Christians to whom they related had kept safe. The mass movement had always stayed to the west and south of Arrah. The flood was mainly to the east and north.

Chitambar and Pickett never made it to Ranchi. By the time train service resumed, Bishop Fisher had already left. Five days after the flood arrived, Chitambar was able to go home by ballast train. Ruth and the girls returned as soon as regular trains began running. When the waters subsided, Pickett set about finding funds to make repairs to the buildings. The structures had survived, but not without substantial damage.

Where had the mystery flood come from? Only when the ordeal was over did the city learn that a tremendous cloudburst, 400 miles away, had caused it. A wide valley that narrowed for about 60 miles had, like a sluice, conveyed the water into the Shahabad District. About 50 miles from Arrah, the flow reached a plain and poured into—and over-flowed—the British-made irrigation canal that passed by the edge of Arrah. Thus, as Pickett would later put it, the Arrah flood waters appeared "after a dozen rainless days and wrought their worst destruction under the steady gaze of a cloudless sky."

ON SUNDAY, AUGUST 26, A WEEK TO the day after the day the flood appeared, the Methodist Church of Arrah gathered, as usual, on the commodious veranda of the Pickett bungalow. This Sunday, though, a good many Hindus joined them too. Despite the severity of the previous week, the theme was thankfulness to God. The offering given that day was the most generous in the history of the church, although it was not a total anomaly, for the giving of the church had more than doubled that year and, for the first time ever, the church had been able to cover their pastor's support in full.

In the weeks to come, Waskom and Ruth were not only faced with cleanup, repairs, and the replacement of personal effects due to the flood but with the end of their term in Arrah. From November 3-12, Waskom and Ruth attended their last district conference in Bihar. The assembly met under a *shamiana* (a large tent) at a picturesque setting in Shanti Bagh. Among those addressing them were Fred Perrill and J.R. Chitambar. Mary Perrill addressed the women's conference on topics related to childcare. On Friday afternoon, special tribute was paid to the Picketts, just as it had been paid to the Perrills at Waskom and Ruth's first Bihar district conference meeting in the old Tirhoot District.

From the district conference, the Pickett family returned to the bungalow in Arrah to finish packing and to prepare for their successors. The following week, Waskom preached 40 miles away, in Patna, at the new Union Church, of which the Methodists made up one unit. Lutherans, Baptists and Anglicans were also participants. The church met in a room on the veranda of a member's house. The room had been specially furnished in true Indian style. The entire congregation of about 60 sat on the floor, the men occupying the room and the women the veranda. Pickett was impressed by the multi-denominational and multilingual makeup of the church. Both Bengali and Hindustani *bhajans* were sung. But, although the congregation was able to follow Pickett's sermon in Urdu, he noted that Hindi would have served them better.

From the start of his career, Pickett viewed competitive denominationalism as a handicap. What he said in his eighties, he could and probably did say when he was in Arrah: "In the presence of Hinduism, Islam, Sikhism, Buddhism, Animism or any other religion, the differences between and within evangelical Christian churches fade into insignificance." Nevertheless, when it came to calls for organic church union, Waskom had been a skeptic. Just three years prior to his visit to the new union church, he articulated his doubts in an address to the Bihar and Orissa Provincial Christian Council. While spiritual union was imperative, he said, organic church union was fraught with dangers. However, this new exposure in Patna seems to have deeply impressed him, and in due time he lent his unreserved support to the church union movement. As he would later reflect, "We obtain salvation not by becoming Methodists, Presbyterians, Baptists or Roman Catholics, but by faith in Jesus Christ—making Him Lord of our lives and becoming His disciples."

In the final days of November 1923, Pickett wound up his local responsibilities and wrote his report for the fourth annual meeting of Lucknow Conference. Included was a summary of developments in Arrah since his and Ruth's arrival, including a strong affirmation of Emanuel Sukh in his new responsibility as Superintendent of the Buxar District. He was especially delighted to be able to report that his and Ruth's "dream of years" had recently been realized in the purchase of the nearby Solano estate for the girls' school:

This is a magnificent property which has been coveted for the Christian enterprise by every agent of the Church that has seen it. For several scores of years the property has been in the hands of Europeans who without any thought of its ultimate use for the work of the Church have nevertheless prepared it for our needs. It is beautifully wooded, and 4 wells are located thereon. One third of the property has been purchased by the Women's Foreign Missionary Society and two-thirds by the Board of Foreign Missions.

December of 1923 combined a needed vacation with final preparations for the furlough to America. Waskom, Ruth and the girls planned to visit Ruth's family in Bombay over the Christmas holidays. Then, right after New Year's, they would sail for America, stopping on the way in Egypt and Europe for meetings connected with Waskom's temperance work. Leaving the Arrah bungalow was hard. On the one hand, Waskom and Ruth were anticipating a needed rest and reunions with loved ones. On the other hand, closing the doors of the big bungalow for the last time meant leaving behind much they had come to love—including many friends. Also, much remained undone. Although the district's growth had been phenomenal, the potential for growth was by no means exhausted. Moreover, the enormous job of nurturing the district's thousands of new believers had barely begun. Nonetheless, as always, Pickett the optimist refused to see the future in anything but positive terms. After setting down his last annual report from Arrah, he added these words:

I wish to express my grateful thanks to God for the privilege of having spent seven years in Arrah . . . I shall turn the work over to my successor with confidence that the building of the Church of God in this wonderful district will proceed at a greatly accelerated rate.

As for Ruth Pickett, she wrote in the family guest book: "The end of Chapter One. 1916-1924 in Arrah."

The Lucknow Years (1925-1935)

Block containing the Lucknow Publishing House; the publishing house in on the left.

The Pickett family in 1932

Top: Road to Mussoorie
Middle: Fir Clump, interior
Bottom: Eastwood veranda

Wilmore, Kentucky, 1932

Top left: B.R. Ambedkar
Top right: Donald A. McGavran
Right: John R. Mott
Bottom: Methodist Church at
Jubbulpore (now Jabalpur) where
Pickett was consecrated as bishop on
January 5, 1936

13 *The Indian Witness*

From 1925 to 1929, J. Waskom Pickett edited the *Indian Witness*, the most visible job in Indian Methodism. But had the Methodist Board of Foreign Missions gotten its way, the arrival of the Picketts in America, in early 1924, would have marked the end of their Indian odyssey. Not that anyone schemed it. In those days of wilting budgets, you kept your top-drawer fund-raisers in the top drawer if you possibly could.

The Picketts' furlough offered a change of scenery but little rest. For one thing, before leaving India, Waskom had agreed to help his old friend, J.R. Chitambar, raise 100,000 dollars for Lucknow Christian College. When Chitambar became president of the college in April 1922, he inherited more than new administrative and academic responsibilities. A new science hall, two large hostels, an enlarged and remodeled main building, and new athletic fields had burdened the fast-growing school with a heavy debt—one that would not be fully lifted until 1942.

With Wilmore as home base, Waskom immediately began collecting gifts to help pay the debt. He wrote to anyone who might help. He went to any church that would hear him. He made a small booklet about the college and its need. He even designed special stationery. The top corners contained the names of "Fred Fisher, President of the Board," and "Jashwant Chitambar, President of the College." Then came the centered name of the school followed by the words: "The Only Methodist College for Men in Southern Asia." Beneath those lines were three parallel blocks of information. The left one stated the campaign's financial goals. The center one gave Pickett as the representative in America and included the Board of Foreign Missions' address. And the block on the right said the school had 964 students and served a Christian community of 500,000. The bottom of the letterhead announced that "$250 names a room in a new dormitory" and that "$2,000 endows a scholarship." With that information made prominent, Pickett was free to make his handwritten appeals more personal, or even to discuss entirely different matters, without neglecting the opportunity of making visible the school's need. Of course, the LCC campaign wasn't Pickett's sole concern. The Methodist Board of Prohibition, Temperance, and Public Morals was paying half his furlough salary. And, as time and health allowed, he was committed to recruiting and fund-raising for the mission board.

In early June, Pickett suffered a malaria attack in Abilene, Texas. He thought it was residually connected to a bout with malarial fever back in India. "I . . . must have stopped taking quinine too soon," he conjectured. Although it was more likely triggered by overwork, the relapse hardly slowed him down. Enforced bed rest meant canceling some appointments, but it also meant more time for writing letters.

In September, Pickett led a fund-raising workshop for the mission board at Wallace Lodge in New York. He urged both staff and trainees not to make their message "a calamity howl." He told them to be positive and inspirational, and to "make the people visualize the work of the kingdom in terms of individuals. This they could do by using "human interest stories and stories of real people." He had learned, he said, that supporters of missions were especially responsive to

> anything that shows the way the people themselves are rallying to meet their own need, the larger efforts of the people in evangelistic work, [and] the way in which they assume the burdens of self-support.

He gave an example: "I might tell them that the very shoes I wear on my feet were made by village converts in factories established to [get] the people on their feet." Similarly, he urged them to "make people realize that our missionaries are not on the field permanently." They must demonstrate that "our very definite purpose is to help people in the largest possible measure to help themselves." Pickett's own fund-raising modeled this approach. For instance, in his appeals for Lucknow Christian College, he would tell how, in the beginning, students found it impossible to get jobs in government offices and industry. Then he would tell them how college responded by starting a commercial school offering training in shorthand, typewriting, and adapting shorthand to the Indian vernacular. The result, he would say, is that "one man earns more in a month than his grandfather was able to earn in several years."

Pickett had some final advice for his class at Wallace Lodge. Don't appear "petty" by talking about your own work as if that were everything, he told them. Let people realize you are presenting "a part of the great work of the church" with which you happen to be familiar.

THE PICKETTS' AMERICAN FURLOUGH HAD begun only a few weeks after disclosure of a 200 million dollar debt at the Board of Foreign Missions. The debt was due in part to the disparity between pledges to the Centenary Fund drive and what came in. But incompetency had played a part too. Those in charge of disbursements had been operating as if the promised money was already in the coffers. Because of the crisis, Pickett's fund-raising reputation was of special interest to the mission board. In fact, his bosses at the board were so taken by his methods that they mapped out a new role for him in New York. Pickett, however, resisted their pressure to remain in the U.S., and on January 31, 1925, he, Ruth, Elizabeth, and Miriam boarded the S.S. Aurania for the first leg of their return voyage to India.

Before sailing, Pickett learned that he had been appointed editor of the weekly *Indian Witness,* the official publication of the Methodist Episcopal Church in India. In 1861, American Methodists had begun a publishing operation in Bareilly, which they moved to Husainabad, Lucknow in 1866. There the *Lucknow Witness*—along with *Kaukab-I-Hind*—was first published by a staff of six people with one hand-press. In 1882, the paper was moved to Calcutta and, under James Thoburn's editorial direction, renamed the *Indian Witness.* In the 1920s, the editorship of the *Indian Witness* was an esteemed appointment. A 1920s history of Asbury College called it "a stepping stone to the bishopric," and, indeed, it had been—most lately for Pickett's predecessor. In December 1923, the Central Conference had named India-born Brenton T. Badley, then 47, as editor. However, his term lasted only until May, when he was elected bishop. From then until Pickett's arrival, 17 months later, the task had fallen to a succession of acting editors.

Waskom's selection to the post meant the Pickett family would have the happy opportunity of living in Lucknow, for the *Indian Witness* had been returned there in 1914. The Methodist Publishing House, where the paper was printed, was in Hazratganj, a fashionable shopping area of the city. "The Publishing House Block," as it was known, was just a short bicycle ride from the Pickett bungalow. Much of the ornate, block-long, brick-and-plaster structure was rented out by the Methodists. At the midpoint of its protracted facade was a grand two-story portico—the entrance to Whiteaway Laidlaw & Co., which claimed to handle general merchandise from all over the world. Flanking the store were several awning-shaded businesses, which, like their larger neighbor, catered mainly to Europeans and Americans. The Publishing House itself, situated to the left of Whiteaway Laidlaw and to the right of an American dentist, displayed a procession of three painted signboards. Above the awning, the top sign announced "Methodist Publishing House." Immediately underneath, a larger one read "Job Printing." The third notice, on the awning itself, advertised "Books and Stationery."

The newly appointed editor of the *Indian Witness* had come a long way since arriving, 15 years earlier, at the Lal Bagh Church in Lucknow. Indeed, the 35-year-old's knowledge, experience, and maturity commanded the respect of the most seasoned Methodist leaders in India, as shown by the appointment itself. In welcoming him, acting editors, R.C. Rankin and Myron Insko wrote:

> His experience in various phases of missionary work, and the intense earnestness which has characterized his connection with his duties of every sort, are the best guarantee that he will make the paper interesting and attractive and a real force in the life and thought of India.

Pickett began officially in March of 1925. His editorials caught attention almost immediately. The new editor showed from the start that he was not afraid to criticize social evils, propose missiological innovations, or promote the advancement of women. The articles he published, if not reportorial, tended to be analytical. He intended to stretch his readers, to make them think. His favorite Bible verse to quote was, "Love the Lord with all your mind!"

The amount of mail Pickett got astonished him. Most of it was positive, but not all.

> The stream of mail that flows across the desk of the editor of a Christian weekly brings communications of many sorts . . . Some are formal and flow to the files, to some other desk, or to the waste basket with only routine attention. Some voice criticism and except in a very few cases are read with profit and gratitude.

A few denounce the editor, or some recent contributor, for something written, or supposed to have been written, or because something else was not written, and are read with regret. Now and then one is anonymous and not read at all, unless the fact of its anonymity is not suspected until a part of it has been read. Many bring help in the form of articles or reports or news-items or suggestions, and are read with admiration and thankfulness for the spirit of co-operation and devotion to the Kingdom that caused them to be written. But the letters that mean the most to the editor are those that tell of help received from the paper.

PICKETT'S DUTIES REQUIRED PERIODIC TRAVEL, mostly to church conferences, whose proceedings and decisions he reported. But he also made trips in connection with his continuing temperance work and as the newly appointed secretary of the United Provinces Christian Council.

One memorable journey was to Bareilly in October 1925 for the dedication of the new Warne Baby Fold. Its opening meant that 34 children would be quitting the old rented quarters at Clara Swain Hospital for a setting more conducive to their well-being. Pickett had been associated with the ministry from its beginning in the flu epidemic of 1918-19. Perhaps he breathed a sigh of relief that day. But not for long. Minutes after the provincial governor, Sir William Marris, declared the baby fold open, the board huddled and appointed Pickett as financial agent. The baby fold was open, but they still needed 20,000 rupees to pay off the 42,000-rupee cost of the structure. Who better than Waskom Pickett to raise the funds? But his extra commitments were stacking up.

WHEN PICKETT TOOK A BREAK from his exacting routine, it was often to unwind with a book. From his youth, when Mama Ludie drew from him the promise to read at least a book a week, he had steadfastly sustained the practice. Because he wanted his readers to be better informed about Indian affairs and culture, and about other countries too, he encouraged them to make reading a priority as well. By reserving two hours after dinner, four nights a week, he assured them that they could read a book of 300 pages each week. Pickett's own reading ranged from Chinese culture to the poetry of Narayan Vaman Tilak. However, he read little fiction. The better books he reviewed in a regular feature of the *Indian*

Witness called "The World of Books." Those with the greatest reader interest, like E. Stanley Jones' *Christ of the Indian Road*, and V. S. Azariah's *Christ in the Indian Villages*, he featured. Of the Jones book, he wrote, "There is not a dull or unprofitable page in it." And, although he frankly confessed that "we disagree personally with a number of Dr. Jones's conclusions," he was quick to add, "we do not on that account find the book less helpful." Of the Azariah book, of particular interest because it described one of India's best-known mass movement areas, he pointed specially to the last chapter, called "Conclusions." He urged every missionary to read the whole book, but to "study" the final chapter.

Sometimes, as with Katherine Mayo's controversial *Mother India* (1927), Pickett would feature a book in a front-page editorial. "Miss Mayo," as he respectfully called her, had written a muckraking account of the Indian Government's apathy toward the horrific conditions in which people were subsisting. Her commentary, first published in New York, was partly true, but it was unbalanced and full of inaccuracies. By the time Pickett reviewed the volume, it had already produced bitter protests in India. Even Gandhi had decried it, although his criticisms were milder than many. Pickett, who thought the book should have been titled, "The Sins of Mother India," wished aloud that he could have spoken with the author beforehand "to give her another side of India." Although he feared the book was not only perpetuating old prejudices but sowing new ones, Pickett thought it could possibly do some good by causing people to pay more attention to India's voices of reform.

> If these influences [for reform] that are now so apparent in their early stages mature and result in hastening the abolition of child marriage, the adoption of humane standards of treatment for women in child-birth, the renunciation of enforced widowhood, the recognition of the need to treat animals kindly, the liberation of the depressed classes from social and economic bondage, and the development of an appreciation of sanitation, education and economic prosperity, India will have abundant reason to remember Miss Mayo and her book with gratitude, despite her mistakes, and despite the book's bad effects.

Pickett's dislike of Mayo's muckraking style did not mean he ignored suffering and injustice. Often, he couched his social critique in applause for reformers, but, just as often, he spoke his mind directly. And, while

Mayo's sardonic tone unsettled him, those who closed their eyes to evil unsettled him more—and, especially, if they thought *he* should do so!

There are people in India, both nationals and foreigners, who do not like to have social evils in India denounced in a Christian paper edited by a non-Indian. They believe, or pretend to believe, that a Christian from the West should be restrained by the fact that social evils still exist in Western countries. That opinion is utterly repellant to us. We are not in India as Missionaries of Western civilization, nor to preach the morals of Western nations. We recognize no obligation to restrict our preaching in India to such parts of the Christian message as have found full acceptance in some Western land. If we did, we would have nothing to preach. If we denounce falsehood, it does not imply that every one in America or in England is truthful. If we command justice, it is not because justice reigns and injustice is unknown in London, or New York.

Pickett wrote more than 100 editorials and short articles a year while with the *Indian Witness*. Many were suggested by a news item or a book. Sometimes they sprang from a personal encounter or experience. Some focused on spiritual matters, such as: the absurdity of faith as the mere acceptance of a creed; the spiritual helpfulness of some Hindu *bhakti* literature; or the centrality of Christ. Others were salutes to people, including Indian Christians, martyrs, Indian politicians who had taken courageous stands on social issues, and recently deceased missionaries. Most of his editorials, though, focused on matters of conscience, such as: the neglect of children; education and literacy; and failing to treat servants with dignity and respect. Pickett had great compassion for the poor and summoned the Bible, church history, and conscience in their behalf. To those who callously remarked, "God must love poor folks since he made so many of them," he rejoined, "God is blamed for a great many things for which He is not responsible." He allowed that "there are a lot of poor people in the world and God made them all," but he reminded his readers, "[God] did not make them all poor" and chastised those who amassed riches on the backs of the destitute. He warned that even those "with high standards of personal morality . . . are crushing others under an appalling load of poverty." How? "By sinful practices in industries which they control."

Pickett ranged broadly, spotlighting, *among other things,* the prevalence of inhumane working conditions, illiteracy, racism, preventable epidemics, and child marriage. He condemned hatred and hostility, urging ministers, for example, to avoid bitterness toward Arya Samajists who pressured new Christians to recant, and toward *zamindars* (landowners) who persecuted new Christians. He wrote, "No minister was ever helped by an attitude of hostility and none was ever hurt by an excess of friendliness."

As for the hostility of war, Pickett, who labeled himself "the next thing to a pacifist," called it the worst kind of violence. He reminded his readers of the cost of World War I—not just financially but in the loss of life, morality, and spiritual values. "There is no excuse for such an orgy of violence," he wrote, adding:

> Men and women of every faith should join to attack the war spirit and all that provokes it and continue that attack until war preparations shall cease and permanent peace based on mutual respect, tolerance, equal justice and fair dealings for all people shall have been established throughout the earth.

To those who rationalized that war had the side benefit of controlling population growth, he countered: "War is the least efficient method ever advocated for the control of population . . . The prevention of births not the destruction of life is the right method to control the growth of population."

Pickett condemned not just war but even the spirit of militarism. The unfailing companions of militarization, he asserted, are higher taxes and greater poverty. The cost of a single battleship, he said, could save the lives of millions in China's famine area. In the same vein, he denounced suggestions of military training in schools and colleges. Praising Gandhi's example, he instead supported "education for peace."

> India has stood before the world in recent years as a believer in non-violence. Her great son, Mahatma Gandhi has inspired and strengthened opposition to militarism . . . For her own good and for the sake of peace and right throughout the world, India should remain loyal to the ideal that so stirred her when Mr. Gandhi propounded it . . . and keep her soul free from the spirit of militarism.

Although he was often at odds with Gandhi's positions and attitudes, when Pickett thought Gandhi was right, he was quick to affirm him. When, for example, Gandhi, in *Young India*, urged banning purdah, the practice of screening women from men or strangers with a curtain or veil, Pickett not only applauded the Mahatma but reprinted his entire essay.

Not just war, but any pointless violence, dismayed Pickett: riots, retaliation, communal strife—all of it—offended him, particularly when lives were endangered. Disturbing to all had been the premeditated massacre at Amritsar in 1919, where, in the Jallianwala Bagh, Brigadier-General Dyer had, in effect, laid down the death penalty for some 400 by ordering his troops to fire on protesters with nowhere to run. But, for Waskom, the execution of even one individual was objectionable: "As long as the State kills," he wrote, it will be impossible to establish the sense of the sacredness of human life, which is the best protection against murder."

WASKOM'S *DAFTAR,* his *Indian Witness* office, was not at the publishing house but at home, at 37 Cantonment Road. The Pickett bungalow was in a cluster of four houses, all owned by the Methodists. There Pickett wrote and studied, dictating official correspondence to Mr. Cornelius, his secretary, and penning personal letters and notes by hand. There, also, he hosted the many who came for advice or just to visit.

The bungalows, three of them large, and one small, surrounded an expansive lawn with wonderful shade trees—or from the perspective of the children of the dwellings, trees just right for climbing. Although not identical, the bungalows were similar. Each had a ten-foot tall flat-roofed veranda whose main feature was its row of arches. Rising above and behind the veranda was the high-ceilinged main part of the house. Farther back, like the top tier of a wedding cake, was a smaller second story.

Ruth Pickett kept no less busy than her husband. Besides caring for the children, she worked with Waskom in the office and spent much time entertaining visitors. "We always had a full guestroom," remembered daughter, Margaret.

> Mother was very adept at running the home. It was attractive and comfortable. She got along well with her servants, as all missionaries had them in those days. Having lived in India as a

child she was good in Hindustani and in understanding Indian people. Really, she was a great helpmate to Dad.

Ruth also kept daily accounts of all household expenditures,

> writing down in her own special "hisab" [account] books all of the transactions reported by them [servants] and periodically checking in the bazaar to see that their transactions were reported without padding. At the time of monthly salary payments she was meticulous in accounting for all advances and for deducting moneys loaned to the servants for various purposes. Usually funds to help support kids in school or college were gifts and not loans—handed as direct payments to the institutions.

In 1926, when Miriam and Elizabeth Pickett were seven and eight, and again in 1929, when they were nine and 10, the arrival of a new sibling enlarged the family. Elizabeth and Miriam were thus blessed with a convenient source of charges for playing house. Like their older sisters, Margaret and Doug spent the winters at the compound climbing Neem trees, absorbing the local vernacular, making friends with the constant stream of guests, and listening to Waskom's tales about Billy Binkins, a fictional character of his invention. Although the stories themselves have been long forgotten, the characters—Billy, his goat, and his shrewish wife—are still remembered. So are the Pickett children's own pets. Margaret had Siamese cats named Jinx and Winkie Poo; Doug had a goat named Brownie. In addition, chickens and rabbits resided in a small pen on the property. And although not part of the official menagerie, vagabond peacocks regularly paraded through the compound too.

For most of the year, Elizabeth and Miriam were at school in the hills. During the winter months in Lucknow their playmates were the Badley children next door and the Wellons and Ballenger children, whose parents were at Lucknow Christian College. Sometimes the girls would bike to Isabella Thoburn College, always with the *chaprassi* following on his bike. The sisters had many 'aunties' among the Isabella Thoburn faculty. They included Roxanna Oldroyd, Marjorie Dimmitt, Florence Salzer, and especially their beloved Aunty Shannon, then principal and their mother, Ruth's dear friend.

Chand Bagh (Moon Garden), the area where Isabella Thoburn College was located—and the locals' familiar name for the college itself—was also the destination for recitals, Christmas pageants and Sports Day. Other family destinations included favorite picnic sites like Tamasha Bagh (Big Show Garden). Then there was Dilkusha (Contented Heart), a huge garden complex established by Nawab Saadat Ali Khan in the early 19th century. In the 1920s, Dilkusha was a well-kept expanse of lawns, trees, and flowers, the perfect setting for a moonlight Pickett family outing.

Very much a part of the family were the servants, who included Chedi Khan, the cook, who was a bit of a rascal though excellent in the kitchen, and Mrs. Tika, the children's dear old ayah. Mrs. Tika, who was from a poor village family and whose mouth was stained red by *pan* (betel leaf), had an unending repertoire of fairy tales. The children were as devoted to her as much as she was to the family. Even as an adult, Douglas remembered some of her Hindustani nursery rhymes and her wild story about a crow. And then there was Ram Lal, who was with the family for as long as any of the children could remember—perhaps even from Arrah days—and who would go on with them, in 1936, to Bombay. Ram Lal was, in Douglas' words, "a lovable, gentle, quiet-spoken man . . . faithful and loyal in all matters, completely honest and scrupulously hard-working." His two sons, Kalu and Behari, both a little older than Douglas, could perform feats Douglas could never equal, like eating one hot chilli after another and climbing up an unsupported bamboo pole without causing it to topple!

AMONG THE HEROES of Methodism in Lucknow, none surpassed Isabella Thoburn. Her Lucknow Women's College—posthumously renamed Isabella Thoburn College but still Chand Bagh to the locals—was the first institution of higher learning for women in the Eastern World. Both Waskom and Ruth (who, as a girl, had met her) admired Thoburn greatly. Moreover, her Chand Bagh legacy—a frequent rendezvous during their engagement—was the setting of many fond memories. Ruth was not only an alumna of Isabella Thoburn College, having begun her college education there, but also claimed, as her high school alma mater, another school Thoburn had helped start: Wellesley Girl's School in Naini Tal. She and Waskom knew well, therefore, the story of Thoburn's pioneering efforts in education for young women in India, beginning with "six little Christian girls and a man with a club outside the door to protect them."

Waskom often addressed the Chand Bagh student body or conferences held there. His frequent salutes to Isabella Thoburn and other women—including Clementina Butler, American Methodism's first woman missionary to India; Maria Bolst, the first Methodist martyr in India; Lois Lee Parker, whose prayer was the capstone of his ordination day; and Clara Swain, the first woman missionary doctor—were emblematic of his and Ruth's unconcealed ardor for an enlarged role for women in society and the church. Isabella Thoburn's dream of first-rate schools for women of the East, and her philosophy—"the best possible is always the right thing to do"—had nurtured Ruth and Waskom's own vision for the Sawtelle School in Arrah, which they co-founded in just their second year of marriage. But it was another woman who first nurtured the desire and expectation in Waskom for a wider role for women: his own mother, Ludie Day Pickett, who, during each of her son's years as editor of the *Indian Witness*, not only edited her own paper, the *Kentucky White Ribbon* and led the Kentucky WCTU's charge against the liquor trade, but leveraged national clout besides.

With this company of women to inspire him, Pickett regularly brandished his vision of a more prominent social role for women. He did so, not by assailing gender inequities in the fashion of a later generation, but by spotlighting and affirming advocates for women, as well as women who themselves were making breakthroughs. So when Mrs. Muthulakshmi Reddi, deputy president and first woman member of the Madras Legislative Council, called for an end to the practice of dedicating girls and young women to Hindu temples, where under the name of *devadasis* (servants of the divinity) they lived as prostitutes, Pickett urged the Government of Madras to stand with her. "Government," he wrote, "cannot dictate what its citizens shall believe, nor control or purify religion, but it can protect its citizens and more particularly its citizen-children from being made victims of degenerate religion." And when Mrs. George Cadbury, a Quaker and member of the famous Cadbury chocolate family, was selected as the first female president of the National Free Church Council of Great Britain, he noted: "This is the first time . . . a woman has ever held such an office in Britain. And evidently she is filling the post with great credit to herself." And when a couple of months later he read that Drew Theological Seminary had conferred, for the first time, the degree of Doctor of Theology on a woman, Miss Olive M. Winchester, he congratulated her and advised the scandalized of their need of an attitude adjustment. Yet Pickett was not willing just to be a voice for women. He encouraged them to use their own voices. So, the pages of the *Indian Witness* regularly displayed the bylines of the brightest women in the church, including those of Indian women like Satyavati Chitambar, wife of J.R. Chitambar.

ALTHOUGH, AS EDITOR, WASKOM no longer lived and breathed evangelism as he had in Arrah and his first term in Lucknow, he nevertheless kept a deep interest in discovering and commending God's ways to India's heart. From communication to contextualization to controversies, he served up a smorgasbord of issues and insights especially for missiological palates. Though written in the 1920s, many of his missiological concerns sound contemporary. Consider the following:

On Ethnocentrism and Missions

[October 1927] To some ardent nationalists in Asia, the sending of missionaries from the West implies racial pride and arrogance. He would be a bold man and a mistaken one who would say that there has been nothing of that sort among the supporters of missions. An oft-used Urdu expression fits here as though it were made for this situation: *Kyá Kábul men gadhe nahin hain?* (Are there not asses in Kabul?) Kabul is known for its superior horses but presumably there are some humble asses there also.

[October 1928] "Foreign" is not a suitable word to incorporate in the names of Mission Boards and Societies that are international in spirit and outlook. And unless the missionary organizations that work across national boundaries are international in spirit and outlook, they can achieve little in the conditions that are developing and will shortly prevail . . .

When Jesus taught a lesson on the need of inter-racial sympathy and practical helpfulness he described the good man who helped the needy one of another race as a "neighbor." He did not emphasize the distance between them in residence and race by calling either a foreigner but their nearness to each other in common humanity. The church must think of the whole world as a neighborhood.

In an earlier plea for scrapping the "foreign" in missions, he used a funeral motif:

We would like to bury the Board of *Foreign* Missions and the Women's *Foreign* Missionary Society . . . As their successors, and heirs we would propose a Board of International Missions and the Women's International Missionary Society.

He reminded his readers that the Methodist Church in 1927 was American, Indian, Chinese, German, Swedish, Malaysian, Philippine, Mexican, and Chilean. He pushed them to think of this global church as "a bond" that could hold nations together and make for "peace and understanding."

On Open-air Preaching

[November 1929] A majority of the people now living in India will never hear a Christian sermon unless there is a revival of open-air preaching . . . Open-air preaching is difficult. The chief reason that it is not so highly esteemed now as it ought to be is . . . that its difficulty has not been recognized. There is a feeling that one can preach in the bazaars and *melas* and that no sort of preparation is necessary. Pastors who would not think of appearing before their congregations without hours of preparation, if they engage in open-air preaching at all . . . begin to speak without having more than the haziest idea of what they will say.

On the same theme, a year earlier (November 1928), Pickett outlined a plan for open-air preaching, which he urged not sound like a sermon one's seminary professor of homiletics would approve. Instead, he advocated three to six-minute sermonettes, conveying one vital truth and avoiding platitudes to which all will assent. Pickett proposed that an open-air service begin with a friendly gesture and informal opening remarks, followed by a *bhajan* or *gazal*, a well-spoken sermonette, the sale of Scripture portions, and, then, the repetition of the cycle. He urged that Scripture portions be sold and tracts be given free, but that the distribution of tracts should wait until the conclusion of the service.

On Intolerant "Tolerance"

[December 1928] When in Europe the Inquisition was committing thousands of heinous murders in the name of religion in a diabolical attempt to impose uniformity of belief, Mysore and many other Indian states were practicing a broad tolerance in matters of creed.

India has a right to be proud of this record, and should jealously guard it against destruction. The record is in danger now from a quarter from which attack has not been expected. Intolerance is manifesting itself in the stolen garb and name of tolerance. Pretending to see intolerance exhibited in every act of proselytizing, some advisers of the nation would prohibit all changes of community affiliations and all expression of changed convictions . . . Here is a very serious exhibition of intolerance.

Pickett's missiological interest was also on display in his choice of articles for publication. They ranged from "Indianizing" the church, to the villager in the city, to expressing the gospel as a story in song. Often, he featured series of articles on Christian witness and Indian religions and cultures. They included Cyril Modak's insightful set of pieces on "Hindu Bhakti and Christian Worship" and Gertrude V. Tweedie's four-part series on "The Middle Class Moslem Woman of Lucknow," followed five months later by her three-part, "Inter-Penetration of Islam and Hinduism in India." Pickett also published articles on indigenous music, cultural contributions of the missionary enterprise, and missionary reports from other lands.

Pickett's own articles ranged from maximizing the symbolism of Christian festivals to extolling the advantages of drama in communicating the gospel. "In India," he wrote, "drama should be able to serve the church even better than in Western countries. It has never been in conflict with religion here." Contrasting drama with other methods of presentation, he asked: "How many children of Christian parents are unconverted and uninterested in religion because the presentation of Christian teaching to them has been dull and has never gained their attention!"

Pickett's articles and editorials not only revealed his interest in missiological issues, but showed the depth of his insight. Take the following discussion of form and meaning:

Generally speaking Indian Christians are far less inclined than in preceding years to regard as sacrosanct the forms in which truth has been expressed . . . There is a growing appreciation of the fact that the fundamental truths of the Christian faith may be expressed in many different ways, all of them effective but some more effective with one group than with others.

Another example of Pickett's support of efforts to contextualize the gospel was his response to a Vengal Chakkarai proposal in the *Christian Patriot* in 1925. Chakkarai was appealing for funds for a Christian version of a Hindu temple:

> I make a special appeal to non-Christians who would like to see Christianity in India freed from foreign control and costume . . . To me and others such a temple for communion with the Lord and for establishing spiritual contacts has long been the cherished object of their life, and some of them would pass from the world in peace, if they could see this scheme materializing before their eyes.

Pickett wrote:

> Mr. Chakkarai is the leading spirit in the Christo Samaj of South India. He represents a small but active group. They have proven themselves to be independent, fearless and animated by a passionate conviction of the soundness and importance of their views . . .
>
> We welcome this proposal as we welcome every action that may draw anyone to Christ and may reveal him more clearly to anyone.

Pickett was not free of anxiety, however. He was comfortable with the idea and said he hoped that the construction of the temple would proceed, but only if they guarded against the "Hinduising of . . . Christians"—that is, "making Christ . . . to them merely one among a number of Hindu gods or *avatars*." With only the proviso that it did not compromise allegiance to Jesus Christ, Pickett lauded creative Christian thinking in the service of naturalizing Christianity.

Though he was not trained in theology, Pickett was often theologically insightful. Consider, for example, this passage on the meaning of conversion:

> The difficulty [with conversion] is to frame a definition that is sufficiently comprehensive and yet definite and concise. Starbuck's famous definition is that "conversion is the process by which the God-consciousness hitherto marginal and vague

becomes focal and clearly defined, passing from its former position as an accessory to its new position as the most real and penetrative influence in life." This is not entirely satisfactory because it is undeniable that some people have experienced conversion after years of God-consciousness that was both focal and clearly defined. Paul of Tarsus is an illustration; John Wesley is another. Religion was the most real and penetrative influence in Wesley's life long before his conversion experience, when his heart was "strangely warmed" and he became a new man in Christ Jesus.

Pickett esteemed practicable responses to missiological challenges. For example, concerning village evangelism, he wrote:

Village men and women generally have more time for leisure in the exceedingly hot weather than at any other time in the year. They are very fond of sleeping in the middle of the day and of sitting around and talking until a late hour each evening, particularly when there is moonlight. The preacher who conquers the lassitude that the heat inevitably brings and goes night after night to the villages where his Christians live, to talk with them and to teach them, is gloriously rewarded, for he finds an opportunity such as it is very difficult to secure in other seasons of the year.

An ongoing emphasis in Pickett's writing was the holistic imperative of complementing verbal witness with acts of love and kindness. He never tired of reminding his readers that Christ had fed the hungry, befriended the outcast, and healed the diseased. Because of this emphasis, some criticized him for giving "undue attention to social service." But, though he prioritized the spiritual needs of people, Pickett refused to divide spiritual needs and social concern: "The preacher who fails to keep the spiritual uppermost in his ministry . . . sacrifices his best opportunity of helping [village converts] out of their material troubles."

Not surprisingly, this complementary emphasis brought salvos from the other side too. A Hindu acquaintance insisted that Christian service was enough. "Leave the people to go their own way religiously," he said. Pickett regarded the counsel as friendly and worthy of a respectful hearing but, ultimately, as bad advice. He reminded the man that Jesus "healed the sick and the afflicted, comforted the sorrowing and fed the hungry"—but "[he] did not leave people to go their own ways religiously." In one editorial, Pickett described a village of untouchables. Eager to learn about Christ, they contacted a Christian minister. The minister observed rightly that they also had great material and health needs, to which he addressed himself. But he ignored the need for which the villagers were most hungry: the knowledge of God, which is to be found in Christ. Pickett was totally convinced that, along with other tangible expressions of love, "the obligation to reveal Christ is continuous." In fact, for him, that was the quintessence of evangelism: "simply revealing Jesus."

Pickett argued that "everyday is a good day for evangelism," and he could never understand Christians who found it distasteful.

> A Christian who doesn't believe in evangelism is a contradiction in terms; he doesn't believe in himself, for all Christians are made through evangelism [nor] does he believe in his Lord Jesus [who] was preeminently an evangelist and trained his disciples to be evangelists more than all else.

To those who found certain methods of evangelism distasteful, Pickett argued that true evangelism is more love than duty. He stressed what he called, "Golden Rule Evangelism." He contended that if Christians shared their faith on the basis of the Golden Rule, "there would be a great increase in the amount and a vast improvement in the quality of evangelistic effort." By Golden Rule evangelism, Pickett meant a commitment to sensitive, non-manipulative ways of commending Christ. He argued that one should apply the test of love to all methods of evangelism.

> It is a deplorable fact that evangelism has seemed to some people an ugly thing because they have witnessed attempts at it that have not been in harmony with the Golden Rule. It is possible to make truth horrible and charity insulting and evangelism repulsive, but it would be as foolish to turn against evangelism as against truth and charity.

For Pickett, Golden Rule evangelism was not restricting but liberating. It emancipated evangelism from the confines of the pulpit, the Sunday school, and even the home.

> The Golden Rule Christian . . . doesn't confine his efforts at all. He extends them. He welcomes an opportunity to indicate what Christ Jesus can do for men and women who need him, wherever it comes: on the street, in the shop or office, the school room or the railway carriage, on the playground or in the drawing room. And in all these places he considers the fitness of things. He respects people's opinions and even their prejudices where he can do so without condoning wrong.

In Pickett's mind, Golden Rule standards of evangelism, which bar pejoratives, refuse to trivialize others' faiths, and abominate ethnic and racial condescension were also the best response to the charges of proselytism. To take Golden Rule standards seriously was to both take others seriously and to keep an open mind. But one should not go too far, he cautioned: "The mind ought to be always open for selected truth, but there is never a time when it ought to be open for whatever comes along." He explained:

> There can be no healthy mental or moral life where there are no convictions. Mental growth depends upon accepting certain approved facts and refusing to entertain or grant admittance to any doubts about them . . . We accept the axiom that the whole is greater than a part and our minds do not open for a contradiction of it.

14 Mott's Proposal

In the spring of 1925, when the Picketts were returning to India for Waskom's new job as *Indian Witness* editor, they met Allen Parker and his wife, Irene in Liverpool. Like the Picketts, they were changing ships for Bombay. Parker was the principal of Woodstock School in Landour, Mussoorie, in the foothills of the Himalayas. He had arrived in India as a Presbyterian missionary in 1918. After stints at an agricultural institute and as principal of Jumna Christian High School in Allahabad, he had, in March 1922, come to Landour. Perched atop a 7,000-foot ridge, the little cantonment town of Landour, above, beyond, and still distinguishable from Mussoorie, contained a military barracks and infirmary, several private estates, Kellogg Church, a cemetery, and a bazaar. Woodstock, on lower part of the steep, southern slope of Landour Hill, was originally a multidwelling estate. In the mid 1850s, a group of British women had bought it and converted it to a girls' school. Later, after the Presbyterians had become owners, the visionary Parker came on the scene. Parker had already set in motion a series of big changes. These included amended objectives and a development program. Also in the works was a new building program that, by providing both girls' and boys' hostels, would make Woodstock coeducational. Moreover, the school, which had been Presbyterian, was becoming interdenominational and international. All this Parker shared with Pickett on the voyage to India—along with a question: would the Methodists be interested in participating?

The following year, when the financially strapped school in Naini Tal, with which the Methodists had been cooperating, decided to join with Woodstock, American Methodist acceptance of Parker's proposal was inevitable. On Saturday, June 19, 1926, a group of Methodist missionaries constituted the Methodist Woodstock Association, with Pickett as secretary-treasurer. They proposed that the Methodist Episcopal Church accept Parker's invitation on the same basis as other invited missions from

America which, by then, included the Disciples, the Baptists, the YMCA, and the Mennonites. The five Methodist annual conferences in India had already agreed to come up with nearly half of the required annual outlay of 12,400 rupees to pay three teachers they hoped to appoint.

Some large estates were for sale close to the school. Several of the cooperating missions, including the Methodists, would soon purchase them and divide the houses into smaller units for parents whose children were enrolled. After that, the Landour community swelled—especially from April to July, the hot season on the plains. Each estate had a name: Mt. Hermon, Oakville, South Hill, Abergeldie, and Eastwood, the one purchased by the Methodists. Here is how Pickett described it when they were getting set to purchase it in 1926.

> It contains 35 or more acres immediately adjoining Woodstock and has a wonderful house with five or six suites . . . hard-wood floors and very fine furniture, including a piano and a billiard table, which may be sold for some hundreds of Rupees. Also there is a lovely cottage with ample accommodation for two of our families, a tennis court, electric lights in both houses, ample servant houses, one additional building site cleared [and] ready for construction to begin, another building site almost ready, and several sites that can be made available by cutting away the hill sides and erecting pushtas [retaining walls].

Eastwood was owned by a widow. The estate had been developed by her husband, an engineer. Though it had reportedly cost the couple between 80,000 and 100,000 rupees, it was available for only 50,000 rupees. To the Picketts and the other families, whose children would soon be students at Woodstock, Eastwood's availability was providential. All that was needed was a modest down payment and some up-front money for improvements. The balance could easily be covered by rental fees, which each family would pay with its hill allowance. First, however, the Board of Missions would have to approve the plan. Pickett sent off a formal request. Word of the board's approval came two days after Christmas.

Eastwood House was also known as *dudh walli kothi* (the milkman's house), no doubt a reference to the original owner. The Methodists converted it to six apartments, and—though not in the beginning—the Picketts would stay in one of them for several years. Overestimating the importance of Eastwood and Woodstock in the Pickett family pilgrimage would be hard. Ruth and the children, of course, spent the most time there, but nearly every year, Waskom himself came for a few weeks too. On this pattern, followed by many missionary families of that era, Pickett wrote the following:

> Many needs combined then to draw missionaries from different Churches, Societies and lands of origin to summer resorts in the Himalayas. Among these were vacations, respite from the extreme heat of their stations on the Plains of India during May, June and July, visits with their children who were in boarding schools for nine months of the year, and need to exchange understandings, hopes and fears with people of like motivation and purpose who were then, or at some time had been, dealing with more or less comparable undertakings and problems.
>
> Few missionaries spent more than a month there in any year but a succession of Conferences, and school and community gatherings insured valuable opportunities for all visitors throughout those three months.

For most families, enrolling their children in Woodstock School was the beginning of a long tradition, for after their children's two kindergarten years, 10 more were required for graduation. Thus, every year, in late March or early April, the whole family—except the father, who would come for a few weeks during the hottest part of the summer—would journey by rail to Dehra Dun, 125 miles northeast of Delhi. From Dehra Dun, they would travel by bus five miles across the plain to Rajpur, and then several more miles up a narrow switchback, with scenic views at every hairpin turn. Partway up the mountain, at the Sunny View bus terminus, they would get off and continue on foot the rest of the way to Landour. Coolies carried the luggage.

By May of 1927, seven Methodist families were already living in Eastwood House and Cottage. The Picketts, however, were in Fir Clump, owned by the Raja of Tehri. Fir Clump was next to Eastwood Estate, and when the Methodists purchased Eastwood, Parker consented to take a lease on the raja's house, get it set up for three families, and allow the Methodists to rent it at a reasonable price for a prolonged period.

By the time he joined the family at Fir Clump, in April, Pickett was near collapse. Though temporary, an urgent personnel need had arisen at the publishing house. So, besides his full plate of editorial and other commitments, Pickett had, for nearly half a year, been serving as associate manager of the Lucknow Publishing House. "That made my fifth major job, and for the five months . . . I hardly knew when night came," he confessed to the mission board's A.E. Chenoweth. "Even now [late June], more than two months after turning it over to Aldrich, I do not feel rested."

An important item of Woodstock business for the Methodists was to find two missionary teachers for the next school year—preferably one who could teach domestic science and another who could take charge of one of the grades and could also teach high school mathematics in a pinch. One of those they came up with was Robert Fleming, a 24-year-old bachelor. Fleming had no classroom experience, but he did have an M.A. from Drew University and came highly recommended. He also had a great love for the outdoors. Fleming would eventually become as identified with the history and lore of Woodstock as his principal, A.E. Parker was. And Fleming and the woman he would eventually marry would introduce Pickett to one of the most exciting chapters of his life.

Another pivotal person with whom Pickett would become friends in those early summers at Woodstock was Donald A. McGavran, a young Disciples missionary. The McGavrans lived in the Ellengowan House near the Kellogg Church, where Pickett preached regularly in the summers of the 1930s. McGavran had first come to Mussoorie as a child, when his own parents—missionaries in central India—made their annual pilgrimage there.

OF THE YEARS FOLLOWING WASKOM'S return to Lucknow, none was more notable than 1928. The year began with the meeting of the Southern Asia Central Conference, which focused much of its attention on the ongoing mass movement controversy. As one might expect, after seven years of working with a mass movement himself, Pickett gave the proceedings plenty of coverage in the *Indian Witness*. In fact, he featured the entire 4000-word text of a plenary address by Clyde Stuntz, which offered insights from Stuntz' mass movement experience in the Punjab.

At the heart of the controversy was the claim made by some appraisers of the mass movements that it could now be shown that supporting them had been a mistake. After 40 years, they argued, it was apparent that the masses of village Christians had made little progress—spiritual, cultural, or economic. The issue of "arrested development" even came up in the

Bishops' Address, written that year by the outspoken and controversial Bishop Frederick Bohn Fisher. The address encouraged less emphasis on numbers and more on character. "Character is not created in the mass," wrote Fisher. Pickett was not ready to reject the surmise of the mass movement critics but felt that a careful study was needed. He reminded the critics that a minority of mass movement believers had found the courage, or gotten enough education, to move beyond the demeaning existence to which they were ascribed by the caste system. In response to one critic, who lifted up the alternative model of an indigenous, self-supporting city church he admired, Pickett pointed out that the pastor, most of the church's officers, and at least 80 percent of the members had come out of conversion movements.

IN THE SPRING OF 1928, WORD CAME that L.L. Pickett had died. On May 9, he had been preaching at Middlesboro, Kentucky, a small community on the Tennessee line near the Cumberland Gap. Mama Ludie was with him. When, after the service, they had returned to the house where they were staying, they sat up with their hosts discussing the second coming of Christ until about 11:00. When they finally got to their room, L.L. told Ludie he was feeling numb. She called for help, but he lost consciousness. Forty hours later, he died. He was 69. At the funeral, in the Administration Building of Asbury College, Mama Ludie wore white, as L.L. had once requested.

After the death of her husband, Ludie Day Pickett became even more involved in the prohibition movement. In late June, she went to Houston as a delegate to the Democratic National Convention. In a speech to the assembly, she implored the delegates not to nominate the frontrunner, Governor Al Smith of New York, who opposed prohibition. To appoint Smith, she warned, would be perilous for the party. When Smith was nominated on the first ballot, she went home to work for his defeat. She was no doubt greatly reassured when, in the election, Herbert Hoover won all but eight states—including Al Smith's own state of New York.

Earlier that Spring, over Easter, the Jerusalem Conference (or as William Paton of the International Missionary Council preferred: not a conference but the meeting of a council) had met on the Mount of Olives. It was the first expanded meeting of the International Missionary Council since its evolution in 1921 from the Continuation Committee of Edinburgh 1910. Although he was not one of the 240 in attendance, Pickett followed the conference with great interest. He published details of it in several articles, one of them a feature story by E. Stanley Jones.

In June, however, Jones himself became the story. Word came that the General Conference wanted to make him bishop and had begun to vote for him, but that Jones had withdrawn his name. Nevertheless, reasoning that even though Jones did not "choose to run," he would surely acquiesce to a draft, they elected him anyway. Jones reluctantly accepted, apparently regarding their persistence as a call from God. However, once he got away from the crowded floor of the assembly and had a chance to reflect further, he concluded that it was not God's will after all. In the next edition of the *Indian Witness*, Pickett defended Jones' decision:

> Many of our readers had hoped that Dr. Jones would return to India as one of the bishops of this Church. The Church wants and needs as its bishops men who are not seeking the office and are spiritually strong enough to refuse it. But a man would be in a tragic position if he tried to administer the responsibilities of the Episcopal office with the conviction that in doing so he was obeying man rather than God. And the church in India will be better served by having Dr. Jones return to his evangelistic work with the assurance that he did what God wanted him to do than to episcopal administration robbed of the strength and glow of his religious experience by the fear that he had obeyed man at the cost of disobedience to God.

WHEN, IN AUGUST OF 1928, THE INDIAN All-Parties Conference assembled in Lucknow, the meeting's proximity and Pickett's fascination with politics practically foretold his presence. As editor of the *Indian Witness*, he wrote in advance for a press pass and immediately got back a ticket for all the sessions.

The conference was in direct response to Britain's recent appointment of the Simon Commission, but to get a fix on its place in the stream of Indian politics in the 1920s, one needs to go to early February 1922, when Mahatma Gandhi was planning a massive civil disobedience campaign in the Bardoli district of Gujarat. When word came of a terrible clash on February 5, at Chauri-Chaura, 80 miles east of Lucknow, Gandhi was shaken. The clash had resulted in the deaths of 17 constables and 172 farmers. Although it was widely regarded as an anomaly, Gandhi abruptly called off his non-cooperation movement. The move disappointed and chagrined up-and-coming national leaders, including, especially, young Jawaharlal Nehru. After Gandhi's move, Jawaharlal's father, Motilal Nehru, C.R. Das, and others who had hoped that the non-cooperation movement would squeeze the British into important concessions, felt compelled to adopt a substitute strategy. By using obstructionist tactics within the legislative councils, they resolved to dismantle Britain's self-serving 1919 reforms. However, because Gandhi and some others were not convinced this was the way to go, Motilal Nehru and C.R. Das formed a new "Swaraj [self-rule] Party." Then, in November 1927, Britain announced that a commission under Sir John Simon would tour India with a view to future constitutional reforms. Out of bald hubris or, perhaps, indecision on account of the splintered state of politics in India, the British failed to include any non-whites on the commission—even though Indian leaders had been the ones insisting on such reforms. Ironically, though, that omission gave the factions the incentive the needed to overcome their differences. Calling for a boycott of the Simon Commission, they presented a united front for the first time in years. When John Simon and his party arrived in Bombay in February 1928, therefore, the citizens of the city greeted them with black flags, mass protests, and indignant processions. An all-out *hartal* stopped work and closed shops. Wherever the Simon group went—from Bombay to Calcutta to Madras—they got the same reception.

The gathering Pickett attended was one of two meetings of an All-Parties Conference of Indian leaders whose explicit purpose was to respond to criticism from British Secretary of State, Lord Birkenhead. Birkenhead had appointed the Simon Commission and later criticized Indian politicians for failing to provide any broadly supported proposals for constitutional reforms. Pickett regarded the chance to attend the Lucknow meeting as "one of the great privileges of my life." He was especially impressed, it seems, with the debate between father and son—the moderate Motilal Nehru and the radical Jawaharlal. By then, Jawaharlal and other young lions of the Congress Party, like Subhas Chandra Bose and Srinivas Iyengar were convinced the Swarajist strategy did not go far enough. They called, therefore, not just for a new constitution and dominion status but total independence from Britain. Pickett favored the moderates' stance but seemed as interested in the debate as the issues.

Motilal presented the proposals of his group and advocated them with all the skill and finesse of a great lawyer. Hearing him I thought his report would surely be accepted and approved. Then Jawaharlal would arise and begin speaking slowly and in a low voice, very precise in all he said, and gradually increase the vigor and passion of his speech until the whole audience began cheering.

Though they cheered the son, they followed the father. The official report, called the "Nehru Report" was to be debated at the Calcutta All-Parties Convention in December. Largely the work of Motilal, it defined dominion status as the accepted goal for India. It opposed separate communal electorates (commending, instead, loyalty to the nation as a whole), affirmed voting privileges for all adults and equal rights for women, and objected to reserved seats for Muslims in majority provinces (causing most of the Muslim community to withdraw its support). Pickett liked the statement:

It has been so skillfully prepared and represents such a victory of statesmanship over communal and party bickerings that we believe many who had expected to attack it, have had . . . to admire it.

Still, he wasn't completely satisfied:

It does not go as far as we would like to protect the interests of minorities, nor to assure the depressed classes a chance to come into their rightful share of the good things of life.

AROUND THAT SAME TIME, PICKETT GOT an unexpected communication from John R. Mott. As part of an eight-month, globe-circling tour, whose purpose was to interpret the message of the Jerusalem Conference, Mott was coming to India for the Madras meeting of the National Christian Council of India, Burma and Ceylon. The NCC had replaced the National Missionary Council (1914-1922), which emerged from Mott's unifying sojourn in India in 1912.

In preparation for the New Years event, Mott planned to be in India for three to four months. He wondered if, ahead of the Madras meeting, he could meet with Pickett for a day or two to discuss the state of missions in India, especially the uncertain status of mass movement work. Pickett consented but wondered why Mott would want a personal conference with him.

A visit from Mott was a big deal. As both chair and symbol of the International Missionary Council, and as the key figure at Jerusalem '28, Mott powerfully influenced the mission scene. One missionary described him as "the father of us all." When he came calling, Mott was 63; Pickett was 38. Mott wanted to know about Pickett's background in mass movement work and what he now thought about the movements. Pickett related his experience in Bihar, highlighting the results obtained in areas where Emanuel Sukh and Ishwar Dayal had worked. Mott said that he was anxious for the church to come to one mind about conversion movements. Were they, as some said, from God? Or were they, as others insisted, the main obstacle to the evangelization of India? He asked what Pickett would think of requesting the National Christian Council to conduct an impartial, scientific survey of 10 or a dozen Christian conversion movements in India. Since Pickett had that spring and fall published two editorials underscoring the need for sound social research, Mott probably already knew his answer! The aim, said Mott, would be to gather the facts needed to respond, once-and-for-all, to the long-standing conflict of opinion about the value of mass movement work.

Mott's proposal was not entirely unprecedented. In fact, the Church Missionary Society had just assembled surveys of its mass movement work in the central Punjab, Travancore, Tinnevelly, the Telugu area, Western India, and the United Provinces. But although informative, the CMS surveys were meant as much for financial supporters of the mission as for those directly connected to the work. The surveys in the series typically included historical and descriptive overviews, some statistics, generalizations about issues and trends, and an assessment of needs. But though they purported to be dispassionate and free from "purple patches of eloquence or emotion," in fact, they frequently lapsed into just that, as the following paragraph illustrates:

Would that we could transport you . . . to the plains of Tinnevelly. There you would see the long lines of laborers, men and women, in the fields—their backs bent, their faces to the soil. It is a parable of their life. As they go to their work, the unimaginably lovely lights of early dawn surround them, but their souls are dark. The singing of birds is heard, but their ears are deaf to the songs of liberty. At evening the flags of sunset stream across the sky and the mountains stand in holy stillness, but not for them!

Mott, however, envisioned a more thoroughgoing, objective survey—one less susceptible to misapprehension and distortion in its production. In the United States, the Social Survey Movement was flourishing. A new kind of survey had come into its own, one that employed combinations of direct observation, interviewing, onsite data-gathering through questionnaires and schedules, and data-producing experiments. A contemporary description of this new kind of survey defined it as

> a cooperative undertaking which applies scientific method to the study and treatment of current related social problems and conditions having definite geographical limits and bearings, plus such a spreading of its facts, conclusions and recommendations as will make them, as far as possible, the common knowledge of the community and a force for intelligent coordinated action.

It was this sort of survey—including: (1) data gathering with a view to resolving a specific issue, (2) tabulating and summarizing the data, (3) drawing conclusions or "findings," (4) making recommendations, and (5) publishing the results for those who stood to benefit from them—that Mott was contemplating, and with which, as chairman of the board of the Institute for Social and Religious Research, he was intimately familiar.

Throughout his career, Mott had possessed a keen sense of the importance of preserving valuable data and documents, and of doing sound research. As early as 1911 he had asked his friend, John D. Rockefeller, Jr., for help in establishing a missions research center. He had already recruited newspaperman Charles H. Fahs as his personal researcher, historian, and archivist. For the past few years, Mott had realized his fact-finding passion through the work of the Institute for Social and Religious Research, headquartered in New York City. The organization's roots lay in the Interchurch World Movement's survey department. When the IWM closed shop, the department survived, through the vision of Mott and four other incorporators (and Rockefeller), as the new ISRR. Their goal, said the incorporators, was to apply "rigorous scientific methods" for the advancement of the religious, educational, charitable, and moral well-being of society. Throughout its history, Mott served as president of the ISRR and as chair of its board of directors. From start to finish (1921-1934), Rockefeller money undergirded the organization. Most of its research projects involved the Protestant church in the U.S., but some of them—the *World Missionary Atlas*, for instance, and the *Fact-Finding for the Laymen's Foreign Missions Inquiry*—reflected Mott's global interests.

So when Mott broached his idea, he was not projecting the CMS genre of surveys but a study that would employ the state-of-the-art social survey methods being applied in the projects of the Institute for Social and Religious Research—one that promised to provide the data needed to settle mass movement fact from fiction once and for all.

Pickett's response was that such a study would be invaluable, which was what Mott wanted, and probably expected, to hear. But would Pickett be willing to support it publicly? The editor said that he would.

Preceding the December National Christian Council meeting in Madras was an October 9-11 Cawnpore meeting of the United Provinces Christian Council, of which Pickett was secretary. At that gathering, John R. Mott proposed that a missionary with mass movement experience be added to the staff of the National Christian Council to oversee a scientific study of the movements. The gathering agreed and further decided that Pickett should be their spokesperson at the national meeting in Madras. But Pickett had no idea what he was getting into.

15 The Mass Movement Study

The six-day meeting of the National Christian Council of India, Burma, and Ceylon, got underway on December 29, 1928, a Saturday. The venue was the Women's Christian College of Madras—chosen for its facilities and setting, but mainly because it showcased the collaboration of 12 separate missions. Since this year the program called for responding to the Jerusalem findings, nine representatives each (instead of four) came from the 10 provincial councils. The NCC also coopted 10 more than the customary 20 at-large delegates—but just for the extra agenda. So, through Wednesday evening there were 120 participants. Then, for the last two days and the regular agenda, there were the usual 60.

The enlarged Monday to Wednesday sessions were crammed with reports and discussion groups. The delegates, therefore, looked forward to the inspirational times that framed each day.

As much as anything, they were inspired by the setting—the domed college chapel. Next to the colonnaded path on which they approached the chapel was a lovely garden with a magnificent tree and square pond, but even these did not rival the appeal of the chapel's elegant curves and welcoming doors and porches. From the first evening, its simple charm and blend of East and West drew the delegates in. As they drew near the sanctuary, residual conversation from an hour of introductions and socializing broke off and, in Pickett's words, "quietness descended."

Upon entering the chapel, they sat, Eastern fashion, directly on the polished floor of black slate and white marble. Except for a couple of benches in the back there were no seats. And except for a thick, blue curtain that traced the curve of the apse, there were no decorative additions. In front of the delegates, though, was a plain, wooden cross, subtly accented by the glow of a small lamp, a reminder of the college motto: "Lighted to lighten."

In that first chapel session, John R. Mott spoke exuberantly of rising tides of religious interest everywhere he went. Unprecedented numbers of people were on a quest for truth, he reported, and the churches must not fail to respond. It was just the sort of message Pickett had hoped for, one that he wished every Christian in India could have heard. It struck him as an eloquent and much needed counterbalance to the pessimism that since the war had become, in his words, "more endemic . . . than influenza."

Mott's upbeat message set the tone for the week. It persisted not only in the public addresses but also around the dinner table and in private conversations. Everywhere, one overheard glowing echoes of the Jerusalem IMC Conference, and Mott did everything he could to make the present gathering feel like an extension of it. That is not to suggest that there was no disagreement or debate during the week—there was plenty of both. Overall, however, Mott's positive note pervaded the conference, including even the final business sessions, where uncommon cooperation and a newfound optimism prevailed. New proposals for rural reconstruction and empowering the younger churches found acceptance. Innovative ideas for Christian education and a fresh resolve to tackle racism got their due. And evangelism, which the social gospel had forced to the ropes in recent years, rebounded with approvals for both the proposed mass movement study and the appointment of a mass movement secretary. Moreover, the elections of Bishop V.S. Azariah of Dornakal to the NCC presidency and John Z. Hodge, a missionary of the Regions Beyond Missionary Union, to the secretaryship—both of them friends of evangelism—offered hope that the mood and initiatives would last. Christian India, it seemed, had its own rising tide. Hope was in the air.

Nevertheless, when the proposal for the mass movements study came up, the voices were by no means all assenting. In fact, as the debate progressed, Pickett thought that the one downbeat intonation of an otherwise upbeat conference might be the study's rejection. The thought did not last long though. After two successive persons had spoken favorably, Mott signaled Pickett to seek recognition from the chair. Once invited to the platform, Pickett pressed for the study as the way to at last resolve the perennial mass movement debate. His argument proved creditable. A substantial majority passed the following resolution:

> The Council considers that as soon as possible a Secretary should be appointed to initiate, in close consultation with Provincial

Christian Councils, a study of the work in Mass Movement Areas, and asks the Executive to prepare proposals regarding the choice of a Secretary and the raising of funds, outside the regular budget of the Council, for his support.

By their March 25-26 meeting, the executive committee of the National Christian Council had settled on Pickett to direct the study, a development he had not expected. Meanwhile, John R. Mott, having concluded his 13-weeks stay in India, was taking his Jerusalem review to Burma, Siam, the Philippine Islands, and Japan. After concluding his Asia tour with visits to Korea and China, he sailed home from Shanghai, via Japan, on May 24. In New York, Mott presented the NCC resolution to the directors of the Institute for Social and Religious Research. They agreed to consider a formal proposal for funding at their fall meeting and came up with a list of questions. Mott decided to take no chances. With NCC Secretary Macnicol on the mend from a bout of illness, and Secretary-elect John Z. Hodge not yet on the job, he saw to the production of the proposal himself. Later that summer, aboard the *Mauretania*, he and William Paton, secretary of the International Missionary Council, prepared a draft and forwarded it to Macnicol. "Do not be alarmed by the extensive nature of the proposal," Paton wrote in his cover letter. "You cannot get money out of this crowd unless you ask for a lot, and we put down every conceivable thing we could think of in case it might be needed." Paton added that the appeal had to come from the NCC and that, after making corrections, Macnicol should sign it on NCC letterhead and send it back. Paton, substitute secretary for the ailing Macnicol, would as head of the International Missionary Council be representing other requests to the ISRR. He was anxious that his role be seen as that of an "ex-Secretary of the Indian NCC (1922-1926), who just happened to be at Madras when the business came up."

In October, Mott wrote to Paton concerning the ISRR's disposition on the mass movement study proposal. The ISRR board had given preliminary approval, and the proposal was now with the staff for detailed review and project blueprinting. Final approval would likely come at the board's January meeting. Meanwhile, Mott would apprize Pickett of the staff's need to confer with him during his time in America.

PICKETT'S BIGGEST TASK WHILE in the U.S. was to be a second round of fund-raising for the still financially troubled Lucknow Christian College. In the October 31, 1929 issue of the *Indian Witness*, newly appointed acting editor, Fred Perrill—Pickett's choice—announced that J. Waskom Pickett was now, after five years, "On Leave . . . " from the *Witness*, the Board of Temperance, the United Provinces Christian Council, the Methodist Woodstock Council, and the Warne Baby Fold. However, the whole headline read: "On Leave—to Work." As Perrill put it, Pickett was not vacationing but taking on a task that would call for all the "psychological wizardry" he possessed. No doubt, Perrill had in mind news stories—just out—of Wall Street's Black Thursday, October 24, when stock prices began the precipitous plummet that, by November 13, would remove 30 billion dollars from the American economy. With Pickett's fund-raising trip for LCC just days away, a more dispiriting development was hard to envision. Yet, even though the timing was terrible, LCC was fortunate in securing Pickett. In spite of the crisis, his "wizardry" would work enough magic to bring in many thousands of dollars for the debt-ridden school.

Upon reaching New York, Pickett went to the offices of the ISRR on Seventh Avenue to begin a crash course in the institute's policies, procedures, and methods—requisite to successfully directing the mass movement study. When he left for Christmas in Wilmore, Galen M. Fisher, the executive secretary, gave him two assignments: first, prepare a memorandum describing, more fully than the original proposal, specific needs the mass movement study would address; and second, prepare a revised, more realistic budget.

Pickett's response to the first request included the following aims, with a paragraph of elaboration for each item: (1) an agreed upon definition of the mass movement; (2) more detailed information on the involved tribes and castes and the mass movement's impact on them; (3) a better understanding of the causes of group lapses and reversions; (4) an assessment of the degree to which oppression intensifies for converted depressed-class people; (5) a review of the relationship of converts to their kin-groups and communities; (6) a read on whether the mass movement tends to produce churches divided along caste and tribal lines; (7) an analysis of the influence of the mass movement on higher caste Hindus and Muslims; (8) and a feel for general public reaction to mass movement conversions.

The institute staff's response to Pickett's revised budget was that it was still lean. They enlarged it further—more than doubling for instance the 2,500-dollar annual salary he had suggested. The move was not extraordinary; it merely reflected the institute's policy of making sure no study prematurely exhausted its funds. Typically, they insisted that the budgets for their studies include such things as:

(1) renting and equipping an office including desks, chairs, telephones, typewriters, adding machines, filing cabinets, etc.; (2) salaries of workers and expense of holding meetings and conferences; (3) cost of supplies such as correspondence paper, stamps, tabulation forms, printing of schedules and question-naires, purchase of maps, books, magazines, etc.; (4) traveling expenses; (5) special costs such as having tabulations made by a commercial agency, making of graphs and charts, paying advisors, hiring an editor, etc; (6) costs of writing and printing the report; (7) expense of making the results of the study known to the public including magazine and newspaper publicity, holding of conferences, etc.

Besides all these, the ISRR habitually appended a reserve fund, amounting to a minimum of 5 percent of the total.

Delighted, as much as astounded, by the generous provision of the institute—never before nor afterward, in his view, did he work on an adequately funded project—Pickett nonetheless held firm on the pay raise, refusing the increase. To accept the higher salary, he maintained, would lead his colleagues to think money motivated him.

By mid-January Pickett was again up north for the 37th gathering of The Foreign Missions Conference of North America, which since 1893 had been bringing together mission society representatives for consultation and cooperation. In most respects, this year's conference was a litany of the familiar—the same faces, the same voices—a scenario that probably delighted Pickett, since among the conference speakers were Mott and another of his heroes, Robert E. Speer. Speer, a Presbyterian layman known as "the incarnation of the spirit of the Student Volunteer Movement" had like Mott been prominent at Jerusalem.

The one notable innovation at this year's conference was the fact that a woman—Helen B. Calder—was chair. She called the meeting to order in the Viking Room of Atlantic City's Haddon Hall on Tuesday evening,

January 14. She would wrap it up Friday noon. One of the addresses—given on the first morning by Dr. William Adams Brown,
professor of systematic theology at Union Theological
Seminary—provoked a comment from Pickett. Brown spoke on the
challenge of humanism as a form of secularism. While underscoring the
inevitable insolvency of secularism, he spoke empathetically of those who
embraced it without compromising their principles. Given the opportunity
to respond, Pickett said:

> I am . . . grateful for the declaration of Dr. Brown that we must
> meet the challenge of humanism in the same spirit of sympathy
> in which the Jerusalem Conference viewed the great ethnic
> religions. Out in India, I have been compelled to feel very keenly
> that many of the declarations that are being made with regard to
> humanism and the whole wide range of secularism have hardly
> been fair. There have been suggestions that it is incumbent upon
> the Christian forces to unite with the forces of other religions to
> crush secularism. The fact is that secularist forces, as I meet them
> in India, are more akin to us in spirit and in program than the
> forces of organized religion with which we are in contact there.
> Many of the very finest spirits of India have been driven into
> secularism by the abuses of religion, and I feel that it is wrong
> to call the Christian forces to any alliance with those forces
> against which these fine spirits are in revolt, in order to crush
> them.
>   Call attention certainly to the dangers of that secularistic
> outlook, but let us not be unfair to those people, as I feel and as
> I know that some others in India are feeling. We have been unfair
> in some of our declarations.
>   More than that, let us not ally, or seem to ally, Christianity
> with the forces that have been guilty of oppression. I feel that we
> can do nothing that will more definitely check Christian progress
> in India than to say to India, or seem to say to India, that
> Christianity is an alliance with all religious forces, for India is
> awake today to the evils that some of these religious forces have
> forced upon them. She is in revolt against them, and she will not
> think more highly of our Lord because we, His disciples, seek
> today—in our appreciation of the finer things of the ethnic
> religions, and in our repentance, shall I say, of the older attitudes

that we have taken towards those religions—to ally ourselves
with them now.

A few days after the Foreign Missions Conference, Pickett got word
that the ISRR board had approved the revised mass movement study
proposal. Selecting a technical consultant was the next step. Pickett's
choice was C.H. Hamilton of the Virginia Polytechnic Institute. However,
while negotiations with him were going on, he had to back out apparently,
and Professor Warren H. Wilson of Union Theological Seminary in New
York was chosen instead.

In India, some church leaders were concerned that a technical
consultant from America might hinder as much as help the study—that
such a person might exert too much Western influence on it. Mott,
therefore, wrote to the new NCC president, V.S. Azariah, assuring him
that appointing a consulting expert was customary and was "in no way
[meant to] fetter or embarrass Pickett and those associated with him in
the actual conduct of the survey." Nevertheless, for 20 years, Wilson had
been used to directing studies, not serving in an advisory capacity.
Moreover, he was a take-charge person.

Pickett would also learn after his arrival that Wilson came with
definite assumptions about mass movements and mass movement work.
But, of course, Pickett was partial too. He was not chosen to direct the
study, as some have supposed, because he had been critical of it. Upon
the contrary, anyone who knew his seven-year history with the small mass
movement in Shahabad or had read his *Indian Witness* editorials knew that
he was an advocate of mass movement work. Why, then, did the NCC
choose Pickett? They chose him, in part, because he had a reputation for
getting things done. Also, he had brought the proposal. However, one
suspects that the main reason Pickett got the job was because John R. Mott
wanted him to have it!

For political reasons, Mott also wanted Bishop V.S. Azariah to be
designated ex-officio chair of the study. "It does not demand any undue
demands on your time," Mott assured him.

It will, however, identify the Indian Church with the undertaking
... which, I am sure, you will agree is most desirable. Moreover,
it will give added confidence in many quarters because it is so
widely recognized that you are an outstanding authority on all
that pertains to the Mass Movement.

Following the Foreign Missions Conference of North America, Pickett devoted the rest of the winter and spring to an array of tasks: meeting with prospective Lucknow Christian College donors; giving speeches, including one at the Methodist New England Conference; guest preaching in Methodist churches; contacting missionary societies with workers in mass movement areas; becoming, under Warren Wilson's tutelage, conversant with the current methods of survey work; and working out details for the projected launch of the survey in the fall. Meanwhile, Mott, on tour again—Greece, Scandinavia and the British Isles—enlisted William Paton to get key endorsements for the survey. And at various gatherings—like the CMS conference at High Leigh, near Manchester, England—Mott exploited every opportunity to praise the mass movements, which he called—along with the Five Years Campaign, just beginning in China, and the Kingdom of God Movement in Japan—one of the three greatest evangelistic movements in the world.

ON JUNE 22, 1930, PICKETT, FRESHLY honored with a D.D. from Asbury College, sailed for England and Bombay. In London, he converged with his father-in-law, Bishop Robinson, who, too, was returning to India. However, they would not sail on together. The venturesome bishop, who had missed the Titanic's maiden voyage by a blink, had arranged instead to travel by "air mail," which meant flying with Imperial Airways, the forerunner of the British Overseas Airways Corporation (BOAC) and British Airways. Imperial had taken over the carriage of mail to India in 1927 and had started every-other-week service in 1929. The journey would have been long and tiresome. The carrier flew several types of craft over segments of the route and had to resort to surface travel to link segments together. In all likelihood, Robinson flew from London to Basel by Armstrong Whitworth Argosy and continued by train from there to Genoa. From Genoa, the three-engine Short Calcutta flying boats operated the route to Alexandria—via Ostia, Naples, Corfu, Athens, Suda Bay and Tobruk. From Alexandria, another train was needed—down to Cairo. In 1930, the Cairo to India legs were being flown in De Havilland Hercules to Karachi and Jodphur. That left one last leg to Bombay, the end of the line. In spite of the tortuous route, however, Robinson beat his son-in-law by thirteen days!

When, on July 23, Pickett's ship, the SS *Pilsna*—on which Gandhi would return from the Second Round Table Conference the next year—docked in Bombay, he had the "great joy" of finding Ruth waiting at the pier. After a brief stay with the Robinsons, Waskom and Ruth returned to Lucknow by way of Poona where, on the 28th, Waskom reported to the National Christian Council secretariate, "full of plans and enthusiasm," said J.Z. Hodge. The Picketts got home two days later, but, within a few more days, were off again, by train, to Dehra Dun and up to the cooler heights of Mussoorie and Landour. Pickett set to work immediately, sending follow-up letters to Lucknow Christian College subscribers, arranging for the start of the mass movement survey in October, and resuming his responsibilities as Secretary of the Methodist Woodstock Association.

In Bombay, Poona, and Lucknow, Pickett had found the political air less restive than he had feared. During his time in the U.S., the Indian National Congress' relations with Britain had stiffened. Before his departure, the harsh British reaction to Simon Commission protests and the mulishness of British Conservatives toward Indian aspirations had so exasperated some Indian leaders that even a new, friendlier British regime and an October 1929 pledge by the new viceroy (Lord Irwin) of dominion status and a soon-to-be-convened round table, could not prevent the metamorphosis of Congress into a more combative form. It was Mohandas K. Gandhi, though, who swayed and shaped the Congress that met in Lahore in December of 1929. The cheers Pickett had heard for Jawaharlal when the All-Parties Conference met in Lucknow were, with Gandhi's pre-Congress negotiations, translated into votes, putting young Nehru at the helm of Congress for the first time. Likewise, in response to Lord Irwin's round table invitation, Gandhi had forged a set of preconditions for cooperation. However, since no one, the Mahatma included, expected the British to comply, Gandhi's conditions merely served as a thin excuse for a new all-out campaign of civil disobedience. The launch had followed "Independence Day," January 26, when Congress members adopted a pledge of *purna swaraj* (complete independence). To help muster the masses, the 61-year-old Gandhi had announced a march to the sea to make salt—which, by law, Indians could not make or sell. The long trek got under way on March 12 amidst the protests of Congress members who considered it rattlebrained and the ridicule of local British officials. There were a mere 79 in the procession when it began. However, a little more than three weeks later, when Gandhi and his followers reached the Arabian Sea, the 79 had become tens of thousands, and the whole world knew about it. The Salt March was the signal to crank the engine of civil disobedience into high gear, and that is what happened. Demonstrators placarded for independence; government and railway workers quit; companies withheld taxes; and thousands boycotted British goods and businesses. By May, the flags and colors of Congress were everywhere.

However, it didn't last. By the time Pickett returned to India in midsummer, the fervor had already begun to fade. For one thing, the British had clamped down hard with arrests. They had jailed 60,000 Congress Party members, including Gandhi. For another thing, many Indians did not share Congress leaders' cynicism of the new viceroy's round table move toward dominion status. Moreover, even some early supporters had become unhappy with having to put up with the turmoil and heavy economic strain of the campaign. Thus, while Gandhi and the Nehrus (father and son) refused to take part in the round table unless Lord Irwin met their latest litany of conditions, more than 50 Indian leaders chose to go along with the proposal. Among them were Sir Tej Bahadur Sapru and Srinivas Sastri representing the liberals; the Aga Khan and Mohamed Ali Jinnah, the Muslims; Sardar Ujjal Singh, the Sikhs; B.S. Moonje, the Hindu Mahasabha; K.T. Paul, the Indian Christians; a representation of princely rulers; and Bhimrao Ramji Ambedkar, representing the depressed classes.

Since the Congress-inspired civil unrest was copiously covered by the press in America and Britain, Pickett had expected on his return to find a populace up in arms—another 1921. But he, himself encountered "not the slightest sign of ill-feelings for Europeans or Americans." In his view, the situation was "incomparably better than . . . 1921." He observed, "While Britain faces a very difficult situation . . . she does not stand to lose much if she will definitely grant Dominion Status within a short period." Nonetheless, the calm surprised him. He hoped, for the sake of the coming mass movement survey, that it would last, for cooperation from both Indians and local British authorities would be essential.

16 The Survey Underway

Pickett spent September of 1930 in Landour, eager for October and the arrival of Warren Wilson, the technical adviser. Wilson was to arrive in Bombay on the first. From there he and Pickett would go to the Dornakal diocese—east of Hyderabad—where they would begin the study.

John Z. Hodge, the new National Christian Council secretary, planned to meet them there to see the launch. Pickett had known Hodge since his days in Bihar. Hodge had been one of the four young Harley College men (the other three were Hicks, Banks and Wynd) who had taken on an area composed of Champoran and Saran Districts north of the Ganges in an agreement with the Baptist Missionary Society, which had failed to make any real impact on the area. While serving there, Hodge had provided accommodation for Mahatma Gandhi and his wife during the early days of Gandhi's crusade on the peasant farmers oppression by some of the indigo planters. Hodge was running an English Bible class and Gandhi used to attend the class and gave talks on the Sermon on the Mount. Gandhi's wife was unwell then, and the missionaries tended to her needs.

The choice of Dornakal seemed apt. In the words of John R. Mott, it was "the largest, most efficient, and most productive piece of Mass Movement work in India." Also, Bishops Azariah and Whitehead, the most visible exponents of the Anglican showpiece, had just published a book on the mass movements that was already entering its second printing.

In a way, coming to India was to complete a vow for 62-year-old Warren Wilson. More than 40 years before, as a first year student at Oberlin College in Ohio, he had been an early signer of the SVM pledge, dedicating himself, if possible, to missionary service. After graduating from New York's Union Theological Seminary, Wilson had pastored two churches. The second one, in Brooklyn, gave him the chance to take graduate courses in sociology at Columbia University. There, under the tutelage of Franklin H. Giddings, the dean of the modern social survey, he was introduced to social research. In fact, he became one of the first students to get his doctorate under Giddings. His dissertation, "Quaker Hill: A Sociological Study," was the second study ever in the sociology of rural life in America. From 1910, Wilson was the superintendent of the Department of Church and Country Life of the Presbyterian Church, USA. Starting that year, he recruited young theological students to make a series of social and religious surveys in a dozen states in nine geographical regions. Since 1926, Wilson had been a lecturer on the rural church at Union Seminary. He also headed the Presbyterians' summer institutes for rural pastors. Thus, from an American perspective, he seemed the perfect fit to advise a study focused on village India.

Wilson landed in Bombay on September 23, a Tuesday. But because he was a week early, no one greeted him. On hearing Wilson was in Bombay, Pickett, who was still in Landour, hurried off to meet him. However, on the train he became ill and on arriving in Bombay was admitted to the hospital with appendicitis. They operated on him the next day, the first of October. Unfortunately, Hodge had already gone to Dornakal for the start of the survey. Wilson notified him by wire of Pickett's condition. After the surgery and another wire from Wilson, Hodge relayed word of Pickett's progress to William Paton, adding the technical consultant was now "at large somewhere." While Ruth Pickett attended the patient, Wilson was getting acquainted with two mission stations in that part of the country.

When, later that month, Hodge got to Bombay, Pickett was looking fit and was just a day away from being released. He reported that he had already been working on revisions required by the delay. The plan to survey five selected areas remained intact. Nevertheless, with the postponement, Pickett had found it necessary to juggle the dates and move the first field testing from Dornakal to Etah, in the North. From his room, Pickett had already written to A.E. Slater and William H. Wiser—both of the American Presbyterian mission—about coming to Etah in the United Provinces for the trial study. Despite the short notice, he was confident that they would extend an invitation, for the Presbyterians had hoped to be included all along.

Wilson was by now back from his tour. In a letter to Paton, Hodge described his first impression of him:

I spent a day—a very warm day—in Bombay and had the rare privilege of looking for the first time on a "technical consultant" in the person of Dr. Warren H. Wilson. It was a relief to find him a man like ourselves, a little more dogmatic perhaps, . . . a man accustomed to the measuring rod, who at a moment's notice can reduce our multifarious Christian activities to £.s.d.

There at the hospital, the three met for two hours, completing the changed calendar through May, when Wilson's connection to the study was to end. No doubt, they also discussed possible side effects of the political situation. In contrast with the calm Pickett found on his return to India in Bombay, Poona, and Lucknow, Hodge, on a just-completed visit to Nagpur, had found nationalistic feeling running high. Also, in London, the first of three Round Table Conferences for negotiating arrangements for a new, federal constitution—was about to meet.

The next day, Waskom and Ruth set off for Lucknow, followed a few days later by Wilson. From there, Pickett and Wilson attended a mass movement conference in Cawnpore, then traveled on to Etah, 47 miles northeast of Agra and the Taj Mahal.

THE TRADITION OF SOCIAL SURVEYS into which Pickett was about to plunge was very old: as old as the survey of England ordered by William the Conqueror in 1085 and recorded in the *Domesday Book*, as old even as the census of Caesar Augustus, which brought Joseph and Mary to Bethlehem. Still, the present-day survey movement's roots were fairly new, beginning with Charles Booth's 17-volume study—begun in 1866—of London's poor, and the 1907-08 Sage Foundation's Pittsburgh Survey, which sought to go beyond hypothesizing about urban forces by collecting the facts of labor and life in the city. By the 1920s, the American Social Survey Movement, largely the offspring of the Pittsburgh Study, was in full flush, with innovations coming in an almost continuous flow. The staff of the Institute for Social and Religious Research kept abreast of these, routinely seeking the best possible matches of procedures and instruments to surveys under their sponsorship. In addition, they adopted the correlative practice of tailoring what they borrowed to the specific needs and contexts of each survey.

The NCC survey would be much in this tradition. Preliminary interview schedules (questionnaires) would be field tested and adjusted. Then, the formal survey would get underway, with the teams interviewing in the villages and recording responses for tabulation and review. Added data would be obtained from church records, censuses, and other public records. All of this information would find its way into compilation books, which would eventually be used to tell the story of the survey and provide the basis for the findings. These would be published in book form, with a set of recommendations. Although the book would generalize on the overall study, as each survey area was completed, the director (Pickett) would prepare special reports for sponsoring agencies and their workers.

WILSON BROUGHT WITH HIM FROM America a survey method he had refined over two decades and in which he took much pride. Though some of the data he used was from existing records and documents, most of it came from interviews that employed various schedules (questionnaires). Though notables like Charles Josiah Galpin of the USDA, Edmund deS Brunner and H. Paul Douglas of the ISRR, and George F. Warren of Cornell University had developed the schedules for rural America, Wilson claimed that, with some minor adjustments, they would be equally suitable for India. When missionaries and Indian church leaders voiced their skepticism, he countered that they were confusing "findings" with methods:

> Missionaries have data, the "findings" drawn from many experiences, conferences, conversations; and at the first they refused to believe that American survey processes could be adapted to India except by one who possessed these data and had participated in these conferences and experiences . . . The method of Survey is entirely different from the findings; the essence of method is adaptation. Social survey is a flexible technique of inquiry suited to change, in any particular, at a day's notice.

When the missionaries raised questions about using American-made survey instruments, Wilson was offended. But their hesitancy was more caution than suspicion. They knew that the social sciences, though promising, had not achieved the status of "exact" (physical) sciences. They knew, too, how easily villagers misinterpreted what missionaries said and how often missionaries misread villagers. Later, under the heading, "Statistics Do Not Tell the Whole Truth," Pickett would give three examples from the survey of misleading statistics.

Wilson deflected questions about the "foreign" interview schedules by insisting, first, that they were not fixed and, second, that they were not the main thing. At the heart of his approach, he said, was a "social sequence" study of (1) the physical habitat (2) the economic basis of living (3) the social organization (4) community institutions, and (5) the schools and churches of the research subjects—in that order. As long as the sequence was followed, the schedules could be adjusted. That combination, Wilson believed, made his method foolproof. It could be applied with equal effectiveness "in a London suburb or an African Kraal."

The evolution of the Household Schedule, which became the centerpiece of the questionnaires used in the mass movement survey, was an example of the flexibility Wilson boasted of. "I have never before surveyed households," he later reported, "but after conversations with missionaries in Gujarat and Kolapur State, I recommended a schedule of investigation of Households which we have steadfastly followed." Another example of the flexibility he featured was the freedom to add subschedules when desirable. For instance, when exploratory conversations in the villages around Etah revealed the prevalence of *jajmani* economic relationships, involving the exchange of food production for goods and services, it became clear the Household Schedule needed supplementing. So, with the expert counsel of William H. Wiser and John E. Wallace, the Etah team came up with a *jajmani* subschedule, a single sheet that could be inserted into the Household Schedule as needed.

Wilson believed the flexibility shown by incorporating the *jajmani* subschedule should put missionary reservations to rest. In his words, the liberty to adapt the schedules based on local input and field-testing made his method "of no nation." Further, Wilson argued that no one was more sensitive than "the technician" to the need to put aside "the conclusions arrived at in the study of one country . . . [while studying] another people and another manner of life."

PICKETT AND WILSON ARRIVED IN ETAH for the test survey on Saturday, November 8, 1930, as did E. Graham Parker, who would serve as subdirector, and Parker's wife, who would serve as host. More helpers arrived Monday, the day the field testing was to begin. They would spend the first two weeks interviewing people in 52 nearby villages. In the first week, only the Household Schedule was ready for testing. However, two more schedules, still with the printer, were expected any day.

The first day of the Etah survey was a practice day, with everyone trying out the Household Schedule, which could supply more than 350 pieces of information. It covered family members, religious status, church participation, religion in the home, creedal knowledge, caste relationships, moral and social stances, idolatry and superstition, house and lot, animals owned, sources of income, record of income, debts, and contributions to the church. From day two, the survey team's routine included dividing into two groups, going by car to the Christian *mohallas* (caste or occupational sectors of the community), and asking to meet with the men. (They used the Household Schedule to interview family heads.) Whenever possible one or two of them would find the headman of the village, usually a *zamindar*, and interview him with what they called the "Bystander Schedule." They also had schedules for upper class Hindus and Muslims (what they knew and thought about their Christian neighbors), Christian women and their families, superintendents of churches and missions, and pastors (about their work, congregations, and families). At day's end, they copied the interview data into transcription books.

During the second week, work began on the compiling books. Wrote Wilson: "These had to be made so the whole array of material could be seen in its correlations, and in a form convenient for summarizing and comparing." Pickett, who had gone to make arrangements at the next survey site, arrived back in Etah at the end of the third week, on November 29. As Wilson explained, by then the data was well enough organized to let Pickett review the results so far, and preview what the summaries might contain.

It is necessary in a social survey to foresee the end at the beginning. The data as secured must be kept in orderly form so that they will from the very first inform the mind of the Director as to the conclusions he will arrive at in the end. For this reason we have from the first transcribed and compiled the data coming in day by day, in order that the Director might daily see the trends of the investigation and might devise means to discover any truths that lay just beyond the edge of our Inquiry.

Wilson thought a survey should grow and be cumulative in nature. Picturing where the data was leading and starting an early draft of the final write-up showed what they needed to find out, what they were overlooking, and what they were wasting their time on. They could also critique and confirm tentative conclusions, and add anecdotes and comments—all while the day was still fresh in their minds.

Because he needed to lay the groundwork for the next place, Pickett could not be present much of the time. His advance work consisted of two parts. First, he needed to galvanize the local superintendents and pastors into a team. This he did by stressing the importance of the survey and explaining what it would take to do it well. After that, he enlisted their help in formulating a plan, recruiting the best people to help, arranging for lodging and cooks, finding a car or two to get around in, and buying needed supplies. Depending on its geographical size and the number of villages involved, this advance work could take several weeks.

A few days before each survey started, the local superintendents and pastors called on the village headmen to arrange for the visit of one of the teams, explain how they would proceed, and answer questions. So when the workers arrived, they typically found village representatives waiting outside the village for them—as often as not with a welcoming band, typically consisting of a wooden flute and some percussion instruments. After greeting the team, the local leaders and the band would lead them through the village so everyone knew they were there. When they arrived in the Christian *mohalla* which, because the Christians were untouchables, was outside the main part of the village, their hosts washed team members' hands, offered them *charpoys* (lightweight, portable bedsteads) to sit on, or made them feel welcome in some other way. Then the interviewing began.

ALTHOUGH WILSON WAS PROUD OF THE flexibility of his method, ironically, he was uncomfortable with the changes Pickett and his team made in the interview schedules. They must have been extensive though, for Pickett described the revamping at Etah as "radical," suggesting the instruments they finally adopted could no longer be regarded as unalloyed importations. Even so, weaknesses remained. For instance, the Household Schedule assumed a correspondence between Bible memorization (specifically, the ability to recite the Lord's Prayer and Ten Commandments) and spiritual achievement. However, in some survey locations, the emphasis of the missionaries and Indian church leaders was not on Bible memorization, but on Bible knowledge—that is, familiarity with Bible stories.

SURVEY INSTRUMENTS ARE NEVER BETTER than the interviewers who use them. That Pickett recruited helpers who were familiar with village protocol and etiquette is not in doubt. That he made sure they were trained in the use of the questionnaires is not in doubt either. We also know the field-workers shared insights they picked up while interviewing. For instance, Pickett spoke of how they learned to interview heads of households with their relatives and neighbors present, because, often, they interjected corrections or volunteered extra information. We don't know if Pickett and Wilson made their survey takers aware of issues like the inclination of respondents to give agreeable answers when the reputation of someone present was at stake. For example, would an interviewee be likely to offer criticism of the church if either the pastor or a missionary was there? Of one difficulty, everyone was aware—that of having to translate interview questions from English into the local vernacular and the response into English. To help them in this, Pickett and Wilson used Indian college graduates as interpreters.

Without computers and modern tabulation procedures, the task of copying the thousands of daily data entries into transcription books and assembling summaries and correlations of all the information into compiling books, must have seemed daunting. But there was no effort to restrict the number of interviews. By survey's end, the household interviews alone numbered 3,800. That was as Wilson wanted it—large and impressive. In his own words,

> Quantity production is necessary in a Survey. The readers must be impressed with the numbers of instances studied. The investigators themselves must base their conclusions upon a very large number of instances in order that they may be positive that the trend of the social process has been discovered.

IN MAY OF 1931, SIX MONTHS AND 1,500 interviews after the project had gotten underway, Wilson returned to America as planned. The following October, Pickett and his associates completed the last survey in the Ghaziabad district near Delhi. Officially, Wilson reported that it had been "a joy and a satisfaction to follow the energetic and able leader . . . in his masterly organization of the material and his executive administration of this wide reaching study." In fact, though, Wilson seemed to have left with a fair amount of resentment. Two months after his return, he vented his frustration in a letter to the ISRR's Galen Fisher. Offering advice for a similar situation, he declared that making a missionary director of the survey had been a mistake. "The responsibility for the scientific processes involved ought to be committed to the person who knows how to do surveys," he wrote, "and there should not be left any doubt, or possible question, as to his authority." Getting around in a remote field, printing the questionnaires, and taking care of business matters was one thing. But the survey itself, Wilson insisted, should be left to "the Technical man," who should have responsibility for "the selection of localities, scope and adequacy of particular studies, number and type of workers to be employed—and other manners and methods to be employed in securing the data." Further, he contended, the technical man should write up the survey story, having responsibility for the facts, the methods used to get them, and even their "effect upon the mind of the reader." Wilson added that he was not questioning Pickett's competence for administrative management ("I have found no missionary better fitted for this responsibility"). Nor did he say how certain other ingredients might factor in choosing a director—like relational and leadership skills, or knowledge of the culture and its languages. Instead, he digressed from his recommendations to an attack on Pickett himself. He complained that Pickett was slow to embrace his advice, unwilling to give him the credit he was due, and given to adding material of his own—though some of it, he said, was "excellent."

It was probably inevitable that Pickett and Wilson would lock horns at points. First, they had different ideas about the purpose and use of the survey. Pickett and the NCC were interested in the survey's implications for the future of mass movement work. That was why they set up the survey. But Wilson's interest—reflecting his personal priorities—was the survey's implications "for those whose desire to devote their lives in the most efficient manner to the office of the Pastor serving a well-defined Parish with a certain number of people under his care." So, while Pickett wanted data for evaluating the effectiveness of mass movement evangelism and disciple-making, Wilson wanted data for helping pastors shepherd their fixed flocks. While some information would be useful for both aims, the perceived purpose of the study was bound to shape the content of the schedules, the final database, and, of course, its interpretation.

A second area of disagreement between Pickett and Wilson was their divergent views of the missionary's role. Pickett thought of the missionary as a change agent, as one interested in altering the worldview, faith, self-image, and hopes of those who lived in constant fear, followed false gods, depreciated themselves, and were shackled by fatalism. Wilson, on the other hand, favored a more passive role. He marveled, for instance, that, in contrast to India's cities, he had seen no beggars in the villages. So, the caste system seemed to work—leave it alone: "Let no American or European scorn these methods of organization [the village caste system] until he has pondered the fact there is no breadline in India," he scolded after his return. Similarly, on the poverty and indebtedness of untouchables, Wilson argued:

> The debt situation in India which is so generally deplored should, I believe, be looked at from the poor man's point of view . . . The money lenders are not the only cunning men in India. The peasant who borrows has often no intention of repaying until he is compelled. He is the only man in India who gets prompt service under the inflexible and rigid credit system of that country. His wants are attended to. He gets money when he needs it. He pays it back when he is compelled. It is true that since the Indian peasant is a bad risk he pays a high rate of interest. The principal comes back to the lender in the form of excessive interest. But it seems to me that we should look upon it from the point of view of the Indian peasant, and not of the American economist or reformer.

Perhaps Wilson's view did not reflect callousness towards untouchables as much as the functionalist notions of French sociologist Emil Durkheim that dominated his era. If it worked, you didn't tinker with it. So, in contrast with missionaries like Pickett who thought of themselves as bearers of the gospel and agents of social change, Wilson wanted to see "the Indian village organization be preserved," as he put it. In classic functionalist form, he stated: "The preservation of it would mean that a beautiful and competent culture by which men are fed and clothed and housed shall be preserved for the future." Thus, one can imagine a very different mass movement report had Wilson directed the study and interpreted its findings instead of Pickett.

Another difference between Wilson and Pickett centered on Wilson's insistence that good method insured the dispassionate detachment of the social scientist. The result, according to Wilson, would be a value-free investigation—something that (by implication) could not be expected of missionaries. Pickett not only took issue with the contention, but alleged that Wilson "came out from America . . . supposing his chief contribution to the study would be to question some assumptions that seemed to him to provide motive power for the Mass Movements." Of course, Wilson was no less disapproving of the biases of the missionaries and Pickett From his point of view, Pickett's tendency to veto his recommendations and go his own way constituted clear evidence of such bias.

PICKETT BEGAN WRITING HIS book-length report of the survey in the summer of 1932 while on furlough in Kentucky. Asbury College provided an office in its Morrison Library. Except for the daily visit of his daughters, Elizabeth and Miriam, he worked uninterrupted. When the summer was over and the Pickett family had moved into a missionary apartment in Ventnor, New Jersey, Waskom completed and edited the book with the help of Wilson and the ISRR staff.

Throughout the process, Wilson continued to complain—especially to NCC Secretary Hodge, who heard from him "frequently and voluminously." Hodge reported Wilson's apprehensions in a letter to ISRR director Galen Fisher, but Fisher assured Hodge that steps had already been taken address Wilson's concerns. Wilson, however, may not have been convinced of that, for he evidently stuck with a request he had made two years before: that his name not be included in the report. "To do so," he told Fisher at the time, "may make it easier for Dr. Pickett, who finds it difficult to estimate justly the value of the services of an associate." No doubt that is why, except for a brief mention of his contribution in John R. Mott's Foreword, Wilson's name does not appear in the first American edition of *Christian Mass Movements in India*. However, in an Indian edition, Pickett included this tribute:

> Dr. Warren H. Wilson was selected as technical consultant and the Board of National Missions of the Presbyterian Church in the United States most generously released him with a portion of his salary for a year. His experience in survey work in American Home Missions and the freshness of his approach to the Mass Movements in India enabled him to make an invaluable contribution to the study.

WHEN IT FINALLY APPEARED IN LATE November, *Christian Mass Movements in India* brought Pickett's name to prominence in missions. But as Pickett wrote in his opening pages, many besides him were responsible for the final product: John R. Mott, the instigator; various NCC personnel; consultants in India (like Wiser and Wallace); ISRR staff members, local leaders who helped make arrangements; the 83 people who worked on the surveys; and the thousands who agreed to be interviewed. Nevertheless, because Pickett coordinated the study, wrote its story, helped interpret its results, and made the recommendations based on them, the name most closely associated with the 1930-1931 survey is fittingly his.

To exaggerate the impact of *Christian Mass Movements in India* on the Indian church scene would not be easy. When it appeared, "a chorus of praise" greeted it. None of the cheering was more enthusiastic than that of Dr. Donald A. McGavran, who wrote: "There has come a book sent by God, and its name is Christian Mass Movements in India." He also described it as the missiological book of the century, although, at the time, only a third of the century had come.

Pickett's book led many mission boards and Indian churches to rethink and alter their priorities and methods, with mostly good results. By today's standards, the Pickett study had a number of weaknesses, some of which were recognized even then. Still, a review of social surveys up to that time shows it to be the most ambitious survey of its kind ever carried on outside the West. The nearly 4,000 interviews by Pickett and his colleagues resulted in the largest database ever amassed on Dalit Christian society. To this day, it remains the seminal record of the Indian mass movements. But it was important for another reason too: its legitimization of employing the social sciences in missiological research. Data gathering and analysis was now seen as vital to laying bare false assumptions and revising the missionary agenda. Up to that time, those fundamental ideas had not been widely acknowledged. *Christian Mass Movements in India* had a lot to do with changing that. It served as a wake-up call, alerting churches and missions to mistakes of the past—often destructive mistakes—and the path to more fruitful evangeliza tion in the future.

17 Applause and Dissent

While Pickett was overseeing the National Christian Council's mass movement survey, another missions study, the Laymen's Foreign Missions Inquiry, was underway in India, Burma, China, and Japan. Ironically, it too was inspired by John R. Mott, funded by John D. Rockefeller Jr., had interdenominational endorsement, and was guided in part by Galen Fisher and the Institute for Social and Religious Research. The inquiry advanced by stages. The first, in 1930, was an investigation phase. "Fact-finders" under Fisher's direction gathered an extensive collection of historical, financial, sociological, and administrative information from the four Asian fields. Then, in 1930-1931, in a compressed and digestible form, the ISRR put what it had gathered into the hands of a denominationally representative, but independent, "Commission of Appraisal." It was chaired by William Ernest Hocking, a philosophy of religion professor at Harvard. After its own whirlwind tour of the same four countries and many interviews, the commission made an assessment of mission programs and policies and gave recommendations for mission executives and boards. Next, it published *Re-Thinking Missions*, a summary of findings, in which the views of Hocking himself loomed large. Beginning in April 1933, the commission also issued seven supplemental volumes at the rate of one per month. These contained information from the field studies they had used in preparing *Re-Thinking Missions*.

Just before the release of *Re-Thinking Missions*, the Laymen's Inquiry leaked some of its more provocative findings. These were given to the press in a series of bulletins. On one level, their publicity ploy worked phenomenally. It evoked sensational headlines, feature articles in the papers, a slew of interviews with Commission members, editorials, and even sermons. With its call for a speedy devolution of missionary work and other revolutionary ideas, the commission was thus able to stimulate great interest in its work even before the report came out. However, while the puffery whetted appetites, it also raised eyebrows. For some, it lessened confidence in the objectivity of the Laymen's Report.

Re-Thinking Missions—the full title was *Re-Thinking Missions: A Laymen's Inquiry after One Hundred Years*—reflected the new liberals' ecumenical ideals and growing skepticism of the theology and methods of the missionary movement. Doubts about the exclusivity of the gospel, appreciation of certain facets of non-occidental faiths, and an evolving vision of a future faith consisting of a mosaic of the most sapient insights of various world religions had been making headway for some time among the liberals. Ernst Troeltsch's *Die Absolutheit des Christentums und die Religionsgeschichte* (1901), which had questioned the absoluteness and finality of Christianity had foreshadowed the trend, but only in the 1920s, alongside the Fundamentalist-Modernist controversy, did it begin to attract broad-based notice. Professor Hocking's opening chapters of *Re-Thinking Missions* fueled the skepticism, calling forth a mixed response. For some, his analysis was a welcome breath of fresh air. But others thought his promotion of religious dialogue and mutual influence among the world's religions would torpedo the future of missions. Financier John D. Rockefeller, Jr. in New York and new Nobel laureate Pearl S. Buck (who had hosted Hocking in China during the inquiry and who would become romantically involved with him) both lauded the report. On the other hand, respected mission leaders like Presbyterian Robert Speer, though appreciative of some parts of it, were troubled by its agenda-laden aspects. And some denominations that earlier had backed the inquiry now sought to distance themselves from it.

In general, the Methodist Episcopal Board of Foreign Missions greeted the Laymen's Report favorably. Of special interest were the four volumes of fact finders' evaluations, which prompted the board and its missionaries to review whether Indianization in the Methodist church was more apparent than real, whether enough progress was being made toward self-supporting churches, and whether church expansion had been too rapid and too scattered. However, their response to Hocking's *Re-Thinking Missions* was less enthusiastic.

At the time, Pickett said little publicly about the Laymen's Report. But, later, in response to an inquiry from John R. Mott, he told why he thought it got a mixed reception:

Its unsatisfactory results were due, I think, to the following facts among others:

(a) Over-confidence in their own judgements.
(b) Inadequate preparation for their task.
(c) Undue discrediting of the Church as an institution and of its appointed ministers.
(d) Overestimation of the significance of much of the testimony received from non-Christians and an indiscriminating, even naive, acceptance of the testimony of certain non-Christians as objective and friendly, when it was in fact influenced by a desire to weaken the motivation for Christian missions.
(e) Too little sense of responsibility, too much readiness to express judgements reached in their discussions with regard to their possible harmful effects and without counsel with men and women who might have helped them to wiser decisions.
(f) The importation of divisive theological issues that should have been rigorously excluded from the report.

Pickett himself had been interviewed in Lucknow by members of the Laymen's Inquiry as he was finishing his own study. But if he hoped for any encouraging note in their report on the mass movements, he was sorely let down. Instead of an opportunity, it presented the mass movements as "an outstanding and difficult problem" and encouraging them as expediency, misguided zeal, or buckling to pressures to put up good numbers.

[It would be] easy to dismiss the whole mass movement as a mistake due to the readiness of missionaries to follow the lines of least resistance and to their zeal for enrolling large numbers of converts, a zeal intensified at times from pressure from the home base for statistical results.

As if that were not ice water enough, they added:

Zeal has outrun discretion; the work of the missionaries has been lamentably over-extended geographically; groups and individuals have been taken in wholesale without adequate preparation and, too often, left with little or no religious nurture. Baptism has been used with scandalous unrestraint, in a fashion without justification in either the theory or the practice of the Christian church.

A final dousing concluded that the missionaries' errors could be

> corrected only by a rigid policy of concentration which seeks quality rather than quantity and does not measure success by statistical results . . . It is significant how many of the best leaders in missionary service, both in India and in China, have approved the suggestion of a moratorium on statistics.

ON NOVEMBER 29, 1933, FIVE DAYS after the annual meeting of the Methodist Board of Foreign Missions, held in Brooklyn, Pickett sailed for India. Despite the smell of fresh ink in his suitcase—his book's gestation period at Abingdon Press having come to its terminus—he was as frustrated as he was buoyed. He had hoped the mission board would help him make the most of his last weeks in America by finding him opportunities to engage church leaders in the implications of his study. There was, for example, a series of interdenominational gatherings in progress. But the hoped-for openings did not come, and even at the annual meeting his input was relegated to a short slot on the final afternoon—and that following Arlo Brown, president of Drew University and a member of Hocking's commission.

When he got to Lucknow in early January, Waskom was greeted by Ruth and the children. Their arrivals there had not long preceded his, for on returning to India at the end of summer, Elizabeth, Miriam, and Margaret had gone off to boarding school in Mussoorie, and Ruth and young Douglas had gone to stay with Ruth's parents, John and Elizabeth, at the episcopal residence in Delhi. Since Elizabeth was not well, Ruth had waited until December to go to Lucknow and prepare for the arrivals of the rest of the family.

From America, Pickett brought with him the first notices of his book. The publisher, Abingdon Press, had nested them strategically in a bevy of other notices that together added up to a full-page ad. One said:

> We have heard a great deal about the Indian Mass Movements and we have heard them connected with the gibe "Rice Christians." At last we have a scientific approach to the whole question of the Outcastes of India, their background, their social, economic and religious disabilities under Hinduism during centuries, and their future in Christianity. Dr. J. Waskom Pickett,

with twenty-three years of missionary experience in India has intensively studied the Forgotten Man of India, as the Outcaste may be called, and for the first time in centuries we see the Forgotten Man finding himself in a movement that has challenged the attention of Mahatma Gandhi.

The reference to Gandhi alluded to the Mahatma's intensifying criticisms of missionaries, whom he described not only as wrongly seeking to convert people from one religion to another, but as duplicitously using humanitarian services like education and medical help as bait. What missionaries *should* be doing, he offered, is to help the Hindu or the Muslim be "a better follower of his own faith," which, he said, implied "belief in the truth of all religions."

ON MONDAY, JANUARY 15, 1934, a week after Waskom got home, an earthquake surprised the city. Waskom, Ruth, the children, and a neighbor child were at home on the front veranda when the magnitude 8.4 seism struck. It was 2:15 in the afternoon. The first signal was a low rumbling. Then the ground started to heave with a motion like ocean waves. Seconds later, they heard the noises of things falling inside the bungalow. However, although the earthquake's effects stretched all the way to Lucknow, its epicenter was 300 miles away, in eastern Bihar. There, along a stretch 80 miles long by 20 miles wide, nothing was left standing. People casualties were many. When the convulsing stopped, nearly 11,000 Indians and Nepalese lay buried in the quake's debris. The fact that it had come in the afternoon was the only solace. Had it come at night when everyone was inside and asleep, the toll would have been many times higher.

By mid-February, 1934, it had become clear that Pickett's book was starting a seismic upheaval of its own—both in sales and influence. Although it had only been available for a few weeks in India, it was nearly sold out. Moreover, the initial reviews described the book in nothing less than earthshaking terms. None were more enthusiastic than Donald McGavran's *Sahayak Patrika* review (the *Sahayak Patrika* was the Mid-India Christian Council's weekly paper), but many of them were unusually generous in their praise. Methodist educator, W.D. Schermerhorn, wrote that no one could adequately understand the Christian mission in India without Pickett's volume. More than one Indian publication offered chapter-by-chapter summaries of the nearly 400-page tome. (In 1936, J. Holmes Smith would write a 72-page digest of it to make the facts of

Christian mass movements available to a larger public.) In any number of places, groups adopted *Christian Mass Movements* as a study book. Seeing the interest, the Methodist Board of Foreign Missions distributed 140 paper bound copies to missionaries and nationals in India and 60 copies to missionaries on furlough and in other countries.

Pickett also heard from friends with extensive mass movement experience. Even H.J. Sheets ("Schutz" until World War I came along), Pickett's former superintendent in Arrah, and now a professor at Bareilly Theological Seminary contacted him: "I thought I knew nearly everything pertaining to mass movements, but the further I read the humbler I become."

INEVITABLY, THE BOOK WOULD ALSO have its critics. Pickett, no doubt, was disappointed (though probably not surprised) by the icy reception of his former bishop, Frederick Bonn Fisher—now in America. Without naming either Rockefeller or the ISRR, Fisher inferred in a *Christian Century* piece the "lavish" backing Pickett got had inevitably affected "the tone of the survey and the character of the findings." Overall, Fisher's review was less a review than an occasion for trumpeting admiration of Gandhi's embrace of all religions and for touting *Re-Thinking Missions*. Pickett's recommendations, wrote Fisher, were "in line with modern . . . missionary administration," but lacked "prophetic imagination." Moreover, they were "conceived in caution and expressed with timidity." He said "the next step ought to be a cooperative study under the leadership of modern Hindu idealists and patriots who have caught Mahatma Gandhi's vision of social reconstruction." He added, "Would that they might have the same financial backing!" The rest of his piece critiqued Pickett's narrow focus on "conversion [a term Fisher found 'irritating'], baptism, and a break with old associations," in contrast with the "more liberal and humble attitude" of an interreligious solution.

In India, the *Guardian* of Madras struck a self-described "discordant" note too, but for different reasons. It confessed that

the large collection of facts, figures, impressions and opinions leave us bewildered and the reader can hardly venture to form a judgement of his own. He has either to accept Dr. Pickett's judgement or if he is inclined to be skeptical about it, he is left in suspense.

The review went on to suggest:

> In our opinion, a *survey* should have been the major effort and
> not a *study*. The former would have provided . . . pictures of
> separate mass movement areas—the peculiarities of the field,
> historical development of the work, the policies followed, the
> methods adopted, their strong points and defects. Such separate
> pictures would suggest comparisons and enable us to assess
> motives, methods and achievements, and understand the features
> of each system.

The reviewer was probably unaware that Pickett provided what he was
calling for in separate survey reports to the supervising missions of each
study area. No doubt he was pleased that Pickett's next book, on mid-
India—co-authored with Donald McGavran and George H. Singh—did
adopt that approach.

The most thoroughly unfavorable review of *Christian Mass
Movements* came not in 1934 but some 14 years later in a book by Manilal
Parekh, a "Hindu Christian" from Gujarat. In a nearly 70-page chapter
called "Christian Mass-Robbery," Parekh argued that many mass-
movement converts were never really converted at all and that encouraging
mass movements, therefore, amounted to endorsing proselytism. He
contended that missionaries who promoted mass movements were
interested only in numbers. Quoting at length from Fisher's *Christian
Century* review, and criticizing E. Stanley Jones' support of Pickett's book
as "inconsistent" with earlier statements, Parekh characterized Pickett's
"masterly" defense as "a sinister attempt to defend these mass-movements
of Hindus and others into Christianity" and "a thorough-going
rationalization . . . a masterpiece of propaganda."

Although Parekh's review was, in a way, more assault than review,
it probably had less to do with Pickett than with Parekh's own deeply-held
beliefs, which included a strong aversion to proselytism and the conviction
that following Christ was about being a better Hindu, not a former Hindu.
R.C. Das responded that while Parekh's critique of the spirit, motives, and
methods of modern missions was not without foundation, he ignored "the
inherent missionary urge for self-expression and communicativeness in
the message of Christianity and personality of Christ." Das added:

Until he [Parekh] recognizes this self-propagating character of Christian life, and its moral right to opportunities for full development in the whole world, his criticisms, however in order within limits, will remain merely negative, one-sided, and so unfair.

18 Lessons from the Survey

Christian Mass Movements in India was a trove of statistics, information, and interpretation. To make them easier to digest, Pickett divided the book into specific discussions. Into them, he wove fascinating facts, clarifying anecdotes, simple lists, and practical proposals.

Pickett described the term, "mass movement," which he dated to 1892, as confusing and unfortunate. He pointed out that people commonly got the wrong idea and, further, that it was inaccurate. Impressive as it sounded back in America, none of the movements were of society en masse. And none of them were heterogeneous turnings. When a Hindu "village" became Christian, "village" invariably meant the section where the outcastes lived, which was really outside the village. Americans pictured these "villages" like the small towns and steepled churches they knew. But, in no sense, was the church like the church in an American village, with a centrally-located place of worship to which all in the village were invited. If the converted Christians were untouchable Chamars, for example, the church would be restricted to the Chamar mohalla, outside the village. And nobody from the clean castes—even the lowest clean-caste neighbors—would even think of joining them for worship. Of the inevitability of this residential segregation, Pickett quoted a missionary who said, "The man born in the outcaste village may as soon think of building his house in the other group as a pig may think of going to live in his master's front room."

Regrettably, degrees of pollution demarcated even the untouchable castes. In one North Indian village, a group of Chamars changed their minds about becoming Christians because that would have meant throwing in their lot with some recently baptized Sweepers—beneath even them on the pollution scale. Until Pickett's book, the term "mass movements" obscured these caste distinctions—distinctions which, except for a few places in South India, persisted into the church. Pickett's objection to the term, and his reasons, helped to dispel some of that fog.

Though Pickett regretted the expression and preferred "group movement," he nevertheless kept "mass movement"—at least for the time being—because it was the term people knew and were accustomed to. He defined a mass movement as "a group decision favorable to Christianity and the consequent preservation of the converts' social integration." He added:

> Whenever a group larger than the family, accustomed to exercise a measure of control over the social and religious life of the individuals that compose it, accepts the Christian religion (or a large portion accept it with the encouragement of the group), the essential principle of the mass movement is manifest.

Pickett made five observations on how group conversion movements begin. First, they start within existing social units—he also used the term "homogeneous"—within specific untouchable castes.

Second, the immediate stimulus is usually a catalytic leader connected to the group. Though some identified movements with missionaries, Pickett indicated that is was a misconception.

> The real founder of the church in Travancore was not Ringeltaube but Vedamanickam. In Kistna it was not Darling but Venkayya. In Sialkot it was not Gordon, but Ditt.

Third, the movements emerge in groups with unaddressed grievances. So, the untouchables' interest in Christianity was as attributable to what their caste Hindu neighbors were doing (or not doing) as to what the missionaries were doing. Of the groups from which Christian mass movements have come, Pickett wrote, "all were in one respect or another underprivileged and had a grievance against the social order in which they lived."

Fourth, Pickett underscored the role of hope in sparking conversion movements. The expectation of a brighter future for themselves and their children through education, social uplift, and the like were key attractions for untouchables thinking about Christianity. However, according to Pickett, the expectation was not rooted in the missionaries' hopeful words as much as in the changes the caste groups observed over time in other groups who had become Christians.

Finally, Pickett observed that conversion movements spread from group to group:

> News of the conversion of a group travels far and fast. In thousands of villages, the first word about Christ ever listened to with real interest came in the report that some group had begun to follow him. If members of the group appear to be happy in their new life as Christians, other groups begin to consider whether they would not find happiness in following Christ. To group conscious people the action of a group is incomparably more important than the action of many isolated individuals, the corporate witness to Christ transcends in significance the personal witness.

Today, missiologists take Pickett's five observations for granted. But, in the early 1930s, his cluster of ideas was new on the missiological landscape.

ONE OF THE MOST PERSISTENT QUESTIONS raised about mass movement work had to do with the motives of those who turned to Christ. To many, it was clear that these new members of the faith were motivated by secular, not spiritual, impulses. Pickett took their point seriously. He admitted the matter of motives was complex:

> Many Christians think it necessary to examine with great care the motives of all who seek entrance to the Christian Church . . . Others fearful of placing themselves in the position of a judge, take the attitude that whosoever will may come, and while trying to stimulate motives they consider proper, scrupulously refrain from prying beneath the voluntary declaration of the inquirer.

Pickett, himself, was inclined to grant some latitude:

> Some of us see in the desire of the Sweepers . . . to be treated like respectable people, to secure for their children some other work than the cleaning of cesspools and privies, and to obtain help

against oppression, not evidence of unworthy motives, but rather, support for their claim that they have admitted Jesus to their midst.

Then, he quoted from the Census of India: "The hope of a decent life on earth is not any more or less a bribe than the hope of a blissful eternity hereafter."

One of Pickett's aims in the survey, therefore, was to ask converts about their motives in turning to Jesus. What he hoped to do was compare so-called "spiritual" and "non-spiritual" motives with the interviewee's Christian growth and achievements. Having heard from 3,947 outcasts their reasons for turning to Jesus, Pickett sorted their answers into four groups: (1) spiritual motives (2) secular motives (3) social reasons, and (4) natal influences. In Group 1, he placed responses such as the following: "seeking salvation"; "convinced by the preacher"; "to know God"; and "because of faith in Jesus." In Group 2, he put answers like these: "sought the help of missionaries"; "in hope of education for the children"; and "for improved social standing." In Group 3, among similar replies, he included: "family was being baptized"; "my relatives were Christians"; and "my people told me to." And in Group 4, he included grounds such as: "my parents were Christians when I was born."

In a way, the range of reasons were similar to what Christians might give anywhere. However, on dividing the inventory and correlating the four resulting groups of motives with the later attainments of the converts, some surprises turned up. In a nutshell, the Christian commitment and growth of those who had come to Christ for purely secular reasons, like wanting help against oppression, compared favorably to those whose motivations were spiritual. The same was true for those who became Christians because other family members had decided to do so.

According to Pickett, the comparisons showed that "God uses social forces to bring . . . [people] under the influences of the gospel." He concluded that having spiritual motives for becoming Christians, as opposed to secular or social ones, did not give converts any significant advantage in their spiritual formation and development. What made the difference was what happened after they were baptized. Immediate and ongoing post-baptismal training was the key.

But how did they measure spiritual formation and development, what Pickett called "Christian attainment?" Before a correlation between initial motives and Christian growth could be made, he needed to know that.

Pickett acknowledged that, "in the truest sense it is not possible to measure Christian attainment." One cannot devise questions that precisely show how "Christian" a group has become. "But," he argued, "it is possible to measure response to many requirements and recommendations of the church, and it is reasonable to interpret the results as indications of Christian attainment." So Pickett and his helpers watched for household shrines or other evidence of idolatry in the homes of the Christians. And they asked questions devised for that purpose. They tried to learn how much the Christians still relied on charms. They asked if their faith had helped them conquer fear of evil spirits. They asked about the creeds of the church, key scripture passages, and Sabbath observance. What about their use of alcohol since becoming Christians? Had their been any improvements in home life (such as greater love and respect for wives)? What were the men's present relationships to the old *biradari* ("brotherhood," that is, the local caste organization)? Another important indicator of attainment came through asking their Hindu and Muslim neighbors what, if any, changes they had seen in them.

FROM HIS DATA, PICKETT DEVELOPED a list of observations.

1. *For many, group movements "constitute the most natural way of approach to Christ."* While Pickett fully recognized that other forms of evangelism were also needed and that group movements were not the best way to reach all of India's people, he nonetheless adopted this inference as the central principle in his doctrine of evangelism for village India. As he further observed, "The more individualistic way preferred in Western countries is not favored by people trained from early childhood to group action."

2. *Group movements prevent "social dislocation."* This conclusion lay at the heart of Pickett's critique of the mission station philosophy of winning individuals and isolating them from the "heathen" influences of the past. In contrast, Pickett saw the segregation of converts from their people as more harmful than helpful:

> Single conversion unfortunately leads usually to a complete break of the convert with his group. This involves him in economic loss and mental anguish and deprives him of valuable restraints upon

wrong-doing and supports to right living. Unless he finds compensations in fellowship with other Christians he is likely to break under the strain.

3. _Group movements foster indigenous churches_ by helping to overcome what Pickett called, the "strong tendency to identify Western social patterns and customs with Christianity." Pickett claimed the village church (unlike many urban churches) was almost always the product of a group movement and naturally became "thoroughly Indian in social patterns and customs."

4. _Group movements aid in the conversion of others_. Pickett based this conclusion on the fact that conversion movements grow group to group.

Pickett had some negative observations too—that is, he also recognized certain dangers in the mass-movement approach to winning village India. Here are the key ones:

1. _Neglect of "personal religion."_ By "personal religion" Pickett meant what Christians now call spiritual formation. Pickett wanted to be sure those who went with the decision of the group to follow Christ had a personal testimony of rebirth and the help they needed to become mature disciples.

2. _Importing caste barriers into the church_. As long as only one caste was involved, this problem did not show up. But when groups representing different caste levels began coming into the church, it was apparent that conversion could not be counted upon to be a magic solvent for transforming old caste prejudices.

3. _Arrest or retardation of the movement_. Pickett noticed that some group movements slowed to a snail's pace or came to a halt as soon as the first wave was baptized, while others grew even faster. One important factor was that in encouraging people to take literacy classes, adopt more sanitary living patterns, or work for more financial stability, you might, unawares, be encouraging them also to break their group ties and obligations, thereby depriving the group of needed leadership and perhaps even setting the group back by the subtraction of a capable individual or family. The trick was to encourage individuals to grow but also to stay.

Another set of dangers were related not to the movements themselves, but Christian follow-up. In fact, Pickett called them "weaknesses" because he thought missions and churches were not doing an adequate job. They were: (1) an underestimation of the obligations involved when baptizing groups of converts; (2) inadequate contextualization of support and pastoral methods; (3) low standards and expectations; and (4) inadequate administration. Of these, the third was of most concern to him. He wrote, "In no other respect is the contrast so conspicuous between the most successful and the least successful mass movement work."

THE INTERVIEW DATA, CORRELATIONS, and observations led Pickett to the following recommendations for missionaries and Indian church leaders:

1. *Prioritize spiritual aims.* Missions must minister to temporal needs, he said. Not to do so would be to ignore the example of Jesus who fed the hungry without fear of criticism he was baiting them. But "there should be no question about the primacy of the spiritual aim," said Pickett. For him, evangelism was the heart of mission, though mission could not be reduced to evangelism.

2. *Develop local leaders,* While Pickett conceded that, in the beginning, it would be necessary to bring in leaders from the outside, the goal always should be to raise up strong lay leaders from within groups of new disciples.

3. *Develop programs specially suited to mass movement work.* Pickett commended programs that would: (a) nurture the spiritual life of the group (daily worship using indigenous forms, for instance); (b) reduce social tensions between mass movement converts and their neighbors; (c) assist with socioeconomically; (d) better coordinate the mission's various ministries; (e) allow for experimentation; and (f) utilize more Indian leaders.

4. *Reallocate resources according to receptivity.* Pickett wanted to shift money and personnel from mission stations and unproductive fields to mass movement areas. Of course, he was not the first to advocate the notion. Even John Wesley, the founder of Methodism, had done so. But

in Pickett's day, the principle had fallen between the cracks of evangelistic strategy.

5. *Work cooperatively with other missions.* For Pickett, the gospel trumped denominational interests. Thus he urged ending overlap and competitiveness, loaning proven personnel to rekindle faltering ministries, and shifting overloads to missions with more available personnel and resources.

THOUGH MUCH HAD BEEN LEARNED from the mass movements, Pickett was not yet satisfied. In particular, he had learned that in Telugu country the conversions of untouchables and their changed lives were apparently stimulating interest in Christ in groups of Sudras. So, for him, the study was not over; it had just begun.

19 Sudra Movements

January 1934 marked the start of a three-year extension from the Pickett's mass movement research under the NCC. A key goal was to follow up on his earlier, cursory look at Sudra movements. Sudras were members of the fourth, or lowest, division of the recognized Hindu castes. But they were not, like untouchables, outcastes. In March, Pickett spent 10 days at the United Lutheran Theological College (Gurukul) at Guntur. The college was inaugurating a department of extension and research. While there, Pickett inquired about several centers of Sudra church growth in the South. The first was in the northwest corner of the Guntur District, where the American Lutheran and American Baptist churches were working. The second was less than 40 miles from there in the Kistna (or Krishna) District. It was a CMS mission. The third was in the Nizam's dominions surrounding Hyderabad, where British Methodists were at work.

Pickett continued to do some work for the Methodists as well. In June, he went to the Belgaum and Gokak Districts, 240 miles south of Bombay near the Western Ghats—part of the Methodists' old "Kanarese Mission." Because the two districts were supposed to have reverted to animistic Hinduism, the Reverend E.A. Seamands, who had once been the preacher-in-charge of those areas, was recommending the Methodists withdraw. At the mission board's request, Pickett looked into the situation, visiting 10 villages. He was surprised to find that all the baptized people called themselves Christian and were known as Christians. More than half knew the Lord's Prayer and the Ten Commandments. Most had a good knowledge of the life of Christ and went to worship services regularly. Why, then, had Seamands concluded they had reverted to Hinduism? Perhaps because where these untouchables lived (the Christian Madiga and Holeya *kheris*), they worshiped on the wide verandas of what were ostensibly Hindu temples—with the idol in a small room in the back. Pickett reported:

> Where all the group who own the temple have become Christians, they can remove the idol. I was told that it has been done in several villages, though I saw no temple from which the idol had been removed before our coming. But in one village on a challenge from us, the people removed the idol and asked that the temple be rededicated as a Christian church. I suggested a service of purification and several architectural changes and a whitewashing, to be followed by a big service of dedication in which Christians from other villages would be invited to participate.

On that errand, Pickett, who concluded that Methodists should not withdraw, traveled nearly 2,000 miles, just as he had on his March trip to Guntur.

Pickett wished he still had time for the surveys he had in mind for the Guntur, Kistna, and Hyderabad Sudra movements. But the southwest monsoon had set in, and the roads had become too muddy for motorcars. Because it was planting season, potential interviewees would be scarce too. He would have to wait.

Pickett spent July and August with Ruth and the children in Landour. When late September came, he headed south. In central India, he led a small survey of Satnami territory, south of Raipur. Satnamis were a 100-year-old monotheistic sect, comprised mainly of Chamars. The survey was to test the waters for a potential group movement. One of the helpers was Donald McGavran. It was McGavran's first chance to observe Pickett at work. The results must have seemed promising to McGavran, for afterwards he disclosed in a circular letter to American supporters: "Our area in Chattisgarh [the Disciples of Christ's Bilaspur District] calls for a mass movement work amongst the Satnamis with definite expectation that some day the entire group of 600,000 will decide for Christ."

THE NEXT MONTH, October 1934, A.C. Brunk of the American Mennonite Mission, wrote in a letter:

> I have been invited by Dr. J.W. Pickett . . . to accompany him
> in a study of a movement of the middle class (caste) people
> toward Christianity in South India. We feel that this will be a
> splendid opportunity to learn how the movement was started and
> directed and thus we may learn better how to direct our
> evangelistic work . . . I will be leaving tomorrow.

A.C. Brunk and four other Mennonite workers from the Dhamtari area, near Raipur, had just heard Pickett speak at a meeting of the Mid-India Christian Council. As Pickett described the mass movements, George J. Lapp, who was Brunk's bishop, asked, "Dr. Pickett, why does not that sort of thing happen here?" Now a few days later, with the opportunity to accompany Pickett to the Guntur and Hyderabad areas, Brunk hoped some light might be shed on his bishop's question.

As Pickett hoped, the weather cooperated. After months of rain and clouds, a week of bright sun marked the approach of the cold season when activities of all kinds picked up. The team's first stop was in northern Hyderabad state, where they visited the first of three Sudra movements Pickett was targeting. By the time they completed their circuit of villages and interviews, Pickett was sure that here in Telugu country "a remarkable work of grace" was in progress. It may even have reminded him of the revivals of his youth in Kentucky, for he wrote:

> Some of the stories of conversion are as remarkable as any in
> church history. A strong emotional element is common to many
> of these conversions. Visions, dreams, intense consciousness of
> wrongdoing and ardent longing for a sense of God's presence and
> favor are frequently encountered.

Pickett and his team then moved on to Andhra Desa, first to the northwestern corner of the Guntur district. This was the largest of the three Sudra movements. Here 10,000 Hindus had turned to Christ, and there were many more inquirers.

Of special interest to Pickett was how often Sudra movements emerged where untouchable movements were already established. He wanted to know how much the untouchable Christians had influenced the Sudras. If he found a pattern, it might be the key to reaching caste Hindus throughout India.

With this "trickle-up" theory (which he shared with Anglican bishop Azariah and others) in mind, Pickett paid close attention to what Hindus and Muslims thought about their Mala and Madiga (untouchable) Christian neighbors. Frequently he got the answer he hoped for: that Muslims and Sudras had, indeed, become open to Christ through their untouchable neighbors.

Shortly after Pickett interviewed three Muslims who were so-influenced, they returned with 18 more. Pickett reported:

> Their spokesman declared that they had no mosque, no priest or teacher, and knew more about the Christian religion than about their own, and that they felt it would be better for them to throw in their lot with Christians and begin to worship God under the direction of a Christian minister whose character showed that he had an experience with God.

From the two smaller Sudra movements in Hyderabad and Kistna came similar stories. In each place, there were 7,000 to 8,000 caste converts. In Kistna, two men told Pickett the Christian outcastes of the village were changed in every respect. So Pickett asked if they had seen any change for the better in converts of their own castes. "Yes," answered one of them, "the change is even greater . . . In one year they have changed as much as the outcastes did in five." Had they ever seen such character changes within Hinduism? "Never." The conversation ended with Pickett asking if they, themselves, would like to seek the help of Jesus Christ and openly confess him as their Lord. One immediately responded in the affirmative. The other said he would if his family agreed. Both men and their families were enrolled as inquirers that evening.

AMONG THE MOST vexing criticisms of mass movement work was that every success with untouchables further stigmatized Christianity as an outcaste religion. Pickett was encouraged that proof of the trickle-up phenomenon would help put that argument to rest—that is, if it was determined to be a pattern. By the time he reported on the present surveys in his 1938 book, *Christ's Way to India's Heart,* he was sure the evidence did support the trickle-up theory he and Bishop Azariah had proposed. Azariah summarized it this way:

Dr. Pickett mentions an area where out of 187 villages with caste converts, 170 villages had already Christians of outcaste origin. In a neighboring mission district, it has been seen that caste conversions followed outcaste converts in 69 out of a total of 76 villages. In the Dornakal Diocese there is no caste convert in any village where there were no Christians of outcaste origin.

Besides observing that Christian outcastes had influenced Sudras, who were Hindus of the lowest caste, Pickett also described growing interest in the Christian faith among "upper caste" Sudras. But if Sudras were the bottom caste ("the feet") and only untouchables were lower ("the dust around the feet"), what did he mean by his oxymoronic assertion? Pickett explained:

The lower caste Sudras are the artisans, the higher caste Sudras the land owners. In the Telugu country some eighty percent of the Hindu population is made up of the Sudras. The Telugu country is unique in that respect. The landowners there are Sudras; they are the real men of power, the ruling class, and many of them are well-to-do.

This also clears up Brunk's report that "people of comparative good financial position [were] coming into the church." That is, there were poor and rich among the new converts, but they were all Sudras.

SUDRA MOVEMENTS, WHILE encouraging, also presented problems. For example, you now had untouchable Christians giving leadership to a church into which their social superiors and former oppressors were coming. Moreover, the place of worship was where the outcastes lived, in the Madiga *kheri*, or Mala *kheri*. Given their incompatible backgrounds, the intractability of caste in the Hindu worldview, and the labyrinthine complicatedness of the social infrastructure—far and away more complex than Western villages—these social distinctions were not likely to recede anytime soon. Salvation could not be counted upon to act like a magic solvent, immediately dissolving generations of thinking caste and of living with the embedded socio-economic and political manifestations of caste. Nevertheless, how the sponsoring missions responded to caste differences at this early stage would be crucial. It would likely set the course for a long time.

That is not to say that there were not reasons for optimism. As Pickett noted, even though they still could be imperious, the new Sudra converts insisted "the converted outcastes [had] seen the power of Christ":

> I have had interviews [in 28 villages] with almost a thousand of the middle caste converts in which I have asked them what led them to Christ, and they have replied that they have been convinced of the reality of Christ's claims by what they have seen in the outcastes. I found great numbers who have not yet become Christians who said something like this: "It looks as though the virtue has gone out of our own gods. We have lost our faith in them. The future is with these Christian people. They are God's people."

Nonetheless, Sudra converts to Christ found it hard to feel at home in the established outcaste churches. The following reasons are summarized from a Pickett letter. First, cast converts were disposed to aloofness—to perhaps connect up with the missionary for spiritual sustenance but not leaders lower on the social ladder than themselves. Second, churches made up of outcastes did not always welcome Sudra converts. As Pickett observed, "With the background they have, the depressed class converts have a tendency to oppress others. They sometimes take the position that now the higher caste convert is in their control." Third, the church is in the outcaste quarter; soon the caste converts have a feeling that they should no longer have to go there. They ask the church be relocated in the caste part of the village. Fourth, when caste Christians become ministers and school teachers, they assume that their work should be with other caste people, not untouchables. In Pickett's words,

> They believe that, because they have a background of privilege, they can present Christ to the caste man as the minister from the outcastes cannot, and sometimes they take very unchristian attitudes toward their fellow ministers of outcaste origin, and yet with no element of conscious guilt involved.

Pickett also noted that caste converts did not support the church as the outcastes did. He wrote:

> They do not average as much in per capita giving as the older Christians from the poverty-stricken outcastes. They think the preacher is one of the outcastes and is taken care of by them. It is extremely difficult to establish them in the church and have them assume responsibility for supporting the preacher from the outcaste groups.

In addition, there were social relationship issues to contend with:

> Many converts from the higher castes rationalize so that they come to feel that in order to win other higher caste people to Christianity it is well not to have too much to do with their fellow Christians from the outcastes, and outside of the church they don't want to have any social relationship with them.

"Must these groups merge socially, must we work toward a unified social life?" Pickett asked.

> Is this part of our . . . obligation, or shall we be happy when one man thinks of himself as a redeemed outcaste, while the cast convert has a different pattern of Christian consciousness altogether? . . . What will be the ideal of Christian consciousness before us here? There are certain social customs that the new converts are bringing over from Hinduism that are incompatible with Christianity.

Pickett concluded the church needed help with these issues—that is:

> [the] cooperation of the mission boards . . . even some pressure . . . to think these things through, to do research, to challenge assumptions, and to solve some of these complicated problems.

Most of the questions Pickett raised are still not solved, nor have they gone away. How do Christians with distinct worldviews, assumptions, patterns, and language differences show the unity of the church? And what is the meaning of the scriptural phrase "one body" in a country where the reality of caste relationships so rigorously and exhaustively dominates every aspect of life?

WHEN, NINE OR TEN MONTHS earlier, Donald McGavran read Pickett's *Christian Mass Movements in India,* he had just begun his second term as field secretary for the 70-missionary India mission of the United Christian Missionary Society. He later wrote:

> As I read Waskom Pickett's *Christian Mass Movements in India,* my eyes were opened. I suddenly saw that where people become Christians one by one and are seen as outcastes by their own people, as traitors who have joined another community, the church grows very, very slowly. The one by one "out of my ancestral community into a new low community" was a sure recipe for slow growth. Conversely, where men and women could become followers of the Lord Jesus Christ while remaining in their own segment of society, there the gospel was sometimes accepted with great pleasure by great numbers.

Upon reading Pickett's book, McGavran immediately decided to investigate the growth of the church in the mid-India area, where British, Swedish, American, and German missions were at work. When he discovered that only 11 of the 145 mission stations were growing and the overall rate of growth was less than 1 percent a year, he persuaded the interdenominational Mid-India Christian Council to engage Waskom Pickett for a fact-finding survey. The Council agreed, with the stipulation that McGavran accompany Pickett. By the time they disbanded, the Mid-India Christian Council had set up a 24-person Mass Movement Continuation Committee, with McGavran as its chair. In that role, he edited a new stencil-duplicated Mass Movement Bulletin, which came out monthly. He also began a regular correspondence with Pickett, who had agreed to lead them in a planning retreat during the first week of April 1935.

Since this development took place just before he left for his current Sudra surveys in Telugu and Andhra Desa country, Pickett had to begin thinking ahead about a very different kind of setting than the one he now found himself in. There, after decades of effort, the church essentially consisted of employees and dependents of the missions. With Brunk and other mid-India recruits helping in the Andhra survey, no doubt conversations drifted in that direction often.

CHHINDWARA, THE VENUE for the mid-India planning retreat, was 62 miles north of Nagpur. Including the leaders, 34 persons participated in the April gathering. A major focus was prayer—especially group prayer. Pickett regaled the group with exciting stories of revivals in other places. "It seemed," reported the Reverend T.N. Hill of Jubbulpore, "that we were listening to a modern Acts of the Apostles." On the third day, Pickett led the group in thinking about the decades of limited impact in mid-India. Hill reported: "Over and over the questions confronted us: 'What shall we do about it? What is wise? How shall we make the most of our opportunities?'" On the final day, Pickett described the amazing Sudra movements of the Telugu field.

Out of the retreat came a substantial document of findings. However, the importance of Chhindwara was not the findings so much as the role the retreat played in helping to envision the survey to come—a survey that would mark decisive turning points for both Pickett and his new protégé, Donald McGavran.

WHEN HE GOT BACK TO LUCKNOW, Waskom learned that Ruth's mother, Elizabeth Robinson, whose health had been precarious for some time, was gravely ill. In late May, she was admitted to a Delhi hospital. She died the morning of June 17, 1935.

The loss of Elizabeth Fisher Robinson was deeply felt, not just by the family, but by dozens of friends in Lucknow, Bombay and Delhi. She had not had an easy life, but she had lived it splendidly. She had been married to John Robinson nearly 44 years. In her second year of marriage, their infant son got dysentery and died. It was a great loss, but she was thankful to know he was safe with the Father. Cholera was bad then, and a few days later she saw a Hindu father carrying his dead baby. She wrote to a friend: "His wails were most pitiful to hear as he cried out, '*Mera baba, Mera baba mar gaya.*' He would stop and uncover the child's face and kiss him and then his wails would begin afresh. I wanted to tell him of our hope in Christ." Twelve years later, her youngest daughter, Miriam, got dysentery too, and for a while it seemed she would not recover. But Elizabeth's faith and constant care brought her through.

Elizabeth sacrificed much to help her husband in his difficult work. As another bishop's wife, Satyavati Chitambar, wrote of her, "Mrs. Robinson was one with Bishop Robinson in his work."

One of Elizabeth's great loves was growing flowers, which she loved to give away even more. Her generosity, in fact, was legendary. Once, when invited by the women of the church to a surprise tea-party on her birthday, she brought a check which she gave them as she left. "This is my birthday gift to the WCTU," she smiled. That's how people remembered her all along the Robinsons' journey from Lucknow to Bombay to Delhi—the same road to Delhi that Waskom and Ruth would trace.

FOR NOW, THOUGH, WASKOM AND RUTH'S path took them out of the fierce summer heat to Fir Clump, their Landour, Mussoorie retreat. The previous summer Waskom had preached regularly at the Kellogg Church in Landour. This summer—1935—he had agreed to serve as acting pastor. He would continue in that role—preaching and lecturing to the many missionaries and Indian churchmen who were part of that congregation for a few weeks each summer—well into the 1940s. This year, between June 30 and September 1, he would counsel with more than 40 of them on some aspect of their ministry, and he would preach 19 sermons. The text of the first sermon was Simon Peter's affirmation: "Lord, to whom shall we go? thou hast the words of eternal life." The text of the last one was Paul's admonition to Timothy: "Keep that which is committed to thy trust." Pickett did not mind the preaching responsibility and, in fact, enjoyed it. Landour's best gifts to him, though, were family time and enough seclusion to work uninterrupted on his heavy correspondence and mass movement reports.

Although in the summer of 1935 Pickett was giving some thought to the future, he had no idea just how pivotal the next few months would be. Because of the NCC's precarious finances, he knew, as he put it to R.E. Diffendorfer at the Mission Board, he might not be able to continue in the mass movement work.

I desire . . . that my service to the church in India may be in the position in which I may do the best work for the kingdom as a whole. Whether that field of service will lie in our own church or in interdenominational work I cannot say. Since returning . . .

> I have received from all branches of the church a response to my presentation . . . of the mass movement study that is most gratifying, but I have labored under the most discouraging handicaps financially . . . I have often had to wait for weeks for my salary and expense bills. Whether it is likely that money will be forthcoming to carry on this mass movement work much longer is I think doubtful.

When Diffendorfer asked if Pickett had considered the possibility the episcopacy might be in his future, he said he very much doubted it:

> With regard to the possibility that Central Conference may ask me, as you suggest, to enter the episcopal office, I believe that is not likely to happen. While I have not been in a position for many months to learn much of the talk among our people on the subject, I understand from the few who have spoken of the matter to me that there is general feeling that the Central Conference is not in a position at this time to commit itself to the support of a second bishop . . . Also there seems to be considerable doubt whether the Central Conference . . . ought ever to elect non-Indians.

20 Ambedkar

On October 13, 1935, something happened that set India abuzz, including all the missionaries. In the little town of Yeola, 131 miles northeast of Bombay as the crow flies, where the depressed classes of the Bombay Presidency were holding their annual conference, Dr. Bhimrao Ramji Ambedkar made a startling announcement. That 12,000 untouchables had come together that year was startling in itself. In recent years, such meetings had become more common, but this was the largest. The word was out that Ambedkar, their leader, would put caste Hindus on notice that a new day had arrived. News of the planned announcement had come even to Lucknow. According to Pickett, a group of 30 untouchable leaders had gathered there to await confirmation of the declaration so that, when the news came, they would be ready to pass and publicize a resolution of agreement.

DR. BHIMRAO RAMJI AMBEDKAR, the 14th child of a Mahar family, had been unusually fortunate for someone of untouchable background. His keen mind and hard work came to the attention of the Maharaja of Baroda, who sponsored him for studies in Britain and America. The sponsorship led to a Ph.D. in Economics at Columbia University, New York, and a D.Sc. at the University of London. Ambedkar became a Bombay barrister. He first came into the public eye in a 1927 conference of untouchables at Mahad, about 70 miles south of Bombay. There, as in other places, untouchables had to pay caste Hindus heavily to draw water for them from the local tank. Since, however, the Chawdar tank, as they called it, was technically a public tank, they had a legal right to get their own water. So, Ambedkar led the 5,000 to the tank, helping them to assert their rights in a way they had been told from birth they could not do. The little rebellion had heroic impact. Delegates went back to their own places with a new vision of themselves. Many of them persuaded their fellow untouchables to begin dressing like touchable Hindus and to stop begging for bread. In some places, they started schools. In others, untouchables demanded that existing schools take their children. Meanwhile, by the following procedure, the Sanatanist Hindus in Mahad purified their invaded tank. First, they drew 108 *ghagars* (jars) of water from it. Then they stirred cow dung into it. Finally, after the priests in charge said mantras over the mixture, they poured it back into the tank. Only then could the tank be declared "purified!"

IN 1930, BRITAIN'S NEWLY ELECTED Labor Government called a series of Round Table Conferences in London to discuss constitutional reform. B.R. Ambedkar and Rao Bahadur Srinivasan represented the nation's 43 million untouchables, whom Ambedkar described poignantly:

> The depressed classes form a group by themselves, which is distinct and separate from the Mohammedans, and, although they are included among the Hindus, they in no sense form an integral part of that community. Not only have they a separate existence, but they have also assigned to them a status which is invidiously distinct from the status occupied by any other community in India. There are communities in India, which occupy a lower and subordinate position, but the position assigned to the depressed classes is totally different. It is one which is midway between that of the serf and the slave, and which may, for convenience, be called servile with this difference, that the serf and the slave were permitted to have physical contact, from which the Depressed Classes are debarred. What is worse is that this enforced servility and bar to human intercourse, due to their Untouchability, involves, not merely the possibility of discrimination in public life, but actually works out as a positive denial of all equality of opportunity and the denial of those most elementary of civic rights on which all human existence depends.

At the second conference, in 1931, Gandhi came insisting that, as the only elected national leader at the table, only he among those present had the right to speak for Indians—including Indian minorities. The others at the table, he insisted (which included Ambedkar), spoke only for minority, sectarian interests.

Nevertheless, Muslim leaders made it clear that they would support an Indian federation only if there were built-in political safeguards that would prevent a Hindu stranglehold on government. And Ambedkar insisted on the same guarantee for untouchables, arguing for separate electorates, which would let untouchables elect their representatives separately. Gandhi, however, would have none of it. He argued that untouchables were Hindus. Therefore, no special representation beyond himself and Congress was needed.

With the Round Table impasse and no political protection for minorities forthcoming, in 1932 the British came up with their own plan, a *Communal Award* detailing how Muslims, Sikhs, Anglo-Indians, Europeans, Indian Christians, and untouchables would be represented. When Gandhi learned the plan called for untouchables to be separated from Hindus in their own electorates, he was irate. He dashed off a letter to Prime Minister Ramsey McDonald demanding the plan be rescinded. McDonald replied that only the untouchables could do that. So, a month after the announcement, on September 18, 1932, Gandhi announced a fast to death.

It was a brilliant maneuver—as one writer put it, "an almost Machiavellian move." As the now-recognized leader of the untouchables, Ambedkar was suddenly put in the position of direct responsibility for Gandhi's life. Even Gandhi's son begged Ambedkar for his father's life. The Mahatma's trap gave Ambedkar no choice but to negotiate with Gandhi. To refuse to concede was to be forever the villain.

Gandhi's fast ended when Ambedkar—complaining of black-mail—worked out a concession with the Hindus. The accord, called the Poona Pact, scrapped the goal of separate untouchable electorates. It did provide a quota of seats in the provincial assemblies for depressed class candidates, but only for 10 years. Though it was an ostensible victory for Ambedkar, in reality, it was a bitter pill.

GANDHI PRESSED ON FOR CHANGES WITHIN Hinduism that he believed would eventually erase the stain of untouchability. But Ambedkar continued to regard the Mahatma's reforms as cosmetic. Gandhi's protectionist approach—insistence on voluntary change, aversion to mobilizing the depressed classes, refusal to recognize untouchables as a minority, advocacy of symbolic change over structural change, and antipathy to erasing caste—was, in Ambedkar's mind, pious idealism. It would do nothing at all. Yet, Gandhi would not budge. He insisted that reform from within was the only acceptable path and that, since caste Hindus were the cause, only they could provide the cure. Untouchables, therefore, should do nothing–except trust him and Congress. Proof of their trustworthiness would be opening the temples to untouchables.

In 1932 Stanley Jones went to visit Gandhi in jail and ran into Ambedkar. They had never before met, but soon they were engaged in a long conversation at the jail gate. When Jones brought up Gandhi's approach of purifying Hinduism through voluntary reform by caste Hindus, including opening temples, Ambedkar responded:

> We are not interested in temple entry . . . What we want to know is whether they will do away with caste . . . Will they or will they not give us social equality?

AMBEDKAR ADDRESSED HIS YEOLA AUDIENCE for an hour and a half. He underscored the lack of movement on the part of caste Hindus to accept any changes. He said that it was now time to make a definitive step. And since the indignities untouchables had to endure came from within Hinduism, not from the outside—the course was inevitable:

> The depressed classes have been unsuccessful in their efforts to bring about a change of heart and it is futile to waste our energies and money in further trying to get redress and work in harmonious cooperation. After deeply pondering the way out, I have come to the conclusion that the best way is complete severance from the Hindu fold.

Ambedkar then said that he was born a Hindu and there was nothing he could do about that. But he could do *something*! Taking a deep breath, he boomed, "I solemnly assure you, I will not die a Hindu!"

As director of the National Christian Council's Mass Movement Study, Pickett was much interested in Ambedkar's statement and the response it provoked. He learned of it while on a speaking tour in South India. On returning home to Lucknow at the end of October, he wrote T.S. Donohugh at the Mission Board:

Hindus are maneuvering desperately to stop what may well be a general exodus of these classes from Hinduism. The Mohammedans are making desperate efforts to capture them, the Sikhs and the Buddhists are also competing for them, but there can be little doubt that Dr. Ambedkar's own purpose is to turn his people towards Christianity. He is quoted as having said privately to several people that he is personally a firm believer in the gospel of Jesus Christ and plans to confess the Christian faith and seek admission to the Church sooner or later.

From many parts of India I am being urged to drop other work and go to Bombay in order to help direct these people to Christ and help the Christian Church to fit itself to receive them. Unfortunately the Church in the Bombay Presidency is poorly equipped in spirit and staff to meet this challenge.

With his letter, Pickett enclosed several related clippings.

LIKE AMBEDKAR, PICKETT REGARDED Gandhi's position dubiously. "I think it is clear," he wrote to Diffendorfer, "that the main body of Gandhi's associates have a religio-political purpose which is stronger than all their other purposes."

They are driving to get Hindu temples open to the Harijans. But the men who are doing that are themselves not in the habit of going to the temples for worship. The orthodox, devout Hindus who go to the temples want to keep the Harijans out. But the secularized politicians who want to keep the Harijans within the Hindu fold to increase or safeguard Hindu political power are demanding that the temples be opened. They are working hard in areas where the Harijans have become Christians and when occasionally they get some temple opened to the Harijans, then they put pressure upon Christians to go there to worship. In some cases they have printed postcards renouncing Christianity and have put pressure upon men in their power because of employment, or debts, or for some other reason, to sign those cards. Most of those who have signed have immediately informed the Church that they did so under compulsion and want their renunciation to be ignored.

Pickett continued to hear from those in the church who thought he should drop everything and go to Bombay to meet with Ambedkar. Among them were Jones, Azariah, and Hodge. In early November, he agreed and wrote to Ambedkar, sending with his letter a copy of *Christian Mass Movements in India* and a brief account of his current studies. However, he thought it as important to confer with church and mission leaders in Bombay about the church's readiness to receive a large influx as it was to see the man who might bring it about.

Meanwhile, Ambedkar's movement continued to gather steam. On Monday, November 11, Pickett wrote to Diffendorfer:

> This Harijan movement away from Hinduism is assuming huge proportions. Nothing quite so far-reaching has happened in India in generations. The accompanying clipping will give you an idea of the intensity of feeling and the absoluteness of the break with Hinduism.

Around that time, Pickett went to Jones' Lucknow ashram to hear supporters of Ambedkar explain their leader's reasons for turning from Hinduism. Their spokesperson, who was not an untouchable but an upper class Indian, spoke passionately and eloquently in Hindi on the grievances of the depressed classes. He also spoke of their "utter lack of confidence in the Hindu Mahasabha and in Mr. Gandhi," accusing Gandhi and those promoting temple-entry and anti-touchability of being politically motivated. The consensus of the gathering was that Christianity was the one force that had eased the burdens of untouchables and given them hope.

Afterwards, in a five-minute conversation with two of the leaders, Pickett described his studies of untouchable Christians. The two men were immediately interested and wanted to come by his house. When they showed up at 10:30 the next morning, they had four others with them. They included the president, general secretary, and four other members of the United Provinces Depressed Classes Association's executive committee. To more than one person, Pickett described their meeting as, "in some ways the richest two hours of my life."

The group had come to talk about parts of Pickett's *Christian Mass Movements in India*. When he told them about his current study of Sudras following untouchables into Christian faith, they got excited and said, "that is what we want, not a mere change of religion, but one that will make us and our people leaders of a new movement for the regeneration of India."

The spokesperson said, "You must put these facts before Dr. Ambedkar." Showing their seriousness, they immediately telegraphed Ambedkar to set a time.

The men said they were clear about leaving Hinduism and becoming Christians. But they added that they were not ready to go public with those intents until they had a million people ready to move forward together. Their first step toward this critical mass would be a three-day All-India Conference in Lucknow starting Christmas Day. They asked Pickett to serve on a secret committee planning the event. They also suggested a second conference for their leaders, leaders of the Indian church, and missionaries.

Pickett reported his meeting to both Diffendorfer and Stanley Jones. He told Jones that while the men admitted that some of their followers were leaning toward Islam rather than Christianity, Muslims had never shown any empathy for untouchables, nor offered any help as Christians had.

Despite his excitement about the potential of this ultimate mass movement, Pickett continued to be troubled by the ill-prepared state of the church to receive such large numbers should they follow Ambedkar into Christianity.

> This appears to be a situation of unrivaled importance. We spend hundreds of thousands of dollars spread over a generation to try to get the people of a single city like Calcutta or Bombay interested in the Christian Gospel and now when the leaders of 70 million people determine to abandon a religion of idolatry and caste to seek one that offers reality and equality, we do not have the funds to provide literature and few men to warm their hearts with personal testimony and service. One of the most serious handicaps is the immobility of missionary resources; people and funds are bound down to specific purposes and the biggest and best opportunities pass by neglected.

Other Christian leaders shared this concern. The prospect of any large part of India's untouchables turning *en masse* to Christianity was as unnerving as it was exciting. Organizing to receive them and to help them understand a faith greatly different from the one they knew would be a monumental task requiring personnel and financial resources not presently available. Also, some worried the commonly met perception of Christianity as low-caste religion would be reinforced by such a move from the depressed classes. Others resurrected the old fear of the paganization of the church. How could *masses* of people make such a decision and be real Christians? Real Christian faith, they reminded everyone, is a matter of *personal* decision. Still others questioned the motives of Ambedkar, suggesting that if he and his followers made such a move, it would be more an abandoning of Hinduism than an embracing of Christianity

THE BIG MEETING WITH AMBEDKAR came on the evening of November 24, 1935. With two of the depressed class leaders from Lucknow, Pickett met with Ambedkar for two hours. He complimented Ambedkar for his leadership of the untouchables, his work at the Round Table Conference, his negotiations leading to the Poona Pact, and his Yeola declaration. Dr. Ambedkar was equally gracious. He said he had already read with interest and encouragement the first, second, third, fourth, fifth, eighth, and last chapters of *Christian Mass Movements in India*. He planned to finish the book in the next few days.

Pickett asked if Ambedkar had been much in contact with Christians. Ambedkar said that, while in London, he attended church often—in fact, regularly, for about a year. While a doctoral student at Columbia University in New York, he had become friends with the librarian and a couple of the professors at nearby Union Theological Seminary, and he studied the history of the papacy. He also mentioned Isaac Foot, a Christian member of Parliament who had assisted him greatly at the Second Round Table Conference. And he said that he had recently been studying the Gospels and the letters of Paul.

From there Ambedkar's conversation turned to Christian missions. He asserted that missions had poorly represented Jesus in India. He deduced three reasons:

First, many missionaries had compromised with Brahmins, giving Hinduism a respect it didn't deserve. Instead of always listening to the Brahmins, they should have, like Jesus, been attuned to the cries of the oppressed.

Second, Christians in India were too "otherworldly." Jesus was interested in all kinds of human need, but missionaries seemed more concerned with salvation from a speculative hell.

Third, missionaries had not adequately adapted their methods to the Indian social order and had, thus, produced leaders with little social conscience. He described church leaders in Maharashtra of being self-centered with no sense of duty to anyone, "not even their fellow Christians in the villages." He said, "I would not care to accept responsibility for producing any more Christians of that type." But Christianity in the New Testament, said Ambedkar, "touches me deeply . . . It has the sort of dynamic that my people need."

Pickett responded that, in contrast to what Ambedkar had seen in Maharashtra, New Testament Christianity was working in some places. He gave examples of converts from the depressed classes bringing higher-caste Hindus into the church and even serving as their ministers.

"That is what I want—equality and the removal of all discriminations based on caste," said Ambedkar. But he added that he was not interested in evolutionary change. He had once gone to see the Pope about the complaints of the Adi Dravida converts in South India, and the Pope had responded that those problems would take generations to resolve. Ambedkar said he left disgusted.

"I want to know what the Christian can do and is prepared to do to remove the disabilities under which my people live," he said.

When Pickett responded that no one could promise him the Christian church could do more than it was already doing and that his people's escape from their troubles would ultimately depend on their turning to Christ, Ambedkar said that he was glad to meet someone who hesitated to promise what he couldn't deliver. Certain Mohammedans, he offered, had promised him everything in heaven and on earth.

Ambedkar told Pickett he could not now state which faith was his goal, because it would risk alienating some who were friendly to him.

> I have an open mind but not an empty mind. I know where I would like to lead my people, but I might possibly compromise and go elsewhere if they would not go with me.

But he could never remain a Hindu.

> Hinduism is not a religion but a disease. People of every caste should flee from it as from the plague. When Hindus have extracted nectar from poison, let them begin to talk of extracting salvation from Hinduism.

Shifting the conversations slightly, Pickett told Ambedkar that he had heard he was an atheist. Ambedkar responded, "Sometime ago I would not have been insulted by such a statement, but I do not think it is correct."

Pickett then said, "Your opponents say you are not interested in religion but are playing politics."

Ambedkar answered quietly, "Yes, that is the Hindu line to discredit me. But I have attacked the central need of my people, which is a decent religion . . . that has the power to lift." Momentarily moving the conversation in a different direction, he spoke of missionaries who had come under the influence of Hindu propagandists like Gandhi and Natarajan. He pitied them, he said. Especially C.F. Andrews. Then, returning to Pickett's question, he added, "What politics could be played that way? What could I or my people gain . . . by such a move? All of my personal interests point the other way, and I am sacrificing them for the sake of religion."

"Do you ever pray?" asked Pickett.

"I am not a man of prayer, but sometimes I feel compelled to pray." He gave an example. At the Round Table Conference—when the Hindus opposed him, the Muslims showed nothing but self-interest, the British kept quiet to pacify the Hindus, and Gandhi would grant him nothing—"Then I prayed, and some power outside of myself came to my help." Still, Ambedkar seemed uncertain whether his resorting to prayer was a strength or a weakness.

Twice in the conversation Ambedkar said he was not interested in theological religion. "I want to save my people from the hell they are living in [now] and am not worrying about any hell to which the theologians may assign them." He added, "We must have a religion that works to uplift and free, just as Hinduism works . . . to debase and enslave."

Ambedkar affirmed the value of churches and pastors: "The church is essential, for our religion must be communal and social, but every congregation will need a leader, a trained man." Then he retrieved a theme from earlier in the conversation and spoke of the need of carrying most of his people with him. Unity, he said, was vital. He would regard it as a tragedy if millions of his followers became Muslims, while other millions became Buddhists, and still others Arya Samajists. Therefore, churches and missions should make more contacts with his people, he said. "I can't carry them alone. I may have to go with them in a direction I do not choose."

When Pickett asked Ambedkar if he knew that 125,000 untouchables were becoming Christians every year, he said, "I'd be glad to hear that 250,000 have become Christians this year."

As for himself, Ambedkar admitted, "I might have difficulty in being an orthodox Christian." However, he assured Pickett that he had no wish to promulgate his philosophical difficulties.

Pickett felt Ambedkar had been direct and honest with him. In his notes of the meeting, which he wrote shortly afterwards on a train to South India, he said Ambedkar seemingly felt that his life was not his own, that he had been given the privilege of an education and other advantages for a reason . . . for some special destiny. "He believes," wrote Pickett, "that the hand of God is upon him."

Pickett was the first person to dialogue with Ambedkar who, in Pickett's words, "in any sense represented the Christian movement as a whole." Ambedkar told him that others had approached him since Yeola. But they were, in Pickett's words:

> unrepresentative people who got to him on their own responsibility and presented a type of appeal to the Christian faith that was very disturbing to Ambedkar. He could get no response out of the minds and hearts of these men to the ills of his people and he was repelled.

During the interview, Pickett arranged a meeting between Ambedkar and Stanley Jones for early December. Jones came away encouraged and hopeful. Pickett and his two companions were similarly encouraged after their meeting. They left convinced that Ambedkar was leaning toward Christianity.

The November 24 meeting would not be Pickett's only in-depth conversation with the erudite leader of the untouchables. The following year, 1936, Pickett would move to Bombay, and the two would become good friends. In fact, after the move, Ambedkar would come to the Pickett apartment for dinner about once a month. They would talk politics, religion, and books. Ambedkar, who loved books, always left with one or two under his arm. Sometimes, before they parted, they would pray together.

21 The Mid-India Survey

Waskom Pickett's big post-Christmas event was to be the mid-India survey with McGavran and Singh. Between Christmas and the survey—December 28, 1935 to January 6, 1936—he would attend the 17th quadrennial session of Central Conference. In 1928, Central Conference had been given authority to elect its own bishops and it had elected J.R. Chitambar. With Bishop Robinson's retirement anticipated in May 1936, there was a strong consensus that a new bishop was needed. When the Picketts learned the election of a bishop was on the agenda, they were sure the Conference would, and should, choose another Indian. Nonetheless, despite those sentiments and the knowledge that two-thirds of the votes would come from Indians, they knew there was a chance Waskom's name would come up. So, he and Ruth made a pact. If asked, Waskom would decline. With one bishop in the family, they knew too well the demands and sacrifices of the office.

However, according to the *Indian Witness*, when the time came, the people were of one mind as to the person they should select. The paper reported:

> There were several present in the conference who might have been chosen and who would have filled the office with credit. This was widely recognized but there was very general agreement that in a very special way, "The hour and the man" had met. On the first ballot the Reverend J. Waskom Pickett, D.D., received more than the necessary two-thirds of the votes cast and was declared elected.

When the result was announced, it was received with great enthusiasm and rejoicing, except by Pickett. But, though he did not want to be thrust into the episcopacy, "since the election took place on the first ballot with no one else getting more than eight votes," he felt he could not judiciously withdraw. When Ruth heard, she went to her room and cried.

JARRELL WASKOM PICKETT WAS consecrated as a bishop on Sunday evening, January 5, 1936, in Jubbulpore's English Methodist Church. The church was packed with delegates and friends. The dignity of the service befitted the occasion. While the congregation stood, singing "How Firm a Foundation," the procession of those taking part in the service marched in pairs to the front: Reverend U On Kin and the Reverend Amar Das leading, then Bishops J.W. Robinson and B.T. Badley, Bishop J.R. Chitambar and Bishop-elect Pickett, Drs. L.O. Hartman and E. Stanley Jones, and the two presenters, the Reverends S.K. Mondol and Fred M. Perrill. Upon arriving at the altar rail, Dr. Pickett and the presenters stopped, while the rest went onto the platform and stood facing the audience. Then came another congregational hymn, "The Church's One Foundation," led by Bishop Chitambar; the Collect, led by Bishop Robinson, and so on until the laying on of hands and the final hymn, "All Hail the Power of Jesus' Name," led by Bishop Badley. After the service, L.O. Hartman presented a message on preparing for greater spiritual triumphs, Christ making them possible.

Despite the moving service, however, in some ways the most poignant event of Central Conference that year was the tribute given to Ruth's father, Bishop J.W. Robinson, whose retirement would come in May.

A WEEK LATER, AS PROMISED, Pickett was en route to central India to join Donald A. McGavran and George H. Singh in what looked to be his last survey. Because of his new episcopal duties, however, he had to shorten his commitment from six and a half weeks to five. Stanley Jones had pressed him hard to give up all but three weeks.

The mid-India study survey began with the team's arrival at Harda on the night of January 13 and ended on February 18 at Champa. Two criteria had helped narrow the study areas: (1) the rate of conversion growth had to be 200 or more percent over the past decade (1921-1931); or (2) the mission needed to be in a situation that looked highly promising.

With Pickett's enormously full schedule of writing, speaking, and consulting during the previous months, it had been left to McGavran to do most of the organizational work. However, because of his experience with the Satnami survey, he knew Pickett's routine. To help finance the study, each mission paid one half of 1 percent of their evangelistic budget.

The 38-day tour would be an exhausting one for all. Travel, set-up, interviewing, evening conferences, debriefing—every day would be packed full. A typical day unfolded as follows:

1. *The team would arrive and unpack.*

2. *The first set-up meeting would take place.* This involved a careful analysis of the situation with the English speakers. In this meeting they reviewed population maps, census statistics, and mission records in order to understand where the caste under consideration lived, what its numbers were, how it was distributed through the area, how many had been reached so far, how many were logistically reachable, and how the missionary force was presently organized and distributed. The team wanted to hear statements about the work and to see documents to support the statements. They were interested too in the history of the work, about failures or reversions and their causes, how many castes were now in the church, how they were progressing spiritually, and about the mission's estimates concerning the future. They also asked in advance for maps to be prepared indicating where the growth was taking place, for accurate historical statements on past attitudes of the mission toward group movements, and for records showing how they used their evangelistic money. The team also asked if converts were being removed from their villages, if leaders from among the converts were being used, how the churches were being organized, what methods of instruction were being used, what requirements there were for baptism, and if there were any giving requirements. Some information would have been mailed to the team ahead of time: print materials about the work, communications with the sponsoring board or society, policy papers, regular reports—anything that would "throw light on the . . . history of the work." These were all sent to McGavran who made a checklist of each item received so that they could be returned upon the team's arrival.

3. *The second set-up meeting would happen.* This was essentially a conference with Indian co-workers in Hindi, during which Pickett and other team members asked more questions about the work and the field.

4. *Village visitation would get underway.* With their helpers, they would travel to selected villages for the day's interviews. When, because of the distance, road conditions, or something unseen, important villages were not accessible, arrangements were made ahead of time for representatives to come to the interviewers.

5. *Inspirational services would be conducted.* These took place whenever possible, but the schedule did not always allow for it.

6. *A debriefing would occur.* The debriefing meeting usually lasted an hour. During that time, they reviewed the interview schedules, shared impressions, and discussed questions that had come up during the day.

AFTER PICKETT'S ELECTION TO the episcopacy, McGavran had done his best to rework the schedule, but with 10 fewer days, there was no way to visit all the fields. Two important ones remained. It was agreed, therefore, that McGavran would oversee and write the reports for those surveys.

HAD PICKETT NOT BEEN ELECTED bishop, he would have kept busy for years following up on invitations like the one to oversee the mid-India survey. He had already received similar requests from Catholics in India and missionaries in China. McGavran, it seems, was not the only one to recognize the promise of his insights and knowledge.

Some have thought that McGavran was overstating or just being generous to a favorite mentor when he said, "I lit my candle at Pickett's fire." But the number of Pickett accentuations in *Christian Mass Movements in India* and his other writing that would later be absorbed into the corpus of Church Growth literature is substantial. Among them are such Pickett themes as these: (1) the need for research and getting the facts; (2) his focus on groups and group (people) movements; (3) the power of group identity (homogeneity); (4) the destructiveness of social dislocation and the value of new Christians remaining in their social networks; (5) the hazards of Western individualism; (6) the need to abandon the mission station approach; (7) the concept of social lift; (8) the expediency of reallocating resources according to receptivity; (9) the critique of the term, "mass movement"; (10) the need to avoid foreignness and to adopt indigenous forms and symbols in the liturgy and worship of the church; and (11) the focus on the masses as more receptive than the classes.

How many of these concepts were original with Pickett is harder to say—perhaps not many. For example, long before Pickett's day, John Wesley had grasped the principle of allocating resources according to receptivity. And advocating the use of indigenous forms was certainly no new thing, although, in Pickett's day, he was one of the exceptions in advocating it. Developing missionary strategy from the results of social science investigations was a new thing, however; and Pickett was without question among the pioneers.

This we can say with certainty: Pickett's application of this particular panoply of principles around a core emphasis on group conversions was groundbreaking. The sum of the parts in his panoply was, as McGavran noted in his review of Pickett's 1938 book, *Christ's Way to India's Heart,* a radically new philosophy of missions—a fresh paradigm.

THE REPORTS THE PICKETT-MCGAVRAN-SINGH mid-India team prepared for the participating missions included highly useful analyses and recommendations. Historian and sociologist John A. Lapp, for instance, described the study of A.C. Brunk and Bishop George Lapp's mission as "one of the most sober, penetrating critiques of the American Mennonite Mission ever produced."

For McGavran, the mid-India survey proved to be "most revealing"—that is, it uncovered many fresh opportunities. More important, it confirmed his belief that Pickett really was onto something—that by questioning old assumptions, he had managed to blaze a fresh path. It would be nearly two decades until McGavran published his *Bridges of God,* the book with which he began to stir the missiological world. But had he not, early on, realized the value of Pickett's insights, and had he not, later on, discovered their international relevance, and had he not tirelessly worked at refining and communicating the concepts until the missiological world could no longer ignore them, Pickett's powerful ideas would probably have died in 1930s India. Thus, without Pickett's ideas, we might never have known McGavran, but without McGavran, Pickett's ideas might never have met their potential. With Pickett moving from research into the demanding administrative and oversight responsibilities of the episcopacy, it was going to take a McGavran to keep his insights from fading and, more than that, to bring them into full bloom.

The Bombay Years (1936-1944)

Robinson Memorial Church, Bombay. The bishop's apartment was on the top floor below the right tower; it extended to the back of the building. The two tower rooms served as a guest room and the bishop's office.

Day of Dad's return, November 1936

Douglas and Margaret with Grandpa Robinson, 1938

Eastwood House, Landour, 1936

Kellogg Community Church, Landour, where Bishop Pickett often preached in the 1930s and 1940s

Christmas, 1941

Waskom and Ruth, 1941

22 Politics and Conversion

On February 29, a few days after Pickett's return from the mid-India survey, the Methodist Episcopal Church of Lucknow held a reception and farewell for him and Ruth. With Bishop John Wesley Robinson's retirement becoming official in May, and Bishop Badley's appointment as his replacement in Delhi, everyone knew the Pickett family would soon be moving to Bombay. Between 400 and 500 guests greeted them when they arrived on the lawn of the Lal Bagh Girls' High School. Besides fellowship and refreshments, the reception included tributes by local leaders, music by the Lucknow Christian College Orchestra, and an Urdu poem written for the occasion. A few days later, in the *Indian Witness*, Fred Perrill reflected:

> The welcome extended to Bishop and Mrs. Pickett in Lucknow is typical of the regard in which they are held by all members of the church in India. They will be welcomed in Bombay and should some future day bring them back to Lucknow . . . they will discover that their welcome has grown with the years.

From Lucknow, Waskom, Ruth, Margaret and Douglas retreated to Landour. In May, with the family remaining in the hills for the hot season, Waskom would go to General Conference in Columbus, Ohio.

ONE OF THE DEPRESSED CLASSES GROUP, with whom Pickett had spent "the richest two hours of my life," and who arranged for Pickett's first meeting with B.R. Ambedkar, was B. Baldeo Pershad Jaiswar, apparently of Chamar background. Adopting names like Koril, Aharwar, Jatiya, Dhusiya and, especially Jaiswar, was how some groups of Chamars sought to escape the stigma of untouchability. Since that memorable meeting in

November and their time with Ambedkar, Pickett and Baldeo Jaiswar had kept in touch. And when Baldeo learned the bishop would be going to America for the Methodist's General Conference, he gave him a letter to read.

On Thursday, May 7, 1936, the sixth day of the Columbus, Ohio gathering, following fraternal greetings from a messenger of the Korean Methodist Church, the moderator, A.B. Leonard, give Pickett the floor. Pickett unfolded the letter—a greeting from the All-India Adi Hindu Depressed Classes Conference of Lucknow. It was dated 4th March, 1936. He explained the letter contained a declaration he had been asked to share. It began:

> Christian missionaries have come to our rescue. Many of our number have received the gospel and embraced Christianity. Some have reached high positions and are looked on with respect. The rest of us who have received education, and are now at the forefront of the fight for the rights of our brethren, are largely the product of Christian missions.

The letter described the Hindu opposition to the conversion of untouchables: "Caste Hindus . . . want us to remain their slaves. They object when anyone tries to help us." It affirmed that

> liberty . . . can come only through the grace of the Lord Jesus Christ . . . He served the poor and needy all His life and at last died in their cause. His followers are bound to be our friends and helpers.

The final paragraph was a plea for prayer:

> We beg to ask that the General Conference, the Missionary Council, and the Christians of America pray the almighty Father to save us from our oppressors and to enable us, realizing his will for our lives, to achieve in Jesus Christ the destiny for which God made us.

TWO WEEKS AFTER BISHOP PICKETT read the letter, its authors gathered in Lucknow with delegates from seven provinces for a two-day All-

Religions Conference. It could not boast the order and decorum of the American meeting in Ohio; on the contrary, it was more like a protest rally. On the public day of the conference, most of the 14 guest speakers spent their podium time condemning Hinduism. They used metaphors like "poison," "chloroform," "a chain," and "traffic with the devil." The mood was one of intense detestation as person after person described acts of oppression and duplicity by Hindus and Hindu reform movements. The clamorous assembly had been advertized as a forum in which untouchable leaders could hear the case for each of several alternatives to Hinduism. Instead it was short on information and long on incitement.

More disappointing, though, was the absence of Ambedkar, who was ill—"Hamlet without the Prince," commented one reporter.

> What was hoped for was a responsible panchayat . . . [What transpired was] a noisy mass meeting, wherein Moslems predominated to the extent of 75 percent of the audience, and Harijans were largely at a numerical discount.

Nonetheless, in the two days that followed the 14 presentations, the untouchables who were present adopted several resolutions: (1) they affirmed their confidence in Ambedkar and his declared exodus from Hinduism; (2) they resolved to follow Ambedkar out of Hinduism. The conference also appointed a study committee to recommend an alternative religion. Ostensibly, they would come to a consensus on their new religion at a conference planned for mid-1937. One of those appointed to the study committee was Baldeo Jaiswar.

When the Lucknow All-Religions Conference was first announced, some—including leaders of the NCC—had been reluctant to get involved. They were afraid a Christian presence would give the wrong impression. It might come off as if the Christian faith were a commodity in competition with other religious commodities. Other Christian leaders, however, saw an opportunity, if only to show solidarity with the plight of the depressed classes. Among them was the Reverend John Subhan, a Methodist pastor and one of the 14 presenters at the conference. Using Pickett's mass movement study, he showed that Christianity offered more than personal salvation. It also offered the possibility of social transformation. "It is the glory of Christianity to fuse both . . . into one," he said.

Although the All-Religions Conference did not accomplish all it set out to do, it did garner publicity for the depressed class movement. Fred M. Perrill, for example, thought the conference significant enough to devote most of two issues of the *Indian Witness* to it. And a group of missionary attendees, including Donald McGavran, came out of the conference with a set of recommendations for promulgation and action. Among NCC leaders, they were tagged "the Lucknow group."

The All-Religions Conference was notable not only for its strong anti-Hindu rhetoric but, also, for its anti-Gandhi sentiment. One of its resolutions was a rejection of Gandhi's label "Harijan" as abhorrent and insulting, with a request that others not use the term. The same resolution said: "This conference further expresses its dissatisfaction with the Harijan Movement launched by Mahatma Gandhi." Not surprisingly, therefore, Hindu criticisms of Ambedkar and his followers became harsher than ever in the weeks following the event.

MEANWHILE THE METHODIST General Conference in America had confirmed what Methodists in India already knew, that from September 1936 Bishop Pickett would be assigned to the Bombay Area, consisting of the Bombay, Gujarat, Hyderabad and South India Conferences. However, the Pickett family would not move there until after his return from America in late October or early November. In the interval, Pickett addressed a series of large gatherings—in Boston, Philadelphia and New York, including one at Norman Vincent Peale's Marble Collegiate Church—telling about the mass movements.

However, it was the address he gave in London on his way back from the U.S. that got trumpeted in India. The setting was Central Hall, Westminster, on October 8, 1936. His Grace, the Archbishop of Canterbury, was presiding. The event, arranged by the International Missionary Council and the Mildmay "Movement for World Evangelisation," was conceived as a fund-raiser for supporting a successor to Pickett in the mass movement work of the NCC.

William Paton introduced the meeting. Paton depicted the situation among the untouchables as a problem and challenge. The Archbishop of Canterbury then reminded the audience the movement of untouchables to Christ was prior to and independent of what they had read in the papers about the Ambedkar phenomenon and the new political movements on behalf of the untouchables. "We are not going to take part in any auction among political parties in India for the souls of India's people," he assured the audience. Then, praising Pickett's *Christian Mass Movements in India*, he described Pickett's years of work studying the mass movements. Pickett's speech followed. It was filled with stories from the mass movements. He said that, like the Archbishop, he had no wish to see the "wholesale and indiscriminate baptisms" of the age of Charlemagne repeated in India. Neither would he want to see multitudes taken into a church unable to care for them. But, referring to the Yeola event, he said that he saw great significance in the decision of 12,000 untouchables to leave the Hindu faith.

For 45 minutes, Pickett mesmerized the audience with a blend of facts and anecdotes of the movements. One reporter wrote: "We drank in every word." Most of the church papers, including the October 16 issue of the *Church Times*, reported the speech. The *Times* headline read, "No 'Auction' for the Souls of Indians.'" When Gandhi read the article and the transcript of Pickett's speech, he was indignant.

THE DAY THE *Church Times* article appeared, Pickett flew into Karachi on Imperial Airways. He had left London's Croydon Aerodrome—"gateway to the Empire"—seven days before on a slow-flying H.P.42—pilots used to talk about its "built in drag." His air journey to Karachi took him through Paris (Le Bourget), Basle (Birsfelden), Genoa, Naples, Corfu, Athens (Phaeron Bay), Tobruk, Alexandria, Gaza, Rutbah, Baghdad, Basra, Bushire, Lingeh, Jask, and Gwadar. It included several overnight stays and stops at unattended fuel stations in the desert. By today's jet-age standards, the trip would have seemed interminable. However, the bishop called it "most enjoyable."

From Karachi, Pickett went directly to Landour. After a week of relaxation, he, Ruth, and Douglas left for Lucknow to arrange for shipping their effects to Bombay. The date was October 26. They drove to Bombay via Jubbulpore, where Pickett spoke to the Mid-India Provincial Council. McGavran was there. So was John R. Mott (in India for his fifth visit).

The new Pickett residence was in one of the twin towers of the Robinson Memorial Church—named for John E. Robinson and built by Ruth's father, John Wesley Robinson. It was on Sankli Street in Byculla, a middle-class enclave in the northwest part of Bombay.

The decade-old church was unusual in that it housed church offices, residences for a missionary family and several pastors, rooms for missionaries who were passing through the city, a hostel for young men, rooms for community social service, and a shared worship space for English, Marathi, Kanarese, and Telugu-speaking Methodist congregations. The scarceness and high cost of housing in the city made it seem wise to include the episcopal residence as well.

WHATEVER LEISURE TIME PICKETT managed in November soon vanished. His December 1936 calendar included three round-trips by train totaling 3,000 miles. From December 3 to 4 he participated in the National Christian Council's Conference on Mass Movements in Nagpur. After that, he went to the South India Annual Conference at Kolar, 40 miles from Bangalore. Finally, at month's end (from December 29 to January 1), he journeyed to the NCC's Biennial Meeting in Nagpur.

The first of the three meetings was not as partisan as some had hoped for. A few had pushed for restricting the meeting to mass movement workers. However, Hodge, Mott, and Pickett recognized that with a few NCC leaders voicing misgivings about Ambedkar's motives, broader representation was called for. So besides the mass movement regulars, they invited all the NCC Executive and "a seasoning of Indian leaders who carry weight in their community." But that was the limit. They dismissed a proposal to invite Gandhi's friend, missionary C.F. Andrews. And when Agatha Harrison, assistant to C.F. Andrews, asked to come as part of her efforts to ease tensions between anti-conversion Hindus and Christians, John Mott told her no visitors were allowed.

The Mass Movement Conference began on a Thursday with Bishop Azariah presiding. One hundred twenty were present, 45 of them delegates. Among those present was Alexander McLeish of the *World Dominion* in London, the main sponsor of Pickett's second stretch as NCC Mass Movement Secretary. Presiding was Bishop Azariah, whose opening remarks underscored the goal of reaching a common mind on some of the issues raised by Bishop Pickett's research. He added that the widespread unrest among the depressed classes, heightened by B. R. Ambedkar's declaration, gave their deliberations extra import. Mott, who delivered three luminous messages, was in top form as the keynoter. Besides Mott's speeches, highlights of the conference included a report by Pickett on his mass movement research in the Andhra country and one by Hodge on the NCC's new Forward Movement in Evangelism.

Although mass movement work was high priority, the NCC's new five-year Forward Movement signaled a shift from missionary to church-initiated evangelization. The intention was to place the mantel of evangelistic responsibility squarely on the Indian churches, thus realizing the ultimate goal of Indianization.

Pickett's report on Sudra movements in Andhra country was a preview of his *Christ's Way to India's Heart*, to be published a little over a year later. It highlighted the widening opportunity created by the influence of the changed lives of Christians from the depressed classes. He pleaded for more cooperation, greater emphasis on indigenous worship, and raising up more Indian leaders.

Donald McGavran also spoke, summarizing the recent mid-India study. However, to the embarrassment of many, he directly challenged John R. Mott to go home and tell the mission boards what India needed was *three* full-time mass movement secretaries, not just one. McGavran pointed to the mid-India survey as a model of what could be done cooperatively by a provincial council. The central lesson of the survey, he said, was the rebirth of hope through embracing the reality of group movements.

The overall mood of the Nagpur convocation was expectant. Participants seemed to sense the Indian church was on the threshold of great advances for the Kingdom of God. Everyone present listened with deep emotion as Azariah and others reported on the movement of God's Spirit in various areas of the South. With the Biennial Meeting of the National Christian Council coming within the month, it was decided that Bishops Azariah and Pickett, and Mr. Hodge, would immediately write a summary of the conference. To the question, "What can be done to stimulate greater interest in the mass movements among the churches?" the delegate body came up with the following ideas: trading stories and lessons learned through inter-visitation; strengthening Indian leadership; publicizing the needs of the mass movement work in city churches; getting students involved in the work; making greater use of vernacular literature; encouraging visits to mass movement areas; sending delegations from mass movement areas to the city churches; doing more surveys; and producing more literature about the mass movements.

A WEEK AFTER THE CONFERENCE, Pickett was in for an unpleasant surprise. In his paper the *Harijan*, Gandhi launched the first of a series of

broadsides on missionaries involved with mass movement work, on Pickett
in particular. Using a question and answer format—the questions having
come from "visitors interested in Christian mass movements"—Gandhi
said in response to the question, "Do you see a reason for Christian
workers in the West to come here, and if so what is their contribution?":

> In the manner in which they [missionaries] are working, there
> would seem to be no room for them . . . They do . . . harm to the
> whole of India. They present a Christianity of their belief but not
> the message of Jesus as I understand it.

To the question, "What would happen if there is an increase in the process
of multiplying Christians?" he said:

> If there is an appreciable increase there would be blood feuds
> between the Harijans themselves, more savage than the feuds we
> have in Bombay. Fifty per cent of the residents in Segaon [a
> small town 260 miles northeast of Bombay] are Harijans.
> Supposing you stole away 10 Harijans and built a church for
> them, you would set up father against son, and son against father
> . . . That would be a caricature of Christianity.

Against Bishop Pickett's speech at Central Hall, Westminster, the reader
was told that Gandhiji regarded reports of an uprush of spiritual hunger
among millions of untouchables as absurd. When he read what Pickett had
said in the *Church Times*, it had shocked him. Clearly agitated, Gandhi
said, "He has made such extravagant statements that I would want a
demonstration of them—even of the statement that millions were seeking
to be converted."

In the next issue of the *Harijan*, Gandhi again inveighed against
Pickett's statistics. Quoting from the *Church Times* report, he said, "I have
rarely seen so much exaggeration in so little space."

> A reader ignorant of the conditions in India would conclude that
> the figures relate to the conversions due to the movement led by
> Dr. Ambedkar. I am sure Dr. Pickett could not have made any
> such claim. He had in mind the figures to date commencing from
> the establishment of the church in India hundreds of years ago.

But the figures are irrelevant to the general claim said to have
been advanced by the Bishop.

Gandhi then asked,

> Where are "the multitudes in India who marvel" at the
> transformations in the lives of "four and a half millions of the
> depressed classes"? I am one of the multitude having practically
> traveled more than half a dozen times all over India, and I have
> not seen any transformation on the scale described by Dr.
> Pickett . . . I should like to know the Brahmins "who have
> testified—albeit reluctantly—to the power of Christianity to
> transform the characters and lives of people whom they once
> thought incapable of religious feeling."

Gandhi claimed that, in contrast, he could point to plenty of Brahmins who
were ready to testify to the power his own reform movement to change
the lives of Harijans.

Gandhi implied that Pickett's speech contained other unbelievable
elements, which he had no time to answer. Then he launched one last
volley:

> I should like to know the hundreds of high-caste Hindus who "are
> now coming into the church in areas where this transformation
> of life has occurred among the untouchables." If all the
> astounding statements Dr. Pickett has propounded can be
> substantiated, truly it is "one of the great miracles of Christian
> history," nay, of the history of man.

23 The McGavran Controversy

After Christmas, the 1936-37 Biennial Meeting of the NCC got underway. Those who hoped the mood of the Mass Movement Conference three weeks earlier would carry over were let down. This time Agatha Harrison *was* there. And this time, supporters of mass movement evangelism were the minority, numbering, at most, a third. The strong missionary voice that once dominated NCC meetings was no more, but though the better part of the 60 delegates were Indians, that was not the fly in the ointment. The impediments were, instead, these. First, many representatives were from city churches where putting money and personnel into village work was out of favor. Second, a vocal handful of non-Indian, Gandhi sympathizers was present. Among them were Mr. and Mrs. Carl Heath of the India Conciliation Group (ICG). Representing the Mahatma's posture, they insisted on a moratorium on evangelizing the depressed classes in favor of internal Hindu reform. Bishop Azariah found the notion of their "wanting us to take our directions from Mr. Gandhi" distasteful, but in his role chair, he kept the sentiment to himself. Thus, despite Azariah's prominent presence in his purple robe, those who came from the Mass Movement Conference with high hopes were soon dispirited. Their mass movement recommendations fell on deaf ears. Evangelism, they were told, is more than mass movements, and it would be unwise to overemphasize special interests.

The mass movement enthusiasts were also disappointed by the conference's failure to appoint a new mass movement secretary to carry on with Pickett's work. G.S. Ingram and some others were lobbying to get McGavran appointed, which everyone knew McGavran wanted. They were also pushing for a mass movement board. But the Executive Committee liked neither the "board" proposal nor the idea of McGavran as Pickett's successor. And since Frank Whittaker—the man they did want—had not yet agreed, they took no action.

On the last day of the conference, Azariah happened on Ingram, McGavran, McLeish, and Thomas Donohugh who was visiting from the Methodist Board of Foreign Missions in New York. They were intently discussing the McGavran brush-off. Donohugh was clearly agitated because the Methodists had just voted to help fund the position at the NCC Executive Committee's request. Azariah tried to quell their frustration, to no avail.

When William Paton got Hodges's report of the meeting, he too became "seriously exercised" over the failure to appoint a mass movement secretary, for the Executive Committee had also appealed to him. In response, he had solicited funds from the British missionary societies. Paton wrote to Azariah and Hodge demanding an explanation. "We were asked to help a specific plan," he bristled "and now find something else has been proposed, rather vague and indefinite, with no clear recognition of the change of policy involved." To both Donohugh and Paton, it appeared that Azariah as president and Hodge as secretary had deliberately let the matter of a replacement for Pickett fall between the cracks.

But Azariah had an explanation. He said they were negotiating with someone and that although McGavran had been lobbying for the post and had some backing, they were clear that he was not their choice:

> He has not done any Mass Movement work himself in his own mission. He has made a survey of the mid-India area; but when he introduced the report of the survey, he used language that would estrange anyone from the cause he advocated.

Azariah's response would not have surprised Pickett. A month and a half before the meeting he had written to Diffendorfer:

> I think it is doubtful whether Dr. McGavran will be invited to join the staff of the National Christian Council. He has been regarded as insufficiently considerate of work and workers not directly related to Mass Movements. Personally, I think most of the criticism to which he is being subjected is unfair, but it cannot be ignored.

In support of the NCC's not having appointed a mass movement secretary, Pickett wrote to A. Livingston Warnshuis, IMC co-secretary with J.H. Oldham, that although the NCC had been criticized, in fairness, there were not yet enough funds in place. Moreover, Hodge, Azariah, and he were agreed on a candidate if he was able to accept, and a backup candidate should he decline. But he added:

> I regret that neither Hodge nor Azariah considered McGavran as acceptable. I recognize, however, that some of McGavran's pronouncements during this year have given cause for fear that he would not be able to command united support.

On the last day of the NCC meeting, Agatha Harrison approached Pickett. She wanted to talk about Gandhi's attacks on him in *The Harijan*. The next day, Pickett described their conversation to R.E. Diffendorfer:

> If you receive "The Harijan," you will discover that in three recent issues Mr. Gandhi has accused me, the C.M.S. Secretaries, and the Bishop of Dornakal of exaggeration. His personal representative, Miss Agatha Harrison, was present throughout the session of the Council and on the last day told me that she had become fully convinced that Mr. Gandhi was in error. She showed me a hand-written statement from Mr. Gandhi that if he was convinced of the incorrectness of his charge he would offer a handsome apology. She has asked that the Bishop of Dornakal and I meet Mr. Gandhi next week. I agreed to do so if the Bishop of Dornakal agrees, but I will not see him alone.

On January 17, Bishop Azariah sent a thank-you to Miss Harrison and signaled that Secretary Hodge was already arranging to bring the Mahatma to Nagpur. His letter contained a strong and unapologetic defense of the Christian position on conversion. He stated that he realized Mr. Gandhi did not agree with conversion but that "since . . . [conversion] is a fundamental characteristic of Christianity, it is impossible for us to alter our position." On comments Harrison had made about a conversation with Indian politician C.R. Rajagopalachariar, Azariah wrote:

> Mr. Gandhi and Mr. Rajagopalachariar . . . see that thousands are accepting the Christian faith and transferring their allegiances from their ancestral Hindu religion to Christianity. Mr. Rajagopalachariar intensely dislikes this. Since 1932, i.e., since the report of the census of 1931 was published, he has publicly

urged Hindus to wake up and give up their social inequalities in order that the depressed classes may not be driven from Hinduism.

Mr. Gandhi and Mr. Rajagopalachariar vehemently attack missions and missionaries for redoubling their efforts at such a time as this. It is realized that the possibility of conversion of large numbers to Christianity is even greater today than ever before. They therefore attack foreign money, the foreign missionary; and not only these but also all indigenous propaganda work as they have never done before.

What, I ask, is our duty at this time—as followers of Christ and as Indian nationalists? First and foremost it is our duty to be loyal to Christ, and therefore we must proclaim Him to all our people as the Way, the Truth, and the Life . . . Christ and His message always arouse opposition . . . Conflicts are inevitable when His followers are loyal to Him. On the other hand, if unworthy methods are used in this work by any particular mission or church or in any particular area, it is our duty to discover these and rectify blunders. But the remedy for a mistaken method of work is not to stop the work!

My conclusion is therefore this. Mr. Gandhi and Mr. Rajagopalachariar must first abandon their attitude of antagonism to change of religion as such. Each religion stands for certain truths. When a man genuinely seeks after truth, he will come to a point where truth must win his obedience. This obedience must mean abandoning one religious system and uniting with another. If a man fears this result, he will either affect a compromise with the truth as he sees it, or yield to an unreality, professing to see in his old religion the new truth he has found in the new religion.

It is our love of country and countrymen that makes us redouble our efforts at this juncture and call for help from Christians all over the world. If Mr. Gandhi's objective is the uplift of the village, the removal of social disabilities . . . and not merely the propping up of Hinduism—let him show his greatness and genuineness by sympathy with us in our effort. Hating conversion and hating the Christian propaganda are not becoming of a true lover of India's poor.

It is this point of view that I shall make clear in our interview.

On the same day, from his office at Robinson Memorial Church, Pickett wrote the following to Warnshuis:

> The Hindus are watching every movement of the Christians with the greatest concern. Mr. Gandhi is devoting a very large part of his energy to an effort to hold the depressed classes in Hinduism. He has attacked me . . . Bishop Azariah and the Church Missionary Society. These attacks, first published in the Harijan, have been copied very widely by the Indian press. Mr. Gandhi has interpreted all effort to win converts from the depressed classes as a political movement to strengthen the Christian community and to weaken Hinduism as a political force. Some politicians have gone as far as to threaten to make all efforts to win converts illegal as soon as they have achieved power.

Pickett indicated in the letter that he and Azariah were to meet with Gandhi in Nagpur on February 17 (although the meeting actually seems to have occurred on the 12th). He added:

> Fortunately Mr. Gandhi's attacks on Bishop Azariah and me can be easily disproved. He accused me of exaggeration because I said that in the Telugu country the transformation in the character of many of the converts from the depressed classes had so commended the Gospel that many neighbors of the middle and high castes are becoming Christians. To this he replied that he has met very large numbers of Indian Christians and that they are not better than the Hindus. His attack upon Bishop Azariah is based on the latter's statement that 40,000 of the middle and upper caste peoples have become Christians. He argues that since he had not known this it couldn't be true.

Besides Pickett, Azariah, and Gandhi, four observers were present at the meeting: John Z. Hodge and Mrs. Hodge, Miss M. Reid, and Gandhi's secretary, Mahadev Desai, who took notes "for his own files." Since Desai's report has, so far, not been found, and since the parties agreed not to publish any reports of the meeting, all that is known comes from piecing together a few details leaked out over the next couple of years.

PART OF WHAT LEAKED OUT became engulfed in scandal. More than a year later, in 1938, in the London-based publication *World Dominion*, Donald McGavran published three articles entitled, "The Battle for Brotherhood in India Today." McGavran described the evils of the caste system and the Hindus fight to keep it alive and well. Introducing the Ambedkar factor, and underscoring the opposition of Gandhi, he stated that the present focal point of the battle was the Christian ingathering of untouchables through conversion movements. The outcome of the battle and the fate of Hinduism will largely be decided, he wrote, by "where 70,000,000 'untouchables' go in their search for brotherhood." McGavran closed the series of articles with a dramatic account of the battle of words between Pickett, Azariah and Gandhi in their meeting at Nagpur:

Mr. Gandhi recently came to Nagpur to see Bishop V.A. Azariah, the great Christian Indian leader of the Christian forces in India, and Bishop J.W. Pickett, the author of that epochal book *Christian Mass Movements in India,* in regard to the movements to Christ numbering two hundred thousand per annum from amongst the oppressed classes. "We shall not allow conversions to continue," Mr. Gandhi exclaimed in conclusion of a three hour conference. The Christian leaders pointed out to Mr. Gandhi the unquestioned improvement which had come to the oppressed class people who became Christians, and tried in every way to induce him to say that he was in favor of any amelioration of their lot. But his position remained adamant, namely that it was better for the oppressed classes to suffer in Hinduism than to be relieved in Christianity. Of course he would not say this. He simply refuses to admit that the oppressed classes who have become Christians are at all improved. At the conclusion of the conference, Mr. Gandhi said to Bishop Azariah, "You Christians must stop preaching to and making disciples amongst the Depressed classes. If you do not, we shall make you. We shall appeal to the educated Indian Christians; we shall appeal to your home constituency; and if those fail we shall prohibit by law any change of religion, and will back up the law by the force of the State."

McGavran's account of the until now shrouded meeting was immediately quoted in the Madras *Guardian*. It was accompanied by an editorial note, which stated:

Stray references have been made to the Gandhi-Dornakal interview, in speeches and papers. The foregoing report is a more coherent account than what we have seen on other occasions . . . Dr. McGavran has evidently had access to information that has been denied to the public . . . The statements published point to serious developments in the future that are far-reaching in consequences to many interests. It is unfair that secrecy of this kind should be maintained on this issue, while a few people are at liberty to publish disjointed versions of the interview.

When Azariah and Hodge learned what McGavran had written, they were incensed. Azariah wrote a strong letter to the *Guardian* denying there was any substance at all to the quotations ascribed to Gandhi:

Every statement—without exception—attributed to Gandhiji by Dr. McGavran is *wholly and absolutely untrue* . . . [Gandhi] did not say or suggest, directly or indirectly, anything like what is attributed to him in this article. The whole, as far as our interview in March 1937 is concerned, is a cruel fabrication.

Hodge confided to Paton that, "This thing has worried me more than anything else during my association with the NCC."

McGavran, who said he was unaware of the agreement not to publish what was said in the meeting, admitted in the *Guardian* that he had made up the quotations and that his account of the meeting was pieced together "from a dozen different sources." But Pickett admitted to Hodge that he was the likely the sole source, "that McGavran may have laid hold of something" he had said at the Landour Conference the previous year.

McGavran received severe written reprimands from Azariah, Hodge, and Paton, the last intimating that without an acceptable apology, McGavran's entire career would be in jeopardy. All of them made it clear that neither they nor Gandhi considered the first draft of his apology acceptable because it sounded more defensive than apologetic. (In essence, McGavran had said that although he had invented the quote, he had not misrepresented the Hindu denial of brotherhood to untouchables, which had been his point.) However, when Gandhi's secretary, Mahadev Desai, judged McGavran's new apology acceptable, everyone breathed a sigh of relief—although Gandhi apparently wanted it published in all the papers that had quoted the McGavran piece.

Although Hodge backed Azariah's pointed denial, Pickett never did. In fact, on several points, he confirmed McGavran's statements. For example, Pickett wrote to *World Dominion's* Alexander McLeish:

> Confidentially, I am of the opinion that the Bishop of Dornakal has dealt too severely with him [McGavran] and also that the Bishop of Dornakal's denial has gone considerably further than the facts justified. Three of the four statements attributed by McGavran to Gandhi were, in my judgment, reasonably fair indications made by him in the interview, but the Bishop of Dornakal, in his eagerness to prevent a clash on the eve of the Tambaram Conference, has declared that none of these statements were either made or suggested directly or indirectly. I have entered an emphatic protest against the statement which he has sent to the press without consultation, and have insisted that any subsequent statement be issued after agreement between us.

On McGavran, Pickett added: "He should not have published anything about this interview without getting our permission and making sure of the facts, and what he wrote was not an adequate account." But he also said, "Poor McGavran ought not to be further humiliated."

After Pickett took issue with Azariah for being too harsh with McGavran and for his overstated denial, the bishop's reaction seemed to mellow. McLeish wrote: "Evidently Dr. Pickett's protest was made to the Bishop of Dornakal between the two letters we got here [from Azariah]. I am struck by the very different tone of the last letter I got."

WHAT WAS REALLY SAID in the meeting with Gandhi? Several years later in a tribute to Gandhi, Hodge suggested that the Gandhi who showed up that day was a disputatious Gandhi:

> There came a day when the Mahatma and two eminent bishops met in our bungalow to discuss the meaning and implications of

Christian Mass Movements, with special reference to proselytizing. I saw then the well-briefed advocate and practiced dialectician in action—a formidable adversary. But the bishops held their ground.

Similarly, J.F. Edwards, the English editor of *Dnyanodaya*, who seemed to be informed about the meeting and who was the first to let Paton know about McGavran's "partly mistaken" account, called the debate a "stiff" one. Their hints of the tone of the discussion are not out of line with what Pickett wrote in a letter only a month after the Gandhi meeting:

> In the interview with Gandhi which Bishop Azariah, Hodge and I had on the 12th February, he intimated that if we continue seeking conversions from the depressed classes, he will draw away from the Church many educated Indian Christians who share his aversion to the conversion of the untouchables.

More arresting than the reported tone of the meeting, though, is a comparison of what Pickett said Gandhi intimated with McGavran's much maligned "quote": "We shall appeal to the educated Indian Christians." As for McGavran's most controversial suggestion—that Gandhi threatened by legal means to stop conversions—perhaps the Mahatma said no such thing that day. But if he had, how different would it have been from what he said in another meeting two years earlier: "If I had the power and could legislate, I should certainly stop all proselytizing."

So why were Hodge and Azariah so distressed? Gandhi was due an apology, but why was it more upsetting to Hodge than anything he'd faced in all his years with the NCC? And why did Azariah overdraw his denial? The answer, it seems, is that they were afraid Gandhi and the Hindus would exploit the controversy and sink the IMC Conference at Tambaram. For Azariah and Hodge, such a development would have been the supreme embarrassment and disaster. Pickett was certain that explained Azariah's excessive reaction. And on confessing that, "This thing has worried me more than anything else," Hodge immediately added:

> I am still apprehensive that its repercussions may react on Tambaram. We have been studiously endeavoring to prepare a good pitch for Tambaram, and this kind of thing is likely to queer it.

It was not offending Gandhi that concerned them, but what Gandhi might make of it, and the possible repercussions for their hosting of the foremost missionary conference of the decade. That is why Paton, Hodge, and Azariah immediately tried to notify editors not to discuss the McGavran piece in their papers—not just editors in India, but in Britain too. J.F. Edwards, in a letter to Paton, expressed the fear they all shared:

> If any British papers were to discuss openly the issue raised in McGavran's unfortunate article, the discussion would be bound to reach India with fatal consequences for the Tambaram Conference which we all hope and pray may mean so much for the Christian movement in India and the world over.

Although Pickett shared concerns over the McGavran articles' negative effect, he thought Azariah and Hodge were unduly cowered by Gandhi and his supporters. As he had written to R.E. Diffendorfer in March 1937, he had been disappointed with Azariah and Hodge's deportment ever since the NCC Biennial Conference.

> Let me say quite confidentially that neither Bishop Azariah nor Hodge has showed to their best advantage in recent months. Their leadership at the last session of the N.C.C. was halting and uncertain. My judgement is that P.O. Phillip and others who represent the detached, non-typical Indian Christian attitude of hostility to the depressed classes and of a deference to Gandhi and the Hindu Communalists had frightened them rather severely.

AFTER PICKETT'S MOVE TO BOMBAY in 1936, and he and Ambedkar became friends, Gandhi was a frequent subject of their conversations. Pickett's unfavorable estimation of the tactics of Gandhi and his associates was colored as much by these exchanges as by Gandhi's *Harijan* attacks on Pickett, for Ambedkar was far from an admirer of the Mahatma. Beyond disputing Gandhi's claim to represent India's untouchables, he regarded Gandhi as an impediment to improving their status. Likewise, to Gandhi, Ambedkar was both rival and nemesis.

A few days after Pickett and Azariah's controversial 1937 meeting with Gandhi, Ambedkar complained that Gandhi's men were intercepting many letters addressed to him. Pickett listened with interest, but he doubted the story. However, shortly after that, something happened that changed his mind.

In early July 1937, Pickett opened a letter from the office of the All-India Depressed Classes Conference. It was from Baldeo Jaiswar, one of the men who had helped Pickett set up his first meeting with Ambedkar. Jaiswar wanted to know how Pickett was doing and, particularly, about the letter he had sent Pickett in the spring of 1936 to read to the Methodist General Conference in America. On July 8, Pickett responded as follows:

> My dear Baldeo,
>
> I was happy to receive your letter of July 2nd yesterday, and thus to reestablish contact with you after a period of 15 months.
>
> Your statement given to me on the eve of my departure for America was read to the General Conference and released to the Press. It created very great interest throughout the United States. I am sure that the Churches of America are remembering India's oppressed castes continuously in their prayers and are hoping that the next few years will bring a decision to follow Christ made in deep sincerity by millions of them. I may tell you that in my Episcopal Area thousands of your people are now deciding to be disciples of Jesus. In one small area 700 people were baptized in six weeks quite recently.
>
> I hope that you will soon make your decision and will seek an experience of the redeeming grace of Christ Jesus.

But Baldeo Jaiswar never got Pickett's letter. Mohandas K. Gandhi got it instead! A month later, Pickett received an envelope from Gandhi's ashram at Warda. Opening it, he was astonished to find his letter to Jaiswar. With it was a note from Gandhi, dated July 31. It read:

> Dear Friend,
>
> The enclosed was delivered evidently by some error at Delhi at the office of the *Harijan Sevak Sangh* [Harijan Service Organization]. The receiving clerk in the usual course opened the correspondence that came under his charge, put the enclosed before the secretary and the secretary finding that the letter was not meant for him but contained what appeared to be strange statements sent it to me, or to be more accurate, to Mahadev

Desai whom you met with me at Nagpur, who in turn has forward it to me.

Does not the letter contain very strange statements? Can I make public use of them either with or without your name?

Yours sincerely,

M.K. Gandhi

Was Ambedkar's complaint about Gandhi's hijacking mail justified? Was Pickett's letter intercepted as part of a pattern? Perhaps, as Gandhi claimed, it really was an accident. But, for Pickett, Ambedkar's improbable tale suddenly had the ring of truth.

24 From Tambaram

In early 1938, Pickett's *Christ's Way to India's Heart*, based on his 1934-1936 surveys, came out. It was a small book—just 117 pages. Yet, many have considered it his best. McGavran wrote that it was "a sparkling presentation of a philosophy of missions which is . . . capturing the minds of the leaders of Christian India. Seldom does one find philosophy as readable!" He added:

> Bishop Pickett's great contribution to Christian thinking is that he has formulated the theory which lies back of the growth of great churches and is to a considerable degree responsible for it. Without using the following terminology or making the following claim, he has in our estimation written a "Philosophy of the Growth of Churches Which Grow." He has contrasted it with the "Philosophy of the Growth of Churches Which Do Not Grow."

R.E. Diffendorfer read it and immediately wrote to Pickett: "I have just finished your little book . . . The book should be in the hands of every missionary to India and of every Indian Christian leader. It must be given to every candidate for missionary service in India."

Another admirer was B.R. Ambedkar, whose concern for untouchables the book approvingly represented. That year, Ambedkar twice asked Pickett to baptize him—but secretly. The bishop, however, would not consent. He also wanted Pickett to arrange for training 10,000 men and women a year to be pastors to his untouchable followers. Ambedkar, himself, would select the candidates, and Pickett would baptize them. However, despite pressure from some of his friends to agree, Pickett declined that request as well.

AS BISHOP OF THE BOMBAY AREA, Pickett encouraged church leaders in his charge to creatively put into practice applicable lessons from the surveys. He was pleased with the response. In many of the villages, his proposal of every-evening worship was adopted. Teaching on intercaste brotherhood took hold so well that Sweeper children were admitted to at least 20 schools for the first time. All village day schools were put in the care of the woman missionaries, so District Superintendents could be freed for evangelism and other church building activities. New village churches and parsonages were erected at a record pace. Moreover, villagers themselves erected and paid for them—except for the roof, which Pickett found funds for. Pickett exulted: "When village men who have never in their lives earned as much as fifteen cents for a day's work, give fifty cents to nine dollars each for a church in their village, there is convincing evidence of the value they attach to the gospel."

One of Pickett's strengths was as encourager. He also took encouragement when missionaries and leaders excelled in their ministries. But a few came with personal or political agendas. With these, he was unsparing. He had little use for those who "get trips around the world on the promise of missionary service and refuse to render the service or to study seriously to qualify to render that service." And when they began to seek what he regarded as "cheap notoriety" by "denouncing governments of state or church," he felt they did great harm.

But such were exceptions. Many newcomers to the field, like James K. Mathews at the Bowen Church, impressed him deeply. "He has made a very fine beginning," Pickett reported to Donohugh. "Attendance at the church services has markedly increased. At Mahabaleshwar, where he attended language school, he is said to have preached the best sermon heard there in many years."

Pickett liked getting missionaries who, like Mathews, were not yet married. He gave the following reasons: (1) transit costs were less; (2) support was less of a burden for the church; (3) they adjusted more quickly; (4) they learned the language faster; (5) the danger of their leaving the field was halved; and (6) marriage on the field to one who had already adjusted had many advantages.

PERHAPS THE HIGH POINT OF 1938 was Pickett's year-end trip to Madras for the third International Missionary Conference. It was his first IMC conference. Four hundred seventy delegates from 64 countries came. To

Pickett's liking, the keynoter was John R. Mott. One reporter described Mott's address as "a worthy product of fifty years' international service," and Mott himself as one who "stood like a sentinel wearing his seventy-three years as a mantle of youth."

The conference featured Professor Hendrik Kraemer's specially prepared, *Christian Message in a Non-Christian World*. Although not claiming to be a response to *Re-thinking Missions*, everyone considered it as such. The conference theme was the church in the non-Western World. Kenneth Scott Latourette, one of the planners, wrote:

> It was an attempt, in the face of passing Western imperialism and colonialism, to make missions ancillary to the churches which were growing out of the Protestant missionary effort of the preceding century-and-a-half.

Giving a paper on mass movements was Frank Whittaker, the finally-chosen successor to Pickett as NCC mass movement secretary. Pickett was pleased that delegates were introduced to the conclusions and recommendations of his *Christian Mass Movements in India* in digest form.

Immediately following Tambaram, Pickett headed for Central Conference, meeting in Hyderabad. Accompanying him were several key figures from Tambaram. So more of his Methodist colleagues could have the benefit of hearing them, he had arranged ahead of time for them to speak at the Central Conference gathering as well.

After Tambaram, John Mott sought Pickett's assessment of the conference. Pickett highlighted the following:

> In my judgement the things that gave Tambaram distinctive values were (1) its ecumenicity, (2) the contributions of the delegates from Asia, Africa, and Latin America, (3) the respect shown by European and American delegates for the superior qualities of experience and understanding of delegates from what were formerly called "mission fields," and (4) the clarity with which the need for union was seen.

Of the many next steps that were proposed at the conference, Pickett thought priority should be given to four: (1) cooperatively producing an adequate Christian literature for the nonoccidental world; (2) seeing the evangelistic task as the responsibility of every institution of the church and combining resources for evangelism "without regard to considerations relative to denominational advantage; (3) giving priority to developing more adequate programs for the cities; and (4) giving more attention to "the training of an indigenous ministry in every land."

ON SEPTEMBER 3, 1939, Lord Linlithgow, Viceroy of India since 1936, proclaimed India to be at war with Germany, a decision that Gandhi and Congress leaders thought should be the Indian people's, not Great Britain's. Congress' response was the following:

> If Great Britain fights for . . . democracy, she must . . . end imperialism in her own possessions, establish full democracy in India, and the Indian people must have the right of self-determination by forming their own constitution.

Britain, however, was too absorbed with the Continent's darkening skies of war to make concessions to what many thought of as an opportunistic demand. Instead, on October 17, it announced that, following the war, the Government of India Act would be modified and that steps would be taken toward eventual dominion status. The indefiniteness of the announcement resulted in Congress ministers quitting their provincial posts. And after another equally unacceptable offer the following summer, Gandhi led Congress in launching a *satyagraha* to underscore their displeasure. In response, the British interned thousands, including M.K. Gandhi, Jawaharlal Nehru and the radical Subhas Chandra Bose, who promoted the violent overthrow of imperial rule. Bose escaped and was welcomed to Germany by Hitler. The rest were released at the end of 1941. Two-and-a-half months later, Japan entered the war and with breathtaking speed overran much of East Asia.

FOR THE MISSIONARIES, the early part of the 1940s was something like waiting for a storm. They and the Indian church leaders went on with their business but kept alert to the volatile conditions. By then, the war was not just news in the papers but was being felt more palpably in the cost of commodities, a big drop in earmarked gifts from America, slow mail, and the added burden of German missions now under the temporary guardianship of the non-German denominational missions. Other effects were the extra risks and secret routes involved in voyages home for furloughs and, after Pearl Harbor, further depletion of the missionary force.

The two main reasons for the depletion were these. First, once the US was at war, nobody who went on furlough got back. Second, some missionaries, because of their language abilities, were conscripted. Four days before Pearl Harbor, the Picketts' daughter, Elizabeth and her husband, Henry A. Lacy—married the year before—arrived in India as missionaries. "Hank," the son and grandson of missionaries to China, was to be the new principal at Parker High School in Morabad. Before the war was over, though, he would be called up by the Office of Strategic Services—a U.S. Government intelligence arm—because of his knowledge of the Foochow dialect.

Despite their small numbers, Pickett was amply satisfied with the accomplishments of his missionaries and Indian pastors. Nearly every district in the Bombay Area was experiencing growth in church membership and giving. Spiritual vitality was on the rise too. Despite the war, Pickett could report, "Everything considered, the church is standing the test very well."

The bishop's only ocean travel in the war's early years was to General Conference in 1940. The journey also gave him the chance to visit Elizabeth and Miriam, and his mother in Kentucky. His return ship's covert voyage brought him to Sydney via Honolulu, Tahiti, Pago Pago, Fiji, and Auckland. Sydney he found to be much like an American City—American songs on the radio, American funnies in the newspapers, Hollywood movies in the theaters, and American goods in the stores. "The people are apparently all eager for closer relations with the U.S.A.," he wrote. When he got to Sydney, he learned that his ship for Bombay had been diverted for military purposes and that no other ship would get him back in time for key meetings. So, despite the risks, he flew to Rangoon and, after a brief stopover, to Calcutta. He arrived on September 5, one day after the death of his old friend and colleague, Bishop J.R. Chitambar.

Perhaps the most worrisome development in the war was the Japanese occupation of countries in Southeast Asia, which, by 1942, was already complete. The ease and pace with which the Japanese had overrun these Asian neighbors was, in India, alarming. Because of the invasion of Malaya, including Singapore, evacuees poured into India by boatloads. The next incursion of Japan—into Burma—produced still more refugees, many of whom made their way through the jungles to India. Among them were Christians, including missionaries. Pickett and the other bishops gave appointments to escaping Methodist missionaries, including wives whose husbands, by refusing to abandon their work, became prisoners of war. Following those invasions, many believed the bombing of India's big cities in the East was imminent and that, eventually, India would fall too. By the summer of 1942, most Americans in India had heeded State Department advisories and left. But although they, too, had been pressed to return, few of the Methodist missionaries were ready to leave before their regular furloughs. In May, Pickett bragged to Diffendorfer:

> You may be interested to know that the holier-than-thou, emotionally high-pressured, and overheated independents are running faster than any others. The steadiest missionaries represent the denominational bodies.

Pickett, it seems, was more immediately concerned with rising tensions between Hindus and Muslims, a bit of which he had witnessed firsthand recently when he accidentally got caught in the middle of a Bombay riot. Not surprisingly, he blamed recent communal stresses on Gandhi. He wrote,

> Mr. Gandhi some years ago openly and persistently talked of 'Ram Raj.' This aroused the fears of the Mohammedans and a section of them countered with the demand for Pakistan. It also aroused the depressed classes and they are determined that no national government committed to the enforcement of Hinduism as a national religion shall be established. I consider that the present tragic situation is entirely due to Mr. Gandhi and his followers.

One place where tensions seemed to be easing was within the church. In recent years, in some of the large meetings, there had been disputes between missionaries and young Indian leaders—for example, over missionary decisions to sell some church properties. But, now, tensions were dying down. Of the 1940 Central Conference meeting in Delhi, Pickett wrote, "Unlike some recent conferences, there was no clash between Indians and missionaries and Indian leadership was stronger than ever before." He described it as, "in some ways, one of the best conferences I have ever attended."

Pickett continued to encourage innovations, especially those that gave the gospel and the church a more indigenous feel. In October 1941, Methodists of Putamba, 130 miles northeast of Bombay, held the first Christian *Jatra* as a replacement for festivals honoring Hindu gods or saints. On Saturday, late in the afternoon, 1,000 Christians from 40 area villages, accompanied by their *bhajan* bands came singing *Christ Maharaj ki Jai* and met the bishop at the church. Pickett led the procession through the town. Each village carried a flag with the number who had come. After their circuit, they went back into the church. On the platform was a 12-foot-high wooden cross, illuminated with lights. The bishop, local pastor, and a Christian barrister from a nearby town spoke. On Sunday, there was a mass communion for 500. Twenty-one children and 18 adults were baptized. A festival meal followed. The *jatra*, intended to be an annual event, drew thousands of Hindus. But it also helped the village Christians to bond and to realize that their numbers were not as small as they, perhaps, had imagined.

25 Jones' Dissent

In 1944, Waskom Pickett would be the only active bishop from India to attend General Conference. Accompanying him to America would be his daughter, Margaret, who was now 17 and ready to begin studies at Ohio Wesleyan University. When, in late 1943, Waskom put their names on a list for passage, he knew there was some danger, because, for the duration of the war, passenger ships had been converted to troop transports. He did not know that a German homing bomb, launched from a Heinkel 177 aircraft, had just sunk HMT *Rohna,* a troopship bound for Bombay, nor that 1,149 soldiers and civilians had died in the tragedy—134 British and Australian officers and Indian crew members, and 1,015 Americans, the greatest loss of American lives at sea in the war—but he was well aware that every vessel that went to sea, alone or in a convoy, was subject to attack. However, as Jashwant Chitambar discovered in the great Arrah flood of 1923, J.W. Pickett was not a man lacking in courage. He never sought dangerous situations; he was not reckless at all; but he never hid from danger either.

Because of the risk, the comings and goings of troop transport ships were kept secret. One wasn't told it was time to go until it was time to go. As it turned out, Waskom, Ruth, Margaret, Douglas, and Grandfather Robinson could spend Christmas together, but not New Years. On New Years Eve day, the vessel carrying father and daughter slipped quietly out of Bombay Harbor.

Besides returning military personnel, there were 18 civilians aboard, most of them missionaries. The passengers were not privy to their route or even their destination. However, after days of zigzagging, Cape Town appeared, and the rumor spread that they would, in all likelihood, land in New York, Miami, or Los Angeles via the Panama Canal. Toward the end of the month, the days grew colder and everyone knew that it would be New York! The ship docked on January 30, 1944.

Delaware, Ohio, the location of Ohio Wesleyan University, and Wilmore, Kentucky were just the start of a full itinerary for the bishop—one that would occupy him throughout the spring, summer, and fall. However, the main event was General Conference, from April 26 to May 6 in Kansas City, Missouri, preceded by a South Carolina speaking tour and, before that, a debriefing appointment with the mission board's Executive Committee.

To the Executive Committee, Pickett reported on the impact of the war on India, the devastating famine in Bengal, and the widespread food shortages elsewhere. He spoke appreciatively of the support received from MCOR, the Methodist Committee for Overseas Relief. With special affection, he described the devotion and good work of his Indian ministerial colleagues and said he was encouraged by the quality of ministers being produced by Leonard Theological College—especially important with recent cuts in missions personnel.

PICKETT'S SOUTH CAROLINA SPEAKING tour was in early March. Included were several evening engagements at local churches and a series of addresses at the South Carolina Conference. The bishop was in top form, at least in the view of L.D. Hammer, Associate Editor of the *Southern Christian Advocate*, who judged his every utterance worthy of superlatives. But not everyone who read Hammer's glowing report came to the same conclusion—particularly with respect to the following:

> In his messages Bishop Pickett thoroughly "debunked" the Gandhi myth. There have been many in this country who have regarded the so-called Mahatma (Great Soul) as one of Christianity's foremost leaders, who have endeavored to raise him to sainthood . . . There are always those, it seems, who wish to conscript and compel to come into the Christian fold all who have any element of greatness about them, whether or not they accept Christ as their Lord and Saviour. Bishop Pickett clearly pointed out that, to the Christians of India, Gandhi is "Public Enemy No. 1." He tried to compel the Christian leaders to cease their efforts for the untouchables of India. He wants the outcasts to remain outcasts, and not be given the privilege, through Christianity, of rising above the level to which they have been for generations condemned.

And the bishop showed that the Indian Christians are loyal to Great Britain and the war against the Axis powers. Of the Indian army of 2,500,000 volunteers who have rushed to take arms against the Axis, a very large part is Christian, a part of which seems unusually large when the proportion of Christians, 8,000,000 to the total population of India is considered.

A few weeks after the report appeared, Pickett heard from an annoyed Stanley Jones in New York. Jones had plainly seen Hammer's piece and, in a *Christian Century* article on Gandhi and missions, had criticized Pickett's characterization of Gandhi. In response, Pickett had sent a clarification. What he had said was that "depressed class leaders in India [namely Ambedkar] called Gandhi the public enemy number one of their people." In the letter, Pickett had asked to meet with Jones, suggesting that Jones might not be fully aware of all that had been going on recently in India and that it was important that he and Jones "know each other's minds on the situation." In his reply, Jones, a longtime admirer of Gandhi, did not mince his words:

It seemed to me, Waskom, that you were leading the missionary movement into a head-on collision with the national forces of India working for freedom. That would mean that the missionary movement would have no part in a free India . . .

The future belongs to nationalist India and not British Imperialism. If you back British Imperialism, you are backing the wrong horse. Its day is about to be ended as far as India is concerned. A part of our job, as I see it, is to help the Indian Christians to orient themselves to that free India in which they will have to live and function. The progressive Indian Christian thought would agree.

I am sorry, dear Waskom, to have to be at seeming odds with you on so vital a question. I love and admire you and have stood by you. But your attitude has troubled me.

Jones' critique of his old friend was consistent with his own recent decision to abandon public neutrality on political issues for ingenuousness:

When the war came on, I felt I should throw aside a cramping discretion and expose my heart. I did so in many addresses in the

West. For this I was refused a visa when I wanted to return to India in 1944.

Then, again, Jones had been voicing carefully crafted statements like "good government is no substitute for self-government" since 1925. His frequent editorials from London, then New York after the onset of World War II were but bolder amplifications.

There can be no doubt that the British Government's denial of a visa, stranding Jones in New York, wounded him deeply. Yet, much as he wanted to return to India, he did not regret his outspokenness. "My heart is there," he told Waskom. "But I don't want to work in a mouse-trap. I must be free to express my convictions."

Jones' irritation concerning Pickett's Carolina statements turned, it seems, on two key differences: first, disagreement on the veracity of the British Government's commitment to quit India after the war; and, second, contrasting assessments of Gandhi's present initiatives. Or one could say, Jones believed Gandhi more than the British, while Pickett believed the British more than Gandhi. Pickett was not anti-independence, although he was, as his son, Douglas wrote, "in some ways a great admirer of the British, and it is true that he thought India's best interests would be served by the inclusion of the country in the Dominion after Independence." As for his view of Gandhi, it pretty much reflected his friend, Ambedkar's view. Again, in Douglas' words:

> I think Dad, while he admired many of the Mahatma's attributes, nevertheless viewed him as much a very clever, sometimes unscrupulous politician, as a truly spiritual religious leader. I think he felt that of the two men, Gandhi and Nehru, Nehru was the real giant and hero of the Independence struggle. There was certainly a great admiration, even affection, there. I think the feelings were mutual, as it was evident to me in the three meetings in which I witnessed Dad and Nehru interacting.

As for Jones, his views were as colored by Gandhi's influence as Pickett's were by Ambedkar's. Later, Jones would call Gandhi's murder "the greatest tragedy since the Son of God died on a cross." In his life and actions, Jones repeatedly gave Gandhi a place second only to Christ.

The British promise that Pickett was ready to believe was called the Cripps declaration. In March 1942, it made the British intentions clear.

Not disposed to working out the details of independence while they were fighting a war, Churchill's Government had sent Stafford Cripps with a promise to grant independence after the war. But arguing the British presence invited a Japanese invasion, and comparing the Cripps offer to a postdated check from a failing bank, Gandhi had spurned the offer and announced his "Quit India" campaign. The time for negotiating was over, he declared, adding: "This is open rebellion . . . I conceive of a mass movement on the widest scale possible." Then, Gandhi offered this mantra, saying: "Imprint it on your hearts . . . let every breath of yours give expression to it. The mantra is: 'Do or die.' We shall either free India or die in the attempt."

When Congress supported Gandhi's proposed campaign, the British arrested Gandhi, Nehru, and other party leaders. When the news got out, widespread retaliation followed—especially from students. Word that Gandhi's secretary, Mahadev Desai had suffered a fatal heart attack in the first week of the internment aroused anti-British passions even more. Convinced of the mistreatment of the arrested leaders, rioters wrecked railway stations and government buildings, bombed bridges, derailed trains, and cut telephone and telegraph wires in what became the largest civil uprising since the rebellion of 1857. Pickett, living in Bombay, was in one of the most volatile places.

Gandhi put the blame on the British. But, in Pickett's view, the Mahatma's threat to make the country ungovernable and, more recently, his refusal to denounce the escalating violence had inspired its share of the mayhem too. When, a few months later, early in 1943, Gandhi announced a fast of 21 days, and doubts about his capacity to survive it brought India-wide *hartals* and protests, Pickett raised a skeptical eyebrow. British and American newspapers were demanding Gandhi's release. Even the U.S. Government urged the British to let him go. Though also concerned, Pickett, nevertheless, frowned on Gandhi's means of gaining what he wanted:

> We are all a bit anxious about Mr. Gandhi's fast. If he should die, there might be an outbreak of violence. We fear, too, the effect on America's attitude toward her British ally. Mr. Gandhi is attempting to compel the government . . . It is camouflaged violence.

What accounted for the bishop's South Carolina remarks, therefore, was distaste for and distrust of Gandhi's recent tactics. Because of them, Pickett had just left an India that was, in his mind, unnecessarily in a turmoil of disarray and duress.

In his letter to Jones, Pickett had intimated that Jones' zealousness might be tempered if he were more fully apprized of British intentions for after the war, and of the real roots of the past two years' civil unrest. Jones, however, remained unmoved:

> You suggest that I am "not fully cognizant of the situation as it has unfolded in India . . . " The only unfolding of the situation I can see is that imperialism is more firmly in the saddle and Indian aspirations for freedom are more suppressed than ever before and the situation more muddled and hopeless than ever before. If you feel that is an encouraging development, then your sympathies are with British imperialism. That to me, Waskom, is not a development but a degeneration. And the worst of it is that we are tacitly backing it.

There is no evidence of any offense on the part of Pickett over Jones' vigorous criticism. Despite their disagreement, their friendship never faltered. However, their dispute shows the sharp divergence of opinion that existed during the pre-Independence, war years, dividing not just expatriates and friends of India, but Indians themselves.

AFTER A SUMMER filled with meetings, fund-raising, and family visits, Pickett sailed for India at the end of September 1944. When he got there, he left post-haste for a string of December conferences, "large and small." Because Pickett did not immediately report his safe arrival, some in America became alarmed that something may have happened to him on the way. Murray Titus wrote:

> Here it is the first of December and no word has come from you yet of your safe arrival in India . . . I saw a letter the other day . . . in which [Margaret] said that she had received a letter from you from somewhere in Egypt, but that was ages ago, and we are wondering what has happened since.

Soon, however, the explanation came that, although the voyage had been "exciting in spots," the delayed report was the result of an immediately full schedule. Bishop B.T. Badley's December retirement meant that Pickett would be transferred to the capital at year's end. Understandably, therefore, he was eager to dispose of the loose ends of his current assignment in time for Christmas in Delhi, especially since Ruth and Douglas were already there and unpacking.

The new assignment included supervision of the Delhi, North India, and Indus River Conferences. It would prove an awesome responsibility—not just because the territory was so vast, but because the events of the coming years were to prove so momentous. However, as Methodist historian, John N. Hollister would later write: "Pickett's coming seemed to be 'for such a time as this.'"

The Delhi Years (1945-1956)

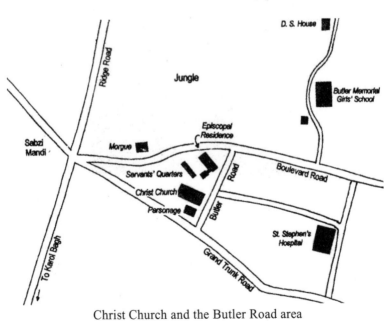

Christ Church and the Butler Road area

Waskom, Ruth, Douglas: camping could mean work or recreation

A village school, a common sight for Pickett as he visited pastors and churches under his oversight

Partition: the Muslim refugee camp at Purana Qila

Bishops Robinson, Subhan, Badley, and Pickett, 1945

Pickett photo of President Prasad and Prime Minister Nehru on the first
Republic Day

The bishop and health minister, Rajkumari Amrit Kaur

Waskom Pickett in conversation with Jawaharlal Nehru; Bishop Marshall Reed from Michigan is next to Pickett; Douglas Pickett is third from the left.

26 Finally, Delhi

An Indian proverb says, "On the road to Delhi I met a hundred men, and they were all my brothers." In Arrah, Lucknow, Bombay, Landour, Mussoorie, and all the far-flung towns and villages through which he had so-far wandered, J. Waskom Pickett had found—especially among the exploited, the sick, and the needy—many more than a hundred brothers and sisters. Now, on the final stop of his Indian Odyssey, he would meet some more.

Though he never neglected the prosperous, and would not in Delhi, Pickett prioritized the poor throughout his ministry. A recent expression of his concern had come in the form of a moving appeal he wrote for presentation to a 1943 gathering of Landour's Christian community. He called the speech, "Our Service to Those Who Serve Us." By "those who serve us," he did not mean the servants who worked for Westerners and well-off Indians, but those with even fewer advantages—those who had known nothing but "grinding poverty all their lives . . . [whose] bodies, minds, and souls [had] . . . been starved." Pickett spoke of the system in which they were caught through no fault of their own . . . of the shortened lives of rickshaw pullers, the backbreaking loads carried by coolies and coal sellers, the social isolation and humiliation of Sweepers, and the wonderful potential of many of them, given hope and help. The scarcity caused by the World War II could not be an excuse he argued. "The Christian, not the Communist, nor the Fascist, nor the Japanese militarist is the pioneer advocate of a new world order."

It was Christ who said, "Come unto me all ye that labor and are heavy laden and I will give you rest." It was Christ who taught men to pray "Thy will be done on earth as it is in heaven." It was he who first organized a society with a program that included mercy and justice for all.

"What is our service to them?" Pickett asked. "What would Jesus do for these needy ones who serve us?" The bishop proposed setting up a second community center—though not like the one his audience had been meeting in for the past 15 years. He proposed a center specially designed to meet the needs of the disadvantaged serving class of the community. It would be a place for recreation, education, and meetings—but more. For example, it would also have links to the church and hospital.

WHEN, IN JANUARY 1945, Pickett began his Delhi-based assignment as Indian Methodism's senior bishop, those in greatest need continued to be his priority. In the coming years, he would give his energies to rescuing thousands of Partition refugees, lobbying for American surplus wheat to prevent a famine, finding support for overfull and financially strapped tuberculosis sanatoriums, and helping birth a unique medical mission in Nepal.

All these would be in addition to his regular episcopal duties, which were formidable in themselves. With its 300,000 members, preparatory members, and baptized children, the Delhi Annual Conference contained the largest Methodist constituency outside the United States. Against the 75 million non-Christians in the region, it might still seem small. But the church was brimming with life and bursting its seams. The challenge of overseeing it all was complex and large.

THE HISTORY OF METHODISTS IN DELHI went all the way back to William and Clementina (Rowe) Butler, American Methodism's first missionary couple to India, in 1856. The first Methodist missionaries to live there, however, the Reverend and Mrs. F.M. Wilson, did not come until 1910. Five years later, the Methodists bought a parcel of land adjoining Delhi Ridge, the northmost spur of the Aravalli Hills. They bought an adjacent parcel the next year, making more than nine acres. The initial property's first buildings included a house for the District Superintendent, a temporary chapel, and some storage sheds. The second property was intended for a young women's school under the sponsorship of the Women's Foreign Missionary Society.

In 1924, recognizing the growing importance of the Methodist presence in the new capital, the Methodist General Conference formed the Delhi Area. To commemorate the work of William Butler, they bought more land for a new church ("Butler Memorial Church," they planned to call it), community center, parsonage, and bishop's bungalow. The five and a half acre plot was across the road from the previously bought parcels.

The first episcopal residents were Ruth Pickett's parents, John and Elizabeth Robinson, who came to Delhi in May 1924. Bishop Robinson, who had already overseen the construction of several key Methodist structures, would also supervise building the houses and church here. By August 15, he and Elizabeth could move into the new episcopal residence, but the other buildings would take longer.

The cornerstone of the new church was laid on April 6, 1930. After a service in the "temporary" church on Battery Lane, the congregation of 400 walked in procession to the new site on Boulevard Road. With them was Clementina Butler, daughter of William and Clementina (Rowe) Butler. Satyavati Chitambar, wife of J.R. Chitambar unveiled the cornerstone. It read: "Christ Church [the new name had been suggested by Miss Butler], a memorial to Dr. William Butler, Founder of the Methodist Mission in India, 1856-1864. Dedicated to the Glory of God, December 20, 1931." At the ceremony, Sir John Thompson, Chief Commissioner of Delhi, congratulated the Methodists on their prime location at the north end of Delhi Ridge. Indeed, when finished, the tower of Christ Church was visible for miles, and from its top, one could see a surprising expanse of both the old and new city.

In December 1944, when the Picketts moved to the Boulevard Road compound, the jungle lands of the escarpment still ran right up to the road. The area around the compound contained much "mutiny history." In fact, just to the north was the Mutiny Memorial. Boulevard Road, which traced the northern boundary of the compound, ended on the property's West side, where, like a spoke in a wheel, it intersected with four more spokes. Moving counterclockwise, the first of them, Ridge Road, went north, past the Mutiny Memorial. Between Ridge Road and the next spoke was Sabzi Mandi, a large vegetable and fruit market. Beyond the market was the famous Grand Trunk Road (or "GT"), India's version of Route 66, only much older, with many more tales to tell. The fourth spoke, the lower end of Ridge Road, ran south toward New Delhi. And the final spoke, Hamilton Road, traced the southern edge of the property and led, after a while, to the walled city of Old Delhi. Not one of the radial spokes, but running north to south and connecting Boulevard and Hamilton along the east side of the parcel, was Butler Road. So, the triangular perimeter of the Christ Church compound was formed by Boulevard Road on the north, Hamilton Road on the south, and Butler Road on the east.

The Christ Church compound contained the church, parsonage, bishop's house, and servants' housing. It was surrounded by a six-foot-high stone wall, with a wide entrance in front of the church. More privacy walls enclosed the houses and their gardens. Together, these formed an elaborate set of perimeters. *Choukidars* (guards) provided added security after dark.

From south to north, along Butler, were the parsonage and Christ Church. Immediately around the corner on Boulevard was the gated entrance to the episcopal grounds. The bishop's bungalow was set back. In front was a circular drive, containing a generous lawn. Along the inside of the drive were flowers and a low hedge. Along the outside were more flowers and taller shrubs and trees. The driveway passed through a porte-chochere at the center of the front veranda.

The vine-draped, brick bungalow was perfect for entertaining guests, and from the start, there were plenty of them. It contained six rooms: an office, living room and main bedroom laterally across the front, and a dining room, sandwiched by two more bedrooms, across the back. From each room, one could go direct to one of the house's two verandas. The back veranda was connected by a breezeway to the kitchen and garage. Stairs at its west end climbed to the roof and a *barsati* suite for guests. The roof also provided a more tolerable sleeping place in hot weather.

Looking out from the front gate across the road, one could see the quarter-mile drive to the Butler Memorial Girl's School building, completed in 1932 and now housing 300 students. A small path behind the school led to the No. 4 Battery Lane Compound, where the District Superintendent lived, and other missionaries and church workers. Looking west from the gate, one could see another building, located just up Boulevard Road, opposite the wall behind the servants' quarters. It was a morgue.

From the start, Waskom and Ruth found 12 Boulevard Road as warm and inviting a place as they had remembered it. It was also fitting that the retired Bishop Robinson, who had built the house, was again living there as part of his daughter's family. Ruth kept the house spotless. She was fond of the saying, "a place for everything, and everything in its place." Throughout the house and on the verandas were potted gardenias and other plants. Many had come from her parents. Local furnishings and fabrics decorated the bungalow. Most of the furniture was cane-seated. In the living room was a fireplace.

Getting oriented to the house and neighborhood was easy; getting oriented to the work was not! The incredible array of responsibilities yoked to the role of India's senior Methodist bishop was, to Pickett, an administrative phantasmagoria. "The demands . . . are enormous," he admitted. "I can't begin to do all that needs to be done."

Pickett did not take time to settle into his office but immediately began visiting his superintendents and pastors—often (as he had 26 times in the Bombay Area) in connection with a building dedication. At dedications, he always reminded the local Methodist community that the only foreign help had been for the roof.

By any measure, ministering to the spiritual and physical needs of this growing constituency was a prodigious challenge. The conference's Methodists included thousands of cultured Indians, some of them well-off. But at least 65 percent were illiterate, and more than that were very poor. Seventy percent had no church building within five miles of their homes. Another three-fourths had no nearby medical services. In addition, food was scarce. In fact, famine had threatened much of India in each of the previous three years—since 1942, when Japan overran Burma and cut off one of India's chief sources of rice. Within the first year of that event, five million Indians had starved, and another 20 million were close to perishing. The food situation, only slightly better when Pickett arrived in the capital in 1945, was of great concern to him.

As Bishop Pickett began touring the churches and missions of the region, he was equally aware of the increasing political strife in the land. There were constant reports of "riots and mutinies." Nevertheless, the bishop was publicly optimistic. In a 1946 summer newsletter to American patrons, he wrote:

Politically this may be a year of glory for India. Independence has drawn near and will likely be established during the year. A National Constituent Assembly will probably meet before this letter reaches you to prepare a constitution for the future government of India.

Besides facing a plateful of new episcopal challenges, Pickett brought with him the responsibilities of the presidency of the National Christian Council, although, by the end of 1945, he hoped to resign so an Indian president could be chosen—perhaps Bishop S.K. Mondol, or B.L. Rallia Ram. "Both of these men," he remarked, "are making good notably . . . Both are doing their work with humble Christian spirits and so effectively that in our own and other churches we hear fine tributes to them."

Another young leader with whom Pickett was impressed was James K. Mathews, who after a term under Pickett in Bombay, had, since 1942, been serving as a Quartermaster in the U.S. Army. Major Mathews, who was then stationed at Chabua, Assam, was being considered, and would soon be appointed—in mid-June of 1946—to the mission board in New York as Associate Secretary for India and Burma. Normally, two terms in India would have been needed for the position, but Pickett enthusiastically wrote: "I vote for his appointment anyway."

Through Major Mathews, Pickett was alerted to the possibility of buying leftover military supplies from the U.S. Army after the war. So, in February 1945, as World War II was winding down and the National Christian Council was considering prospective postwar relief projects, Pickett encouraged the council to pursue the possible purchase and charitable distribution of whatever leftover war supplies the Americans, and the Government of India, might be disposed to sell.

The Government of India had already set up a Disposals Board. When the NCC asked about its plans, the board said that what was not absorbed by provincial civilian hospitals and government organizations was likely to be negligible. Nevertheless, the NCC could put in specific requests if they wished. How the American army proposed to dispose of its war surplus, though, was, so-far, unclear.

The NCC chose two actions: first, it solicited requests for submission to the Indian Disposals Board; second, it appointed Bishop Pickett and Presbyterian leader, Dr. John B. Weir to try to find out the American authorities' plans. Pickett was interested in what the Americans planned to do with their remaining medical equipment and supplies. At that time, Fred Perrill's son, Dr. Charles Perrill, and his wife, Dr. Wilma Perrill, were assigned to the Clara Swain Hospital in Bareilly. Soon after V-E Day in May 1945, Pickett sent "Dr. Charles" to look into the matter. The generals were not ready to act while the war with Japan persisted. They were, however, willing to talk.

By September, preliminary discussions were underway with the American Liquidation Commission. On September 11, 1945, Pickett described the progress of the negotiations to R.E. Diffendorfer:

We are busily occupied just now in the negotiations for surplus war supplies. As chairman of the N.C.C. it falls to me to present the needs of all the Churches. We are trying to set up a Committee to handle all supplies. To do the job correctly and secure the maximum benefits we would need to organize a corporation and run two or more warehouses. That, of course, we can't do, but we are hoping to secure considerable benefits for all missions. [E.C.] Bhatty, one of the newer N.C.C. Secretaries is to be with me tomorrow interviewing various Govt. Officers regarding the remission of duty, transportation charges, term credit for purchases, etc.

Two days later, Pickett, E.C. Bhatty, and E.M. Moffatt got with the commission. They met with a sense of urgency. They had learned the U.S. Army authorities had already come to an agreement with the British Indian Government. For fear of hurting the economy, surplus materials from the war would not be dumped on the open market. Instead, they would be destroyed.

Despite the let down, Pickett was cautiously optimistic that something could still be worked out. Since the National Christian Council was not scheduled to meet for a month, he and Weir arranged to present their report to an ad hoc committee with broad enough representation to insure a thoughtful, well-balanced response. The group of eight met on September 25, 1945. After hearing from Pickett and Weir, they developed a set of findings and recommendations for the NCC. They counseled the appointment of a "United Committee"—including Roman Catholic representatives—to handle the purchase of surplus supplies should there be the opportunity. In view of the urgency of the situation, they also recommended that an interim committee be formed to get a head start. There was no telling when the war would end, and once it did, the authorities would act quickly to dispose of the war's remains. Once formed, the United Committee could serve immediately as a liaison between the churches and the liquidation authorities. It would set up an office in Delhi, to be staffed by workers lent by participating missions and churches. Other recommendations in the proposal addressed such matters as banking procedures, the repayment (through a surcharge on purchases) of the 5,000 rupees needed to open the office in Delhi, and a plan for storing, distributing, and delivering the purchases. In late October, the NCC met and approved the plan. It appointed a seven-person committee with Pickett as chair. One of the seven was Dr. Charles Perrill, who was brought aboard as a technical adviser.

When V-J Day came, the American troops were quickly withdrawn. Left behind in Assam and Calcutta were huge stockpiles. Pickett, Perrill, and the others were heartsick to learn that whole field hospitals were almost immediately bulldozed and buried underground. They also discovered the Americans were paying daily laborers excessive wages to cut up mosquito nets. However, by an unexpected act of Congress, which Perrill was sure Pickett had some behind-the-scenes part in, destroying equipment was halted and civilian charitable institutions were allowed, from late 1945 until April 1946, to buy medical supplies, jeeps and the tools to maintain them, trucks, motorcycles, and much more.

Pickett's United Committee for Surplus Supplies (UCOSS) went to work as an umbrella for numerous institutions. In charge of the Delhi office were Harold Shaw, a Presbyterian, who served as administrator, and Ralph C. Kaufman, a Mennonite, who served as purchasing agent. The purchase-and-distribution involved not just learning what supplies were available, but getting the word out. Among the most popular items were the jeeps. Sergeants from the U.S. Army Surplus Supply took UCOSS representatives out onto the fields at Willington Airport. Pointing to a hundred jeeps, they asked, "Which ones do you want?" However, some of the army's other propositions were less appealing—for example, the offer of 500 donkeys for a dollar apiece. "Until we got them distributed, how would we feed them?" asked Shaw and Kaufman.

Dr. Perrill, who was getting ready to go on furlough in May, was given the job of scouring massive catalogs and endless lists of supplies for the most useful items. He had to decide, for example, "whether or not to order, sight unseen, '75,000 yards of nylon screening.'" At that time, nylon (invented in 1938) was new; no one in the office was acquainted with it or its properties.

The war surplus enterprise was, by all accounts, a remarkable accomplishment. All sorts of equipment, even whole field hospitals, were bought at greatly reduced prices. When the project ended in early summer, 115 charitable groups—Christian, Muslim, and Hindu—had made more than four million dollars in purchases. Pickett, whose son, Douglas—freshly graduated from Woodstock—also aided in the effort, seemed particularly delighted with the medical finds: the generators, x-ray machines, medicines, clothing, and linens bound for hospitals and clinics.

The war surplus project was just one avenue of many that Pickett found for advancing medical care. His kinetic leadership (1936-1956) of the Medical Council of the Methodist Church in India was widely admired. In his episcopal role, he was ever on the lookout for the best obtainable doctors, nurses, and technicians for Methodist medical institutions. Over a lifetime, he raised millions of dollars for Indian hospitals and clinics. Some of them he helped start; others, he almost single-handedly saved from extinction. Pickett was also keen to promote initiatives in health care, and better training for health care workers. As he assumed his new responsibilities in Delhi, he urged "a new emphasis in India upon medical work, both curative and preventative." Typical of this emphasis was his plea for quality health care nurses:

> In some areas two-thirds, or more, of all Indian women nurses are Christians. But most of them are very inadequately trained. Few were high school graduates before entering nurses' training schools. They were the best candidates in their day of training, but better qualified candidates are essential now . . . Public health nursing is a new field for which training of a high order is required.

Many instances could be cited also of Pickett's interest in individuals involved in or aspiring to medical service. For example, Ernest Sundaram, whose family traced its Christian roots to the missionary, William Carey, had dreamed of a medical career from his youth. When, after high school, he took the state examination for the L.C.P.S. (Licentiate of the College of Physicians and Surgeons) certificate, he emerged with the top scores. That insured him a scholarship to a medical college—supposedly! Instead, the scholarship was awarded to another student—a Hindu. Another top-scoring student—a Muslim—was also passed over for a lower-ranking Hindu student. When Pickett heard about the injustice, he took it to his friend, Rajkumari (Princess) Amrit Kaur, Nehru's minister of health. With her help, both boys were awarded scholarships and admitted to a medical college in Calcutta.

It is hard to overestimate J. Waskom Pickett's overall impact on the church's ministries of healing. In the words of Dr. Charles Perrill, "No one did more than Pickett to advance health care in India."

TUESDAY, APRIL 9, 1946, when temperatures back in Delhi were in the mid-90s, Waskom, his son Douglas, and District Superintendent Dhan Singh Chowdhury, set out on a 20-day tour of the Kumaon District in the Himalayan foothills. In all, they walked more than 150 miles, visiting Naini Tal, Ranikhet, Dwarahat, many places in the Katyur Valley (including Phatgale, Dangoli, Charson, and Baijnath), Almora, and Champawat. Along the way, they dedicated a remote mountainside church. However, the main reason for the trek was to study the reported food shortage, which they found acute. With fields dried up—especially in the higher elevations—and the scarcity of food being such that it was impossible to buy, the trio survived on U.S. Army K rations—one of the acquisitions of the United Committee's war surplus effort! On their return, Pickett called a meeting of Methodist leaders to discuss relief options for areas with food shortages. They agreed that what the church could do was limited. For instance, since grain was now a government monopoly and supplies were rationed, they could buy no grain. However, vegetables and meats were not rationed. And what about all those K rations?

The NCC executive committee was also searching for ways to help in famine areas. They, too, felt handcuffed. Under the circumstances, about all they could do was to urge regional Christian forces to work together for starvation prevention, and they came up with a few ideas for intervention in extreme crises. Unfortunately, there was not, in those days—from them, or the denominations, or the state—any consideration given to long-term measures for reducing vulnerability to famine.

After months of unrelieved immersion in his episcopal responsibilities, National Christian Council, and war surplus work—"my busiest and hardest year since I first came to India in 1910"—Waskom was ready for a respite. In mid-May, he, Ruth and Douglas headed north for the quaint Kashmiri village of Pahalgam, nestled 400 miles away along the Liddar River. On May 20, they unpacked their suitcases, removing, with their civilian clothes, some surplus GI apparel—"just right for a vacation in this quiet place," beamed Waskom.

Except for a few days in a houseboat on Srinagar's Dal Lake, the Picketts stayed in Pahalgam in a tent owned by a friend. Few places were more photographic or enchanting. Pahalgam's river was filled with rainbow trout and, in summer, its hills with shepherds and sheep. Surrounding the village was a circle of soaring, fir-covered mountains, and farther on, to the north and east, an array of resplendent snowcapped peaks. "But to be honest," wrote Pickett to James Mathews, "[Pahalgam] means little more than a change of location and an opportunity to concentrate on writing and reading." He added, "We have been here 19 days, including three Sundays. I took one day off for climbing a peak 11,600 feet high [about a 2,500 foot climb], along with Douglas. The other days I have worked. This is [my] 360th letter—all hand-written."

27 Independence!

By the end of World War II, Indian nationalism had become a juggernaut. For that and a host of related reasons, not the least of which was a mounting British weariness with the burdens of maintaining the empire, the new Labour Government was ready to offer India its release. However, quitting India would not happen cleanly or simply. In 1945-46, Muhammad Ali Jinnah's Muslim League won an overwhelming 73 of 78 seats set aside in Parliament for the Islamic electorate, vindicating Jinnah's claim to speak for India's Muslims. As the fact of independence drew near, Jinnah, whose party had called for an independent Muslim state of Pakistan, grew more determined in his rejection of attempts to find a compromise. In August 1946, the inflammatory rhetoric and threats of months of debate between Congress and the Muslim League developed into ugly communal violence. The Muslim League had decided to abandon constitutional methods for direct action. On August 16, 1946, designated as their Direct Action Day, bloody riots broke out in Calcutta. At the end of the day, there were 4,700 dead, 15,000 injured, and 150,000 fleeing the city. From Calcutta, the violence spread to east Bengal and Bihar. In early 1947, riots and killing also broke out in the Punjab. By then, 12,000 had been killed.

By this time, the British were determined to step up the process of quitting India. On February 20, 1947, the British prime minister, Clement Attlee announced the British would leave India by July 1948. The arrival of Louis Mountbatten as viceroy in March would speed it up still more. But the intensifying communal violence underscored the fact that Congress, while successful in shaping a nationalism sufficiently strong to get Britain to quit India, had not figured out how to integrate the Muslims. Independence would come—but with a partition.

Despite the great shifts that lay just ahead, and his great interest in politics, Pickett's letters seem to show a man undistracted. Nevertheless, he was mindful of the changes on the horizon and the need to be prepared. When, at the NCC's 10th biennial meeting at the end of 1946, it set up commissions on "The Church in a Self-Governing India" and "Christian Education in the Future India," Pickett was the meeting's chair.

THE WINTER AND SPRING OF 1947 were filled, as usual, with oversight responsibilities, personnel decisions, meetings with district leaders, official correspondence. But in April a new task was added—an unexpected errand. The errand was an emergency trip to Burma, where the banks were having cash-flow problems and the church schools could not withdraw the money they needed to pay their teachers. On April 2, a Wednesday, Pickett flew to Rangoon with relief funds and the offer of a loan. However, when he got there at noon on Thursday, the bank crisis was already resolved. So, after a weekend blitz, including getting together with all the missionaries, preaching a Good Friday service, visiting all the church properties, preaching in the English and Chinese churches Sunday morning, meeting with Burmese national leaders, consulting at length with Pastor Rathnam of the Telugu Church, and conferring with missionaries on several other matters, Pickett, at 4:00 a.m. Monday, left for the airport and his return flight.

In Calcutta, he hoped to catch a late train to Delhi, but he got there after the last one had gone and had to check into a hotel. After dinner, he phoned an old friend, a railway official whose children had been in school with the Pickett children. The friend invited him over. Since there were no taxis outside the hotel, he hired a phaeton driven by a tall Muslim and his assistant. Soon, however, Pickett sensed that something was amiss. The carriage driver turned off Chowringhee two or three streets early—"a shortcut," he told the bishop. However, when he turned the phaeton onto an unlit street, Pickett demanded he go back. But a man brandishing a large knife appeared and told Pickett to be quiet or be killed. The driver ordered him to turn over all his money. Pickett, who had 1200 rupees (about 375 dollars) on him—more than he had ever before car- ried—refused. The driver struck him in the face and made him stand up. He searched Pickett's pockets and took the money. Fearing for his life, Pickett hit the driver so hard that blood streamed from his nose. Then he wheeled and kicked the man with the knife. When the knife fell from his hands into the street, Pickett thought he would escape, but a third assailant managed to grab him around the legs and hold him. As the thieves forced him toward a lumberyard about 20 feet away, Pickett was sure they intended to murder him. But he succeeded in tearing away from them and ran to the safety of a crowd drawn by the commotion. Members of the crowd walked Pickett back to his hotel. The thieves had gotten all but 30 rupees. The one waving the knife had missed Pickett's throat by only an inch. "That is an indication of the lawlessness now prevailing in India," Pickett later told James Mathews.

IN DELHI, WASKOM WAS MET BY Ruth and her father. A few days later he met, for the first time, a new granddaughter, Jessie Louise Lacy. A few days more and he was off again—driving (80 miles), riding horseback (50 miles), and walking (100 miles) through the Kumaon hills, just as he had the previous year when Douglas and Dhan Singh Chowdhury had accompanied him. On his return, on April 27, he set out almost immediately for a whirlwind tour of the Bareilly District that included Bareilly and nearby Tilhar, and Shahjahanpur and Jalalabad, 45 miles farther south. All in the span of a week, he took part in an education conference, chaired a meeting of the Educational Executive of North India, presided over the annual meeting of the Bareilly Seminary Board, held a cabinet meeting on reshuffling some women's appointments; addressed a *Prem Sabha* (fellowship gathering) of 300; received 60 people into full church membership, interviewed young people about Christian service, laid the foundation for a new church building, did a marriage ceremony at Shahjahanpur; addressed the Lodhipur Community School; led worship at Tilhar and helped with plans for a new village center there. "Life is very full," he wrote on his return.

Life was no less full for Ruth. When her husband went on tour, she packed his suitcase. While he was gone, she was his right hand. Besides managing the house, which was a full-time guesthouse for missionaries, church leaders, and visitors from America—anyone passing through—she read letters, managed accounts, filed carbon copies—did everything but write his letters. Waskom took none of this for granted. He wrote to Ruth every day he was away. Once, though, on an especially full day, he dictated his letter. He felt guilty for days.

ON MAY 30, WORD CAME FROM the Ramsey Hospital in Nanital that Ruth's father had died of heart failure. Since Elizabeth Robinson's passing in

June 1935, Bishop Robinson, though retired, had not been idle. He had, in those 12 years, edited the *Indian Witness*, managed the publishing house, traveled to three continents, filled in as overseer of the Lucknow area, edited the *Indian Temperance News*, created an index to the *Indian Witness* through 1946, and spoken in English and in Hindustani at scores of conferences and churches. Even retired bishops, it seems, knew well how to fill their days! An obituary in the *New York Herald Tribune* called Robinson "the grand old man of Indian Methodism," as, indeed, he was. Two weeks later, in a letter to James Mathews, Pickett wrote of him, "No one knew so well as we who were closest to him what a great man and great Christian he was. I doubt if any man in our time had so much greatness of which he was unconscious. His humility was at times positively startling." In the summer of 1942, the family had helped Grandfather Robinson to celebrate 50 years of service in India. As a remembrance they gave him a book of tributes. Waskom's tribute said much about his admiration for his father-in-law, as well as his love for Ruth:

> What can I write that will do justice to the tributes of love and gratitude that my heart and mind continually pay to you and mother? More than any other who will write, I am indebted to both of you. For Ruth, who enshrines in her character and personality so much of you, my debt is immeasurable. For what I see of you in my children I am unspeakably grateful. In the church that I serve in Bombay Area and beyond, in and out of Methodism, I am continually discovering evidence of your influence making my task easier and the rewards of my office richer. And when I turn my attention within myself, there, too, I am reminded of my debt to you. I like to believe that I have responded to your influence and have taken into myself something of what I have admired and loved in you. Friends sometimes delight me with intimations to that effect. My fondest hope is that I, too, may complete fifty years of service in India.

MEANWHILE, THE BRITISH WERE packing their bags to go home. After arriving in New Delhi in March, Lord Mountbatten, India's last viceroy, had sprinted through a succession of meetings and discussions with Indian leaders. In fact, by April 5, he had met with nearly every key leader, including Gandhi and Jinnah. Gandhi told him that he would rather see a bloodbath in a united India than an India and Pakistan endlessly at odds. Jinnah insisted there could be no India without a "surgical operation" resulting in a Muslim state. In May, as communal rioting intensified in the Punjab, Northwest Frontier Province, Central Provinces, and Calcutta, Mountbatten returned to London. When he returned to Delhi on June 2, he immediately told Indian leaders of Britain's preference for a united India, but he said the decision was in their hands. They had to decide directly though, for the British wanted to transfer power and grant dominion status as soon as possible. One month later, the British House of Commons passed the long-awaited bill granting independence. Both the *Hindustan Times*, the voice of the Congress Party, and *Dawn*, the Muslim League journal, gave the action high praise. The former called it, "the noblest and greatest law ever enacted by the British Parliament."

By this time, however, the Hindu and Muslim political factions were so irreparably split that partition seemed certain. Even Nehru had given up on a united India. A Partition Council, responsible for administratively overseeing the details of the Partition was formed, with Mountbatten as chair. They roughed out the plan of the Partition quickly, but not completely. When Independence Day came, they were still trying to settle on the boundaries. The plan called for a Pakistan consisting of two Muslim majority areas sliced from the northwest and northeast corners of India. Upon receiving independence and temporary dominion status, India and Pakistan would have to decide whether to keep or cut ties with the British Commonwealth of Nations. To these conditions, both sides reluctantly agreed. For the Muslims, who wanted control of each province where they were the majority, even if (as in Bengal) it was only 51 percent, the proposal did not offer enough. For the Congress Party, it gave away too much.

Pickett did not have much to say publicly about the proposal with its "two-winged" Pakistan ("moth-eaten," Jinnah called it). However, philosophically and practically, he was stalwartly for a united India. The prospect of partition raised a plethora of questions and a paucity of answers. In what ways, and to what extent, would the mission board be forced to adjust its policies and procedures? What would become of the Indus River Conference? What other ecclesiastical boundaries would be affected? How would Jinnah's Muslim state look on Christian missions? Would they allow them even to stay?

WHEN MOUNTBATTEN ANNOUNCED that the time for the transfer of power to the governments of the two new states was to be August 14 at midnight, Pickett and his fellow bishops, who were already weighing the long-term implications of that moment, decided to turn their focus to the event itself. Pickett explained their preparations:

> We are busy making arrangements for the celebration of Independence Day and the founding of the two Dominions. The National Flag will be raised on our schools, hostels, etc. But a few of the Christians are protesting this on the ground that symbols in the flags carry so much of non-Christian meaning that Christians cannot accept them. I am strongly advising that all Christians desist from that attitude, for there is nothing in the mere symbols necessarily evil or anti-Christian.

A statement from the bishops urged individual Methodists, no matter what their feelings about Partition, to joyfully welcome independence as "a great advance toward the democratic ideal." It reminded Indian Methodists of their responsibility to pray and encouraged a service of thanksgiving and intercession at every church—or where no church building existed, in homes or any other suitable setting. The bishops also urged all the Methodist schools to have a flag-raising ceremony and to pray for the "peace, prosperity and progress" of the peoples over whom the flags would fly. And they proposed that all Methodist institutions, and even families, plant two trees as living memorials of the day.

ON AUGUST 14, 1947, AT 11:00 P.M., the Constituent Assembly of the Government of India met in a special session in the circular hall of the State Council building. The session was to climax at midnight with the members assuming authority over the new Dominion of India. The chamber was packed, the galleries overflowing with—besides the members—their families, special guests, diplomats, various officials, the press, and anyone else who could rustle a ticket. At midnight, the tolling of the clock evoked the silence and attention of the entire assembly. As the last chime rang out, the deep-toned "oooom" of a conch shell sounded, as they do in Hindu temples "to call the gods to witness some August occasion." With that, the brightly lit hall erupted with cheers and applause. After that, the Assembly members stood and repeated after Constituent

Assembly president Rajendra Prasad an oath of dedication and service to the new India. That was inside.

Outside, rockets streaked meteor-like across the night sky. Factories, trains, and ships filled the air with high-decibel wails and whistles. Delirious crowds competed until they became hoarse. "It was," wrote *Chicago Daily* correspondent, Phillips Talbot, to a friend, "Time Square on New Years Eve." At home, those with access to a radio listened in as the BBC and All India Radio relayed the speeches and cheers over the airwaves. The moment all Indians had longed for had finally come. In Nehru's grand summation, spoken just before midnight, "Long years ago we made a tryst with destiny, and now the time comes when we shall redeem our pledge."

28 Orphans of the Storm

Sometime during that first Independence Day celebration, the New Delhi sky grew dark and there was a shower of rain. However, before long, the sun broke through and a rainbow appeared. To many, no doubt, the bow was God's seal on their newfound freedom. But just as fresh storm clouds threatened to shroud the sun again, so a rising storm of communal violence threatened the Independence Day euphoria. From Lahore came reports of 153 dead and scores of buildings ablaze—including five Sikh temples and 23 shops in the famous Anarkali shopping center. Amritsar, too, was under siege, and smoke rose above hundreds of Punjabi villages. From Calcutta came word of a bomb explosion and the discovery of stockpiles of arms in the area where Gandhi was fasting to end the killing. So, on the one hand, there was dancing in the streets—Muslims and Hindus together—the sun shining through. But not far off, the clouds had turned to smoke, and their initially pale cannonade of thunder was swelling to a crescendo.

Although Gandhi's risky fast worked a miracle in Calcutta, barbarity continued to reign in the Punjab. Barely two weeks after Independence, Pickett was telling James Mathews what Mathews already knew from the New York papers. "I am sorry to say, " he said, "that the communal trouble has again increased . . . and the whole of the Punjab is in a terrible state of conflict." The news was disheartening to Pickett. He had been in the Punjab only days before on episcopal duty. Hearing that Hindus were afraid for their lives and beginning to flee, he had helped organize a committee to work at decreasing tensions between Hindus, Sikhs, and Muslims. It would be headed by the Methodists' best known, most influential missionary there, Dr. Clyde Stuntz.

In the new Pakistan's half of the Punjab were more than five million Hindus and Sikhs, in India's half a similar number of Muslims. On both sides, the corrosive chemistry of communalism, fear, and old grievances proved a volatile mix. On the one side, militant Muslims wanted their new Pakistan—"land of the pure"—purged of the profiteering ways of Hindu shopkeepers and moneylenders, and Sikh *zamindars*. Across the border, the large Sikh community harbored kindred resentments against the Muslims. Though the phrase, "ethnic cleansing," had not yet been invented, the deed had. The forced evacuations and killings that followed left no doubt.

As news of atrocities on one side reached the other, the frenzied bloodletting only intensified. Soon millions—the rich and the poor, the educated and the illiterate—were on the move in a desperate two-way exodus. From late August to late November, convoy after convoy would make the treacherous journey, as would 783 refugee trains. Those evacuating by ship (133,000) and by plane (32,000) were the fortunate ones. Most people had to take to the roads where anything could happen, including ambushes, accidents, exhaustion, thefts, contagion, storms, and starvation. For safety, the exiles traveled together in columns that sometimes stretched more than 50 miles and contained more than half a million people. A pilot described the unnerving feeling of tracing the length of a convoy at 200 miles an hour for 15 minutes before getting to its end. "You had to see it to believe it," wrote one historian. "You had to be there to understand the confusion, misery and pain of the uprooted millions who clogged the roads."

The refugees knew that, at any moment, around any curve in the road, they risked meeting machete-wielding *Goondas* (bandits) or communal gangs with vengeance on their minds. Less expected but equally menacing were the flash floods that came in the night and trapped and drowned hundreds where they slept. In the Punjab—"land of five rivers"—the monsoon swelled all five until they spilled over into the worst flash floods in memory. Hardest to bear, though, was not the dread of disaster but the mind-numbing torment of the march itself: the endless slog, the sharp stones, the empty stomachs and parched throats, the drenching downpours, the grimy garments, the flies, the corpses—the circling vultures.

Travel by rail could be more perilous yet. Looking back through old photos, one sees coaches crammed full of refugees, with scores more hanging onto the sides or clinging to the roof, desperate not to be left behind. *Life* photographer, Margaret Bourke-White, who witnessed the epic tragedy through her camera lens, remembered vividly the scene at Amritsar Station, the last stop before Pakistan—but, for many Muslims, the last stop, period. She got there just after the slaughter of a thousand Muslim refugees, but the carnage was not all she saw:

> I remember seeing a row of dignified-looking Sikhs, venerable in their long beards and wearing the bright blue turbans of the Akali sect, sitting cross-legged all along the platform. Each patriarchal figure held a long curved saber across his knees—waiting quietly for the next train.

Sikhs and Hindūs going the other way were in equal danger. On both sides, rage trumped reason and payback prevailed. As Pickett put it on September 2, "There is no telling which side has produced the longest list of murders."

In Delhi, tensions began to build conspicuously in the final days of August. Thousands of inflamed Sikh and Hindu refugees, forcibly driven from their homes in the North, were beginning to swell the population. From August 24-27, just 300 yards behind the Pickett house at Sabzi Mandi, the vegetable and fruit market, Sikhs and Muslims clashed more fiercely each day. Monday, September 1, while Pickett was at a meeting of the governing board of Vellore Christian Medical College in South India, he got a telegram from Ruth, reporting an outbreak of violence throughout the neighborhood. He immediately excused himself and caught the first plane to Delhi.

Soon after he got home from Delhi Airport, which proved no easy task, a note arrived from a Christian family hiding a terrified Muslim. How could they get him to a safe place? Pickett drove there, hid the man in his jeep under a heap of sheets and dirty clothes, and headed for a government-designated sanctuary. On the way, a roving gang stopped and interrogated him, but the fugitive under the laundry remained undetected. He was the first of many orphans of the storm rescued by the bishop.

By Thursday, September 4, Hindu and Sikh bands were killing Muslims wherever they found them. That day Pickett wrote to James Mathews,

> I have just come from the morgue across the road from our servants' quarters. A score or two of bodies of men killed in Delhi city are on view there and more are being brought in right now . . .

One of the worst features is that the mob is in control of the roads and railroads. Thousands of Moslems have been pulled out of trains and killed. A passenger who has just arrived by train from Ajmer says that Moslem bodies are piled up in all stations and lie along the track for fifty miles out from Delhi.

Friday, Sikhs and Hindus stormed the Moslem community at nearby Karol Bagh. Saturday afternoon, they besieged Moslem mill hands back of Sabzi Mandi. One of those killed was a Methodist lay member, his skull split by a sword or axe.

With the crisis worsening by the moment, Waskom temporarily stayed put, except Sunday when he went with his pastor, J.W. Singh, to check on the roughly 50 Christian families in nearby Karol Bagh. They returned with a Muslim servant, one of several whom local Christians were safeguarding. When, on their mission, he and Singh saw Sikhs and Jats razing Muslim houses and murdering their occupiers—men, women, and children—local Hindus were upset. For a non-Indian to witness such "savagery" (Pickett's word) was a great embarrassment to them.

That night—Sunday, September 7—the area around the compound became a war zone. In the morning he wrote:

The city is having its great killing, modeled on what happened in Calcutta last August, with this big difference that Calcutta's horror was unpremeditated, while this has been deliberately planned by Sikhs and executed by them and Hindus. The aim seems to be to exterminate the Moslems.

A couple of hours before writing those words, Pickett had walked next door to Christ Church and climbed the tower. He counted six big fires raging. With so much of the city burning, it appeared the looters were having their way, though more troops were promised. Later, he went over to the morgue and counted about 200 bodies. As the day progressed, Christian refugees straggled in. From them, Pickett got updates on the larger picture. One of them reported that gangs looking for Muslims had stopped his train nine times in 50 miles. He described hundreds of corpses along the tracks and in the stations. Other accounts were equally horrific. At 5:00 p.m., a column of perhaps 10,000 Muslims shuffled by. They were headed for the safety of a government camp being set up behind the walls of Purana Qila, a four-century-old Mogul fort. Most of the procession was women and children. Pickett surmised the men had been killed. By dusk, the continual gunfire of the afternoon hours was lessening, but not the burning. The six-o-clock news mentioned neither. All it said was, "There have been isolated incidents during the day."

TUESDAY'S NEWSPAPERS WERE equally terse, revealing but a fraction of what was happening. As Pickett guessed, but could not know, overseas papers were more forthcoming. The readers of Tuesday morning's *New York Times* read about the railway station killings, the uncontrolled fires that lit up the night, the mass killings and looting, even the indifference of Hindu soldiers and police officers, many of whom were reported to be "wholly sympathetic" to the bloody retribution. Tuesday night, word came that Gandhi had arrived. Pickett hoped he could do some good, that his moral influence would work the miracle it had in Calcutta, but the rioting was too out of control for optimism. That night, after a visit to "one of the bloodiest areas," Pickett himself was shot at twice, though he surmised the shooters were trying only to frighten him out of helping more Muslims. Someone also fired a bullet into the Pickett residence. By then, more than 200 refugees were sleeping on the veranda, the floors, the beds and under the beds. Waskom and Ruth reserved for themselves the one upstairs room. Getting up to go to the bathroom, Waskom absent-mindedly switched on the light. Immediately, a bullet struck the windowsill, shattered one of the panes, and propelled several shards into his hand. But he managed to reach up and turn off the light.

ON TUESDAY SEPTEMBER 9, the evening of his arrival, a weak and weary Gandhi conferred with the leaders of the new Dominion Government and with Governor-General Mountbatten. Wednesday, he toured several refugee camps. In the coming days, the combined influence of Gandhi's presence, the arrival of more troops, a government warning to soldiers against dereliction of duty, and evacuating Muslims to refugee camps would bring some order. But for now the situation remained grave. Killings were more isolated but still occurring.

On Wednesday, three Muslim women were beaten to death by five Sikhs in front of Christ Church. A fourth woman, left for dead, was taken to nearby St. Stephens Hospital. Five days earlier she had been stabbed and thrust into a fire. Nevertheless, the doctors at St. Stephens thought they could possibly save her.

The bodies of the three women were added to hundreds more piling up at the morgue. By now, the stench had become unbearable. That day several lorries of army troops came and carried the bodies away, but more corpses replaced them. The next day, Thursday, the killers murdered six—all men. Some of them they clubbed to death; the others they shot. They killed two of them on the back edge of the compound. By Friday, the cleared morgue was again full of bodies—50 of them.

Yet, overall, the storm was beginning to break. Though the postal and telegraph services remained closed, thanks to the U.S. Embassy, Pickett managed to get a letter off to R.E. Diffendorfer at the mission board. However, he cautioned, "If you give out any of what I have written, let it be published without credit to either me or yourselves. We have been warned to give out no news." Pickett did find one bright spot: the courage and restraint of the Indian Christians. "Our people have behaved wonderfully well," he wrote.

> The courage and spirit of service of many of them has been very encouraging. The case for the Gospel could not be better demonstrated than it has been in the contrasted behavior of Christians and non-Christians in these terrible days.

Pickett reserved special commendation for his pastor, the Reverend J.W. Singh: "His courage has never left him."

BACK ON SEPTEMBER 1, WHEN Ruth telegraphed Waskom in Vellore, E.C. Bhatty of the National Christian Council had been in town. He had come to talk with members of the Constituent Assembly about concerns over a proposal to bar conversions for those under age 18. Bhatty planned to go on to Karachi, but John Mathai, the Christian representative in the interim Government, urged him to stay three more days, until Thursday (September 4), when Nehru was expected back from a tour of strife-torn East Punjab. With the communal violence worsening in Delhi and East and West Punjab, Mathai wanted Bhatty to hear from Nehru in person about the Government's plans for refugee relief. Though Bhatty got to see the weary Prime minister, they met only long enough for Nehru to urge the NCC cooperation with the Government on refugee relief.

The same day, a dejected Nehru had summoned Governor-General Mountbatten from Simla to ask his help in getting the emergency under control. Mountbatten arrived the next day, and the following morning, Saturday, September 6, conferred with Nehru and Deputy Prime Minister Patel. At their request, he formed an Emergency Committee, which had its first meeting at 5:00 that afternoon—a two-hour, whirlwind session in which a dozen items were handled, including forming a relief committee under Lady Mountbatten.

The following Monday afternoon, September 8, Edwina Mountbatten met with representatives of 14 volunteer organizations that had signaled their willingness to work with the refugees—but not, so far, to work with one another! Her aim was to set up a central organization to coordinate NGO relief help. Present also was health minister Amrit Kaur, a Christian, who became Pickett's friend.

As a young woman, Amrit Kaur was a star tennis player. She was also a musician, avid reader of the classics, and promoter of the arts. The force behind many of India's early welfare programs, she immersed herself in fighting for children in need, victims of poverty, and those suffering from tuberculosis and leprosy. Before independence, she was prominent as Gandhi's secretary and one of Congress' most vocal members. She participated in Gandhi's Salt March and was imprisoned by the British during his Quit India campaign. As founder of the All-India Institute of Medical Sciences, she was responsible for the policy of requiring all medical students to spend at least three months of their internships in a village setting.

After much haggling, the group agreed to call the alliance, "The United Council for Relief and Welfare" (UCRW). Lady Mountbatten herself would chair the Council.

The next day, Bhatty and representatives from other Christian organizations, including the YMCA, YWCA, and Friends Service Unit appointed a provisional Refugee Relief Committee for Delhi and East Punjab, which would include Pickett. But because of a citywide curfew, there was no telling when he could be informed or the committee assembled.

Pickett had heard Bhatty was in New Delhi to arrange for NCC help in the refugee camps. But the crisis at Sabzi Mandi and the need to protect 200 Christians now in the compound kept him from going to Bhatty. He did not learn of the new committee or of his appointment for another week when a Mr. Nasir Alam came to tell him. Alam was a colleague of J.S.

Aiman, the YMCA person on the committee. Bhatty had returned to Nagpur, probably to confer with other National Christian Council leaders. Mr. Aiman, therefore, was eager for Bishop Pickett's help.

Although the roads were still dangerous, Pickett set out for New Delhi on his bicycle that afternoon. Probably he chose peddling over driving his jeep because petrol was getting scarce. On the way, a gang of Sikhs stopped him. They spoke brusquely.

"Where are you going?"

"To New Delhi."

"No, you go back home. You have no business in New Delhi."

Turning around, Pickett tried another route and was again stopped. Trying a third time, he faced the gang that sent him back on his first try. They threatened to kill him if they caught him again. This time he rode far East of the city and found a safe route.

At the YMCA, Mr. Aiman told Pickett the relief committee was, so far, nonfunctional. He and his colleague, Mr. Alam, were doing what they could, he said, but with no conveyance they were limited. He urged Pickett, therefore, to take the lead.

Pickett was able to meet with the prime minister the same day. Nehru told him he did not like the prospect of a bishop getting killed. "We have enough bad publicity already," he said. But when Pickett insisted on going ahead despite the danger, Nehru promised to do all he could to help.

The next day, Pickett helped two medical doctors, D.E. Alter and John C. Taylor, work out the logistics for mobilizing volunteer doctors. With Bhatty in Nagpur and refugees pouring into the camps by the thousands, Pickett set about organizing the Christians of Delhi for running the camps. With Ruth at his side, he met with one government official after another—access that he credited to Nehru's help. He and Ruth discussed needs with them, clarified a role for the NCC, lined up railway passes for workers, got cards for doctors, arranged for supply needs for the camps (spades, trenching equipment, spray guns for DDT, much more), and estimated the cost of running the camps. With Amrit Kaur and Dr. Jiwa Raj Mehta, director of the Medical Service, he and Ruth worked on a list of medicines needed. They focused on essential medicines not made in India: a thousand, million-unit bulbs of penicillin; two million American units of anti-tetanus serum; and one million units of antigas gangrene serum.

Within two days of Aiman's urging him to take the lead, Pickett's initial corps of Christian volunteers were at work. In the days to come, they worked tirelessly. They offered medical care, set up tents from the army, dug drains, improved sanitation, and gave out food. The next day, Thursday, September 18, Pickett dashed off a letter to Bhatty and Murray Titus in Nagpur. He urged Bhatty to return to Delhi as soon as he could and to plan to stay for some time. Describing his conversation with Aiman and the initiatives he had since taken, he wrote, "I hope you will agree that I have acted rightly in taking considerable responsibility... being the only member of the Executive of the N.C.C. here." He added, "The fact that Delhi is cut off from Nagpur by telegraph, and that mails are most uncertain, necessitates this bold course I am following."

Friday, Pickett prepared a cablegram for R.E. Diffendorfer at the Methodist Mission Board. It included an update on the missionaries, a report of the conditions, and a few requests. Sending it was not easy. On reading the message, telegraph operators asked him incredulously, "You want medicine to save these damn Moslems? Let them die!" So, the American Embassy became Pickett's backup telegraph office.

Pickett appealed to the fledgling Church World Service in New York for help. The organization had been formed after the war by several denominations. Its stated aim was to feed the hungry, clothe the naked, heal the sick, comfort the elderly, and shelter the homeless. In 1946-47, it delivered 11 million pounds of food, clothing, and medical supplies to war-torn Europe. Together with Lutheran World Relief, and the National Catholic Welfare Program, it also began what it called its Christian Rural Overseas Program (CROP). Considering the scope of the young organization's commitments already, Pickett probably held his breath. He needn't have! The organization met the challenge wonderfully. Within a few days, a planeload of supplies, including most of the medicines requested by Amrit Kaur had arrived.

In Delhi, Pickett put out an appeal for more Christian volunteers. No one had anticipated the calamity that had now developed. The influx of Hindu and Sikh refugees had doubled the population. Except for the thousands who had been killed, nearly all of Delhi's Muslim population—Pickett estimated it at 150,000—had been forced from their homes. Thousands had already poured into the camps for Muslims. Thousands more were on the way. The first Camp, at Purana Qila, was started by the High Commissioner of Pakistan. But it soon outgrew his resources. The Indian Government then tried to manage it. But the government representatives failed completely in their efforts to get Hindus and Sikhs to help in the Muslim camps. Potential volunteers would have preferred to attack the camps! Christians had to take over. It was the only solution.

When the Purana Qila camp could hold no more people, a second refuge was set up at Humayun's Tomb. The conditions were dismal. Pickett called them "indescribable . . . much worse than war was." Most of September, it rained—sometimes torrentially. On September 18, he wrote:

> They have streamed in today all day long. We have had teams dealing with food supplies and distribution, medical work, sanitation, tents, etc. In the Hospital Section we have a Maternity Department. Several babies were born today; more are due tomorrow. There are cases in the Camp of mothers who had babies at home and got up immediately after the birth and walked for miles to the Camp. We have treated hundreds of wounds today, men, women, and little children with bullet holes through legs, arms and other parts of the body, and hundreds more with sword cuts. Dysentery is rampant and sore-eyes are epidemic. Fortunately cholera has not appeared yet, nor has smallpox.

Humayun's Tomb, like the Taj Mahal, was a mausoleum. Encompassing the pink, sandstone tomb were expansive lawns and grounds, surrounded by a high wall. It was like a park, except that, the park had morphed to a makeshift city of canvas shelters—some with patched sides and bamboo center poles but most with flat ceilings and poles at the corners. Mud was everywhere. So were the vacant eyes of heartbreak and boredom. Not all the volunteers knew Urdu, the language of the camp, but they didn't need to. Grief was the real lingua franca. Everyone brought stories of lost friends and loved ones. All were in mourning. Most had planned to stay in the new India, in the homes they had always known. Now, for many, Pakistan seemed their only hope—if they kept any hope. For everyone—victim and volunteer—the old tomb had become the saddest place on earth.

Because Sikhs and Hindus were more set on storming the camps—as mobs of thousands threatened to do—than on serving in them, the Christian community was the sole source of relief workers. But in the tent city's early days, there was no effective way to broadcast the need. The usual channels were closed. So Pickett's first workers were young men and women from the YMCA and YWCA, members of Christ Church and other local churches, doctors and nurses he had managed to recruit from nearby St. Stephen's hospital, and he and Ruth. Slowly, though, as communication channels were restored and word of the need got out, new volunteers showed up, until finally their numbers reached several hundred. Many of them put in 18-hour days. Adding to their strain was the knowledge that swarms of angry Sikhs and Hindus might invade the camps at any moment, and their only shield was the presence of Indian Christian regiments from South India. Moreover, the volunteers themselves were being threatened. Both Pickett and Bhatty were warned to quit or be killed. Gandhi got wind of the threats and issued a statement of condemnation. So did the Government of India, warning of severe consequences for those who tried to intimidate relief workers. Pickett's responded by canceling September appointments and focusing even more on the refugees. Bhatty, now back in Delhi, working out of an NCC relief office in Constitution House, was equally determined.

On Wednesday, October 1, Pickett reported that, because of Delhi's worst-ever flooding, and concurrent floods in East Punjab, evacuating those who wished to leave Delhi would take at least three more weeks. The implications were most unpleasant to contemplate. Having survived vicious attacks on their homes, and disease and pneumonia in the camps, the refugees, most with only the thin clothes on their backs, would now have to contend with another menace: the onset of cold weather. "Is there no end to suffering?" asked Pickett.

The volunteers knew that providing food, medicine, and medical help was not enough. They would also need to help the refugees pass the long days and nights. So they got involved in educational work, occupational therapy, and recreational activities. They soon learned the nights were the hardest. So, at the UCRW's suggestion, they started showing films. This involved rounding up an elaborate set of hardware, including projectors, screens, microphones, and gas-electric generators. Still, the temporary "therapy" offered by Mickey Mouse, Donald Duck, Our Gang, and the "Careless Charlie Health Films" was invaluable in easing tension and reducing boredom. Relief workers also set up an inquiry center to help the refugees find lost relatives in the hospitals. The Friend's Service organized a post office, where volunteers helped the illiterate to write and send letters.

Throughout September, Ruth Pickett had been as involved as her husband: providing food and shelter to scores of Christian refugees at their home, accompanying Waskom to meetings, and working in the camps.

When October came, she and Waskom were still swamped at Humayun's
Tomb Camp, though the papers said the crisis was easing and promised
things would soon be back to normal. "How can that be?!" she wrote in
disbelief.

Coming on the heels of her father, John Wesley Robinson's passing,
the new burdens were doubly difficult. But Ruth granted that she and
Waskom were appreciative of one grace:

> For the first time we have been thankful and glad that he is not
> here. The terrible happenings of the past month in Delhi and the
> acute feelings of apprehension would have been very hard on
> him, and our anxiety for him would have been very great.

The "month of shame" was an enormous challenge to the Christian
communities of India and Pakistan. But their response—especially those
who volunteered in the tent cities—was remarkable. There were 160
camps. Many of them were virtual cities. Kurukshetra Camp, 50 miles
from Delhi, sheltered 300,000 refugees for a time. From more than a half
century away, those numbers are nearly indecipherable. But this was the
largest transfer of population in human history. Sixteen million people
were uprooted. Seven percent of them (more than a million) starved or
were massacred en route. And besides those in the camps, thousands more,
including many Christian refugees, took refuge in schools, hospitals, and
private homes like the Picketts'.

BY OCTOBER 14, THE CRISIS had calmed enough for Waskom and Ruth
to leave for nine days of visits in the Kumaon District. A highlight was
their visit to Almora where Waskom met with the board of the Almora
Tuberculosis Sanatorium and baptized 22. Fifteen of the 22 were lepers
whose joy, Waskom noted, was "unbounded." Except for a day in Naini
Tal, the couple did not rest. But, as Waskom admitted, "our spirits rose
as we got away from the strain of Delhi."

While the Picketts were gone, some "political Christians," as Waskom
called them, called on the NCC to dissolve its relief committee and leave
relief to the Government and Red Cross. They contended that relief work
in Muslim camps subjected Indian Christians to danger! However, Pickett
happily reported that Christians who were "more Christian" answered the
resolution with a special meeting to thank the NCC. They even presented

a purse for continuing relief work. The November 1 gathering overflowed St. James Church Parish Hall and led Pickett to declare: "There is no doubt that four fifths of the Indian Christians of Delhi have followed their Church and not their self-appointed political leaders."

That month Pickett received letters of thanks from the Town Hall Emergency Committee of Delhi and the Minister of Health for what he, Ruth, and the NCC had accomplished. He also received expressions of gratitude from the NCC Executive Committee and the Methodist Board of Missions. Though Pickett is, and will be, best remembered for other contributions, September and October of 1947 were, in Bishop James Mathews' words, "Pickett's finest hour." As Donald F. Ebright, chronicler of the civilian assistance efforts, wrote of those stormy days: "J.W. Pickett . . . did more than any one non-government person to organize voluntary relief in Delhi."

Another legacy of the work of Pickett, Bhatty, E.D. Lucas (of Church World Service), and the Christian volunteers who responded to the call in those days, was their role in inaugurating an expression of Christian relief which continues to this day through the Church's Auxiliary for Social Action (CASA). At the same 1947 meeting in which the NCC's executive committee thanked Pickett and the others, a Central Relief Committee was started for ongoing emergency needs. When E.D. Lucas left to join Baring Christian College in Batala in late 1948, Pickett became its India-Pakistan liaison. In mid-1949, separate committees for India and Pakistan were established. A year later, under Donald Ebright's direction, the need of something more permanent resulted in CASA, whose work continues.

By November 1947, the madness had subsided enough to allow Pickett to think of it in the past tense. He wrote to Diffendorfer in New York, "As difficult as our experiences were, we have a number of happy memories." He listed them as follows:

- the way in which most Christians responded to the call for service and withstood the pressure and threats to make them quit
- the response of government officials and their manifest gladness to have our help
- the ready assistance of the American Embassy
- the courage of Rev. J.W. Singh and one or two laymen to accompany me (I being in less danger than they) into places

where murders were being committed in order to reassure frightened Christians

- the amazingly quick response of the Church World Service to our plea for help
- the heroism of Helen Buss in looking after the sufferers from cholera, isolating them from their families and neighbors, giving them medicine and water and sending them to the Infectious Diseases Hospital in vehicles which I sometimes 'commandeered'
- the devoted way in which my wife cared for the wounded in the dressing station and their extraordinary success in saving lives.

THE MAIN MUSLIM SANCTUARIES, Purana Qila and Humayun's Tomb, bulging just weeks before with tens of thousands of occupants, were now nearly empty. Droves of their frightened and edgy inmates had headed north. But many thousands, for whom Pakistan was too far or too uncertain, clung to Delhi. Their homes destroyed, their fates uncertain, they were as fearful as those who had left. What would they do now? Unlike an innumerable company of their relatives and friends, they had somehow survived the storm, but it had made them orphans.

29 The Last Days of Gandhi

When, on September 9, 1947, Mahatma Gandhi came to Delhi, he was greeted at Shahadara Railway Station by Sardar Patel and Amrit Kaur, among others. But there were no smiles. On the way to Birla House, where he would be staying, they outlined how far the situation had worsened. Gandhi expressed disappointment that he was not able to stay as he had in the past in the nearby Harijan colony, which was choking with refugees. However, this was not his first stay at Birla House.

The next day he admitted he'd had no idea how bad things were.

I knew nothing about the sad state of things in Delhi when I left Calcutta on Sunday last. On reaching Delhi, I have been listening the whole day long to the tale of woe that is Delhi today. I saw several Moslem friends who recited their pathetic story. I heard enough to warn me that I must not leave Delhi for the Punjab until it had regained its former self.

As Gandhi sloshed through the rain-drenched camps in early September, he was overwhelmed by the numbers and the conditions. But as the days passed, in camps like Kingsway, Okhla, Purana Qila, Humayun's Tomb, and Outram Line, more and more Christian volunteers were arriving with shovels, medical supplies, fresh drinking water, wool blankets, and warm clothing for the children. Whether Gandhi and Pickett met up as Gandhi toured the camps is not certain, but they were certainly aware of each other's activities.

By late October, the violence had finally subsided enough to allow both men to shift their focus—Pickett to postponed episcopal duties, and Gandhi to preventing another eruption.

From October 28 to 30, Bishop Pickett presided over the Delhi District Conference—held successfully even though trains and buses were still not running. In November he traveled to Lucknow to address the United Provinces Christian Council, and to Bareilly for the graduation exercises of Clara Swain Hospital's nursing school and a meeting of the Hospital Board of Managers. In December he went to Lahore, now part of Pakistan, for a meeting of church and mission representatives; their agenda centered on the need for a united Christian effort in Pakistan and East Punjab.

As for Gandhi, plagued by the letdown of Partition and its aftermath, and fearful the present lull was only the eye of the cyclone, he redirected his energies to securing a stable accord among the communal factions. Gandhi wanted Hindus and Sikhs to welcome displaced Muslims back to their communities and homes. And he wanted key community and governmental leaders to get behind reconciliation by pledging their all-out commitment to an India for those of every religious persuasion. Rumors were rife of another big attack on Muslims. He took them seriously. So did Pickett, who worried, "There is much tension in the city and more trouble is likely."

Still, because the turning point seemed to have been reached, most were caught off-guard by Gandhi's January 13 announcement of another fast, this time for the united support he wanted. The early response to his announcement was negative, or at least skeptical. Many viewed it as a pro-Muslim maneuver. Radical Hindus called it treason. When, after a few days, though, it became clear that Gandhi was dead serious, general sentiment shifted. However, only when assurance came from all parties that they would settle for nothing less than an India that included a place for Muslims, was a much-weakened Gandhi, on January 18, willing to call off the fast.

BEHIND THE BIRLA MANSION, where Sardar Patel had taken the arriving Gandhi in September, were an open large lawn and garden. Except when he was fasting and too weak, Gandhi conducted his daily prayer meetings there. Remarkably, on January 20, just two days after ending his fast, Gandhi himself was again addressing the meeting. While he was speaking, a homemade bomb exploded near the compound wall, 50 yards from the dais on which he sat. The blast was intended as a distraction so, in the resulting chaos, the bomber's co-conspirators could murder the Mahatma close up. But the try was botched.

Though the bomber was caught, his confederates escaped. Gandhi remained in grave danger. In the coming days, Nehru, Prasad, Amrit Kaur, and others close to Gandhi tried to persuade him to decamp to a safer setting. But until he was strong enough to seek in Pakistan an agreement like the one in New Delhi, he would not budge.

On Tuesday night, January 27—exactly a week after the murder attempt—Waskom and Ruth were getting ready for bed when they heard someone coming up the front steps. From the bedroom window, Waskom saw a dark figure stepping onto the veranda. Donning his bathrobe, he went to the living room door. Standing there was a high-ranking Delhi police official. When Pickett asked him in, he immediately sought assurance that they could not be overheard. Pickett said that his wife was the only other person in the house and that, since they were a team, he would tell her anyway. Thus assured, the visitor confided that another try on Gandhi's life was imminent, that members of a secret society in Bombay and Poona were committed to murdering him, and that perhaps 600 members of the society lived in Delhi. He had come to Pickett, he said, because he was convinced that Nehru, the one person who might induce Gandhi to move, did not fully understand the danger.

Pickett wanted to know what this had to do with him. The official said he hoped the bishop could persuade the prime minister to more assertively press Gandhi to immediately withdraw to the hills. He wanted Pickett to have the conversation in the morning.

Pickett was caught off balance. Why would a high police official conclude he could get Nehru to act if the Delhi police themselves could not? Nonetheless, at six-thirty the next morning, Pickett phoned M.O. Mathai, Nehru's secretary, and requested, if possible, a speedy appointment. He was taken aback when Mathai, whose office was in Nehru's house on York Road, told him, if he came now, he could have *choti hazri* (early breakfast) with the prime minister. When Pickett balked, asking him what Nehru would think, he replied, "The Prime Minister is right here!" Then Nehru got on and confirmed the invitation.

Pickett arrived at 17 York Road just 15 minutes later, and over tea, chapati, and a banana, repeated the police official's plea. Nehru insisted that he knew the danger and had pleaded with Gandhi for three days to retreat to a safe place. So had Amrit Kaur, he said—in fact, at the same time Pickett was receiving his visitor the night before.

"Then you say that nothing can be done. Doesn't that mean that Mr. Gandhi will be murdered?" Pickett asked.

Nehru admitted that was a distinct possibility. But what could they do? Arrest him? He proposed that Pickett drive over to Birla House and talk to Gandhi. Gandhi, he said, had more regard for him than he knew. With the prime minister's encouragement, Pickett agreed to try.

When, a few minutes later, the bishop pulled his jeep into the driveway of the Birla mansion, he was surprised to find the gate open, for it was still early. He was even more surprised to see a frail, but smiling, Mohandas Gandhi emerge from the house to greet him. Obviously, Nehru had phoned.

"To what do I owe this honor Your Excellency is giving me?" asked Gandhi.

Pickett replied that he was not "Your Excellency" but just a Methodist minister who was concerned for him. Together, they walked to a large room, probably one of the four that made up Gandhi's suite. Gandhi lowered himself to the floor and gathered around him several pillows. "Why did Jawahar send you?" he wanted to know.

When Pickett explained, Gandhi became more serious. "Why should I be afraid to die?" he asked. "All my hopes for a better India are being destroyed. Perhaps Gandhi dead will be more respected than Gandhi alive."

In Pickett's reconstruction of this last meeting with Gandhi, he remembered that, besides their exchange on Gandhi's safety, they discussed how well Christians had showed their patriotism and commitment to peace in recent days. Gandhi said that he planned to publicly recognize this. The meeting ended with Pickett again pleading with Gandhi to move to a safer location. After that, he went home. He had sought for three-quarters of an hour to convince Gandhi not to wink at the danger. But, in his words, "I failed completely."

LIKE MANY, WASKOM AND Ruth remained deeply concerned for Gandhi's safety. However, beyond prayer, there was nothing more they could do. After recounting his sad experience to Ruth, Waskom spent the rest of the day with two secretaries. Then, in the evening, he took an overnight train to Lucknow for a two-day meeting with the Executive Committee of Central Conference. On the first day he reviewed the current situation in Delhi and reported his conversations with Nehru and Gandhi.

On the second day, a Friday, the committee completed its work in time to join in an afternoon student gathering at the Lal Bagh Church.

During the meeting, a young man entered the church and briskly approached the platform. He had been asked to relay an urgent message to Bishop Pickett. He was in tears. Pickett, who was about to address the congregation, turned the meeting over to Bishop Mondol. He followed the messenger outdoors. The young man told Pickett that, as he was walking by the parsonage next door, he had heard the phone ringing. He thought the pastor would be pleased if he answered it. However, the caller was Nehru's secretary, M.O. Mathai, asking for Bishop Pickett. When told that Pickett was speaking in the church, Mathai directed the man to tell him that Gandhi had been shot and killed a half hour earlier at 5:07 p.m. He was also to say Prime Minister Nehru wanted the bishop to fly to Delhi to speak for the Christians at a national memorial service.

Pickett immediately told the congregation the news. Then he huddled with the other bishops. They decided to adjourn until 10:00 p.m. when they would hold a memorial service at nearby Central Methodist Church.

Between the adjournment and the memorial service, Pickett phoned Pandit Nehru. He told the prime minister that he could not speak for the Christians of India because he was not an Indian. Instead, he proposed that Nehru ask Rajkumari Amrit Kaur. But Nehru said that wouldn't work: she was to represent the Government in another service.

Later, at the memorial gathering, all four bishops—Pickett, Mondol, Rockey, and Subhan —spoke of the inspiration of Gandhi's life and service. Much of the time was reserved for prayer and meditation, but, with the bishops' help, the congregation also adopted a formal expression of sorrow and loss to be sent to the Central and Provincial Governments. Two days later, at the regular Sunday night meeting time, a second memorial service was held, with Bishop Subhan—Pickett's successor in Bombay—giving a moving eulogy. A few blocks away, Bishop Pickett offered a similar eulogy for the members of the Lal Bagh Church.

The next afternoon at 3:45, when it was time for Gandhi's cremation at Rajghat, Pickett spoke to the students of Isabella Thoburn College. Gandhiji, he told them, was not of an age but was for all time. The meeting closed with the students singing one of Gandhi's favorite hymns, "Lead Kindly Light."

Ten days later, on February 12, Pickett took part in one last memorial service. Lord and Lady Mountbatten had requested the morning service. It was held in a packed Delhi Cathedral. John Mathai and Lord Mountbatten read the lessons; Bishop Mukerji delivered the message; Bishop Pickett offered prayer.

By now, Pickett was convinced the residue of ill feelings was mostly toward the Hindu Mahasabha, the Rashtriya Swayam Sewak Sangh, and the militant Sikhs—groups held responsible, in most minds, for Gandhi's death and the Partition riots. But like everyone else, he had held his breath after the assassination, fearing a new spate of violence against the Muslims. On arriving at Birla House on the night of the murder, Mountbatten had been told by a scaremonger, "It was a Moslem who did it!" Not knowing who had pulled the trigger, but foreseeing bloody vengeance if it was a Muslim, Mountbatten had retorted, "You fool, don't you know it was a Hindu!"

30 The I-3s

T he new year, 1949, was among the most demanding of Pickett's career.
The main dilemma—new only in scale—was the widening gap between
resources and opportunities. And, as the year began, both finances and
personnel were stretched to the limit. Therefore, when a late-January letter
from James Mathews warned that "dearness allowances" for India were
threatened, Pickett reacted passionately. "Dearness allowances," often
called "DAs," came from grants of the Methodist Committee for Overseas
Relief (MCOR). They were salary add-ons, meant to bring some economic
relief in inflationary times. Mathews' letter suggested there was a chance
the MCOR might eliminate them. Pickett called the prospect "the most
disturbing news I have read in years, adding:

> If now the dearness allowances from the MCOR are stopped
> while prices are still at their current level, and the shortage of
> food supplies, clothing, etc. continues with the present severity
> . . . there will be a train of tragedy that I shrink from contemplat-
> ing.

The dearness allowances had been used to help village pastors, Christian
teachers, and others to buy food for their families. Without the help, many
of them would not have survived at all, and basic Christian services would
have ended. Pickett knew that Americans were concerned about the
situation in Europe following the war, but no country in Europe had
suffered like India. In the 1943 Bengal famine, five million people had
starved. Every year since then, millions more had perished. India had no
Marshall Plan, no army of charitable organizations at work as in Europe.
Therefore, urged Pickett, instead of being reduced, the dearness
allowances ought to be doubled.

The bishop wrote his plea from the Indus River Conference, then in session.

> In the Conference today I have listened to the preachers . . . give their reports. These brethren have passed through a succession of turbulent and dangerous experiences. Practically every man has been in danger of losing his life and the lives of his dear ones. All have suffered hunger. Most have seen neighbors slaughtered or driven in terror from their homes. Their congregations have been threatened and persecuted because of being Christians, have lost jobs or had wages withheld or have been looted. Yet these men have brought their congregations safely through every sort of peril and established them more firmly in Christ than they ever were before. If the MCOR grants had not been available, these pastors could not have continued their work and hundreds of their people would have starved or been driven from their homes or compelled to renounce their faith in Christ to escape death or exile.

The previous week, Pickett had presided over the North India Conference. He painted that scene similarly:

> I have never faced men for whom my heart ached so much as for some of those men at that session. They have been heroes in sticking to their work through flood and famine and dire political disturbances. Without the help of the MCOR, they could not have carried on, and, believe me, thousands of those whom they served would have been ruined.

Although the Delhi area conference was the largest in membership outside the USA, and the opportunity was greater than ever, qualified Methodists leaders had never been in such short supply. This meant added stress for both missionaries and indigenous leaders. For example, at the height of the rioting in 1947, thousands of terrified Muslims had professed Hinduism. Now, with order restored, many of them were shedding their skins of expediency and expressing genuine interest in Christianity. Follow-up, though, was complicated by the already enormous burden of the Indian pastors, most of whose churches were full and overflowing. With so many new inquirers, they needed help.

In March of 1949, Pickett received the good news that the MCOR would continue its India grants and that they would restore a cut made in the fall of 1948. But there remained the problem of the personnel gap.

IN EARLY MAY, WASKOM SPOKE at a Convention for the Deepening of the Spiritual Life at Kodaikanal. Kodaikanal, started by Americans in the 1800s, was the most beautiful of the southern hill stations. More than a mile high, it was the setting for an international boarding school and was surrounded by woods with wonderful hiking trails. Like Naini Tal in the North, it was on a lake and was a favorite vacation spot for missionaries in the region.

Retrieving a title he had used in 1944, Pickett called his sermon series, "The Confirmation of the Gospel." From it, he would, the next year, develop a book which, though never published, remains the best statement of his approach to evangelism and social service. He gave his first message on Monday, May 2. In it he asserted that, as the ministry of Jesus makes clear, "the gospel needs to be confirmed." Tuesday, he showed how ministries of healing (physical, mental, and spiritual) confirm the gospel. Wednesday, he focused on the confirmation of changed lives. In his final presentation, he described confirmation through the church. Throughout the series, he depended heavily on contemporary illustrations from the life of the church in India.

What first got him to thinking along these lines was the ineffectiveness of some of his own early preaching. When he began his missionary work, it was with "an exaggerated idea of the effectiveness of preaching as an evangelizing force." But he was not successful. And, in fact, the plainer he made his message, the more firmly his Muslim and Hindu hearers dismissed it. The effect was disillusionment, which only slowly gave way to "the realization . . . that the Gospel that seemed to me so beautiful and appealing was to most of my hearers entirely incredible." Gradually, through reflecting on the benefits of Jesus' routine blending of sermon and sign—often in the form of a cure from some affliction—it dawned on him that the preaching of the gospel must, in some concrete fashion, be confirmed.

PICKETT WAS BACK IN Delhi by May 8, Mother's Day. That night he and Ruth attended the service at Christ Church. All were given flowers to wear in remembrance of their mothers—red flowers to those whose mothers were still living, and white flowers to those whose mothers had passed on. The bishop wore a red one. Still in good health, Ludie Day Pickett had recently begun her eighty-second year.

As the summer of 1949 grew hotter and other missionaries escaped to the hills, Waskom and Ruth decided to stay in Delhi. The bishop spent most days in the office, dividing them between letter writing and meeting with scores of callers seeking help with various problems. One issue faced that summer was what to do with missionaries to China who were being displaced by Mao Zedong's sweep to the south. Putting some of them to work in India seemed logical and wise; however, there was a housing shortage, available housing having shrunk by two-thirds in just five years. Throughout that summer of 1949, several evenings each week, Pickett visited Methodist services in the city or a nearby village. On Friday, May 27, he drove to a village about 10 miles away in which were 320 Christians, all untouchables. He was astonished, but deeply moved, when the leading *zamindar* of the village, who attended the meeting that night, not only paid high tribute to the Christians, of whom he said, "there are none better in the village," but honored them by asking one of them to bring him a glass of water, which he drank publicly.

Another reason for remaining in Delhi that summer was the continuing needs of refugees. From the time of his return, Pickett had been the Central Relief Committee's liaison between India and Pakistan, and the Church World Service in America. Although by midyear, separate relief organizations were formed, with Don Ebright taking over India responsibilities, Delhi remained flooded with over a million refugees, most of them destined to live on the streets. Along Boulevard Road in front of the episcopal residence, a row of lean-tos and cubicles now traced the compound wall. In them the Picketts' new neighbors—battered and scattered remnants of the storm, many of them widows with their children—struggled to exist. Waskom and Ruth visited with them, heard their stories, and became their friends. Ruth set up a school for the children in the family garage. One never knew where, properly nurtured, the dormant potential in one of the little ones might take them. The Warne Baby Fold had proved that decisively. In fact, one of the orphans there—left on a winter's day in a basket on a missionary's veranda—was now Pickett's secretary and, later, would receive several graduate degrees and an Old Testament professorship at Leonard Theological College.

The presence in Delhi of so many victims of Partition, and the bitter pill of a Muslim state in what had once been home for many of them, made for continued tensions. Many Hindus were committed to Nehru's secular state. Others, however, wanted an India ruled by *Hindutva*. Given its way, one of the organizations promoting this viewpoint, the Rashtriya Swayamsevak Sangh (RSS), whose vision seemed for many more akin to Hitler's Aryan dream than the diverse Hinduisms of India, would have dislodged all the missionaries and sent them packing. Its reemerging popularity, after the release from prison of its leader, M.S. Golwalkar, made some missionaries think that day might yet come. In support of that view, they pointed to events like the August 21, 1949 reception for Golwalkar, in Delhi. Golwalkar, who had once said that non-Hindus in India "must learn to respect and hold in reverence Hindu religion," and, indeed, ought to be "wholly subordinated to the Hindu nation, claiming nothing, deserving no privileges, far less any preferential treatment," was given a hero's welcome. The *Statesman* reported that a quarter of a million showed for the reception. Pickett heard even larger estimates—up to 400,000. He heard, also, that there was talk in the crowd of organizing fresh violence against Muslims. Nevertheless, despite the large show of support and the temptation for many embittered Hindus to replace democracy with sectarian totalitarianism, Pickett was convinced that, eventually, most Hindus would refuse to align themselves with the RSS.

Part of Pickett's optimism resided in the knowledge that the Christian movement was growing too. In fact, Pickett had never seen more interest in the gospel, particularly among educated Hindus and Muslims, and many Sikhs. He had recently reported that, in the year following the terrible massacres of 1947, they had baptized more than 10,000 (mostly Sikhs) in Pakistan. But everywhere he went, he found many inquirers and full churches.

ANOTHER CAUSE FOR OPTIMISM was a new mission board program which gave hope of some relief from the personnel shortage. At the last Central Conference, the executive board of bishops had enthusiastically approved a proposal to open the door of short-term service opportunities to recent college graduates. The previous year, in New York, the Board of Missions had embraced R.E. Diffendorfer's idea of sending out groups of young, short-term recruits for service in various world settings. The first group of 50, affectionately known as "J-3s" and "K-3s," had already gone to

Japan and Korea. Pickett hoped that perhaps they could invite 25 "I-3s" to South Asia during each of the next three years.

However, while Pickett and his episcopal colleagues were enthusiastic, some longtime missionaries were not. When the board agreed to send the I-3s, one missionary wrote to New York to protest their coming for what she deemed "a three-years' 'look-see.'" She described a confab of like-minded missionaries in which "*not one of us* could think how we could put them to work at all!"

> They will not have the language and will not be trying to get it. Neither will they have any proper preparation for any particular type of work which they could do without the language. WHAT CAN they do? We don't know! On the other hand, it's no wonder they 'take it into their hands and ask to be sent out' in this way! It's a wonderful trip for them, why wouldn't they want to come out?

Pickett, however, could think of plenty for them to do. There was a need for stenographers and office secretaries. He wasn't the only one swamped with correspondence! There was also plenty of work to be done in hospitals and schools. Pickett hoped that several I-3s would be disposed to work in evangelism—an urgent need. "Nearly every day, people come to me to enquire about Christ or His Church. I have no one to send to their homes or to give time to helping them." He also hoped for a journalist and photographer among them, "who could take good pictures and write well of India." He was certain that one reason the MCOR was thinking of stopping its grants for dearness allowances was the missionaries' lack of time and temperament for publicizing their work. "They are far better at doing the work than they are at writing about it," he wrote, "and had they written more, they would have done less." He added, "Send us some young people with journalistic training to write up what these dearness allowances have accomplished and the present questioning will cease."

Contrary to the grouses and grumbles of those who could see no use for I-3s, and fretted over the cost of signing up those who would be coming on a lark with no commitment to language learning, college graduates were not flocking to the board for short terms abroad. That is not to say there weren't plenty of idealistic young graduates, motivated to serve where it mattered, but it took serious recruitment to sign them on. As for funding, the cost of I-3s would not compromise normal allocations.

The "threes'" support would come from their home churches and special gifts and would likely be money that would not have gone to missions. As for the language learning, before going to India, short-term recruits were to get a six-week orientation that included an introduction to Hindustani and encouragement to follow through with language acquisition on the field.

Despite the protests of a few, that summer the first group of "45-day wonders" would undergo their training and come to India and Pakistan. Fourteen would come to the Delhi Area and, within just a few months, be described by the bishop as "a grand group . . . far better equipped spiritually and otherwise than most missionary recruits of the past." He must not have been surprised, for he had long before decided the best missionary candidates, like the young James Thoburn, Brenton Badley, E. Stanley Jones, Clement Rockey, James Mathews, and Roland Scott (not to mention himself!), were those who came to the field while they were 20 or 21 years old.

> The advantages of sending candidates to the field to begin their service before they take postgraduate courses are in my judgement—(1) They are able to learn the language of the country more quickly and to acquire a more effective use thereof . . . than at any later period of their lives. (2) The church receives them more happily because they make no pretense of superior attainments . . . [They are] endeared to the hearts of the people by [their] freedom from pretension. (3) The young missionaries are able to form friendships with nationals of their own age group much more easily than they could if arriving in the country with higher educational qualifications and more mature social attitudes.

Pickett estimated that three-fourths of India's eminent missionary leaders had emerged from the one-fourth who arrived at the youngest ages.

WHEN THE FIRST TWO SETS of I-3s arrived, they were not groups of 25, as the pattern had been thus far been, but groups of 50 each. One of those in the first batch was Asbury Seminary student, Colleen Gilmore, who would become Pickett's secretary. The final two slots of the second group were filled by Douglas Pickett and Peggy Moffatt, both already fluent in Hindi and Urdu.

The I-3s were employed in just the kind of roles Pickett had imagined—as staff in the Methodist hospitals and sanitariums, as teachers at Woodstock and other schools, in local churches in a variety of capacities, and as rural development workers.

The "threes" were, in a way, like a Christian Peace Corps. In fact, Methodist Bishop James Mathews later intimated that the program, in part, inspired the Peace Corps. As with Peace Corps recruits, who in due course became the bulk of government overseas workers in organizations like USAID, many I-3s eventually became regular missionaries.

31 Birth of the Republic

Following the Thursday service with the Mountbattens, Waskom and Ruth packed their bags for America. On Monday, February 16, 1948, they flew to Calcutta and, from there, on Pan Am to Bangkok, Hong Kong, Shanghai, Tokyo, Wake Island, Midway Island, and Honolulu. Finally, on February 21—after a 13-hour flight—they landed in Los Angeles. Despite—or perhaps because of—the many takeoffs and landings, they described the trip as "thrilling."

At Honolulu, the sister of their son-in-law, Hank Lacy, garlanded them with lilies. At Los Angeles, they were met by their eldest daughter, Elizabeth (Hank was in class at USC), the Goulds (daughter, Miriam and her husband, Bill), Stanley and Julia Clemes (longtime friends), and Robert Williams. The Picketts planned to stay with the Goulds. After two weeks, they planned to drive to Ohio in their new Dodge, which they intended to bring back to India. However, their plans were dashed. On March 5, in Fresno, a drunk driver, looking back over his shoulder, crossed the centerline and crashed into the new Dodge, damaging it beyond repair. Waskom, who had been on the passenger side—his son-in law, Bill Gould, was driving—lay unconscious for two hours. His head had gone through the windshield. Three days later, his face covered with bruises and stitches, he reported the accident to James Mathews in ironic terms: "I was attacked . . . in Calcutta on Easter Monday last year and was shot at . . . in September last, but I was not touched." Mentioning his 22 stitches and 69 abrasions, he suggested the accident might have a silver lining. "A little squib" in the *Advocate*, he offered, might interest some of his friends and even lead to some checks for the work in India!

Besides some minor surgery connected to the accident, the rest of Pickett's American stay consisted of the usual schedule of preaching, fund-raising, and recruiting. But furlough duties did not preclude furlough joys. These included unwinding at a borrowed cottage in New York, visiting the grave of Dr. Clara Swain (first female missionary doctor to the Orient), and attending the marriage of daughter Margaret to John Sagan in Ventnor, New Jersey. Nevertheless, when October came, Waskom and Ruth were ready to be back in Delhi.

By Friday, October 8, the Picketts' replacement car and most of their baggage were aboard the Norwegian cargo ship, *Hoegh Merchant*, docked in Tacoma, Washington. They sailed that Sunday. After nearly three weeks at sea, Pickett wrote to Mathews, "Never have we enjoyed a voyage more." The leisurely voyage furnished a rare commodity: time to relax and write. During those three weeks, Pickett finished 15 lessons for the Urdu *Upper Room*, several book reviews, devotional meditations for the *Indian Witness*, and two articles. One of the articles was titled, "Hinduism is Changing."

Though Waskom and Ruth relished the opportunity to ease up, the lengthy voyage offered more leisure than their obligations allowed. It took 26 days to get to Manila, and the next day they learned that on the way to Bombay, via Singapore, they would make unanticipated stops in Iloilo, Cebu, two ports in Borneo, and two more in Indonesia. That meant the ETA for Bombay was now December 7, but Waskom had promised to attend Delhi Conference on November 24. Since the conference had already been postponed two-weeks for his benefit, he and Ruth decided they had better leave the ship and fly from Manila. While there, though, Waskom preached at a crowded Knox Memorial Church and brought greetings from India to the Philippine Central Conference.

PICKETT WAS PLEASED with the 1948 Delhi Conference. Despite the turmoil of India's first year of independence, more than 600 new Christians had been baptized and the number of inquirers was growing.

He must have been pleased, too, by the receipt of a letter from an old friend. The letter, which came in mid-December, had at its top a crest, an elephant head on a background map of India. On the wreath that formed the crest's perimeter were the words "Constituent Assembly" on the top, and "India" on the bottom. The sender was H.C. Mookerjee, a Bengali Christian who was then vice president of India's Constituent Assembly. "I was very glad to hear . . . that you are back at Delhi," he wrote, "and that in spite of the accident you had while in the States, you are fully recovered through the Grace of God so that you might have the privilege of continuing the good work to which you have devoted your whole life."

Mookerjee said he had recently moved "because I found life difficult at Constitution House." That would not have been hard for Pickett to imagine, for Constitution House, a series of military barracks, was far from a luxury hotel. Since most Constituent Assembly delegates billeted there, it allowed little privacy, especially for one chairing most of the meetings of the Assembly's sessions.

The Constituent Assembly, elected mainly by the provincial legislatures in mid-1946, was the body charged with framing the constitution for free India. However, its job was even weightier than that, for the creation of a constitution by and for Indians represented the fulfillment of a national dream. As the Indian commentator and author, Arun Shourie, has observed, "The demand that Indians must themselves determine the system under which they would be governed had become part of the Freedom Movement—in a sense it was the essence of that Movement." Thus, even though the resulting constitution has been faulted as too Western, too voluminous, and too-often amended, the fact that it evolved from a process entirely overseen by Indians was nearly as important as the document itself.

The work of the 389-member Constituent Assembly—lessened to 299 after the creation of Pakistan—took 165 days over a period encompassing almost three years. The product was a constitution that mirrored the Westminster parliamentary democracy, with some augmentations such as its enumeration of Fundamental Rights. Given the British educational history of many of the Assembly members, the form of constitution they adopted was not surprising: secular, democratic, federal. It was not the constitution Gandhi wanted: his state would have been rooted in the grassroots and would have been, *in effect,* Hindu. However, it was the constitution Nehru wanted: decidedly secular but guaranteeing a place for all of India's faith communities. It was also the constitution many of the missionaries wanted—secular in nature—because they were convinced that, in a land that was 85 percent Hindu, a common civic identity was the surest path to religious equality.

As part of the deliberation, committees of the Assembly, such as H.C. Mookerjee's Subcommittee on Minorities, listened to the interests of various constituencies. Protestant Christians, though not favoring special dispensations for minorities, were concerned that religious liberties be protected. To represent that concern, the NCC sent Bishop Shot Mondol, one of Pickett's Methodist colleagues, and Professor E.C. Bhatty to Delhi immediately after Independence in August 1947. They met twice with Christian members of the Assembly. Their discussions focused on worries that had surfaced when the issue of religious liberty had come up for debate in the spring session of the Assembly. Most bothersome was a proposed amendment banning the conversion of anyone under 18. Mondol and Bhatty, who were lodging with the Picketts, discussed their errand in after-dinner conversations, Bhatty even referring to the exchanges in the Pickett guest book.

About this time, Pickett himself was engaged in a series of informal dialogues with two key Constituent Assembly members:

> While the Constitution of India was being formulated my good friends Dr. H.C. Mookerjee, a devoted Baptist layman who was Vice President of the Constituent Assembly and its presiding officer at most of its sessions, and Dr. B.R. Ambedkar, chairman of the Drafting Committee, several times joined us in our home for dinner and after-dinner consultations.

Given the participants, those conversations were not, in themselves, remarkable. But, late in life, Pickett's recollection of them, —if his memory was accurate—divulged a remarkable secret. "Some of my suggestions," he remembered, "including the exact words of the section on Religious Liberty, were incorporated in the draft presented to the Assembly and accepted."

THE "WORDS" TO WHICH Pickett referred have been, by far, the most controversial in the Indian Constitution. Eventually, they appeared in Article 25.1:

> All persons are equally entitled to freedom of conscience, and
> the right freely to profess, practise and propagate religion.

Of these words, the surprise is "propagate." Though the Christian community was relieved to see it included, some Hindu delegates had hotly contested it. They warned that its inclusion would lead to the annihilation of Hindu culture. However, those in favor pointed out that the term only reaffirmed what was said elsewhere about free speech.

Religion was not a peripheral issue for the framer's of India's constitution. And language having to do with conversion was especially controversial. Of great concern to Christians, for example, was delegate K. M. Munshi's proposed amendment to a clause stating that "conversion from one religion to another brought about by coercion or undue influence shall not be recognised by law." Munshi wanted an amendment that would prohibit converting anyone under 18. Ambedkar, however, saw a major defect. What about the legal quandary it would create in deciding what to do with children wishing to follow their parents in converting to another faith? In the end, Ambedkar's question defeated Munshi's revision.

Although the proposed language "profess, practise and propagate" also unsettled Munshi and the Hindu majority, there was enough good will toward Christians for the article's passage. But was Pickett's claim to have contributed that wording—a claim made to friends in his later years—true? Is there any evidence to support it?

If the wording of Article 25.1 (draft Article 19) came to the Constituent Assembly from Pickett via Ambedkar or Mookerjee, it was not through Ambedkar. Created August 29, 1947, just after Independence, Ambedkar's Drafting Committee had the task of going over a roughed out constitution the Assembly had already been at work on. Their job was making sure the decisions of the Assembly were faithfully reflected in the document and that other subsidiary and necessary constitutional details were suitably included. Because some members of the Drafting Committee were not always able to come to Delhi, or died, or resigned, much of the load of the revision fell on Ambedkar himself. In fact, at some of the called meetings, only he and his secretary showed. Nevertheless, though the circumstances offered Ambedkar opportunity to include the language of propagation in his draft revision, it didn't happen that way, for it was already in the draft he received.

Where, then, did the surprising language come from? It was not in the Objectives Resolution moved by Nehru on December 13, 1946, the third day of the Constituent Assembly's first session. That statement, the heart of Nehru's contribution to the process, spoke of "freedom of . . . belief, faith, [and] worship." However, only the following April, when it was introduced by Sardar Patel's Advisory Committee, did the language of "propagation" come to the Assembly: "the right freely to profess, practise and propagate religion subject to public order, morality or health, and to the other provisions of this Chapter."

The full name of the committee headed by Sardar Vallabhbhai Patel was the Advisory Committee on Fundamental Rights, Minorities and Tribal and Excluded Areas. The statement on the right to propagate one's

faith came from its members. Besides Patel, they included the heads of
four subcommittees: (1) Fundamental Rights, chaired by J.B. Kripalani;
(2) Northeast Frontier Tribal Areas and Assam Excluded & Partially
Excluded Areas, chaired by Gopinath Bardoloi; (3) Excluded and Partially
Excluded Areas (other than those in Assam), chaired by A.V. Thakkar;
and (4) Minorities, chaired by Pickett's Christian friend, H.C. Mookerjee.

There is no question, therefore, that Mookerjee was directly involved
in bringing this language to the Assembly for debate. But had he discussed
with Pickett the constitution's Fundamental Rights section and the
religious liberty clause? And had Pickett suggested in that context the
wording that appeared in the draft and, later, the constitution itself?
Mookerjee's December 1948 letter to Pickett, which he wrote not just to
welcome him back, but to ask when he might come by for a visit, does
nothing to lessen that likelihood. In fact, Mookerjee's main focus in the
letter was on that very language! He wrote:

> The papers have told you that we have at last passed our
> Fundamental Rights including the right to propagate our faith.
> I congratulate myself that the whole of the Fundamental Rights
> was passed with an Indian Christian in the Chair.

The Assembly vice president also described how, as chair, he had guided
the debate:

> What was most wonderful was that though attempts to either
> curtail or to totally deprive us of what we regard as the most
> precious of our rights were made by people with a strong bias
> towards Hindu Mahasabha mentality, the stoutest champions on
> our side were in all cases drawn from the Brahmin community.
> I picked out Brahmins from every part of India deliberately and
> did not allow a single Sikh, Moslem or Christian to speak,
> because I was quite confident that the goodwill we had acquired
> through giving up voluntarily all claims to special treatment
> would be quite sufficient to rally them to our side, and I am more
> glad that my confidence was not misplaced.

As with many national documents, much of India's constitution
contains language borrowed from elsewhere—most notably, in its case,
from the 1935 Government of India Act, from which some 250 clauses

are taken. Also, the members of Constituent Assembly committees listened to ideas and suggestions from many quarters, from which added clauses may well have come. Whether or not the language of Article 25.1 came from Pickett, its guarantee of freedom to share one's faith is prized by many Indians. Yet it remains controversial. To proponents of *Hindutva*, for example, it is not a freedom to esteem, but an eyesore and impediment to their dream of a national return to radical Hindu principles.

IN OCTOBER 1949, PRIME MINISTER NEHRU made his first ever trip to the United States. His main priority was to work out an agreement for low-cost U.S. wheat to help avoid the growing threat of widespread famine. Getting a good deal was important. India's monetary position was perilous. Unrealistic plans and projections, a trade war with Pakistan, and huge spending on arms had throttled the economy. An accompanying plummet in agricultural production to below the infamous 1939 level was sending prices moonward. Nehru hoped to ease the crisis by importing and storing a million tons of wheat and selling it strategically, thereby keeping its cost down.

With Mao Zedong's great success dominating the news—and widespread distress over the prospects for further Communist gains in Asia—President Truman was eager for friendly relations with India and, in an unprecedented gesture of welcome, sent his personal plane, the elegantly appointed *Independence*, to retrieve Nehru after his stopover in London. When the prime minister arrived at National Airport at 4:30 p.m. on October 11, a 19-gun artillery salute greeted him, and *"Jana Gana Mana,"* played by the Army Band. *"Jana Gana Mana"* (Thou Art the Ruler of the Minds of All People) was from the pen of the Nobel Prize winning poet, Rabindranath Tagore. It was sung first on December 27, 1911 at the Calcutta session of the Indian National Congress. It was not, however, in praise of King George as many assumed, but in praise of God. Nor was it yet the Indian national anthem, as the *New York Times* reported in its coverage of Nehru's arrival. That happened three months later, on January 24, 1950, when the Constituent Assembly formally adopted the first of its five stanzas.

President Truman received the prime minister with these words: "Destiny willed it that our country should have been discovered in the search for a new route to yours. I hope that your visit, too, will be, in a sense, a discovery of America." In his address to Congress two days later,

Nehru echoed the president's speech: "I have come here on a voyage of discovery of the mind and heart of America." But some thought his speech also contained a touch of arrogance: "Like you," he said, "we have achieved our freedom through a revolution, though our methods were different from yours."

Two days later Nehru met privately with Secretary of State Dean Acheson at the Secretary's home. They did not hit it off. Nehru, whom Acheson said "talked to me, as Queen Victoria said of Mr. Gladstone, as though I were a public meeting," began the conversation by broaching the possibility of buying American wheat at lower than world prices. Acheson answered that any wheat deal was up to Congress, adding that he had already been working on it. But Acheson seemed little interested in India's food shortage. Instead, he zeroed in on Nehru's stand on Kashmir. Likewise, President Truman, with whom Nehru met the next day, wanted only to focus on Kashmir. But for Nehru, Kashmir was an internal matter, which the U.N. and the U.S. had no business interfering with.

Neither Acheson nor Truman could know just how deeply he felt about it. Following Independence, the disposition of India's princely states was not yet fully resolved. While clinging to their wealth, most of the princes had waived their right to sovereignty and entered the new India. However, two had not: Hyderabad and Kashmir. Hyderabad's Nizam was a Muslim, but most of his subjects were Hindus. Kashmir's maharaja was a Hindu, but most of his subjects were Muslims. In 1948, Hyderabad's ruler tried to crush a peasant "join India" movement. Seizing the opportunity, Nehru responded with a "police action" and incorporated the state. That left Kashmir. When tribesmen from Pakistan invaded, the maharaja swiftly notified Nehru's Government of Kashmir's accession to India. That allowed Nehru to defend the borders with troops. Pakistan responded with its own troops, plunging the nations into war. Mountbatten pressured Nehru to let the newly-established United Nations mediate. But Nehru regretted his concession. Since Kashmir was the ancestral home of the Nehru family, non-Indians supposed his stubbornness was sentimental. But, to Nehru, Kashmir represented his dream of a nonsectarian India in which Muslims could feel as much at home as Hindus.

As the Secretary listened, a frustrated Nehru insisted that, from the perspective of a secular state, the religious makeup of Kashmir should have no bearing at all on Kashmir's disposition, that India—even after partition—had a large Muslim population well-represented at the highest levels of government. Acheson, however, was unmoved by the logic of "the great man," as he caricatured him. To Acheson, Nehru's "combination of public speech and flashes of anger and deep dislike of his opponents" were distasteful and most unstatesmanlike. He was equally dismayed by the rest of their conversation, which he interpreted as Nehru lecturing him on various world issues. As the late night meeting ended, the Secretary concluded, "I was convinced that Nehru and I were not destined to have a pleasant personal relationship." With Nehru failing, then, to reduce Acheson's already solidifying view of him as stubborn and aloof, it comes as no surprise the prime minister failed to extract any promises on India's food needs. Nehru went home as misunderstood on Kashmir and his stance of nonalignment as when he came. And, of course, he went home empty-handed.

NOVEMBER 26 WAS TO BE A BRIGHTER day for Nehru—in fact, for all of India. That was the day the Constituent Assembly's four years of hard work ended. Under the dome of Parliament House's Central Hall, Constituent Assembly president Rajendra Prasad observed the moment with a speech made memorable by its touching tribute to M.K. Gandhi, the father of the nation. Then came the vote, followed by lengthy cheering and the pounding of desks. But the real celebration was to come two months later, on January 26, when, two days after his election, as called for in the new constitution, Rajendra Prasad would be inaugurated India's first president, and the new republic would be formally ushered in.

BACK IN MARCH, PICKETT had welcomed the news that Dorothy Clark Wilson, author of a popular new novel on Moses, *The Prince of Egypt*, would be coming to India to do research for a new book. The Picketts had already met Dorothy Clark Wilson and liked her. On hearing she was coming, they immediately agreed to make their home her headquarters. When Mrs. Wilson arrived in Delhi on the night of November 8, she had in her bag a letter from Ruth Pickett. It said, "I shall be waiting for you at the airlines office. Don't feel anxious at all." Nevertheless, because her plane was three hours late, Ruth, who had gone home, was not immediately at the Imperial Hotel rendezvous point. The author was reassured though, when, on telling one of the officials the address she would be staying at, he said, "Ah, 12 Boulevard Road? But that is the bishop's house!"

On Wednesday, January 25, the day before the presidential swearing in, Wilson was in Allahabad, gathering material for her book when a telegram came. Of it she wrote:

> The most wonderful surprise! I am to see the inauguration of the first President of India! I received an invitation from Bishop Pickett today telling me of my invitation to attend the ceremony at Government House tomorrow, the day India officially becomes a republic.

But that would not be her only surprise. At the Pickett house the next morning, Ruth Pickett had yet another announcement for her. They had also gotten her invitations to the grand parade at the stadium in the afternoon and to President Prasad's reception the next day.

The swearing-in ceremony took place in the great, round Durbar Hall at Government House. It began at 10:15 with the arrival of Governor-General Chakravarti Rajagopalachari and President-elect Rajendra Prasad. Prasad had begun his day with prayers and a stop at Rajghat to honor the memory of Mahatma Gandhi, who had envisaged this day more than a quarter of a century earlier. When the chief justice had sworn him in, the president made a short speech, first in Hindi, then in English. After that, he was led to the Upper Loggia, followed by the prime minister, deputy prime minister, chief justice, speaker, cabinet ministers, supreme court judges, and auditor general, who, after also being sworn in were presented to the president. Afterwards, the guests—including the Picketts and their American visitor—all moved to the ballroom, were presented by name to the newly sworn president, and served refreshments.

That afternoon, the Picketts and their guest headed for Irwin Stadium where the ceremonial parade commemorating Republic Day would take place. At 3:25 the trumpeters sounded "Markers" and markers and massed bands marched onto the parade grounds:
At precisely the moment scheduled, the band, crimson coated and resplendent, marched onto the field and started the national anthem, the signal for countless ranks of soldiers—every branch of the military including picturesque Nepalese Gurkhas with their curved kukris—entering at six different points and marching toward the center to form a solid line across the field. Presently [at 3:45] the official party

appeared. The president was riding in a horse-drawn landau, with a gold umbrella over his head. In front were strikingly clad lancers on horseback. When the president had inspected the parade and returned to the dais, there came the firing of the *feu-de-joie* and a repetition of the National Anthem. Then, giving Prasad three *Jais*, the parade—beginning with the Navy Band and ending with the Police Band—marched by.

The two-day celebration ended on Friday with a large garden reception for the president at Government House. There Wilson, with Ruth Pickett's encouragement, gave Prime Minister Nehru a poem she had written about him. It was the second time she had seen him up close, but not the last.

Two weeks later, in Viruthampet, North Arcot—not far from Vellore—she got a letter from Ruth Pickett, who had been to a luncheon at Nehru's house. She wrote:

> We asked the Prime Minister if he'd not like to meet the lady who had given him her poem about him ... Well, you are to have a special invitation when you get back. I'm to let him know when the time comes.

The invitation came on March 20. It said: "Dear Miss Dorothy Clark Wilson, the Prime Minister would be pleased if you would very kindly have lunch with him on Tuesday, the 21st March, at his house. Please confirm." She did.

DURING HIS YEARS IN DELHI, Bishop Pickett brought many guests to breakfast or lunch at the prime minister's table. Other visitors met high officials without ever leaving the Pickett house. Dorothy Clark Wilson met health minister Amrit Kaur twice that way. Pickett, however, did not think of his friends in high places merely as government friends, though he enjoyed conversing with them. His friendship with Amrit Kaur, for instance, was also friendship with the refugee, or the leper, or the student who dreamed of being a doctor, because cooperatively he and the Health Minister could help them in ways that neither could alone. Right now, friendship with Nehru meant thinking about how he could help the prime minister convince the Americans to sell some of their surplus wheat to India. Lately, Pickett had been thinking a lot about that wheat.

32 Ambassador-at-Large

With the threat of famine looming large, J. Waskom Pickett came to America in 1950 determined to engage in some unofficial diplomacy. For leverage in getting to those with the power to emancipate some of America's wheat surplus, he would use his mother's friendship with Vice President Alben Barkley and his moral authority as Methodism's senior bishop in India. He planned to appeal to the churches too—not for wheat but contributions to antituberculosis work. There was an alarming surge in TB in India—probably not unrelated to the worsening food crisis. That summer Pickett would visit congregations in 32 states. Nevertheless, his first priority remained to get the U.S. Government to reconsider its refusal to sell wheat. So, in early July, he spent five days in Washington, D.C. meeting with anyone of importance who would listen. He went with the blessing of the mission board, Indian embassy and, back in New Delhi, Amrit Kaur, with whom he kept in touch by phone. During that week, he met with representatives of the State Department three times and addressed a small luncheon in one of the Senate rooms that was arranged by Vice President Barkley. Besides Barkley, seven others were present. They were Special Assistant to the President Averell Harriman; and Senators Douglas (Illinois), Lehman (California), McMahon (Connecticut), Thomas (Utah), Green (Rhode Island), and Humphrey (Minnesota). Pickett reported the meeting that night by overseas telephone to Amrit Kaur. All but one, he told her, had offered their support. Senator Humphrey suggested he organize a Friends of India Society to lobby for wheat and raise a million dollars for tuberculosis relief.

In mid-August, the bishop's initiatives were rewarded with a half-hour conversation with President Truman, which Averell Harriman arranged. Truman suggested that Pickett ask Nehru to reapply for wheat. He also assured Pickett he would revisit the issue sympathetically. Before boarding his plane for New York and London, Pickett made a public plea for

America to share its oversupply of grain with India. He added that, by turning her back the year before, the U.S. had given ammunition to India's Communists. He asked why allow four million tons of wheat to rot when millions were facing starvation.

Pickett arrived back in Delhi on August 22. He described his journey as pleasant, but "tiring." Nevertheless, he had already met with Amrit Kaur to report more fully on his efforts. The health minister confirmed his fears. A series of summer crises had compounded the need. Because of a failure of the monsoon in the southeast, floods in four provinces in the North, and a huge earthquake in Assam—the largest ever measured, six million tons of unharvested food grains had been destroyed. After briefing him, Amrit Kaur offered to give Pickett a statement that he could use to encourage the American churches to step up their relief efforts and put more pressure on the U.S. Government. Kaur did not think, however, that Nehru, who had been deeply hurt by the U.S. Government's indifference to India's suffering, would reapply for the sale of wheat. His relationship with the U.S. State Department had become so fraught with misunderstanding that it would do no good. U.S. Ambassador to India, Loy Henderson, agreed. But he told Pickett the need was clearer than the need for George C. Marshall's European Recovery Plan. The right thing would be for the U.S. to make an outright gift of the wheat.

Word soon got out about Pickett's representations of India's needs. The Deputy Commissioner of Delhi, with whom Pickett had tea one day, thanked him and told him that his initiatives had touched the hearts of more people than a year of any other kind of service he could have rendered. Still, months went by without a breakthrough in Washington.

In late January, Waskom and Ruth had supper with Evelyn Hershey, the U.S. Government's social work attaché in Delhi. She told them that food rations in several provinces had just been cut by another 25 percent and worried that if the U.S. failed to respond soon, friendship with India would be lost, and democracy would be set back for a generation. The conversation with Hershey inspired Pickett to try the next day to phone Vice President Barkley, President Truman, and Senator Humphrey. He also mailed a fresh circular to churches and donors in America, pleading with them, due to the gravity of the situation, to redouble their efforts to help.

February brought news of the death of Dr. R.E. Diffendorfer, a great shock. Diffendorfer, who, it seemed, had been executive director of the Board of Foreign Missions longer than Pickett could remember, had retired only two years before. Other February news, however, was more heartening. Word came that 23 members of the U.S. Congress, including Senator Hubert Humphrey, had met with President Truman and urged him to recommend that Congress send two million tons of wheat to India. A short while later Truman made the recommendation, but holdups persisted.

Believing that if they kept at it, their efforts to persuade the U.S. Congress to act would pay off, Pickett urged every influential person and group he knew to continue applying pressure. A late-March newspaper clipping, found in his effects, with the headline "U.S. Missionary's Efforts to Speed Up Food Aid," described both his earlier efforts and his current barrage of cablegrams urging quick action. At the urging of James Mathews and the Board of Missions, Methodist churches all over the U.S. joined Pickett's cause. Finally, in late spring, word came that the Wheat for India bill had passed Congress. Pickett reported that throughout India the news had been welcomed with great gratitude. To expedite the distribution of the wheat, the Indian Government agreed to cut all the usual red tape.

For Pickett, the wheat victory was not a signal to rest. With India's needs still fresh on American minds, he intensified his campaign for help in combating the tuberculosis epidemic. First, with an endorsement from Amrit Kaur, he renewed his fund-raising efforts by post. Second, he solicited the new American ambassador, Chester Bowles, for Point Four help for two sanatoriums, whose board he chaired. The Point Four Program was a U.S. foreign-aid initiative originally proposed by Truman as the fourth point in his 1949 inaugural address. It was designed to improve living standards in poor nations. Third, Pickett followed Senator Humphrey's advice to found an American society charged with raising a million dollars for the sanatoriums. There were a dozen such tuberculosis facilities in India, but the two whose board Pickett chaired were the leading ones.

PICKETT NOT ONLY GOT INTO THE "wheat business" during this era, but the "dairy cow" business as well. In many places, milk sellers milked their cows at their patrons' homes. Some of them placed a stuffed calf nearby so that the cow, thinking it was its own calf, would be willing to give milk. They insisted this was necessary. Even so, Pickett noticed the cows gave, at most, a single quart twice a day. Over the years, Pickett often suggested importing milk cows from America or Europe to breed with Indian cows.

But the idea of improving milk production through interbreeding seemed to have little appeal among the missionaries and government officials he sought to persuade. With the exception of Dr. Sam Higginbottom, founder of the first missionary agricultural college in India, who had the same idea, he did not find any encouragement. However, on an American visit, Pickett convinced a dairyman in Merced, California to donate four Jersey bulls for interbreeding. Pickett managed to get the bulls to India with the help of a new missionary recruit who cared for them on their voyage. Once they got to India, Pickett arranged to have some of the best Punjabi milk cows artificially inseminated with semen from the bulls. The experiment was a success. Punjabi farmers began lining up to have their cows impregnated. Some Hindus protested that American secular cows should not be interbred with Indian sacred cows. Nevertheless, the Indian Government eventually imported hundreds of more Jersey bulls for that very purpose.

WHEN INDEPENDENCE CAME TO INDIA, Pickett was as loyal a patriot as one could find. As such, he was warmly regarded by many government officials, including Pandit Nehru. Early in 1952, just before a trip to Ludhiana, Pickett phoned the prime minister's private secretary for a brief appointment. Although Parliament was in session and Nehru was busy catching up after a just-finished election campaign, he okayed a meeting for the next morning at 10:15, three quarters of an hour before he and his cabinet were due at a memorial service for the late King George. That day Pickett read with interest a newspaper report that an influential politician from the South had been trying for several days, without success, to see the prime minister. And while Pickett was waiting for his appointment in the office of Nehru's secretary, he overheard the secretary decline several requests for appointments and tell one individual the prime minister would be going out of town in two days, so he was limiting himself to "matters of first importance." Pickett's agenda was twofold. First, he was about to return to America for the Methodist General Conference and wished to know how he could best represent current Indian needs and concerns. Second, he wanted help, if possible, in obtaining a site for a new Methodist Church in the heart of New Delhi. He had followed the channels for finding a suitable location and getting clearance to build but had made no headway. He left the prime minister's office with a promise of help.

By 1952, Pickett was seeing another friend, B.R. Ambedkar, with less frequency. But despite Ambedkar's deteriorating health, they occasionally connected. The last time they met, Ambedkar asked him, if he'd lost hope for his conversion to Christ. Pickett assured him he was still praying for him. Ambedkar's response may have surprised him. He said, "Please keep it up. I am not yet satisfied." It is not certain, though, if that was before or after Ambedkar's 1956 announcement that he had turned to Buddhism.

ON FEBRUARY 20, 1952, WASKOM AND RUTH left by plane for America via Hong Kong, Tokyo, and Honolulu. They were in Hong Kong and Honolulu just long enough for Waskom to write *Indian Witness* articles on his impressions of each place. While Waskom went on to a bishops' policy conference in Arizona, Ruth remained in Honolulu with their daughter Miriam and her family. Waskom and Ruth planned to rendezvous later in California and, after General Conference in San Francisco, visit their other two daughters, as well as Ludie Day Pickett who was now 85. It would be their last visit with Waskom's mother; she died March 1, 1953.

During the spring and summer of 1952, Bishop Pickett spoke in churches ranging west to east from California to New York, and north to south from Michigan to Arkansas. His agenda was two-fold: to raise funds— mainly for medical work; and to stimulate a climate of good will for India.

Due to "misunderstanding and concern" about India's relations with Pakistan, Kashmir, and the United Nations, Pickett soon discovered the second of his aims was even more pressing than he had guessed. So, he said: "I became a self-appointed ambassador for India and did my best to remove the causes of misunderstanding." This was an "appointment" he would never relinquish—even in his retirement.

On August 17th, the bishop was the featured speaker on the Protestant Radio Hour. On September 6, he and Ruth returned to India via Newfoundland (where a cracked cylinder in one engine kept their plane at Gander for 10 hours) and London, arriving back in Delhi on September 12. When their Pan Am Clipper landed, they debarked and found, that although it was 1:00 a.m., a large group of ministers and lay persons had come out to welcome them home.

The bishop returned to a desk piled high with business that had accumulated during his absence. Since he planned to visit several areas for church dedications and other events—all before Delhi Conference in

December—he wasted no time getting into it. Among the work that had accrued were letters to be answered, refused visas for new missionaries to be appealed, and at least one writing assignment to which he had agreed—a chapter for Roland Scott's forthcoming book, *Six Ways of Evangelism.*

Pickett began his chapter by affirming that "the obligation to evangelize belongs to all churches, regardless of location, age or strength. To receive the evangel is to receive an obligation to proclaim the evangel." He, then, outlined from his own experiences three responses of village churches: (1) those that happily accept the responsibility; (2) those that "do something for evangelism but require as much service for themselves as they give;" and (3) those that get in the way of evangelism. He called them, respectively, "spontaneous," "dependent," and "impeding" churches, and he offered examples of each. Some churches in the latter categories were able to turn around, he wrote. He credited such turnarounds primarily to renewed spiritual vitality. However, Pickett's main concern was keeping churches from getting into the latter categories in the first place. One key, he wrote, is to encourage new Christians to begin telling others immediately about what Christ has done for them. In his words:

> The Christian who has gone but a short way . . . toward perfection may make his friends eager to join him on the way . . . To suppose that one cannot be an evangelist unless he has first become a saint is to reverse the true order, for one can certainly not become a saint until he has been an evangelist. Bearing witness to Christ . . . aids in the development of Christian experience and character.

Therefore, he urged churches to:

> give attention to ways and means of using the asset of the new convert's influence with his family, neighbors and caste fellows. The segregation of the new convert, whether to protect him or indoctrinate him, should be recognized as a deterrent to evangelism.

IN EARLY 1953, Ruth Pickett required surgery, so Waskom stayed close to home. Another Pickett was available to offer support too. Douglas, soon to marry Ann Stewart Leeder, another child of missionaries, was working as an I-3 missionary at Pickett Junior High School in Khatauli, only a little over 50 miles from Delhi.

That winter and spring, Waskom followed with interest newspaper accounts of the newly elected U.S. president, Dwight David Eisenhower—especially stories that hinted at his policies towards India and Pakistan. A new president also meant a change of leadership at the American embassy, a prospect Pickett found uninviting because it meant the departure of his friend, Chester Bowles. There would also be a new secretary of state, John Foster Dulles, who, Pickett noted, was about to visit India, presumably "to woo India and Pakistan into the Western defense block."

Pickett could not have known that, over the next few years, he would meet with Secretary Dulles some 14 times, nor that it would not take more than one or two of those meetings for him to decide that he disliked both Dulles and his policies. Pickett's assessment of Dulles' foreign policy was that it was myopically one-dimensional. Because he was so focused on stopping the advance of Communism, Dulles ignored "democratic India" and armed "despotic Pakistan" (as Pickett labeled them)—all because of geography. To Pickett, Dulles' game plan was not only unreasonable, but unconscionable. It did not take him long to decide that Dulles' self-serving nationalism, combined with his mulish intractability, made the secretary "unfit" for his role—a view that in the years that followed, when Pakistan three times turned its U.S. supplied arms against India, only grew stronger.

Pickett missed no opportunity for indicting Dulles' policies, and, thanks to his political connections, his opportunities were extraordinary. Senator Humphrey, who shared Pickett's negative assessment of the Pakistan Pact proposal, offered him the opportunity to air his concerns informally with members of the Senate Foreign Relations Committee. But Pickett did not stop with that. Just as he had gotten an audience with President Truman, so he managed to get one with President Eisenhower on August 4, 1954. Upon hearing Pickett's case, Eisenhower asked him for a memorandum detailing his arguments against the pact. Pickett responded with a closely reasoned outline of his position that ran about 3,000 words. It might not get the result he hoped for, but at least he had gotten a hearing where it mattered most.

33 Mission to Nepal

Dr. Robert ("Bob") Fleming, a teacher at Woodstock School, and his
wife, Dr. Bethel Fleming, a medical doctor, went to Nepal "on the wings
of a bird," as they put it. They meant it quite literally.

Bob Fleming had come to Woodstock School at the end of the 1920s
when the Methodists were desperate to meet their initial quota of teachers
and not lose face with their denominational partners in their new
cooperative venture. Waskom Pickett's request had gotten Fleming to
Woodstock. Now, more than two decades later, Pickett was his bishop.

Over the years Bob Fleming had become a favorite fixture at
Woodstock. His students became enthusiastic collectors of ferns,
butterflies, and snails. Young Douglas Pickett had specialized in beetles.
Fleming himself cultivated an interest in the birds of the Himalayas. For
years, after he came back from Chicago with a Ph.D. in 1937, he had
trekked into the mountains of North India during school vacation
(December to February). There he collected bird specimens, which were
shipped off for study and display in the U.S.—mainly at Chicago's Field
Museum of Natural History. By the early 1950s, he was among South
Asia's top ornithologists.

Dr. Bethel had come to India with the American Presbyterians. In fact,
she was for a time in charge of one of their hospitals. However, when she
and Dr. Bob were married, the Presbyterians found an Indian doctor to
take her place, and she became school physician at Woodstock and a
surgeon at Landour Community Hospital.

For some years, Bob Fleming had been interested in extending his
bird-hunting into Nepal, but the border was closed. He decided to apply
anyway, and, to his astonishment, the Government of Nepal granted him
a six-month permit. He brought the permit letter to Pickett in Delhi and,
after discussing it at length, Pickett helped him draft two more letters: one
to the Field Museum of Chicago asking for financial backing, and another

requesting extra permits: one for a medical doctor for emergencies and the other for an assistant to help prepare bird specimens for boxing and shipping.

With his requests granted, Fleming's first expedition to Nepal took place in 1949-1950. Dr. Carl Taylor, who had once been a student at Woodstock and was the first public health doctor in India, accompanied him. The rest of the party consisted of T.R. Bergsaker of the Norwegian Baptist mission and a teacher at Woodstock, and Harold Bergsma, a Woodstock high school student who returned from furlough in the U.S. with needed equipment. While hunting for bird specimens, the party discovered that there was an enormous need for medical assistance. When people learned that a doctor was in the group, hundreds of ill and afflicted people swarmed their camp. On subsequent treks into Nepal, with Dr. Bethel and the Fleming children along, as well as former China missionary, Dr. Carl Fredericks, the need was equally apparent.

Inevitably the Flemings became interested in starting a medical ministry in Nepal. They sought Pickett's counsel. He not only encouraged them but helped them draft letters seeking permission. The first letter went unanswered. The following year, Fleming posted a second letter, requesting permission to open maternity and child welfare centers in Kathmandu plus a small hospital in Tansen. Tansen, where Fleming had encountered so much human tragedy on the first trip to Nepal, was an important trading center about 150 miles west of the capital. But would the second letter go unanswered too? All they could do was wait.

IN LATE MAY 1953, Dr. Bethel Fleming came down from Mussoorie to see Bishop Pickett. She and Dr. Bob had at last heard from the Nepal Government. And the response was positive! But how would the strapped-for-funds mission board in New York view the notion of setting up medical clinics in Nepal? She admitted she had her doubts.

Pickett told Dr. Bethel that he had no authority to commit the Methodist Mission Board to the Nepal project but that he would immediately write to New York with a proposal he thought they would respond positively to—an idea he had already discussed with the Presbyterian Commission Representative for India, John Weir. Pickett's idea was to invite the various mission and church boards affected by negotiations for church union in North India to join with the Methodist and Presbyterian boards in a joint mission to Nepal. Later, he recalled it like this:

> I wrote to the United Methodist Board of Missions telling them that I hoped that we would not attempt to establish a Methodist Church in Nepal but rather to secure the participation of missions of many Churches in sending missionaries and finances for a wide non-denominational program of service to God and to the people of Nepal.

James Mathews, now a corresponding secretary with the Board of Missions, indicated responsiveness on the Board's part if, as Pickett had proposed, the venture could, indeed, be a joint one. When the United Presbyterian Board of Missions and the Regions Beyond Missionary Union (chiefly British) agreed, followed by several more boards, Pickett also got the backing of the NCC to convene a provisional committee.

Pickett had gone over the Flemings' permission letter from Nepal carefully. It contained four conditions: (1) all of the expenses for the hospital and maternity welfare centers would be borne by the sponsoring boards; (2) the staff would be drawn from Nepalese citizens as much as possible, and they would be given proper training; (3) the hospital and welfare centers would be turned over to the Government of Nepal in five years; (4) distribution of medicine and treatment of all patients would be free. Pickett suggested modifications in the last two items, and at the end of June the Nepal Government agreed.

Before long, Pickett got an invitation from the Flemings to come to Kathmandu to meet and confer with the prime minister. All had been arranged. He was also to address a small audience of friends of the enterprise. When Pickett was introduced, he began with a short statement in Hindi. Most of the Nepalese who were present knew Hindi, but they had never heard a European or American speak it. Pickett reported:

> The result was exciting. People sat forward and listened eagerly and when I shifted to English because there were twenty or thirty Europeans and Americans present who did not know Hindi their interest held.

> The Prime Minister leaned over and asked how long I would remain in Kathmandu. I replied "By your orders, Sir, I must leave

in three days." He replied, "Oh no, please stay at least a year. We need your help."

Pickett agreed to an appointment at the prime minister's office the next day. He repeated his plea for Pickett to stay a year or longer. He even offered an airplane, an American pilot, and an Indian cook—all financed by his Government. Pickett reported that such hospitality was typical of how those representing the proposed mission were treated in those early days. Several weeks later, the Flemings were given the opportunity to rent a palace belonging to one of the royal families.

By the start of 1954, Dr. Bethel had launched the first clinic in Bhaktapur, and the United Medical Mission to Nepal, as it was called at first, was on its way to becoming a unique and enormously successful Christian presence in a formerly closed country. By the year 2,000, the eight mission agencies that formed the mission that year had grown to 39 agencies from 18 countries. Eventually, the work expanded into education and other areas. Members of the mission were not allowed by the Nepalese Government to evangelize; nevertheless, churches emerged everywhere the mission worked.

Pickett's early contributions helped lay the foundation for more than a half century of remarkable ministry. They included: (1) the idea of creating an umbrella under which, eventually, 39 church and mission organizations would cooperate, (2) the unique organizational structure that has allowed UMN to function so well for so long, (3) the early negotiations that brought all the parties together, (4) the wise securing of the imprimaturs of the Executive Committees of the National, Uttar Pradesh and Delhi Christian Councils, (5) the calling together of the first provisional board of managers, (6) the leadership of the regular board for the first three years, (7) keeping the mission free from the control of the churches, and (8) many of the early organizational chores. Ernest Oliver, the first director of the mission, remembered that even his appointment was Pickett's doing.

[Bishop Pickett] was Chairman of a group of missionary societies working on the borders of Nepal preparing for entrance into that closed land. The bishop was a great encouragement to us all, and when the opportunity to enter Nepal came in 1954, it was the bishop who proposed that I lead the United Mission to Nepal, a task which I joyfully accepted.

IN THE SPRING OF 1954, Donald McGavran asked Pickett to give him feedback on a book he hoped to publish. It was called, *The Bridges of God*. Pickett said he would be delighted to see it, and based on McGavran's description of it, he added:

> I am so glad to know that you are emphasizing and restating some of the underlying principles that I declared in my books of 17 years or 20 years ago. It is interesting that you and McLeish are both doing that now.

With the manuscript for *The Bridges of God* came McGavran's announcement of a new career-blueprint:

> I am planning to give the rest of my life to a promotion of the People Movement point of view. Just what that will mean I do not yet clearly see. But for the next 18 months or two years, it means living near New York, and by every way that I can, pressing this point of view on the boards at home.
>
> Now, I shall need major support from the field from someone who believes in People Movements, and from one who has sufficient experience to know that no huge shift in emphasis such as I propose can possible [sic] be brought about except slowly and that by hammering away at it . . . For this major support, I turn to you who lit my candle in the beginning, and who has been such a source of encouragement through the years.

Pickett responded with an assurance of support and endorsement and an offer to meet in New York in the summer to converse further about McGavran's plans. He also gave McGavran generous feedback on the manuscript, whose effect he thought would "prove epochal." He thought some of McGavran's points might have more impact if McGavran phrased them less dogmatically, but, in general, he affirmed his old friend's bold statement and challenge of the traditional one-by-one, mission-station approach to winning new Christians. He reminded McGavran of advice given to him many years before by John R. Mott:

> If you are going to do much good in the church in India you must challenge the assumptions on which you find your associates

working. If those assumptions are right, find out why, and if they are not right, prove them wrong and divert thinking and work into other directions.

AFTER MORE THAN 40 YEARS of missionary service, Pickett was beginning to think about retirement. Others were anticipating it too. Dr. J.C. McPheeters of Asbury Theological Seminary—which like Asbury College was located in Wilmore, Kentucky—wrote to thank the bishop for granting a mid-term furlough for J.T. Seamands so Seamands could teach some courses there. But he also had a proposal:

> Brother Seamands... advises me that you expect to be connected with the Board of Missions following your retirement in 1957. I wish it might be possible for the board to release you to head the department of missions in Asbury Seminary. We are looking forward to building a school of missions as time progresses as an outgrowth of the department. If you could head the department you could be released from our campus for considerable work in the field at large.

Though Pickett did not decide to head the missions department, he would teach at Asbury for a quarter in the autumn of 1962. He taught two courses: "The World Mission of the Church" and "Potential Christian Nations of Tomorrow." He also led a seminar on "India, Pakistan, and Adjacent Countries." On his recommended reading list was McGavran's *Bridges of God*, though he thought McGavran was excessively generous in his references to Pickett and his writing. He was astonished to hear that McGavran told others that he lit his candle at Pickett's fire. When he asked McGavran about it, McGavran responded,

> Yes, I tell people that I lit my candle at your fire—which is quite literally true. Your people movement emphasis back in the mid-thirties came to me with the force of a revelation from God, which perhaps it was.

34 "Leaving Home, Going to America"

As the Middle of the Decade and retirement approached, the Methodist Church in India seemed healthy. In the cities, many educated Hindus were becoming Christians. Village churches were also growing. And though Christ Church, next door to the Picketts, was still the only church building the Methodists had in the city, the prospects seemed bright for a new, well-located place of worship in the heart of New Delhi. As for Methodist schools and seminaries, they too were thriving. Ruth Pickett's Garage School for refugees, which had 80 children in the late 1940s had dwindled to 20. But even that was good news, for it meant those made homeless by the 1947 communal riots were gradually finding places to live and reintegrating into the city's social fabric.

There were two troubling developments though. Recently, the Home Minister had begun denying visas to missionaries designated for evangelistic work. Pickett thought they might get a temporary reprieve by applying some leverage in the right places, but the new policy clearly pointed to the need to wrap up the process of Indianizing church leadership. Pickett recommended that missionaries: (1) not panic; (2) avoid public controversy; (3) not criticize the Government; (4) faithfully persist in the effort to get visas for entry and permits for residence for all missionaries whose services were needed; and (5) cultivate good public relations.

The second, even more troubling, development was the rise of a virulent campaign against foreign missionaries led by the Arya Samaj and the Hindu Mahasabha. Pickett expressed his concern to James Mathews:

> They are creating a great deal of prejudice against Christianity . . . They come in force to a Christian center, denounce missions, accuse missionaries of all kinds of horrible crimes against Indians, threaten the Christians with troubles of

every conceivable sort unless they consent to be restored to Hinduism by a purification rite. In this way they are said to have converted hundreds of our Methodist rural people . . . They staged a demonstration at the Ingraham Institute demanding that the foreign missionaries leave and that the school release the Hindu children which it was alleged to hold against their will.

FROM APRIL 25 TO MAY 7, 1956, Bishop Pickett was at General Conference in Minneapolis. He regarded it as "incomparably better than any other I have ever attended." Pickett warmly approved the Conference's endorsement of continued negotiations for Indian church union—something he had long supported. He was also glad for its decision to admit women to the Annual Conference on the same basis as men. His only regret, he said, was that "I will not be able to appoint any women to the pastorate of churches in India before my retirement." However, to Pickett, probably the most gratifying change was that missionary bishops elected at Central Conferences were now, for the first time, full voting members of the Council of Bishops and were allowed to participate in deciding the content of the Episcopal address. Reversing an earlier decision, the Judicial Council also ruled that there was no constitutional reason for bishops elected at Central Conferences to be barred from presiding at the General Conference. The Committee on the Selection of Presiding Officers followed up by selecting Pickett to be the first to be so honored. Pickett said he wished they had chosen a national, but his Indian colleagues were among those who wanted the distinction given to him. Afterwards, he remarked, "While I cannot claim to be Indian by citizenship, I do claim that in heart and mind my four and one-half decades of ministerial service have made me largely Indian."

Following a family visit in Glendale, California, Pickett left for India on July 1. The next six months would be his last as bishop in Delhi. That did not mean any diminishment of work though. Invitations from all over India for a final visit made it difficult for him to disengage from his Indian odyssey. But with lots of last minute loose ends and fixed commitments like chairing the Centenary Central Committee and preparing his final episcopal address, he had to turn down most of them.

THE BIG CHURCH EVENT OF THE year for Methodists in India was the 100th celebration of the arrival of William and Clementina Butler. It was planned for October 31 to November 3 at Isabella Thoburn College in Lucknow. A Centenary Central Committee was responsible for overseeing the organization of it.

The ambitious program included all the following: inspirational services; dignitaries from America; John. N. Hollister presenting his newly published *Centenary of the Methodist Church in South Asia*; Paul Wagner presenting an original painting entitled "*Jai Krist*"; a testimony meeting led by J.T. Seamands; a youth rally at which Pickett spoke; a music festival that included a "Centenary *Bhajan*" by M.R. Utarid; two films ("India: Crucible of Freedom" and "Transformed Lives," shown by Professor J.E. McEldowney of Leonard Theological College); and a centenary pageant. The pageant was an historical drama by Helen Cady Rockey, wife of Bishop Clement D. Rockey. Called, "The Promise," the five-act pageant showed how God had fulfilled the promise recited by Joel Janvier during the frightening events of 1857: "Fear not, little flock, for it is the Father's good will to give you the Kingdom of God."

Besides the various events, there were lots of displays and demonstrations. There would be exhibits on medical work, the urban church, the rural church, the seminaries, technical and agricultural work, youth work, educational work, Indian art and handicrafts, and Methodist history in India—all of them quite elaborate. The medical exhibit included photographs, posters, and pamphlets, maps, models, and graphs that, together, portrayed the spectrum of Methodist medical work in India—from the village dispensary to the large hospital and training center.

The handicrafts exhibit featured, among other examples, book binding, cane craft, ceramics, fancy work and sewing, metal craft, painting and lettering, scrap craft, toys, woodwork, and weaving.

The historical exhibit included important documents, diaries, pictures and charts; lots of photos, including a time line that had photos of all the bishops; a woodcut and a blotter made from the roof beam of the Butler bungalow; William Butler's Bible; Bishop Frank Warne's gavel; H.J. Adams' coat and set of teeth; and a collection of Indian Methodist publications. Many of the photographs had been duplicated and, along with various handicraft items, were for sale in the centenary store. There was also a tea stall where one could purchase cold drinks, snacks, and tea poured from the historic Butler "Tea Set."

The success of the Centennial was attested by a letter Pickett got from Eugene Smith, executive secretary of the Board of Missions. He wrote, "Several have reported that the programs were considerably more impressive than those of the General Conference at Minneapolis."

MANY OF THOSE WHO CAME to the Centenary Celebration remained for the twenty-third session of Central Conference, which ran from November 3 to 11. In his Episcopal Address, Bishop Pickett spoke of the need to adjust to change.

> The Gospel changes not . . . but because the mind of man, both the individual mind and the mass mind, are forever changing . . . we must seek fresh methods of sharing the Gospel and adapt those methods to the widely differing levels of understanding and bodies of experience of those to whom the Father has sent us.

Pickett also spoke of the ongoing duty of evangelization, arguing "[conversion] cannot be forced but must be permitted." Christians must also be mindful of their duties as citizens, he said, including that of "serving those of all faiths with unselfish affection." He concluded with a word of thanks from Bishop Rockey (also retiring) and himself for the kindness of those they had been privileged to serve.

Bishop Pickett retired officially at the end of the Central Conference. But five days later, in what would be the first of several ambassadorial tours for the Board of Missions, he left for Borneo. He returned on December 1. He and Ruth had lunch that day with Amrit Kaur and her brother. That evening, the Methodist churches gave the retiring couple a farewell. Pickett affectionately responded, "We are not going home, but we are leaving home and going to America."

On Sunday morning Pickett laid the foundation stone for his long-dreamed-of Methodist church in New Delhi—Centenary Methodist Church. In the afternoon he dedicated the Bishop Robinson Parish Hall at Christ Church—conceived in 1924 but only now completed. After another brief trip—from which he returned on December 21—Waskom, along with Ruth, Elizabeth and Henry Lacy and their five children, and Douglas, left for five days of family time. Aboard ship in Bombay and ready to sail, Waskom was given a newspaper. From it he learned that B.R. Ambedkar had died on the 16th. A few minutes later the ship eased away from the dock into the harbor. Thus, came the end of J. Waskom Pickett's 46-year Indian odyssey.

IN A WAY THOUGH, J. Waskom Pickett's Indian odyssey never ended. Throughout his retirement, India was always on his mind. For the next several years, he taught missions at Boston University School of Theology, where future missiologist of note, Gerald Anderson, working on his doctorate, was in one of his seminars. Anderson remembers Pickett as "still very vigorous, very lively, and very eloquent." Says Anderson, "He had a strong voice and a winsome, personable way. He was full of rich experiences that he was prepared to share." A review of Pickett's course descriptions and notes taken in his classes reveal how prominent India was. The orbit of topics was sweeping, including not just the expected "Biblical Foundations for Missions" or "History and Theology of Missions," but such exotic rendezvous as humor on the mission field, finding beauty in poverty, and educating the adult illiterate ("Jesus did not die for the literate!" he told his students). But, no matter what the topic, he always got around to India—to group movements in village India, to a case study of Bishop John Wesley Robinson, or to British imperialism in India. Even when the topic wasn't India, the illustrations often were. Not surprisingly, his bibliographies featured Indian topics and authors too. But there *were* other possibilities—like McGavran's *Bridges of God*!

Pickett did get back to India—several times. The first time was in connection with his new observer-adviser role for the Board of Missions, which took him around the globe during the months when he was not teaching in Boston—106 days in Asia and Africa (1957); 99 days in Africa and South America (1958); 160 days in Latin America and Asia (1959). Besides advising the Board on what he found, he sought to learn the extent to which lessons learned from India were applicable in other places. He looked for new ideas too. For example, he was interested to find out how Japanese Christians planned to evangelize Japanese Americans.

Whether in Tokyo or Nairobi, Pickett aimed to make each visit count. He assumed the area bishops and superintendents would help facilitate that, as he and Ruth had done over the years when officials of the mission board came to India. But not everyone appreciated the visits. One American-born bishop, already tired of church visitors from abroad, let it be known that he was too busy to entertain retired missionaries like Pickett and Jones. In another place, no one remembered—or bothered—to meet Pickett's plane. Nevertheless, in most of the time Pickett was pleased with the opportunities given him.

In August of 1959, having just completed a tour of Latin America, Pickett traveled to Tokyo, Hong Kong, Manila, Singapore, Sibu, Rangoon, Calcutta, Patna, Kathmandu, Lucknow, and Delhi on a tour that would last until December. He was anxious to get to India, because he regarded those days as critical for the church. He predicted that, in the coming years, a key struggle for the church would be with Vedantic Hinduism. How it turned out, he believed, would largely depend on the inner strength of the Indian church. In India, Pickett visited key Methodist leaders, old friends, and friends in government, including Prime Minister Nehru. His meeting with Nehru came just ahead of a state visit by President Eisenhower. What did he and Nehru talk about? For one thing, the arrangements being made for welcoming Eisenhower. Pickett suggested providing free trains into Delhi for those who wished to help greet the American president.

Pickett also told Nehru about a fund-raising campaign he was launching. He had gotten interested in Ludhiana Medical College in the early 1950s. Ludhiana was where, in 1894, Edith Brown had started the first medical school for women in all of Asia. Associated with the college were a nurses training school, a tuberculosis hospital, a leprosarium, a public health department, and a 500-bed hospital. However, Ludhiana was in financial difficulty, and Pickett had agreed to help. When Nehru heard this, he told the bishop if he could raise a million dollars for the hospital, India would match it. In fact, according to Dr. Ron Garst, one-time head of the orthopaedic department at the medical college, "he [Bishop Pickett] raised several million dollars."

Pickett's work as consultant on evangelism with the Methodist Board of Missions ended, as planned, in 1960—but with Pickett rejecting their final assignment. The board wanted him to go to Angola. However, he so despised the Portuguese Government's repression of Angolans that he flatly dismissed the idea.

FROM BOSTON, THE PICKETTS moved to Glendale, California, close to Ruth's sister and her husband, Miriam and Jack Hedenberg. They lived there from 1960 to 1967. During that time, Waskom went up to Northwest Christian College at the invitation of Donald McGavran to inaugurate an annual lecture series on Church Growth at McGavran's institute. Pickett's lectures, published in 1963 as *Dynamics of Church Growth*, were filled with lessons and stories from India. Back in focus were many of his older themes, but expressed freshly, with new insights. An example was his "case for rapid growth"—that is, by people movements—which he said is more likely to result in strong, healthy churches than are "cautiously controlled processes of slow growth." It is fashionable to affirm the opposite, that popular religious movements are "hysterical, shallow, and destructive of spiritual values," he said. But upon what is that notion based—data and observation, or impression? Pickett's counterclaim was that sometimes slow growth "indicates something wrong with the quality of the church" and "produces churches that lack either the urge to make disciples or the faith . . . to translate such urges into effective endeavor." He made his case biblically, statistically, sociologically, and psychologically.

Pickett's other retirement writing included the publication of numerous articles, chapters in two books, and a number of items on the Indian church and Indian missions for the *Encyclopedia of World Methodism*. In 1964, the year Jawaharlal Nehru died, he worked with M. Elia Peter on a small book on Methodist work in India. He received a second honorary doctorate in 1966, this time from Ohio Wesleyan University.

In 1967 Waskom and Ruth moved to Dearborn, Michigan, close to their youngest daughter, Margaret Sagan, and her family. On a 1969 return to India, Waskom and Ruth called on old colleagues and friends, including Sarvepalli Radhakrishnan, then President of India. Over dinner, he asked Ruth where she was born. Teasingly, she said, "I was born in India—I'm an American Indian." Radhakrishnan smiled broadly. "Mrs. Pickett," he said, "You do not look like any other American Indian I have ever seen."

In 1972, the Picketts moved to the Wesley Glen Retirement Home in Columbus, Ohio. Waskom and Ruth returned to India for the last time in 1974. They were accompanied by their daughter Miriam and son-in-law, Bill Gould. At the time, Douglas was director of the Peace Corps in India and Nepal, so they made their headquarters with him and Ann. In New Delhi, they had a last visit with Indira Gandhi, who had succeeded her father as prime minister.

Sometime in the mid-to-late 1970s, Waskom set to work on his memoirs, although, as he told a friend, progress was slow. "My health is not quite as good as I wish it were," he said.

I can put in only two or three hours of hard work daily and my written work was set back by an accident that scattered the pages hither and yon. I don't have it all in order yet. Also I am re-writing a good many pages.

On August 7, 1981, Waskom and Ruth's 65th anniversary, Waskom underwent cancer surgery. He and Ruth hoped it would restore a measure of his health. But it was not to be. After 10 painful days, he passed away at age 91, Ruth holding his hand. When she got home, she wrote in the August 17 square of her wall calendar: "Waskom left us. 3:20 p.m."

Twenty-two Pickett family members came for the memorial service that weekend—even Douglas, all the way from Nepal. At the Maple Grove United Methodist Church, those in attendance were given a printed "Service of Thanksgiving and Praise." Appropriately, the first hymn was, "Oh for a Thousand Tongues to Sing." Alongside the printed order of service was a poem, written by Waskom and dedicated to "India's oppressed millions, the untouchables." He called it, "Whose Are These, Lord?" It began:

> Whose are these, Lord, whom men oppress?
>   To whom do they belong?
> By what right do men of might
>   Call them knaves, make them slaves
>   And do them every wrong?

RUTH ROBINSON PICKETT DIED at Wesley Glen two years later, on October 3, 1983. On October 8, the family had a small graveside service for her in Wilmore, Kentucky. Ruth had requested the service be simple, and for family only, because Waskom's service at Maple Grove, Columbus, had included a lot about her. That, she felt, had been enough.

Abbreviations

BOAC	British Overseas Airways Corporation
CASA	Church's Auxiliary for Social Action
CMS	Church Missionary Society
CWS	Church World Service
GT	Grand Trunk Road
ICG	India Conciliation Group
IMC	International Missionary Council
ISRR	Institute for Social and Religious Research
ITC	Isabella Thoburn College
IWM	Interchurch World Movement
JWP	Jarrell Waskom Pickett
LCC	Lucknow Christian College
MCOR	Methodist Committee for Overseas Relief
ME Church	Methodist Episcopal Church (abbreviated "M.E." in some quotations)
NCC [NCCI]	National Christian Council of India, Burma and Ceylon
NGO	Nongovernmental Organization
NMC	National Missionary Council of India, Burma and Ceylon
RSS	Rashtriya Swayamsevák Sangh
SVM	Student Volunteer Movement
UCRW	The United Council for Relief and Welfare
UMN	United Mission to Nepal
UP	United Provinces
UCOSS	United Committee for Surplus Supplies
USAID	US Agency for International Development
USDA	United States Department of Agriculture
WCTU	Women's Christian Temperance Union
YMCA	Young Men's Christian Association
YWCA	Young Women's Christian Association

Glossary

A Note on Transliteration and Translation

When old spellings are different from contemporary spellings, I generally retain those used in the period being described (e.g., Jubbulpore for Jabalpur, and Arrah for Ara). I also retain old terms and names that have been replaced (e.g., "untouchable" instead of "Dalit" and "Bombay" instead of "Mumbai" (which came into use in 1996). Two other examples: "Ceylon" instead of "Sri Lanka" and "mass movement" instead of "people movement."

However, in a few cases—e.g., where an older term is offensive, or the new spelling is universally known and accepted—I have generally preferred the new term or spelling (e.g., "Islam" instead of "Mohammadanism" and "Muslim" instead of "Moslem").

With regard to non-English words, unless the terms are widely known (like sari), I have defined them in the text the first time they are used. For the reader's convenience, I have also provided a glossary (below).

Definitions of Non-English Terms

Achut [achoot]: untouchable

Ahimsa: the principle of abstaining from all violence (taught in several Indian faiths and championed by M.K. Gandhi)

Anglo-Indian: a person of British and Indian ancestry

Animism: belief in spirits, including those of ancestors and those contained in inanimate natural objects and other natural phenomena

Anna: a 16th of a rupee

Ashram: the home of a guru; a place of religious retreat, reflection, study, and fellowship

Arya Samaj: Hindu reform movement founded in 1875, which looked to the *Vedas* as authoritative for Hindus much like Christians and Muslims look to the Bible and Qur'an. From the movement came support for educational and social reform and emerging Hindu nationalism

Ayah: nursemaid or nanny

Atman: The self (soul) as the subject of individual consciousness, known after enlightenment to be identical with Brahma[n]

Avatar: the incarnation of a Hindu deity

Bagh: garden

Bajra: cat-tailed millet (a species of millet)

Bande Matram: "Hail, Motherland," national song of India

Barsati: one-room or two-room habitation for guests or renting out

Bearer: a domestic servant

Bhajan: a religious song of praise

Bhakti: loving devotion

Biradari: means "brotherhood" and refers to the local caste organization

Brahma [Brahman]: the impersonal supreme being, primal source and goal of all beings

Brahmins: members of the highest division of Hindu castes, traditionally associated with the priesthood (Cf. Kshatriyas, Vaisyas and Sudras)

Brahmo Samaj: a Hindu reform movement begun in 1828; it was based on the Vedas, emphasized monotheism and opposed the use of graven images and sacrifices, and advocated various kinds of social reform

Caste Hindus: Hindus in castes above untouchables

Chamars: a Hindu untouchable caste of leather workers (in Bihar, however, some were farm laborers)

Chand Bagh: literally "Moon Garden" [In Lucknow, the area where Isabella Thoburn College is situated and, consequently, the locals' familiar name for the college itself]

Chaprassi: an office errand runner, used for a variety of jobs such as delivering notes, mailing letters, and carrying files and supplies around the office; sometimes used for depositing and/or cashing checks at the bank, or watching for the safety of the children as well as other such jobs demanding more trust

Charas: hashish

Chaudhris: village leaders

Chela: a disciple of a religious teacher

Choti hair hazri: early breakfast

Choukidar: guard or watchman

Churas: a Panchama (untouchable) caste of the Punjab

Chutiya: a hair tuft which indicated caste

Communalism: strong devotion to the members of one's own religious or ethnic group rather than society as a whole (e.g., allegiance to fellow Muslims, Hindus, Sikhs, etc.)

Coolie: an unskilled day laborer

Daftar: office

Dakhma: a cylindrical funeral building used by Parsis for the disposal of the bodies of the departed

Dalits: those who are broken, oppressed; contemporary designation for those who were once called untouchables or Harijan

Darbar: court

Deccan: the plateau region in South India between the Narbada and Krishna rivers

Devadasi: Dancing girl attached to a temple, a courtesan

Dharma: religious duty, law, or custom

Dhoti: a long loincloth worn by men

Dhusiya: a sub-cast of *Chamars*

Dilkusha: literally, "heart happiness" or "heart's content" [In Lucknow, it is a huge old garden complex near the British Residency ruins. It was established by one of the Nawabs of Oudh long before the Anglo-Indian War of 1857. The Picketts used to go there for moonlight picnics in the 1920s and early 1930s. It was a beautiful, well-kept expanse of lawns, trees and flowers in those days.]

Dravidians: a dark-skinned aboriginal people of southern India and parts of Sri Lanka, including Tamils and Kanarese

Ekka: a pony-drawn vehicle with large wheels, smaller than a tonga [Pickett and his co-workers used them extensively during his Arrah days; though uncomfortable, they were especially useful in traversing narrow, deeply rutted roads.]

Ghagar: water jar

Ghat: a range of mountains

Goondas: bandits

Group movement: a multi-individual decision of persons who have chosen to convert from their old religion to a new one (Cf. people movement)

Guru: Hindu religious teacher

Gurukul: a kind of school consisting of a guru and his students

Harijan: ("child of God") Gandhi's euphemism for untouchables

Hartal: a closing of shops and stoppage of work as an expression of protest or mourning

Hindustani: a standard language and lingua franca of northern India based on a dialect of Western Hindi spoken around Delhi

Hindutva: Hindu principles (derived from *Hindu Tattva*)

Hisab: expenditure

Holeyas: a Hindu untouchable caste of farm and plantation laborers who were formerly known as bonded laborers (also Holaya)

Kanarese: a Dravidian people living mainly in the state of Karnataka, in southwest India

Karma: action or works seen as bringing upon oneself inevitable results (bad or good)

Kayasthas: members of a caste of people who once served the Muslim rulers of India

Khaddar: handspun cloth

Kheri: in Telugu country, a section of a village; see mohalla

Kshatriyas: members of the second of the four divisions of recognized Hindu castes, above the Vaisyas and below the Brahmins; the royal and warrior caste (Cf. Brahmins, Vaisyas, Sudras)

Jajman: patron

Jajmani system: a network of reciprocal relationships between families, at the heart of which is the exchange of food production for goods and services

Jati: the extended family (caste) into which one was born, and in which one was destined to live and die

Jatra: festival honoring gods or saints

Lal: red

Landour: the section of Mussoorie in which the Methodist (and other) missionaries lived and the location of the Kellogg Church at which Pickett preached for many summers

Lok Sabha: the body representative of the people

Madigas: the leather workers' caste in the Telugu country (like Chamars in the North)

Maharaja (or maharaj): the title of an Indian prince

Mahasabha: great assembly; political organization of orthodox Hindus

Mahatma: a person highly regarded for his wisdom and saintly character

Malas: the weavers' caste in the Telugu country

Mass movement: an outdated term used to describe a multi-individual decision of persons who have chosen to convert from their old religion to a new one (now called group movement, people movement, or conversion movement)

Mazhabi Sikhs: a caste of sweepers in the United Provinces and the Punjab who professed the Sikh religion but were not socially recognized as Sikhs

Mela: a fair, often held in connection with a religious festival

Mohalla: section of a town or village; also *basti, tola* (or fem., *toli*) and *para*, depending on the area---and in Telugu country, *kheri*

Mogul: a member of the dynasty of Muslim rulers that dominated N. India and parts of the Deccan from the 16th to the early 18th centuries

Monsoon: the season during which the southwest monsoon blows, bringing with it the rains

Mussoorie: the location of Woodstock School, 170 miles northeast of Delhi in the foothills of the Himalayas

Nabob: any wealthy, powerful, or influential person (see nawab)

Nawab: an honorary title, often conferred upon Muslims of distinction (see nabob)

Naini Tal: a hill station in North India (241 miles from Lucknow) where Ruth Robinson Pickett attended school as a girl.

Nizam: the title of the hereditary ruler of Hyderabad

Noncooperation: a form of civil disobedience established by Gandhi of opposing government policy by refusing to participate in civic and political life or to obey governmental regulations

Padri: corruption of *padre* (Portuguese), a Christian minister

Pan: the leaf of the betel, used to enclose slices of areca nut mixed with lime for chewing

Panchama: untouchable

Panchayat: an elective village council

Pandit: a title of respect and honor, especially for one's wisdom and knowledge

Pariah: an "outcaste"

People movement: a multi-individual decision of persons who have chosen to convert from their old religion to a new one (Cf. group movement)

Pice: one fourth of an anna

Pradakshina: pilgrimage

Prem Sabha: fellowship gathering (love gathering)

Puja: the Hindu worship of a particular god

Purna swaraj: the call for complete independence from Britain

Pundit: see Pandit

Punkah: a large, swinging, screen-like fan hung from the ceiling and moved by a servant pulling an attached rope

Purdah: the seclusion of women from the sight of men or strangers, practiced by some Muslims and Hindus

Pushta: retaining wall

Raj: the British imperial rule of India prior to Independence ("raj" is Hindi for "rule")

Rajah: a prince or king

Rajkumari: an Indian princess

Rupee: an Indian monetary unit, silver coin

Roshan dans: (literally, "light containers"), high glass windows for light and cross-ventilation

Sabzimandi: a vegetable and fruit market located behind the Pickett residence in Delhi

Sardar: (1) title for a military or political leader; (2) a Sikh

Sahib: a gentleman

Sahiba: a lady

Sadhu: a Hindu religious mendicant

Sanskrit: an ancient Indo-European, Indic language, used in Indian religious and classical literature

Sanatanists: a Hindu sect (if a Hindu performs or believes in puja, Krishna, Ram, Hanuman, and other avatars, karma, and reincarnation, then that Hindu is a Sanatanist)

Santiniketam: abode of peace (a school started by Tagore)

Satyagraha: rooted in the notion of *ahimsa*, the policy of nonviolent resistance employed by M.K. Gandhi as a method of gaining social and political reform (literally, "Truth-force," or derivatively, "soul-force")

Sati: the self-immolation of a widow on her husband's funeral pyre

Satnamis: members of a monotheistic mid-India sect, constituted in the 1820s by Chamars wishing to break free from caste distinctions.

Sepoy: an Indian soldier in a European army; an Indian policeman

Shamiana: tent

Shastra: any of the sacred books of Hinduism

Shishya: student of a guru

Shri and Shrimati: Mr. and Mrs. (Also, sri)

Station (e.g., hill station): the area in which the British officials of a district or the officers of a garrison resided

Sudras (also Shudras): members of the fourth (lowest) division of the Hindu castes, the laborers (Cf. Brahmins, Kshatriyas, Vaisyas)

Swadeshi Movement: a political movement that encouraged Indians to buy only goods "of one's own country" and to boycott British goods as a step toward home rule

Swaraj: self-rule, self-governance

Sweepers: families whose work consists of sweeping and scavenging jobs, or who belong to castes traditionally thus employed

Thakur: a Kshatriya caste term of respectful address (chief; master)

Tamash: [or tamasha] means a big show and may describe a variety of events, from a circus to a riot, a temper tantrum to a gala party

Tamash Bagh: a garden in Lucknow [see "tamash/tamasha"]

Telugu: a Dravidian language spoken mainly in the Andhra country of southeast India

Thans: Hindu shrines

Tonga: a light two-wheeled horse-drawn vehicle

United Provinces: old name for Uttar Pradesh; included Agra and Oudh

Upanishad: ("to sit down in front of") Hindu philosophic texts, usually in dialogue form, composed between the eighth and sixth centuries B.C.

Vaisyas: members of the third division of recognized Hindu castes, the mercantile and professional class above the Sudras and below the Kshatriyas (Cf. Brahmins, Kshatriyas, Sudras)

Varna: ("color") any of the Hindu social classes; a caste

Vedanta: a leading (monistic) Hindu philosophy, based on the Upanishadic doctrine of the identity of Brahman and Atman

Vedas: the oldest Hindu scriptures (*veda* means knowledge) comprised of the hymns and ritual texts in the *Rg-Veda*, the *Sama-Veda*, the *Atharva-Veda*, and the *Yajur-Veda*

Zamindar: hereditary landlord

Zenana: the part of the house in which the women and girls were secluded

Ziyat: among the missionaries, a city reading room set up for contacting educated Indians

Sources and Acknowledgments

A Note on Sources

In writing the life of J. Waskom Pickett, I have had the advantage of working in reasonable proximity to the era in which he lived, for as ever more time elapses after someone's death, the harder it becomes to assemble facts of that person's life. Files are purged, attics and basements are cleaned and cleared, and fewer people remain who knew the person up close. When I began writing, Pickett and most of his friends and colleagues were no longer living. However, many who knew him—including all his children—were still alive and available to interview.

Another providence has been the existence of a memoir: *My Twentieth Century Odyssey* published a few months before Pickett's death in 1981. The autobiography was a disappointment because, by the time he began writing it, Pickett was well into his eighties, in frail health, and far removed from most of the details he sought to recall. As Sir Richard Burton wrote, "Autobiographers generally begin too late." Nevertheless, it gave me a place to start.

Pickett wrote *My Twentieth Century Odyssey* by hand from a rough, thematic outline. He recorded events as they came to mind on half-sheets of 8½ x 11 paper. Because he employed a topical arrangement—and did not always stick to that—an orderly telling of his life was precluded. Moreover, his accounts were fragmentary, often repetitious, and, here and there, contained misremembered information. One day, when he was well along on writing it, a puff of wind through an open window scattered the sheets all over the room. He was never able to reorder them satisfactorily and almost gave up. When the book came out, some of what he'd written was missing (for example, the several pages he had written on the start of the United Mission to Nepal, in which he had played a key role), and some of it got in twice! Still, thanks largely to the assistance of his former secretary, Colleen Gilmore and, also, Dr. Charles Reynolds, the book at least got published.

Although the faults of the handwritten patchwork persisted into the book, Pickett's reminiscences are invaluable, not only for what they do tell, but, to a biographer, as a supply of clues for sleuthing sources. In most cases, I have been able to corroborate—with primary materials, interviews, etc.—Pickett's accounts. While the corroborating material has consistently demonstrated both the general accuracy of this and some briefer memoirs, the quotations in them, and some details, must be regarded as loose reconstructions. Moreover, when writing about those he admired, Pickett sometimes slipped into hagiography, and, as he grew older, some stories tended to grow. Nevertheless, as I have said, the reliability of even very late reminiscences is, on the whole, quite remarkable.

I found no shortage of primary documents for establishing the facts of Pickett's life. For example, hundreds of letters from and to him survive in various libraries and archives. Nor did I find any reluctance by those who knew Pickett to tell what they remembered. Several, including his children, generously gave me access to personal records, photographs, and other items in garages, basements, and attics. Some of what they showed me has now been moved to public collections.

One of the Pickett children, Douglas, accompanied me on my initial research trip to India and introduced me to many of the places and people his father knew. Several persons, including Bishop James K. Mathews and Susan Billington Harper, made available yet-to-be-published manuscripts. Others (some via the Internet) gave me useful leads and hard-to-find information of a more general nature. Most of their names, but for brevity's sake, not the details of their help, are listed below.

As I review the assembling of this biography, I am amazed at the variety of sources I was able to profitably make use of: books, letters, maps, newspaper accounts, public records, questionnaires, site visits, photographs, calendars, completed applications, passports, guest books, tape recordings, genealogies, interviews, speech and sermon notes, the Internet, etc. Some discoveries moved me deeply, such as side-by-side life-recollections by Pickett and E. Stanley Jones, tape-recorded in someone's dining or living room in Wilmore, Kentucky in 1971. They had been friends since college days, and this was, likely, their last meeting.

The key sources of background material on JWP's youth, family, and hometown of Wilmore have been the following: (1) *My Twentieth Century Odyssey* (Pickett 1980); (2) the weekly newspaper, *The Jessamine Journal*, which chronicled events in Wilmore, Kentucky during the time JWP was growing up, and, in fact, even the comings and goings of JWP's father, L.L. Pickett; (3) the *Pentecostal Herald*, which published articles by L.L. Pickett and news items about Asbury College and the Pickett family; (4) Asbury College records (although the most important ones were destroyed by fires in 1909 and 1924); and (5) Asbury College histories, especially those by Earl Stanley McKee and Joseph A. Thacker.

The largest single source of Pickett documents is his missionary correspondence with the Methodist Board of Foreign Missions. The original correspondence and documents are in the Missionary files series of the United Methodist Church Archives - GCAH, Madison, New Jersey. The Methodist Global Board of Missions in New York has microfilm copies, organized differently. Other locations of original documents include the archives of Asbury College, Wilmore, Kentucky; Asbury Theological Seminary, Wilmore, Kentucky; and the School of Oriental and African Studies, London [UK] University. Then, there are his books: *Christian Mass Movements in India* (1933); *Church Growth and Group Conversion* (with D.A. McGavran and G.H. Singh, 1956); *Christ's Way to India's Heart* (1938); *Dynamics of Church Growth* (1963); and *My Twentieth Century Odyssey* (1981). For details of Pickett's other writing—books contributions, articles, editorials—and other sources and locations of information, see my "Pickett's Fire: The Life, Contribution, Thought, and Legacy of J. Waskom Pickett, Methodist Missionary to India." Ph.D. Dissertation, E. Stanley Jones School of World Mission and Evangelism, Asbury Theological Seminary, Wilmore Kentucky.

ACKNOWLEDGMENTS

I begin with the late Everett N. Hunt of the E. Stanley Jones School of World Mission at Asbury Theological Seminary, and Darrell Whiteman, now Dean of the school. It was Dr. Hunt who encouraged me to research and write a biography of J. Waskom Pickett and, after his passing, Dr. Whiteman who helped and encouraged me through the bulk of the dissertation work. All of J. Waskom Pickett's children are still living, and, uniformly, they have been of immense help in coming up with many dates and details. Moreover, as my closest links to their father and mother, they have given me—by the character and generosity they have inherited—a glimpse of their parents I could not have found elsewhere. I especially want to thank Douglas Pickett, whom I quickly designated as point person for the family and who graciously agreed to accompany me and my son, John, on my initial research in India. Miriam Gould, Elizabeth and Hank Lacy, and Margaret and John Sagan, the Pickett daughters and spouses, were all equally keen to help.

I owe special thanks to the following library and special collections personnel as well.

In America: Karen Oswalt (Asbury College Archives) who ordered and filed boxes of unsorted Pickett papers and documents just in time for my use, and Tracy Morgan who continued Karen's warm and accommodating tradition; William Kostlevy (B.L. Fisher Library, Asbury Theological Seminary) who guided me to source materials on Pickett's Holiness Movement roots, and Dorothy James, who handled my steady stream of inter-library loan requests; Claire McCurdy and Seth Kasten (Burke Library, Union Theological Seminary); Ernest Rubenstein and Abraham Philip (Ecumenical Library of the Interchurch Center); L. Dale Patterson and Mark C. Shenise (General Commission on Archives and History, the United Methodist Church); Martha Smalley and Joan Duffy (John R. Mott Library, Yale Divinity School); Dennis Stoesz and Ruth Schrock (Archives of the Mennonite Church, which contains a duplicate collection of the documents of the Archives of the United Mission to Nepal); Phillip Stone (The Sandor Teszler Library, Wofford College); Susan Flacks (Department of History and Records, Presbyterian Church, USA); Darwin H. Stapleton and Sharon A. Pullen (Rockefeller Archive Center).

In India: H. Hamilton (Leonard Theological College Library and Archives); Fr. Abraham Oomen (Archives of the National Christian Council); Y.D. Purushotham (Methodist Church in India Archives, Methodist Center, Mumbai).

In the United Kingdom: Tim Thomas (The British Library); Mary Seton and Lesley Price (School of Oriental and African Studies, London University).

Of the non-family members I interviewed about recollections of Pickett, I must mention a few and offer my thanks to the rest: Daniel D. Allen, James E. McEldowney, Donald Rugh, John T. Seamands, and Paul Wagner (missionaries who served under Pickett); Gerald Anderson (student of Pickett at Boston University School of Theology); Burr Baughman (missionary in Sarawak); Prabhu Charam (son of the Pickett's cook in Delhi) and Ghazi [Singh?] (servant in the Pickett household); Drs. Charles Reynolds and Ron Garst (physicians, on Pickett's work in behalf of the college and medical school at Ludhiana); Colleen Gilmore (former Pickett secretary); Tracy K. Jones (mission board official); W.W. Jones and John C.B. Webster (Indian church historians); Ralph C. Kaufman (on the war surplus effort); Sam Kameleson (Indian churchman); Edwin King (Cunard Project); Dennis Kinlaw (former president of Asbury College, knew Pickett well); James C. Lal (Indian churchman who worked under Pickett); James K. Mathews (Bishop Mathews worked both as a missionary under Pickett and as Pickett's corresponding secretary at the Board of Missions in New York); Eunice Mathews (daughter of E. Stanley Jones); Dr. Charles Voigt Perrill (Fred Perrill's son, a missionary doctor who knew Waskom and Ruth Pickett from the time he was six, in 1919, and worked with Pickett as an adult); Godwin Singh (student sponsored by Pickett); and Dorothy Clarke Wilson (author and Pickett guest while she researched a series of articles and a book on Methodist missions in India). Other interviewees included the following: Charles Foreman (on John Weir) and Edgar Metzler (former director of the United Mission to Nepal).

Others who supplied me with information about Pickett, his colleagues and parents, or about specific events, or who offered valuable leads include the following: Christopher R. Christy and Lawrence Silas (retired Indian pastors who remember Pickett); J.F. Conley and Dale E Leathead (on J.Z. Hodge); David Cook (who told me where to find one of Pickett's Household Schedules); Ron Dick (British aviation historian); Menno Diener and Martin H. Schrag (Delhi and Kurukshetra refugee camp workers in 1947); Susan Harper (V.S. Azariah's biographer); Vernon Middleton (Donald A. McGavran's biographer); Ernest Oliver (first director of the United Mission to Nepal); Hal Rockey (son of Bishop Pickett's colleague, Bishop Clement Rockey); Eva Shipstone (longtime teacher at Isabella Thoburn College and friend of the Picketts); and Patsy Woodring (Ludie Day Pickett's biographer). Helping me via the Internet to understand the social survey methods used in the 1920s and 1930s were Martin Bulmer, Jennifer Platt, and Stephen P. Turner; another sociologist, Howard Kauffman, helped me evaluate Pickett's approach and conclusions. Helping me with questions about the Indian

Constitution was James Chiriyankandath. Undoubtedly, I have overlooked others, but I have forgotten the generosity of none.

I want to thank Douglas Pickett, Margaret Sagan, Dr. Charles Perrill, and Asbury Theological Seminary for letting me use photographs from their collections in this biography.

I also owe a debt of thanks to the John and Margaret Sagan Foundation for help with some of the research expenses, including my research in India and the United Kingdom.

I want to express special appreciation to my wife, Evelyn McPhee, and son, John McPhee, both of whom offered me valuable assistance—Evie with editing, and John with research in India, Nepal, and New Jersey. I am most grateful of all, though, for their gift of patient encouragement throughout the several years this project took.

Index

Abbott, Edna 122, 130
Acheson, Dean 352, 353
Agra 41, 53, 59, 61, 63, 118, 119, 200, 383
Ahraura 145, 146
Aiman, J.S. 324, 325
Alam, Nasir 323
Ali, Mahomed and Shaukat 142
All-Parties Conference 182-184, 196
Almora 308, 328
Alter, D.E. 324
Ambedkar, B.R. 157, 197, 237-247, 258-261, 263, 265, 272, 278, 279, 288, 289, 348, 349, 360, 372
Amritsar 138, 166, 317, 318
Anderson, Gerald 373
Andhra area 84, 228, 233, 234, 263, 264
Andrews, C.F. 246, 263
Andrias 119
Anglicans 60, 61, 102, 106, 151, 198, 229
Anglo-Indian War of 1857 40, 51, 56, 58, 101, 301, 380
Anglo-Indians 74, 75, 102, 239
Anglo-Indian War 40, 56, 58, 101, 380
Arkansas Holiness College 22, 31
Army Surplus 304-306
Arrah 8, 82, 89-92, 95-98, 100-106, 109, 114, 115, 117-119, 122, 124-126, 130-132, 134, 139, 142-147, 149-152, 168-170, 215, 286, 299, 378, 380
Article 25 348, 349, 351

Arya Samaj 62, 131, 369, 378
Asbury College 21, 80, 89, 160, 181, 195, 208, 368
Asbury Seminary 343, 368
Attaway, Bertha 80
Azariah, V.S. 163, 189, 194, 198, 229, 242, 263, 264, 267-269, 271-276
Badley, B.T. 10, 73, 127, 128, 160, 249, 258, 292, 297, 343
Ballia 95, 97, 98, 102, 106, 118, 122, 126, 131, 132, 144
Baltic 44, 47, 48
Bangalore 3, 4, 263
Baptists 98, 151, 178, 226, 348, 364
Bareilly 40, 41, 64, 119, 125, 126, 160, 162, 215, 304, 312, 332
Bareilly District 312
Bareilly Seminary 64, 119, 125, 215, 312
Barkley, Alben 356, 357
Bengal 40, 58, 61, 287, 310, 314, 337
Benton, S.O. 36
Bergsaker, T.R. 364
Bergsma, Harold 364
Bhatty, E.C. 305, 322-325, 327, 329, 347, 348
Bihar 8, 82, 89, 90, 95-97, 101, 106, 107, 115, 126, 132, 135, 136, 142, 144, 150, 151, 185, 198, 214, 310, 379
Birkenhead, Lord 183
Birla House 331, 334, 336
Bolst, Maria 169
Bombay 34, 48-53, 67, 68, 125, 127, 128, 135,

152, 168, 177, 183, 195, 196, 198-200, 226, 234, 235, 237, 241-243, 247, 253, 254, 258, 261, 262, 265, 276, 280, 283-286, 290, 299, 303, 304, 313, 333, 346, 372, 378
Bose, Subhas Chandra 183, 282
Boston University School of Theology 373
Bourke-White, Margaret 318
Bowles, Chester 358, 362
Brahmo Samaj 62, 379
Bridges of God 252, 367, 368, 373
Briscoe, A. 126
Brown, Arlo 213
Brown, Edith 374
Brown, Judith 141
Brown, William Adams 193
Brunk, A.C. 228, 233, 252
Buck, Pearl S. 211
Burma 40, 74, 139, 184, 188, 190, 210, 303, 304, 311, 377
Buss, Helen 330
Butler, Clementina 56, 169, 300, 301, 371
Butler, William 56, 57, 300, 301, 371
Buxar 98, 106, 127, 130, 139, 151
Calcutta 39, 41, 50, 61, 68, 76, 77, 90, 104, 112, 127, 128, 160, 183, 184, 195, 243, 283, 306, 307, 310, 311, 314, 317, 320, 321, 331, 345, 351, 374
Calder, Helen B. 192
Carey, William 307

Centenary Campaign 122, 160
Centenary Central Committee 370, 371
Centenary Methodist Church 372
Central Conference 76, 141, 160, 180, 236, 248, 249, 281, 284, 334, 341, 346, 372
Central Methodist Church 45, 57, 335
Central Provinces 314
Chakkarai, Vengal 173
Chamars 84, 85, 95, 99, 110-114, 116, 117, 123, 127, 128, 130, 131, 218, 227, 258, 379-382
Chatterjee, K.C. 38
Chauri-Chaura 182
Chhindwara 234
Chitambar, J.R. 63, 64, 137, 147-150, 158, 170, 248, 249, 283, 286
Chitambar, Satyavati 170, 235, 301
Chota Nagpur 84, 106, 107
Chowdhury, Dhan Singh 308, 312
Christ Church 7, 294, 301, 302, 320, 321, 326, 339, 369
Christian Jatra 285
Christian Mass Movements in India 208, 209, 218, 233, 242, 244, 251, 262, 272, 281, 385
Christian Patriot 173
Christo Samaj 173
Christ's Way to India's Heart 229, 252, 264, 279, 385
Church Growth 9, 251, 374
Church Growth and Group Conversion 385
Church Missionary Society 145, 185, 271, 377
Church Missionary Society (CMS) 185, 187, 195, 226
Church World Service 325, 329, 330, 340, 377
Church's Auxiliary for Social Action (CASA) 329
Clara Swain Hospital 126, 162, 304, 332
Clark, Adam 15
Clough, J.E. 98
Confirmation of the Gospel 339
Congress Party 183, 197, 314
Constituent Assembly 9, 303, 315, 316, 322, 346-349, 351, 353
Contextualizing the Gospel 172, 173, 224
Darling, Thomas 219
Das, C.R. 183
Das, R.C. 216
Dawn 116, 185, 314
Dayal, Ishwar 119-121, 124, 126, 127, 185
Dayal, Priavati 119-121, 124
dearness allowances 337
Dehra Dun 179, 196
Delhi 40, 51, 53, 61, 88, 140, 179, 205, 213, 234, 235, 258, 284, 299-301, 305, 306, 312, 314, 323, 325, 327-331, 333-335, 339-341, 347, 349, 355, 357, 360, 363, 370, 374
Delhi area 85
Delhi Cathedral 335
Delhi Conference 292, 299, 300, 331, 338, 346, 360
Delhi District 331
Denning, J.O. 83, 84, 95, 144
Desai, Mahadev 271, 274, 278, 290
Diffendorfer, R.E. 235, 236, 241-243, 268, 269, 276, 279, 284, 304, 322, 325, 329, 341, 357
Dilkusha 168, 380
Direct Action Day 138, 310
Disciples 178
Ditt 98, 219
Donohugh, T.S. 240, 268, 280
Dornakal 38, 189, 198, 199, 230, 269, 273, 274
Drew Theological Seminary 169
Duff, Alexander 38
Dulles, John Foster 362
Dyer, R.E.H. 138
Dynamics of Church Growth 112, 375, 385
Eastwood 155, 178, 179
Ebright, Donald 329, 340, 342
Eddy, Sherwood 87, 123
Edinburgh, 1910 38, 39, 67, 181
Eisenhower, Dwight David 362, 374
Emden 80
Etah 199, 200, 202-204
Evanston 46, 82, 83, 89, 96
Fahs, Charles H. 186
Finney, Charles 15
Fir Clump 155, 179, 235
Fisher, Frederick Bonn 146, 147, 150, 158, 181, 215, 216
Fisher, Galen M. 191, 206, 208, 210
Fleming, Bethel 363-366
Fleming, Robert 180, 363-366
Fletcher, John 15
Fowles, George M. 32-37, 47
Fredericks, Carl 364
Gandhi, Indira 375
Gandhi, M.K. (Mahatma) 61, 135-138, 141-143, 163, 165, 166, 182, 183, 195-197, 214, 215, 238-242, 246,

261-265, 267, 269-278, 282, 284, 287-291, 314, 317, 321, 323, 327, 331-336, 347, 353, 354
Ghaziabad district 205
Gilmore, Colleen 343
Glendale, California 370, 374
Gokhale, Krishna 135
Golden Rule 175, 176
Golwalkar, M.S. 341, 346
Gordon A.J. 219
Gossner Mission 106, 119
Gould, Bill 345, 375
Gould, Miriam (Pickett) 345, 360, 374, 375
Grey, A.L. 95, 98, 102, 103, 129
Guardian 215, 273
Guntur District 226, 228
Gurukul 135, 226, 380
Hardinge, Charles 58
Harijan 242, 261, 264, 265, 269, 271, 276, 277, 331, 379, 380
Harijan Sevak Sangh 277
Harriman, Averell 356
Harrison, Agatha 263, 267, 269
Hawkins, C.L. 30
Haynes, B.F. 25, 30
Henderson, Loy 357
Higginbottom, Sam 359
hill stations 339
Hindu Mahasabha 197, 242, 336, 350, 369
Hindustan Times 314
Hocking, William Ernest 210, 211, 213
Hodge, John Z. 189, 190, 196, 198-200, 208, 242, 263, 264, 268, 269, 271, 273-275
Hoegh Merchant 346
Holiness Movement 15, 386
homogeneity 251
Hong Kong 77-80, 90, 345, 360, 374

Household Schedule 202-204
Hughes, John Wesley 21
Humayun's Tomb 326, 328, 330, 331
Humphrey, Hubert H. 356-358, 362
Hyderabad 85, 226-229, 261, 281, 352, 381
Hyneman, Ruth 89, 130, 147, 148
I-3s 342, 343, 362
Independence Day 196, 314, 315, 317
India Conciliation Group 267
Indian Temperance News 313
Indian Witness 9, 34, 39, 54, 72, 75, 76, 98, 105, 125, 158, 160, 161, 163, 164, 166, 169, 177, 180, 182, 191, 194, 248, 258, 261, 313, 346, 360
Individualism 251
Indus River Conference 292, 314, 338
Institute for Social and Religious Research 186, 187, 190-192, 194, 200, 201, 206, 208-210, 215
Interchurch World Movement 186
International Missionary Council (IMC) 181, 185, 189, 190, 261, 268, 275, 280, 281
Isabella Thoburn College 39, 55, 57, 65, 167, 168, 335, 371, 377, 379, 386
Iyengar, Srinivas 183
Jaiswar, Baldeo 258-260, 277
Jajmani system 380
Jallianwala Bagh 166
Jana Gana Mana 351
Janvier, Joel 371

Japan 16, 26, 28, 35, 67, 80, 90, 190, 210, 282, 303, 304, 342
Japanese occupation 283
Jerusalem, 1928 181, 184, 185, 188-190, 192, 193
Jessamine Journal 21, 385
Jinnah, Mohamed Ali 197, 310, 314
John N. Hollister 292, 371
Jones, A.P. 31
Jones, E. Stanley 21, 32-34, 36, 39, 45, 47, 48, 52, 53, 55, 57, 64, 71-73, 76, 119, 123, 147, 163, 182, 216, 240, 242, 243, 247, 249, 288, 289, 291, 343, 373
Karol Bagh 320
Kashmir 352, 353, 360
Kathmandu 364, 365, 374
Katyur Valley 308
Kaufman, Ralph C. 306
Kaukab-I-Hind 54, 57, 160
Kaur, Rajkumari Amrit 298, 307, 323-325, 331, 333, 335, 355-358, 372
Kellogg Church 177, 180, 235, 381
Kentucky Holiness College 16
Kentucky White Ribbon 23, 169
Khan, Nawab Saadat Ali 168
Kistna (or Krishna) District 226
Kobe 80
Korea 190, 342
Kraemer, Hendrik 281
Kumaon District 308, 328
Kumaon hills 312
Kurukshetra 328, 386
Kurukshetra Camp 328
Lacy, Elizabeth (Pickett) 283, 345, 372
Lacy, Henry 283, 345, 372

Lahore 68, 127, 196, 317, 332
Lal Bagh Church 45, 53, 54, 56, 57, 64, 68, 72, 73, 75, 161, 334, 335
Landour 177-179, 196, 198, 199, 227, 235, 256, 258, 262, 273, 299, 363, 381
Lapp, George 228, 252
Lapp, John A. 252
Latourette, Kenneth Scott 281
Laymen's Convention, 1917 123
Laymen's Foreign Missions Inquiry 187, 210-212
Laymen's Missionary Movement 34, 88
Leonard Theological College 287, 340, 371
Leonard, A.B. 32, 47, 259
Lord Irwin 196, 197
Lucas, E.D. 329
Lucknow Christian College 63, 94, 147, 158, 159, 167, 191, 195, 196, 258, 377
Lucknow Conference 144, 151
Ludhiana 359, 374, 386
Lutheran World Relief 325
Lutherans 106, 107, 119, 151, 226
Macnicol, Nicol 190
Madras 68, 85, 141, 169, 184, 187, 190, 215, 273, 280
mail trains 53
Manila 346, 374
Marshall Plan 357
Mass movement 83-85, 87, 90, 98, 105, 114, 117, 122, 126, 128, 132, 145, 149, 163, 180, 181, 185, 187-191, 194-198, 200, 202, 206, 207, 210, 212, 215, 216, 218-220, 224, 226, 227, 229,

233, 235, 236, 240, 243, 251, 260, 261, 263-265, 267, 268, 281, 290, 378, 381
Definition 83-85, 219, 381
Mass Movement Bulletin 233
Mathai, John 322, 335
Mathai, M.O. 333, 335
Mathews, James K. 10, 105, 280, 304, 308, 312, 313, 317, 319, 329, 337, 343-346, 358, 365, 369
Mayo, Katherine 163
Mazhabi Sikhs 84, 119, 381
McEldowney, J.E. 371
McGavran, Donald A. 157, 180, 209, 214, 216, 227, 233, 234, 248-252, 261, 262, 264, 267-269, 272-276, 279, 367, 368, 373, 374
McLeish, Alexander 263, 268, 274, 367
McPheeters, J.C. 368
Meerut 40
Mehta, Jiwa Raj 324
Mennonites 178, 227, 228, 252, 306
Men's National Missionary Congress in Chicago 34
Methodist Committee for Overseas Relief (MCOR) 287, 337-339, 342
Mid-India 214, 216, 228, 233, 234, 248, 249, 251, 252, 258, 262, 264, 268
mission station 199, 222, 233, 251, 367
Modak, Cyril 172
Moffat, E.M. 305
Moffat, Peggy 344
Mondol, S.K. 249, 304, 335, 347, 348

Mongolia 81
Moody, Dwight L. 28
Mookerjee, H.C. 9, 346-350
Moonje, B.S. 197
Morrison, H.C. 39
Mott, John R. 28, 29, 35, 38, 67, 68, 87, 106, 157, 184-187, 189, 190, 192, 194, 195, 198, 208-211, 262-264, 281, 367
Mountbatten, Edwina 323, 335, 345
Mountbatten, Louis 310, 313-315, 321, 323, 335, 336, 345, 352
Mt. Hermon One Hundred 28, 38
Munshi, K.M. 349
Muslim League 310, 314
Mussoorie 155, 177, 180, 196, 213, 235, 299, 364
Muzaffarpur 96, 97, 120
My Twentieth Century Odyssey 121, 384, 385
Nagasaki 80
Nagpur 84, 106, 107, 200, 234, 263, 264, 269, 271, 272, 278, 324, 325
Naini Tal 40, 41, 64, 146, 168, 177, 308, 328, 339, 381
National Catholic Welfare Program 325
National Christian Council 9, 107, 184, 185, 187-190, 194, 196, 198, 200, 206, 208-210, 226, 235, 240, 260, 261, 263, 264, 267-269, 273, 275, 276, 281, 303-305, 308, 311, 322-324, 327-329, 347, 365
Nehru Report 184
Nehru, Jawaharlal 61, 183, 196, 197, 282, 289,

290, 297, 298, 314,
316, 322-324,
333-335, 341, 347,
349, 351-353,
355-357, 359, 374,
375
Nehru, Motilal 61, 183, 184
New Delhi 301, 313, 317,
319, 320, 322-324,
333, 359, 369, 372,
375
New York Herald Tribune
313
New York Times 47, 321,
351
Non-cooperation 183
North India Conference 41,
84, 88, 144, 292, 338
Northwest Christian College
374
Northwest Provinces 56, 58,
59
Ohio Wesleyan University
286, 287, 375
Oldham, J.H. 268
Oldham, William F. 88, 89,
123
Oliver, Ernest 366
Oudh 53, 56-59, 61, 63, 68,
118, 144, 380, 383
Pahalgam 308
Pakistan 74, 284, 310, 314,
325, 326, 328-330,
332, 333, 340, 341,
343, 351, 352, 360,
362, 368
Palmer, Phoebe 15
Parekh, Manilal 216, 217
Parker, Allen 177, 179, 180
Parker, E. Graham 202
Parker, Lois Lee 56, 169
Partition 9, 16, 61, 296, 300,
310, 314, 315, 332,
336, 341
Patel, Sardar 323, 331, 332,
349, 350
Patna 101, 133, 150, 151,
374
Paton, William 181, 190,
195, 199, 261, 268,

273, 275, 276
Paul, K.T. 197
Peace Corps 344, 375
Penang 78
Pentecostal Herald 39, 385
People Movements (see
mass movements) 367,
368, 375, 378, 380,
381
Periah 98
Perrill, Charles 82, 96, 304,
306, 307
Perrill, Fred M. 82, 84, 89,
90, 96, 98-100,
102-104, 121, 126,
129, 133, 144, 150,
191, 249, 258, 261
Perrill, Mary 89, 96, 98, 150
Perrill, Wilma 304
Pickett Junior High School
362
Pickett, Ann (Leeder) 362
Pickett, Douglas 121, 167,
168, 213, 255, 258,
262, 286, 289, 292,
295, 298, 306, 308,
312, 344, 361, 363,
372, 375, 376
Pickett, Elbert Deets 16, 20,
47, 82, 89, 138, 139
Pickett, Elizabeth 121, 160,
167, 208, 213
Pickett, Eulice 16
Pickett, J. Waskom
applies to mission board
20
Pickett, James Lowry 16,
20, 47
Pickett, Jarrell Waskom
1918-19 influenza
epidemic 125
about 9
applies to Mission Board
31
appointed District
Superintendent 126
appointed to India 36
arrives at Arrah 95
arrives in Lucknow 54
Asbury Theological

Seminary 368
becomes Bishop Pickett
249
birth 20
Boston University
School of Theology
373
Central Hall speech 261,
262
children of 121
Christian Mass
Movements in India
208, 218, 242, 244,
251, 262
Christ's Way to India's
Heart 264, 279
concern for the poor 116
conversion 24
criticized by Gandhi
264-266, 271, 272
death 376
Dynamics of Church
Growth 375
editor of Indian Witness
160-162, 164, 166,
169, 180, 182, 191
education 21
effects of World War I
106
evangelistic work in
Bihar 105, 111-113
father of Indian
prohibition 141
first mass movement
survey 200-206
first meeting with
Gandhi 142
friendship with Nehru
333, 355, 359, 374
fund-raising work 82,
83, 86, 159, 160, 191,
374
health care initiatives
307
impact of recovery 82
Indian Constitution
348-351
indigenous evangelists
118, 119, 121
Ludhiana 374

marriage to Ruth
  Robinson 89
meeting with Ambedkar
  244-247
meets with Eisenhower
  362
meets with Truman 356
memoirs 375
mid-India study 233,
  234, 248, 249, 251,
  252
move to Bombay 262
moves to Delhi 300
NCC Mass Movement
  Secretary 263
opposition of the Arya
  Samaj 131
ordained 56
Partition riots 319-328,
  330
retirement 368, 369,
  373, 375
robbed in Calcutta 311
sails for India 47
Sawtelle School 122
signs SVM pledge 27
stricken with
  tuberculosis 72
Sudra movements
  226-231
temperance work
  139-141, 152, 159,
  162
United Mission to Nepal
  363, 364, 366
war surplus effort
  304-306
Warne Baby Fold 126,
  162, 191, 340
Wesley Glen Retirement
  Home 375
Woodstock involvements
  177-180, 191, 196
Pickett, L.L. 12, 21, 47, 48,
  82, 86, 89, 181
Pickett, Leroy 16
Pickett, Ludie Day 21, 47,
  53, 82, 89, 162, 169,
  181, 340, 360
Pickett, Ludo 16

Pickett, Margaret 121, 166,
  167, 213, 255, 258,
  286, 291
Pickett, Melissa 17, 25
Pickett, Mellie Dorough 17
Pickett, Miriam Lee 121,
  160, 167, 208, 213,
  283
Pickett, Wilbur 16
Pickett, Willard Lee 82, 83
Piru 114, 115, 123
Point Four Program 358
Poona Pact 239, 244
Porter, Leslie Alexander 59,
  60
Prasad, Rajendra 297, 316,
  333, 353-355
Presbyterians 177, 192, 199,
  208, 211, 304, 306,
  363-365
Punjab 53, 84, 85, 101, 106,
  137, 180, 185, 310,
  314, 317, 322, 323,
  327, 331, 332, 379,
  381
Purana Qila 296, 320, 325,
  326, 330, 331
Putamba 285
Qadir, Julam 63, 64, 119
Quit India 290, 323
Radhakrishnan, Sarvepali
  375
Rajagopalachari (C.R.) 140,
  141, 269, 270, 354
Rangoon 77, 78, 283, 311,
  374
Ranikhet, Dwarahat 308
Rashtriya Swayamsevak
  Sangh (RSS) 336, 341
reallocating resources 251
Refugee Relief Committee
  323
Regions Beyond Missionary
  Union 189
Reid College 39, 57
Republic Day 297, 354
Re-Thinking Missions 210,
  211, 215, 281
Ringeltaube, W.T. 98
Robinson, Elizabeth Fisher

64, 66, 67, 89, 104,
  213, 234, 235, 301,
  312
Robinson, John E. 44, 65,
  88, 262
Robinson, John W. 54, 57,
  58, 64-67, 89, 103,
  104, 195, 234, 235,
  248, 249, 255, 258,
  262, 286, 297, 301,
  302, 313, 328, 373
Robinson, Miriam 46, 64,
  66, 67, 234
Rockefeller, John D. 186,
  187, 210, 211, 215
Rockey, Clement D. 98,
  335, 343, 371, 372
Rockey, Helen Cady 371
Round Table Conferences
  195-197, 200, 238,
  239, 244, 246
Sagan, John 346
Sagan, Margaret (Pickett)
  346, 375
Sahae, D.P. 126
Sahayak Patrika 214
Salt March 197, 323
Sampson, John 95, 98-100
Sapru, Tej Bahadur 197
Sastri, Srinivas 197
Satnamis 227, 382
Satyagraha 135, 136, 138,
  142, 282, 382
Satyagraha Ashram 135
Sawtelle School 122
Schutz, H.J. (also Sheets)
  84, 97, 102, 106, 108,
  117, 125, 126, 131,
  215
Scott, Roland 343, 361
Seamands, A.E. 226
Seamands, J.T. 368, 371
Shahabad 93, 101, 108, 115,
  118, 119, 123, 136,
  150, 194
Shanghai 80, 190, 345
Shaw, Harold 306-308
Sheets, H.J. (also Schutz)
  215
Sikhs 84, 119, 138, 197,

239, 241, 317, 319-321, 324-327, 332, 341, 379, 381
Simon Commission 183
Singapore 77-79, 90, 283, 346, 374
Singh, Babu Kunwar 101
Singh, George H. 216, 248, 249, 252
Singh, Hem Raj 126
Singh, J.W. 320, 322, 329
Singh, Sardar Ujjal 197
Sitapur 53, 64
Slater, A.E. 199
Smith, J. Holmes 214
Social dislocation 222, 251
social lift 128, 251
Soochow (Suzhou) 80
Speer, Robert 192, 211
Srinagar 308
St. Augustine 82
St. James Church 329
Student Volunteer Movement 28, 29, 38, 192
Stuntz, Clyde 180, 317
Stuntz, Homer 35
Subhan, John 260, 297, 335
Sudra movements 226-230, 234, 264
Sukh, Emanuel 119, 127, 132, 133, 139, 151, 185
Sukh, Polly 119, 122
Sundaram, Ernest 307
SVM Pledge 27, 29, 198
Swadeshi Movement 383
Swain, Clara 169, 346
Swaraj 136, 137, 183, 196, 382, 383
Swaraj Party 183
Tagore, Rabindranath 141, 351
Taj Mahal 41, 50, 200, 326
Talbot, Phillips 316
Tambaram, 1938 274-276, 281
Taylor, Carl 364
Taylor, James M. 82, 83,

86-89, 96, 103, 123, 124
Taylor, John C. 324
Taylor, William 75
Telugu area 225, 228, 230, 233, 234, 271
Temperance Clip Sheet 139, 141
temperance movement 9, 140, 141
Tenjo Maru 80, 81
Thoburn, Isabella 59, 168, 169
Thoburn, James M. 35, 38, 126, 160, 343
Thompson, John 301
Tilak, Bal Gangadhar 138
Tilak, Narayan Vaman 162
Tinnevelly 84, 85, 185
Tirhoot 68, 83, 85, 95, 97, 106, 150
Titanic 48, 67
Titus, Murray 291, 325
Travancore 84, 85, 106, 185, 219
Troeltsch, Ernst 211
Truman, Harry S. 351, 352, 356-358, 362
Tweedie, Gertrude 172
Union Seminary (NY) 193, 194, 198, 199, 244
United Lutheran Theological College 226
United Mission to Nepal 9, 366, 377, 384, 386
United Provinces 53, 56, 59, 97, 106, 119, 140, 141, 162, 185, 187, 191, 199, 242, 332, 377, 381, 383
Vedamanickam 98
Vellore 319, 322
Venkayya 219
Ventnor 208, 346
Wagner, Paul 371
Wallace, John E. 202, 209
Warne Baby Fold 126, 162, 191, 340

Warne, Frank W. 47, 54-57, 73, 85-87, 89, 105, 122, 126, 144, 162, 340, 371
Warnshuis, A.L. 268, 271
Weir, John B. 304, 305, 364
Wesley, John 15, 174, 224, 251
Whitehead, Henry 198
Whittaker, Frank 281
Wilcox, Bertrand and Rita 81
Wilmore, Kentucky 21, 47, 82, 89, 158, 191, 287, 368, 376
Wilson, Dorothy Clark 353-355
Wilson, F.M. 300
Wilson, Warren H. 194, 195, 198-208
Wiser, William and Charlotte 99, 199, 202, 209
Women's Christian College of Madras 188
Women's Christian Temperance Union (WCTU) 23, 24, 169, 235
Woodstock School 177, 179, 363, 381
World Dominion 263, 272
World War I 61, 62, 106, 165, 215
World War II 289-291, 299, 304, 310
Wray, Mary Gilbert 32
Wray, Newton 31, 32
Yeola 237, 240, 244, 247, 262
YMCA 29, 38, 178, 323, 324, 326, 377
Yokohama 80
Young India 166
YWCA 323, 326, 377
zamindars 99, 115, 165, 318